**Nominated for 3 EISNER AWARDS including
Best New Series and Best Ongoing Series**

"For fans of literature (from classics to contemporary) this series is worth a read. . . .
The Unwritten is **a roller-coaster ride through a library, weaving famous authors
and characters into a tale of mystery** that is, at once, oddly familiar yet highly original."
— **USA TODAY**

"*The Unwritten* makes a leap from being just a promising new Vertigo title to being on-track to
become the best ongoing Vertigo book since *Sandman*. And given that Vertigo has delivered
the likes of *100 Bullets*, *Y: The Last Man*, and *Fables* since *Sandman* ended,
that's saying something... A-"
—**THE A.V. CLUB**

APOCALYPSE

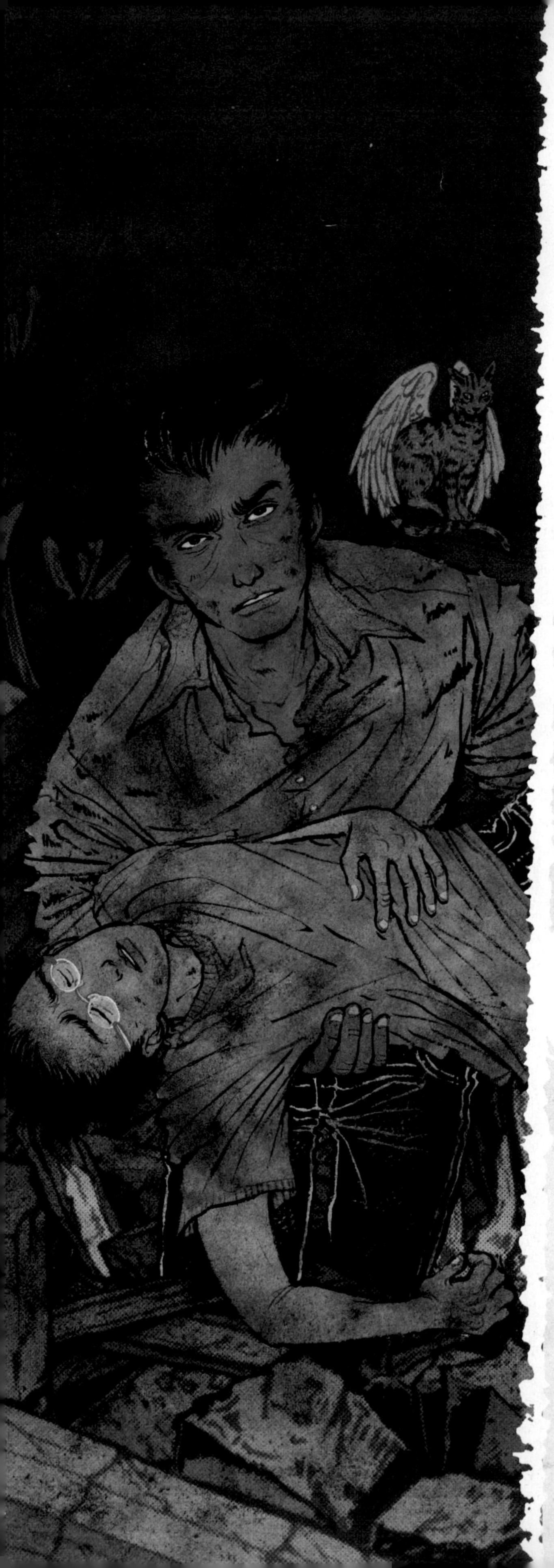

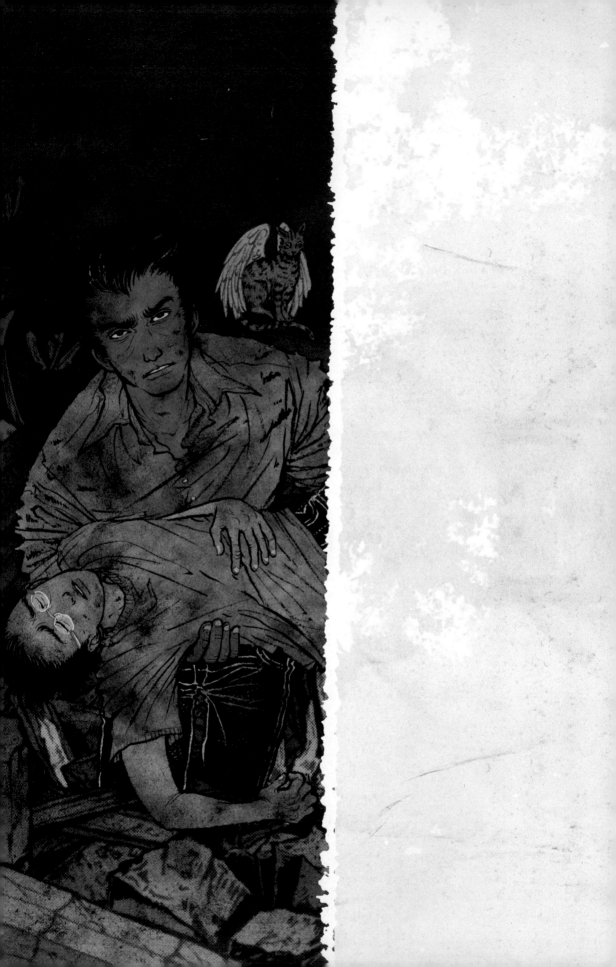

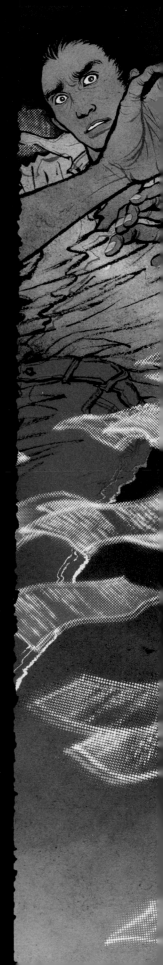

the Unwritten

APOCALYPSE

Mike Carey Writer
Peter Gross Artist Peter Gross Al Davison Dean Ormston Vince Locke Finishes
Chris Chuckry Colorist
Todd Klein Letterer Yuko Shimizu Cover Artist
THE UNWRITTEN created by Mike Carey and Peter Gross

THE UNWRITTEN VOLUME 11: APOCALYPSE

Published by DC Comics. Compilation Copyright © 2015 Mike Carey and
Peter Gross. All Rights Reserved.

Originally published in single magazine form in THE UNWRITTEN:
APOCALYPSE 6-12 © 2014, 2015 Mike Carey and Peter Gross. All
Rights Reserved. VERTIGO and all characters, their distinctive likenesses
and related elements featured in this publication are trademarks of DC
Comics. The stories, characters and incidents featured in this publication
are entirely fictional. DC Comics does not read or accept unsolicited ideas,
stories or artwork.

DC Comics, 4000 Warner Blvd., Burbank, CA 91522
A Warner Bros. Entertainment Company.
Printed by RR Donnelley, Salem, VA, USA. 4/17/15. First Printing.
ISBN: 978-1-4012-5348-6

Library of Congress Cataloging-in-Publication Data

Carey, Mike, 1959- author.
  The Unwritten. Volume 11, Apocalypse / Mike Carey, Peter Gross.
   pages cm
  ISBN 978-1-4012-5348-6 (paperback)
  1. Graphic novels. I. Gross, Peter, 1958- illustrator. II. Title. III. Title:
Apocalypse.
  PN6727.C377U589 2014
  741.5'973—dc23
                                        2014014691

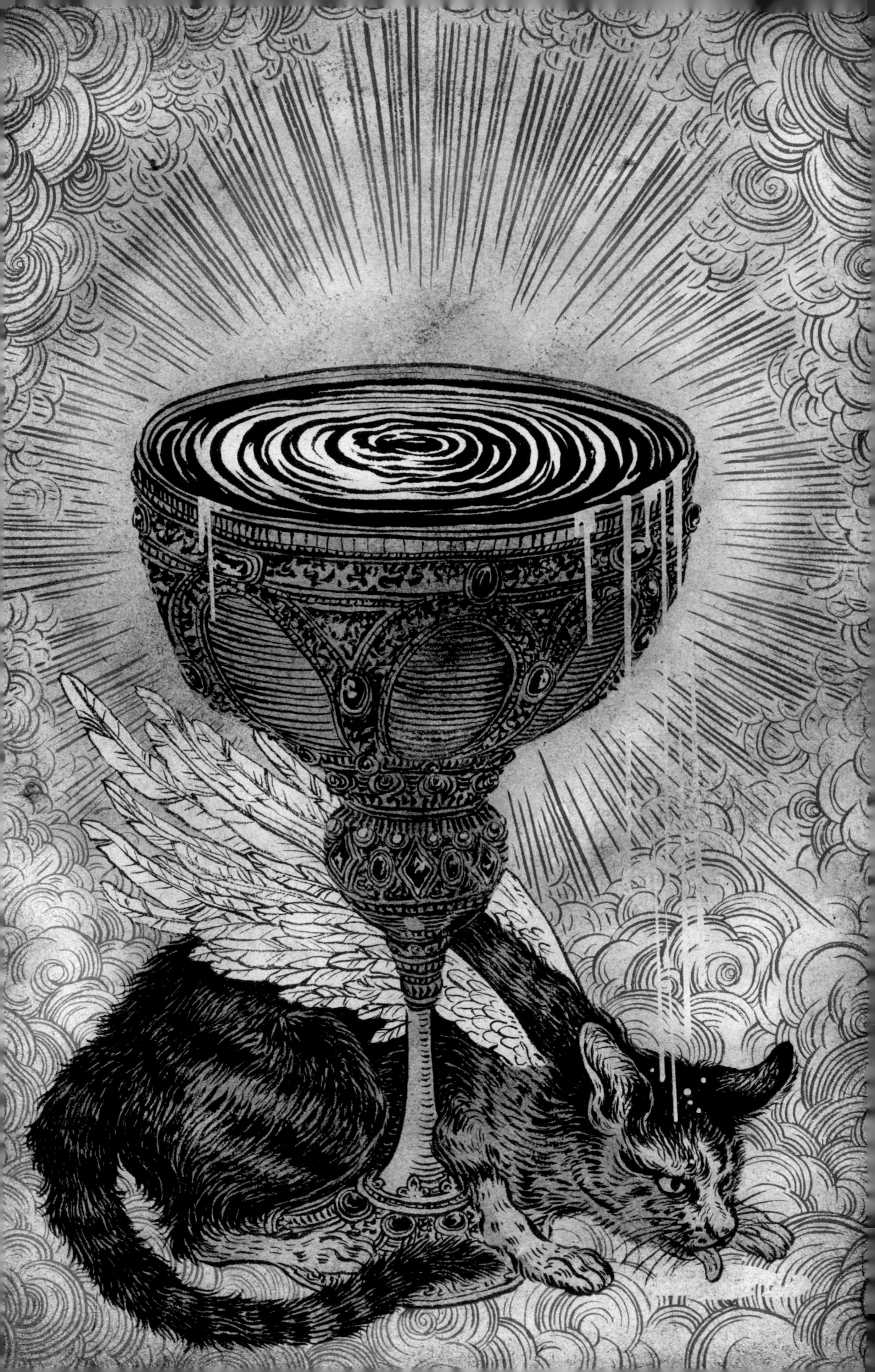

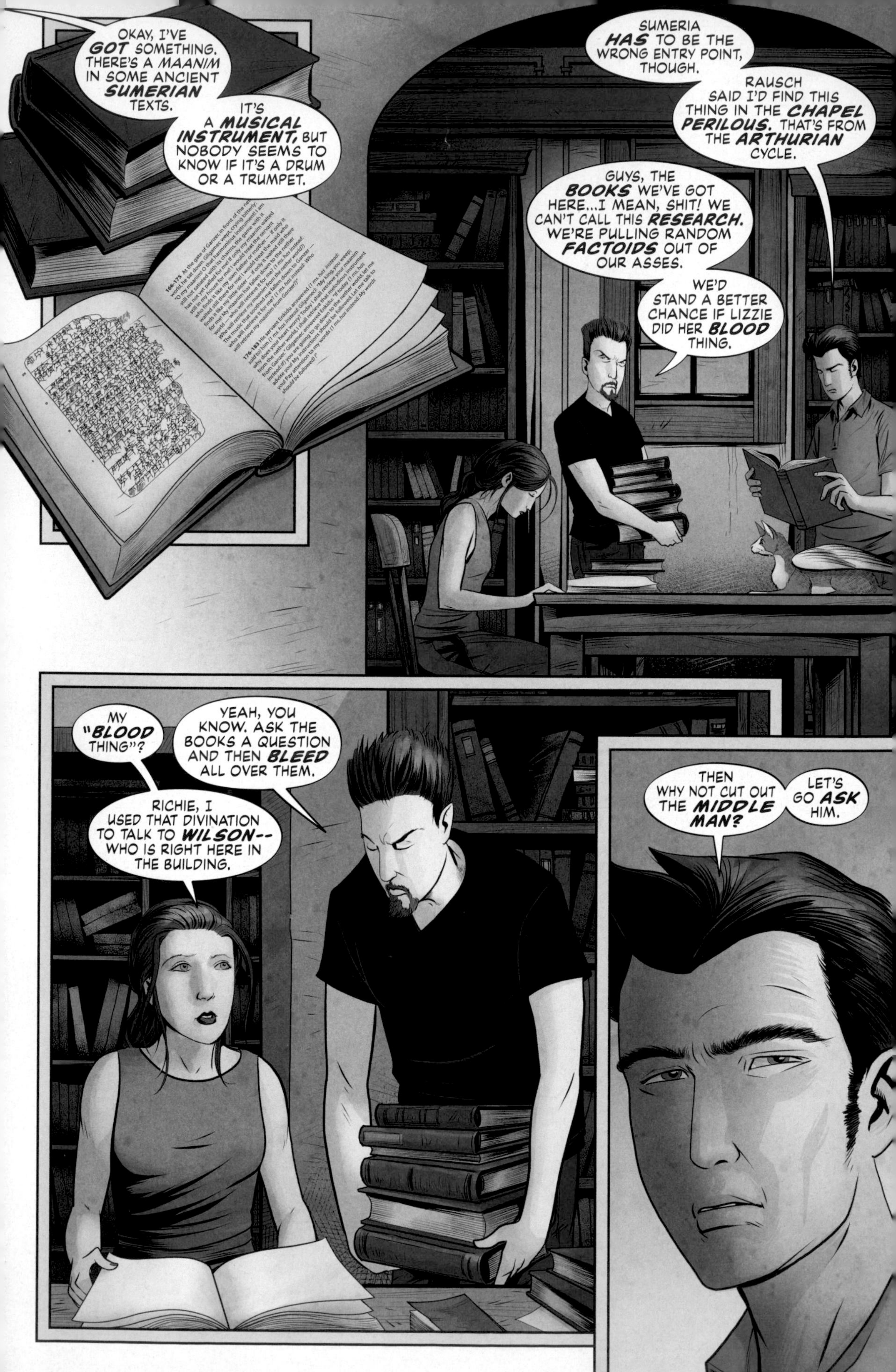
OKAY, I'VE GOT SOMETHING. THERE'S A MAANIM IN SOME ANCIENT SUMERIAN TEXTS.
IT'S A MUSICAL INSTRUMENT, BUT NOBODY SEEMS TO KNOW IF IT'S A DRUM OR A TRUMPET.
SUMERIA HAS TO BE THE WRONG ENTRY POINT, THOUGH.
RAUSCH SAID I'D FIND THIS THING IN THE CHAPEL PERILOUS. THAT'S FROM THE ARTHURIAN CYCLE.
GUYS, THE BOOKS WE'VE GOT HERE...I MEAN, SHIT! WE CAN'T CALL THIS RESEARCH. WE'RE PULLING RANDOM FACTOIDS OUT OF OUR ASSES.
WE'D STAND A BETTER CHANCE IF LIZZIE DID HER BLOOD THING.
MY "BLOOD THING"?
YEAH, YOU KNOW. ASK THE BOOKS A QUESTION AND THEN BLEED ALL OVER THEM.
RICHIE, I USED THAT DIVINATION TO TALK TO WILSON-- WHO IS RIGHT HERE IN THE BUILDING.
THEN WHY NOT CUT OUT THE MIDDLE MAN?
LET'S GO ASK HIM.

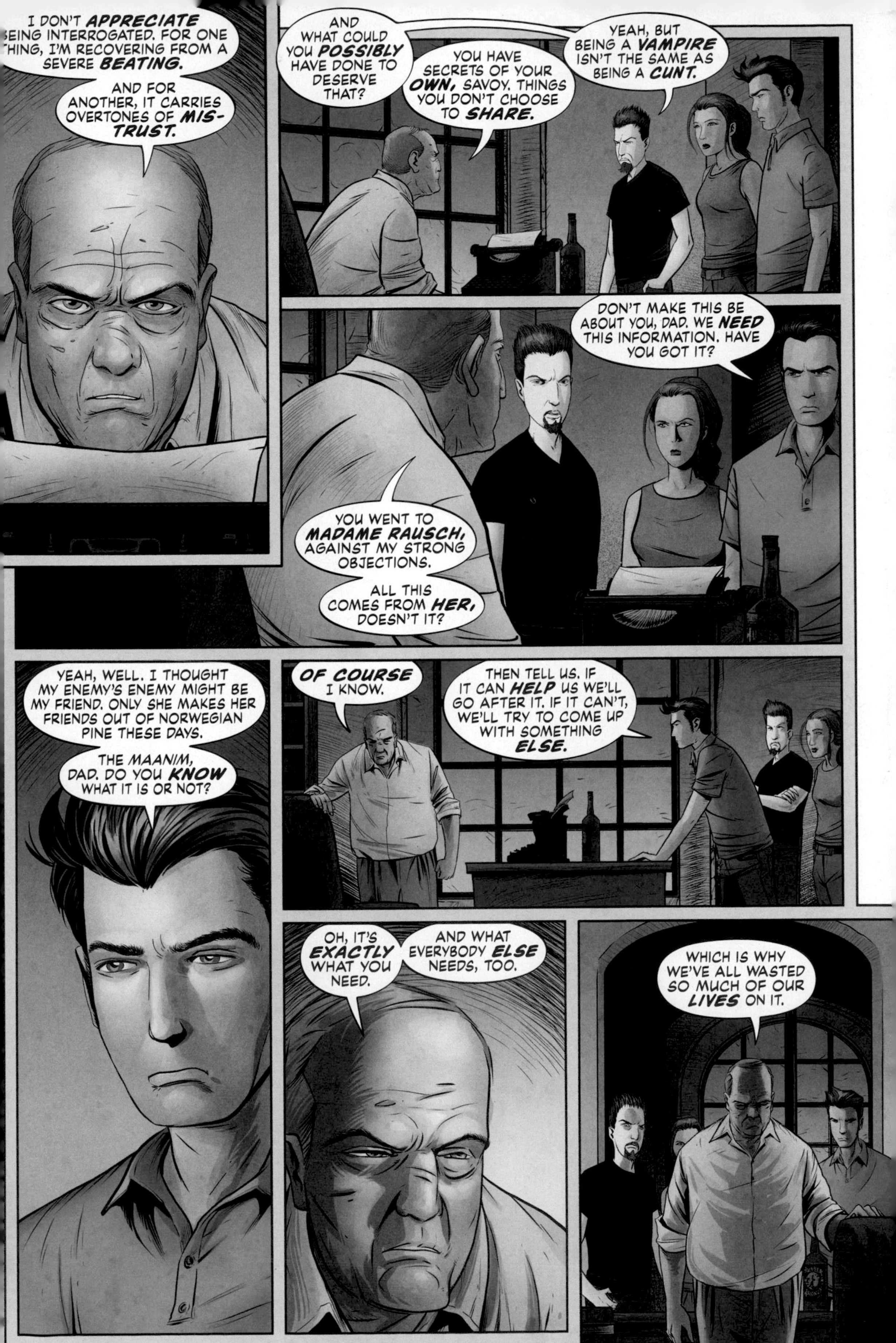
I DON'T APPRECIATE BEING INTERROGATED. FOR ONE THING, I'M RECOVERING FROM A SEVERE BEATING.
AND FOR ANOTHER, IT CARRIES OVERTONES OF MIS-TRUST.
AND WHAT COULD YOU POSSIBLY HAVE DONE TO DESERVE THAT?
YOU HAVE SECRETS OF YOUR OWN, SAVOY. THINGS YOU DON'T CHOOSE TO SHARE.
YEAH, BUT BEING A VAMPIRE ISN'T THE SAME AS BEING A CUNT.
DON'T MAKE THIS BE ABOUT YOU, DAD. WE NEED THIS INFORMATION. HAVE YOU GOT IT?
YOU WENT TO MADAME RAUSCH, AGAINST MY STRONG OBJECTIONS.
ALL THIS COMES FROM HER, DOESN'T IT?
YEAH, WELL. I THOUGHT MY ENEMY'S ENEMY MIGHT BE MY FRIEND. ONLY SHE MAKES HER FRIENDS OUT OF NORWEGIAN PINE THESE DAYS.
THE MAANIM, DAD. DO YOU KNOW WHAT IT IS OR NOT?
OF COURSE I KNOW.
THEN TELL US. IF IT CAN HELP US WE'LL GO AFTER IT. IF IT CAN'T, WE'LL TRY TO COME UP WITH SOMETHING ELSE.
OH, IT'S EXACTLY WHAT YOU NEED.
AND WHAT EVERYBODY ELSE NEEDS, TOO.
WHICH IS WHY WE'VE ALL WASTED SO MUCH OF OUR LIVES ON IT.

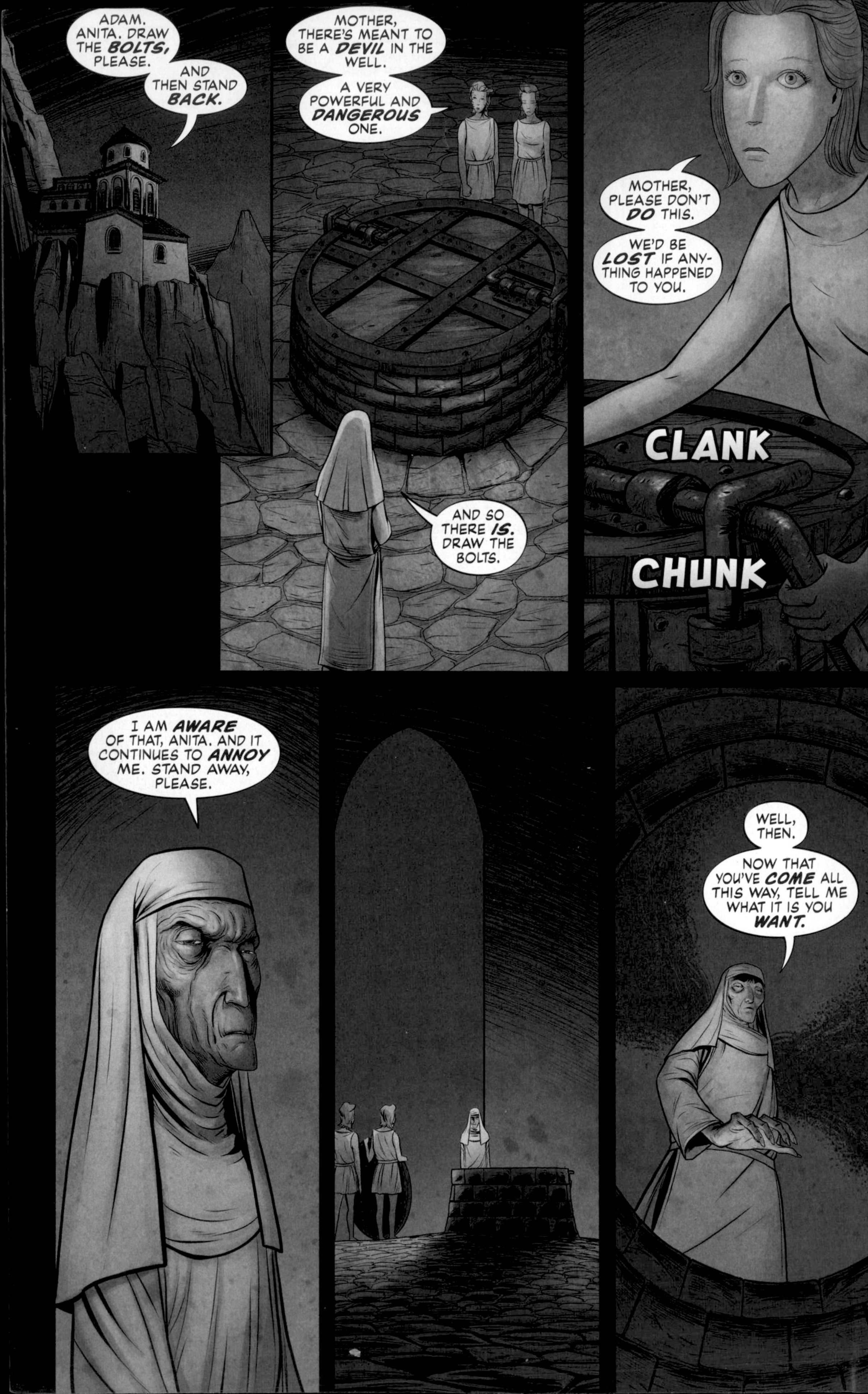
ADAM. ANITA. DRAW THE BOLTS, PLEASE.
AND THEN STAND BACK.
MOTHER, THERE'S MEANT TO BE A DEVIL IN THE WELL.
A VERY POWERFUL AND DANGEROUS ONE.
AND SO THERE IS. DRAW THE BOLTS.
MOTHER, PLEASE DON'T DO THIS.
WE'D BE LOST IF ANY-THING HAPPENED TO YOU.
CLANK
CHUNK
I AM AWARE OF THAT, ANITA. AND IT CONTINUES TO ANNOY ME. STAND AWAY, PLEASE.
WELL, THEN.
NOW THAT YOU'VE COME ALL THIS WAY, TELL ME WHAT IT IS YOU WANT.

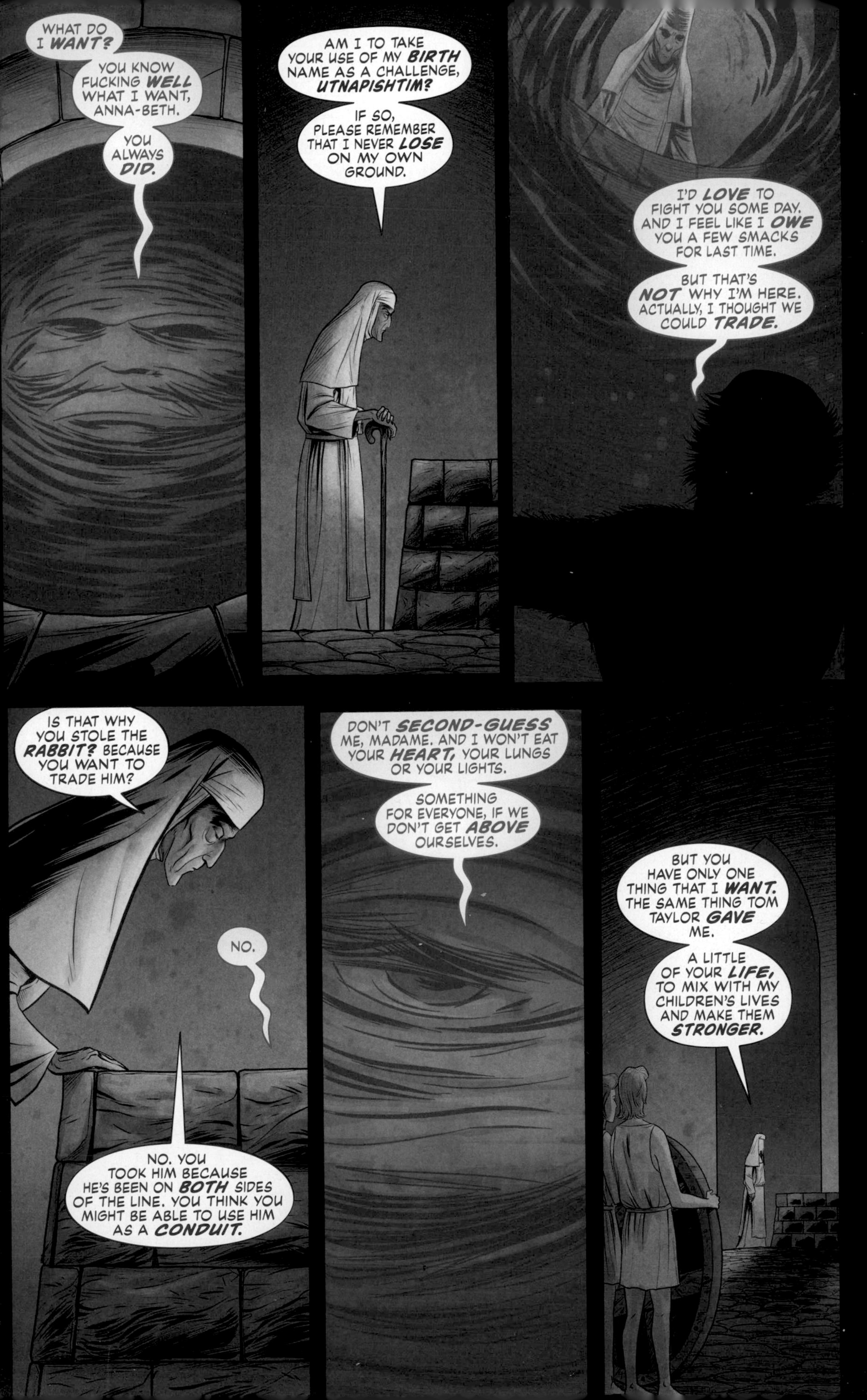
WHAT DO I WANT?
YOU KNOW FUCKING WELL WHAT I WANT, ANNA-BETH.
YOU ALWAYS DID.
AM I TO TAKE YOUR USE OF MY BIRTH NAME AS A CHALLENGE, UTNAPISHTIM?
IF SO, PLEASE REMEMBER THAT I NEVER LOSE ON MY OWN GROUND.
I'D LOVE TO FIGHT YOU SOME DAY. AND I FEEL LIKE I OWE YOU A FEW SMACKS FOR LAST TIME.
BUT THAT'S NOT WHY I'M HERE. ACTUALLY, I THOUGHT WE COULD TRADE.
IS THAT WHY YOU STOLE THE RABBIT? BECAUSE YOU WANT TO TRADE HIM?
NO.
NO. YOU TOOK HIM BECAUSE HE'S BEEN ON BOTH SIDES OF THE LINE. YOU THINK YOU MIGHT BE ABLE TO USE HIM AS A CONDUIT.
DON'T SECOND-GUESS ME, MADAME. AND I WON'T EAT YOUR HEART, YOUR LUNGS OR YOUR LIGHTS.
SOMETHING FOR EVERYONE, IF WE DON'T GET ABOVE OURSELVES.
BUT YOU HAVE ONLY ONE THING THAT I WANT. THE SAME THING TOM TAYLOR GAVE ME.
A LITTLE OF YOUR LIFE, TO MIX WITH MY CHILDREN'S LIVES AND MAKE THEM STRONGER.

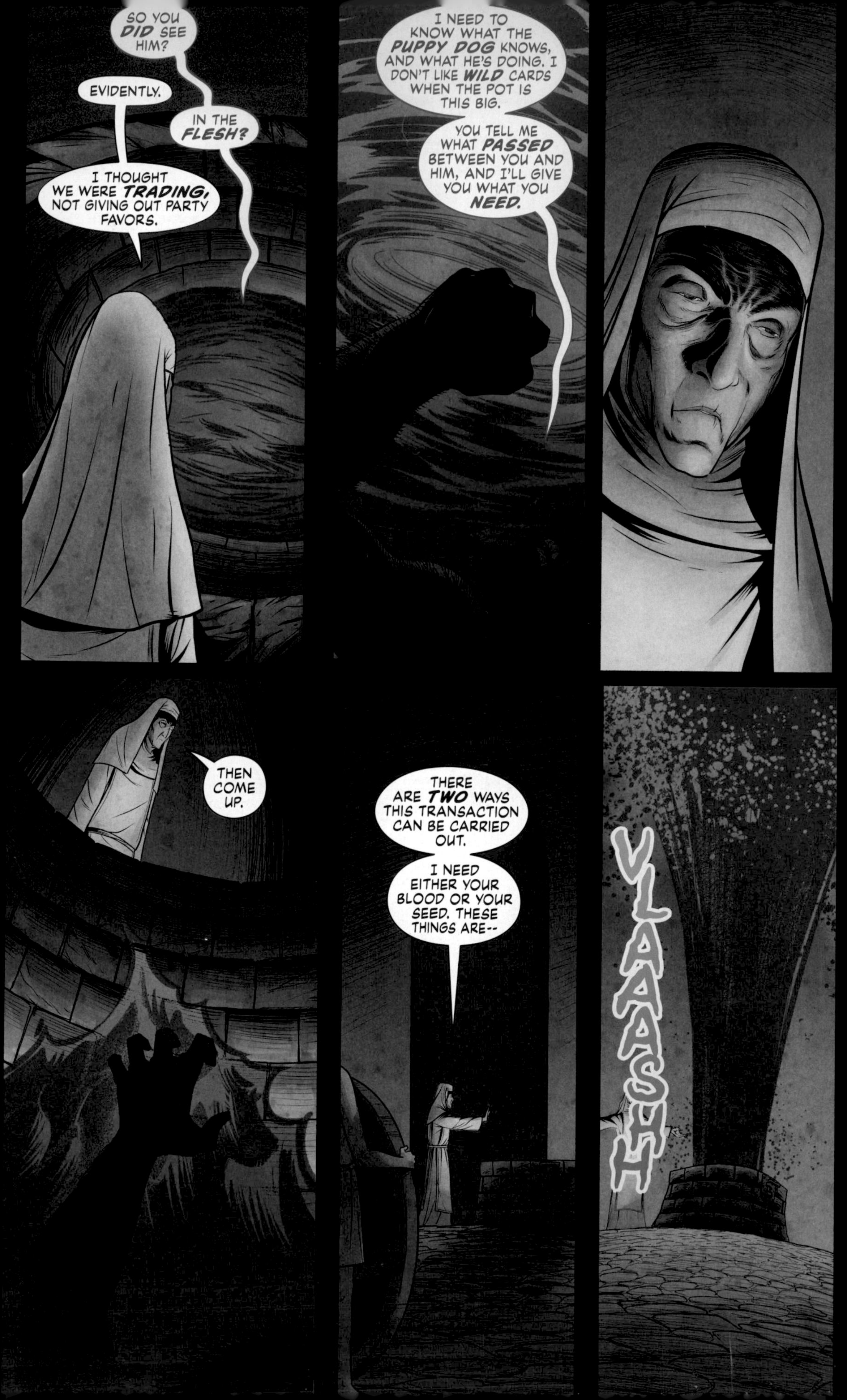

SO YOU DID SEE HIM?
EVIDENTLY.
IN THE FLESH?
I THOUGHT WE WERE TRADING, NOT GIVING OUT PARTY FAVORS.
I NEED TO KNOW WHAT THE PUPPY DOG KNOWS, AND WHAT HE'S DOING. I DON'T LIKE WILD CARDS WHEN THE POT IS THIS BIG.
YOU TELL ME WHAT PASSED BETWEEN YOU AND HIM, AND I'LL GIVE YOU WHAT YOU NEED.
THEN COME UP.
THERE ARE TWO WAYS THIS TRANSACTION CAN BE CARRIED OUT.
I NEED EITHER YOUR BLOOD OR YOUR SEED. THESE THINGS ARE--
VLAAASHH

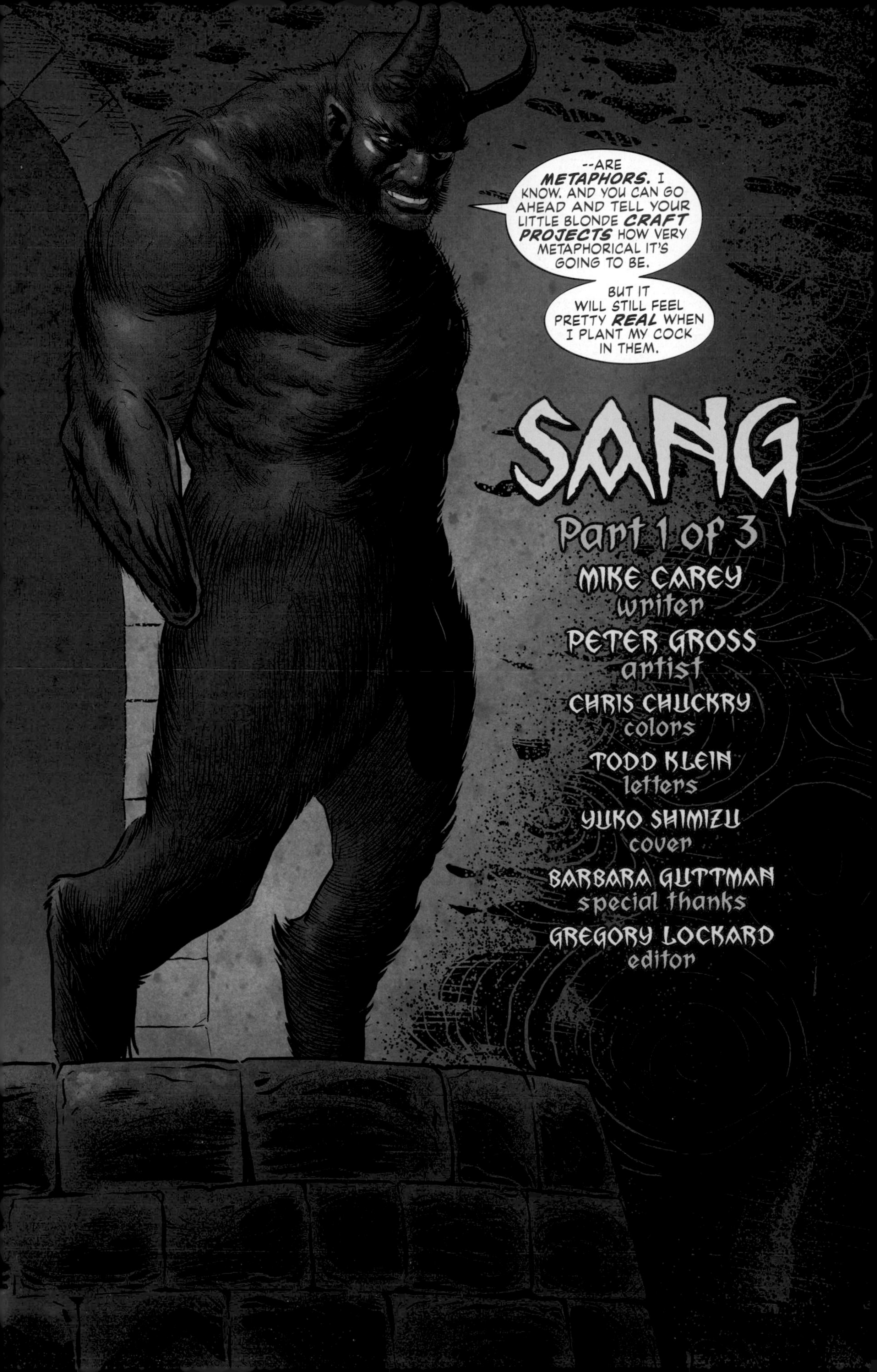
--ARE METAPHORS. I KNOW. AND YOU CAN GO AHEAD AND TELL YOUR LITTLE BLONDE CRAFT PROJECTS HOW VERY METAPHORICAL IT'S GOING TO BE.
BUT IT WILL STILL FEEL PRETTY REAL WHEN I PLANT MY COCK IN THEM.
SANG
Part 1 of 3
MIKE CAREY
writer
PETER GROSS
artist
CHRIS CHUCKRY
colors
TODD KLEIN
letters
YUKO SHIMIZU
cover
BARBARA GUTTMAN
special thanks
GREGORY LOCKARD
editor

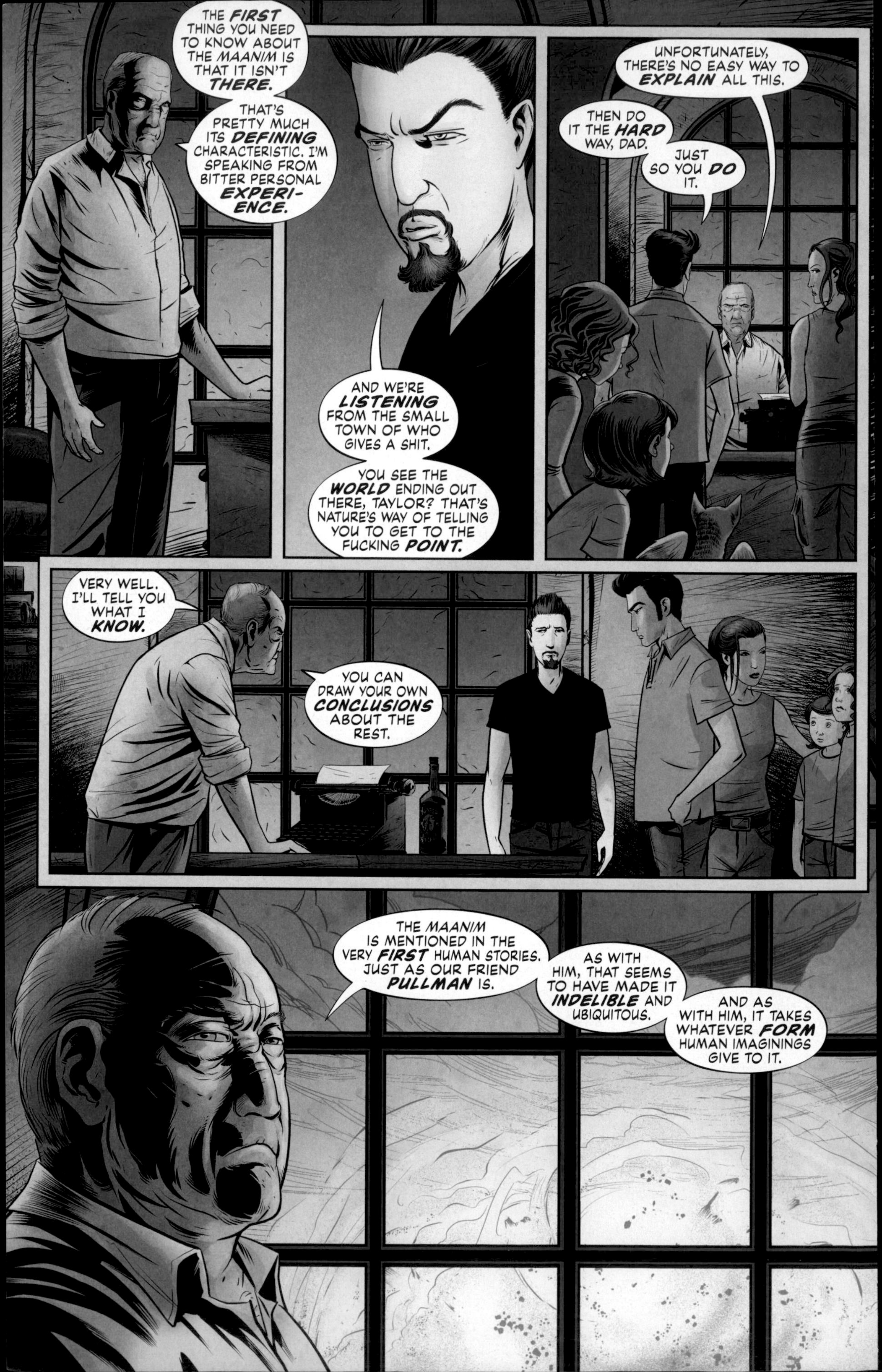
THE *FIRST* THING YOU NEED TO KNOW ABOUT THE *MAANIM* IS THAT IT ISN'T ***THERE***.
THAT'S PRETTY MUCH ITS ***DEFINING*** CHARACTERISTIC. I'M SPEAKING FROM BITTER PERSONAL ***EXPERI-ENCE***.
AND WE'RE ***LISTENING*** FROM THE SMALL TOWN OF WHO GIVES A SHIT.
YOU SEE THE ***WORLD*** ENDING OUT THERE, TAYLOR? THAT'S NATURE'S WAY OF TELLING YOU TO GET TO THE FUCKING ***POINT***.
UNFORTUNATELY, THERE'S NO EASY WAY TO ***EXPLAIN*** ALL THIS.
THEN DO IT THE ***HARD*** WAY, DAD.
JUST SO YOU ***DO*** IT.
VERY WELL. I'LL TELL YOU WHAT I ***KNOW***.
YOU CAN DRAW YOUR OWN ***CONCLUSIONS*** ABOUT THE REST.
THE *MAANIM* IS MENTIONED IN THE VERY ***FIRST*** HUMAN STORIES. JUST AS OUR FRIEND ***PULLMAN*** IS.
AS WITH HIM, THAT SEEMS TO HAVE MADE IT ***INDELIBLE*** AND UBIQUITOUS.
AND AS WITH HIM, IT TAKES WHATEVER ***FORM*** HUMAN IMAGININGS GIVE TO IT.

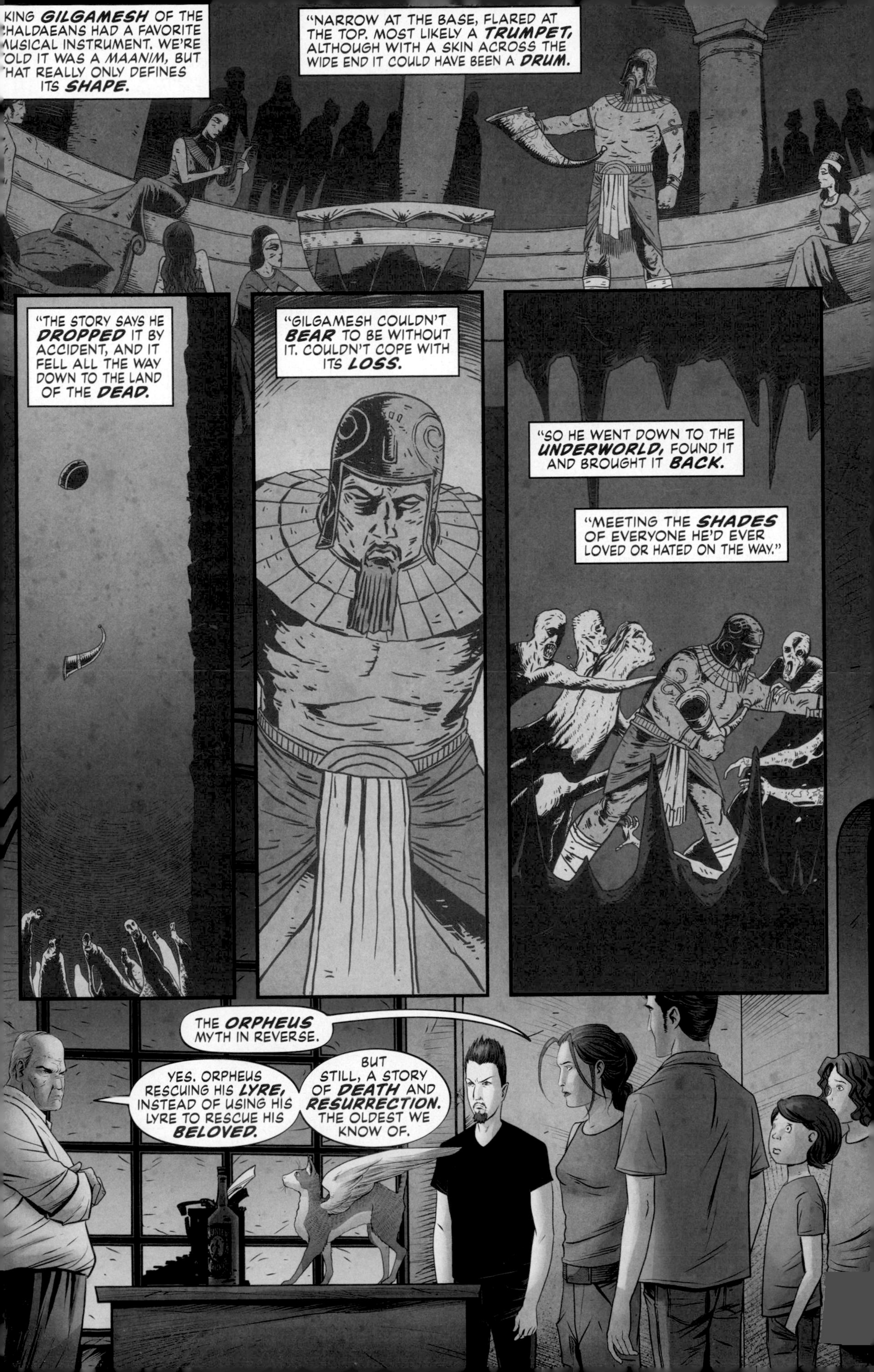

KING GILGAMESH OF THE CHALDAEANS HAD A FAVORITE MUSICAL INSTRUMENT. WE'RE TOLD IT WAS A MAANIM, BUT THAT REALLY ONLY DEFINES ITS SHAPE.
"NARROW AT THE BASE, FLARED AT THE TOP. MOST LIKELY A TRUMPET, ALTHOUGH WITH A SKIN ACROSS THE WIDE END IT COULD HAVE BEEN A DRUM.
"THE STORY SAYS HE DROPPED IT BY ACCIDENT, AND IT FELL ALL THE WAY DOWN TO THE LAND OF THE DEAD.
"GILGAMESH COULDN'T BEAR TO BE WITHOUT IT. COULDN'T COPE WITH ITS LOSS.
"SO HE WENT DOWN TO THE UNDERWORLD, FOUND IT AND BROUGHT IT BACK.
"MEETING THE SHADES OF EVERYONE HE'D EVER LOVED OR HATED ON THE WAY."
THE ORPHEUS MYTH IN REVERSE.
YES. ORPHEUS RESCUING HIS LYRE, INSTEAD OF USING HIS LYRE TO RESCUE HIS BELOVED.
BUT STILL, A STORY OF DEATH AND RESURRECTION. THE OLDEST WE KNOW OF.

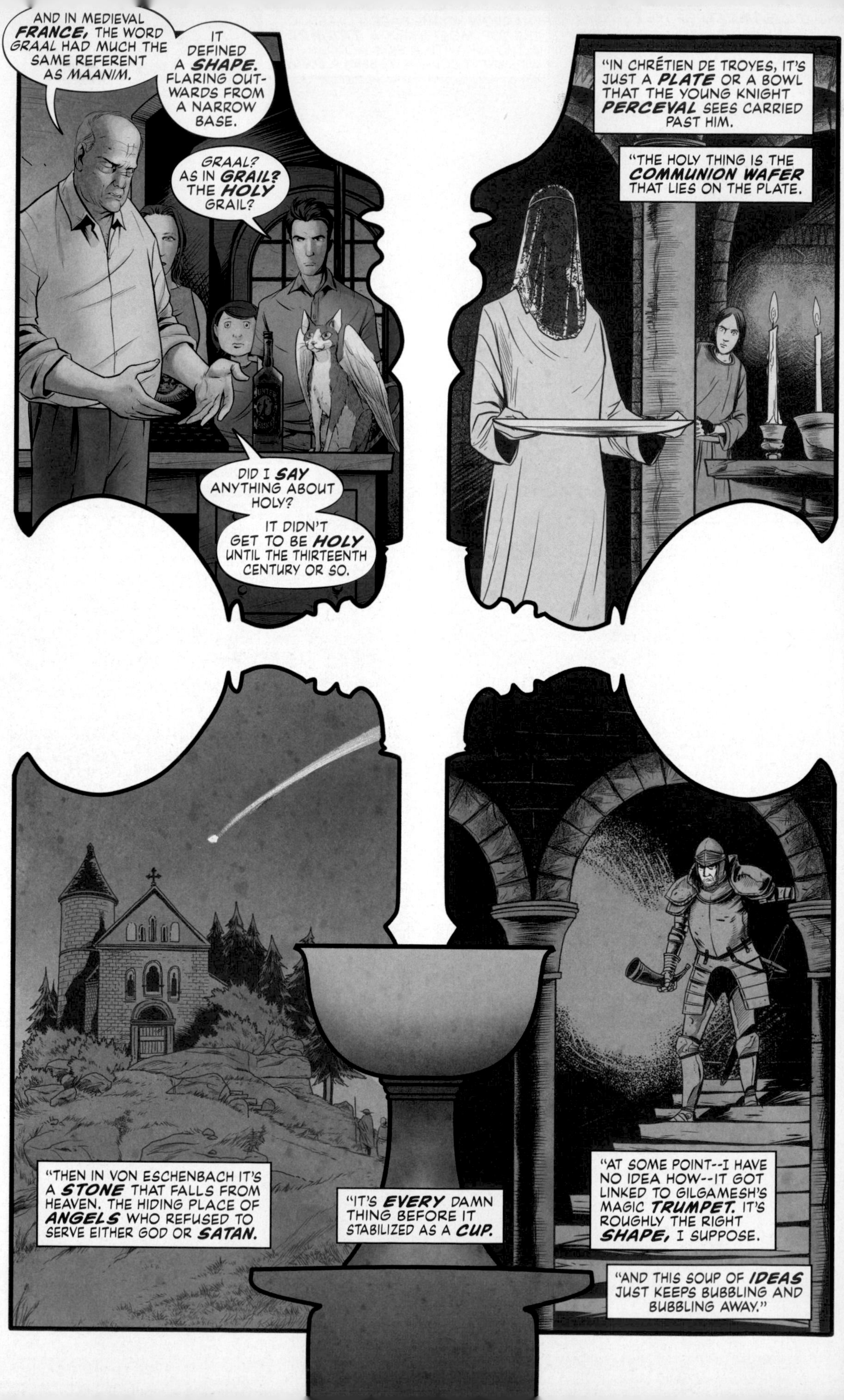
AND IN MEDIEVAL FRANCE, THE WORD GRAAL HAD MUCH THE SAME REFERENT AS MAANIM.
IT DEFINED A SHAPE. FLARING OUT-WARDS FROM A NARROW BASE.
GRAAL? AS IN GRAIL? THE HOLY GRAIL?
DID I SAY ANYTHING ABOUT HOLY?
IT DIDN'T GET TO BE HOLY UNTIL THE THIRTEENTH CENTURY OR SO.
"IN CHRÉTIEN DE TROYES, IT'S JUST A PLATE OR A BOWL THAT THE YOUNG KNIGHT PERCEVAL SEES CARRIED PAST HIM.
"THE HOLY THING IS THE COMMUNION WAFER THAT LIES ON THE PLATE.
"THEN IN VON ESCHENBACH IT'S A STONE THAT FALLS FROM HEAVEN. THE HIDING PLACE OF ANGELS WHO REFUSED TO SERVE EITHER GOD OR SATAN.
"IT'S EVERY DAMN THING BEFORE IT STABILIZED AS A CUP.
"AT SOME POINT--I HAVE NO IDEA HOW--IT GOT LINKED TO GILGAMESH'S MAGIC TRUMPET. IT'S ROUGHLY THE RIGHT SHAPE, I SUPPOSE.
"AND THIS SOUP OF IDEAS JUST KEEPS BUBBLING AND BUBBLING AWAY."

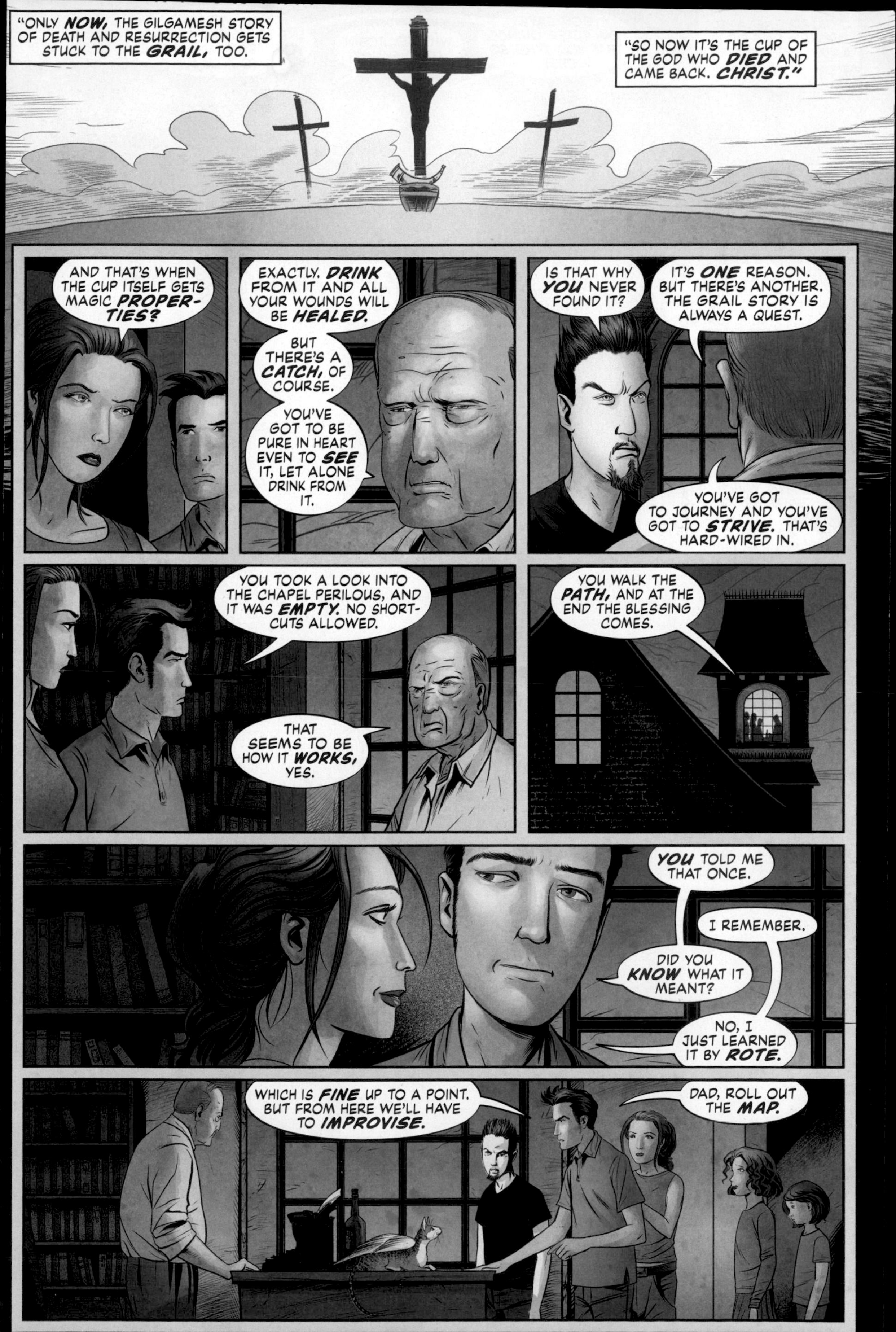
"ONLY NOW, THE GILGAMESH STORY OF DEATH AND RESURRECTION GETS STUCK TO THE GRAIL, TOO.
"SO NOW IT'S THE CUP OF THE GOD WHO DIED AND CAME BACK. CHRIST."
AND THAT'S WHEN THE CUP ITSELF GETS MAGIC PROPER-TIES?
EXACTLY. DRINK FROM IT AND ALL YOUR WOUNDS WILL BE HEALED.
BUT THERE'S A CATCH, OF COURSE.
YOU'VE GOT TO BE PURE IN HEART EVEN TO SEE IT, LET ALONE DRINK FROM IT.
IS THAT WHY YOU NEVER FOUND IT?
IT'S ONE REASON. BUT THERE'S ANOTHER. THE GRAIL STORY IS ALWAYS A QUEST.
YOU'VE GOT TO JOURNEY AND YOU'VE GOT TO STRIVE. THAT'S HARD-WIRED IN.
YOU TOOK A LOOK INTO THE CHAPEL PERILOUS, AND IT WAS EMPTY. NO SHORT-CUTS ALLOWED.
THAT SEEMS TO BE HOW IT WORKS, YES.
YOU WALK THE PATH, AND AT THE END THE BLESSING COMES.
YOU TOLD ME THAT ONCE.
I REMEMBER.
DID YOU KNOW WHAT IT MEANT?
NO, I JUST LEARNED IT BY ROTE.
WHICH IS FINE UP TO A POINT. BUT FROM HERE WE'LL HAVE TO IMPROVISE.
DAD, ROLL OUT THE MAP.

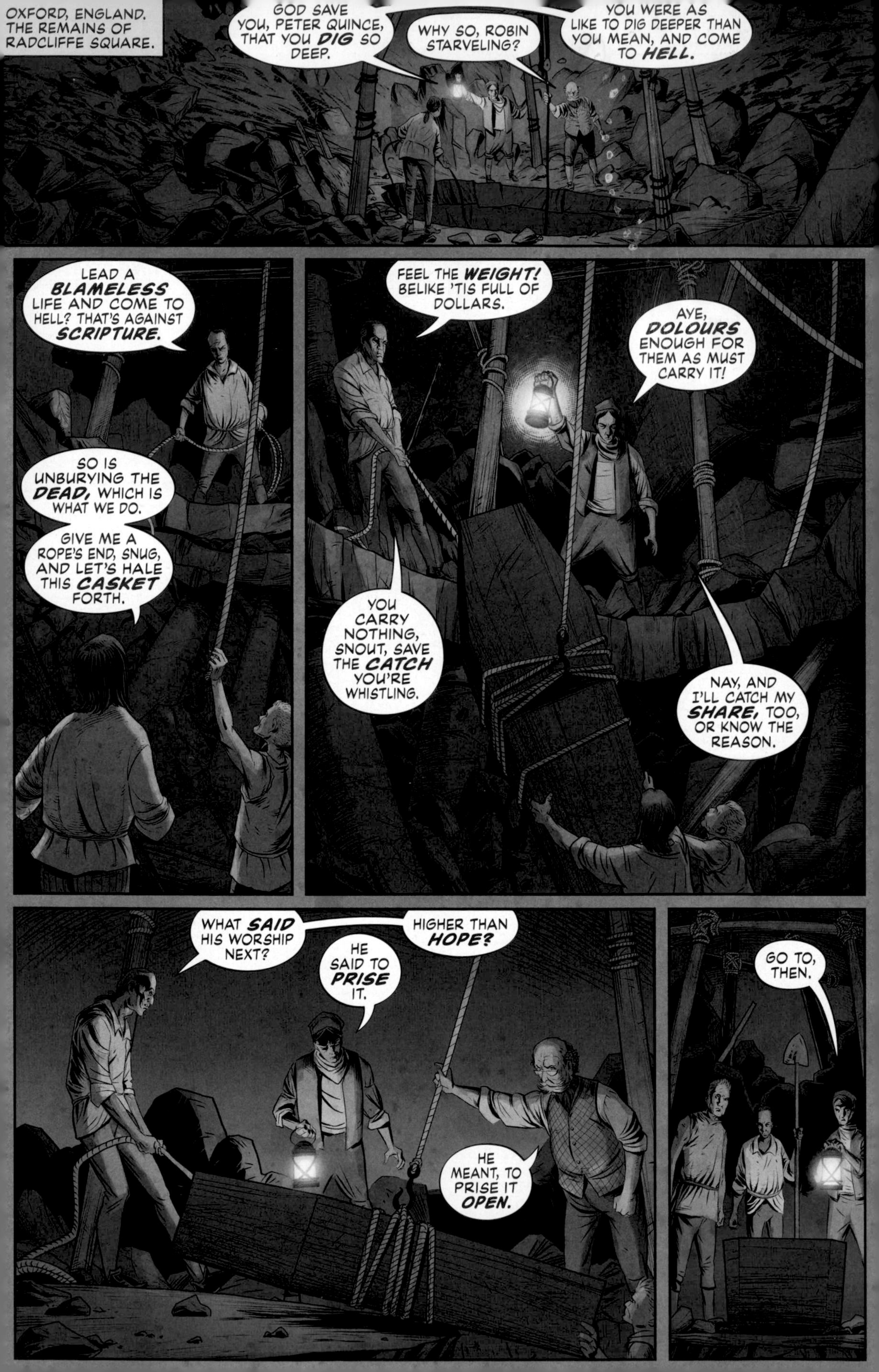

OXFORD, ENGLAND. THE REMAINS OF RADCLIFFE SQUARE.
GOD SAVE YOU, PETER QUINCE, THAT YOU DIG SO DEEP.
WHY SO, ROBIN STARVELING?
YOU WERE AS LIKE TO DIG DEEPER THAN YOU MEAN, AND COME TO HELL.
LEAD A BLAMELESS LIFE AND COME TO HELL? THAT'S AGAINST SCRIPTURE.
SO IS UNBURYING THE DEAD, WHICH IS WHAT WE DO.
GIVE ME A ROPE'S END, SNUG, AND LET'S HALE THIS CASKET FORTH.
FEEL THE WEIGHT! BELIKE 'TIS FULL OF DOLLARS.
AYE, DOLOURS ENOUGH FOR THEM AS MUST CARRY IT!
YOU CARRY NOTHING, SNOUT, SAVE THE CATCH YOU'RE WHISTLING.
NAY, AND I'LL CATCH MY SHARE, TOO, OR KNOW THE REASON.
WHAT SAID HIS WORSHIP NEXT?
HIGHER THAN HOPE?
HE SAID TO PRISE IT.
HE MEANT, TO PRISE IT OPEN.
GO TO, THEN.

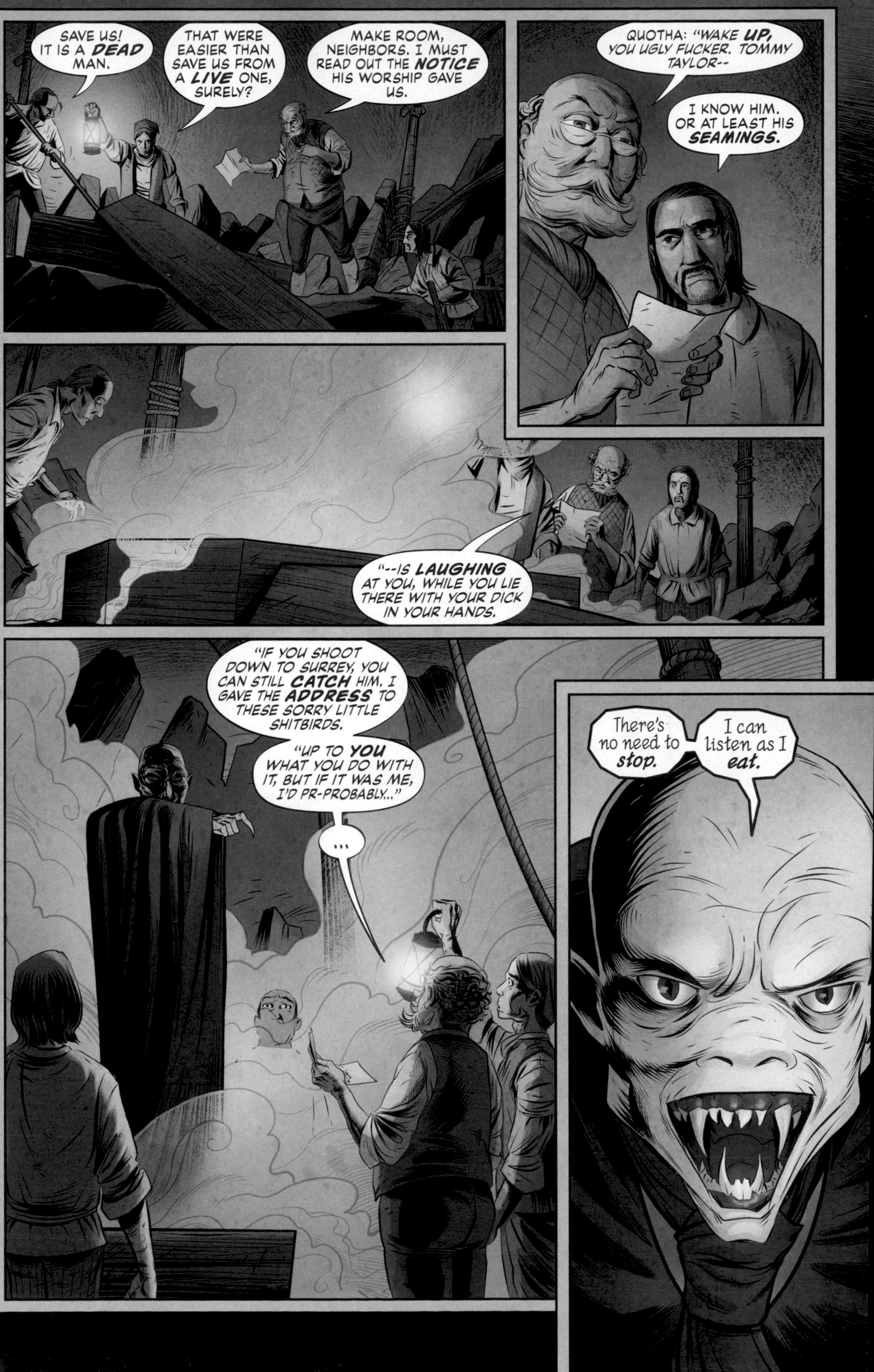
SAVE US! IT IS A DEAD MAN.
THAT WERE EASIER THAN SAVE US FROM A LIVE ONE, SURELY?
MAKE ROOM, NEIGHBORS. I MUST READ OUT THE NOTICE HIS WORSHIP GAVE US.
QUOTHA: "WAKE UP, YOU UGLY FUCKER. TOMMY TAYLOR--
I KNOW HIM. OR AT LEAST HIS SEAMINGS.
"--IS LAUGHING AT YOU, WHILE YOU LIE THERE WITH YOUR DICK IN YOUR HANDS.
"IF YOU SHOOT DOWN TO SURREY, YOU CAN STILL CATCH HIM. I GAVE THE ADDRESS TO THESE SORRY LITTLE SHITBIRDS.
"UP TO YOU WHAT YOU DO WITH IT, BUT IF IT WAS ME, I'D PR-PROBABLY..."
...
There's no need to stop.
I can listen as I eat.

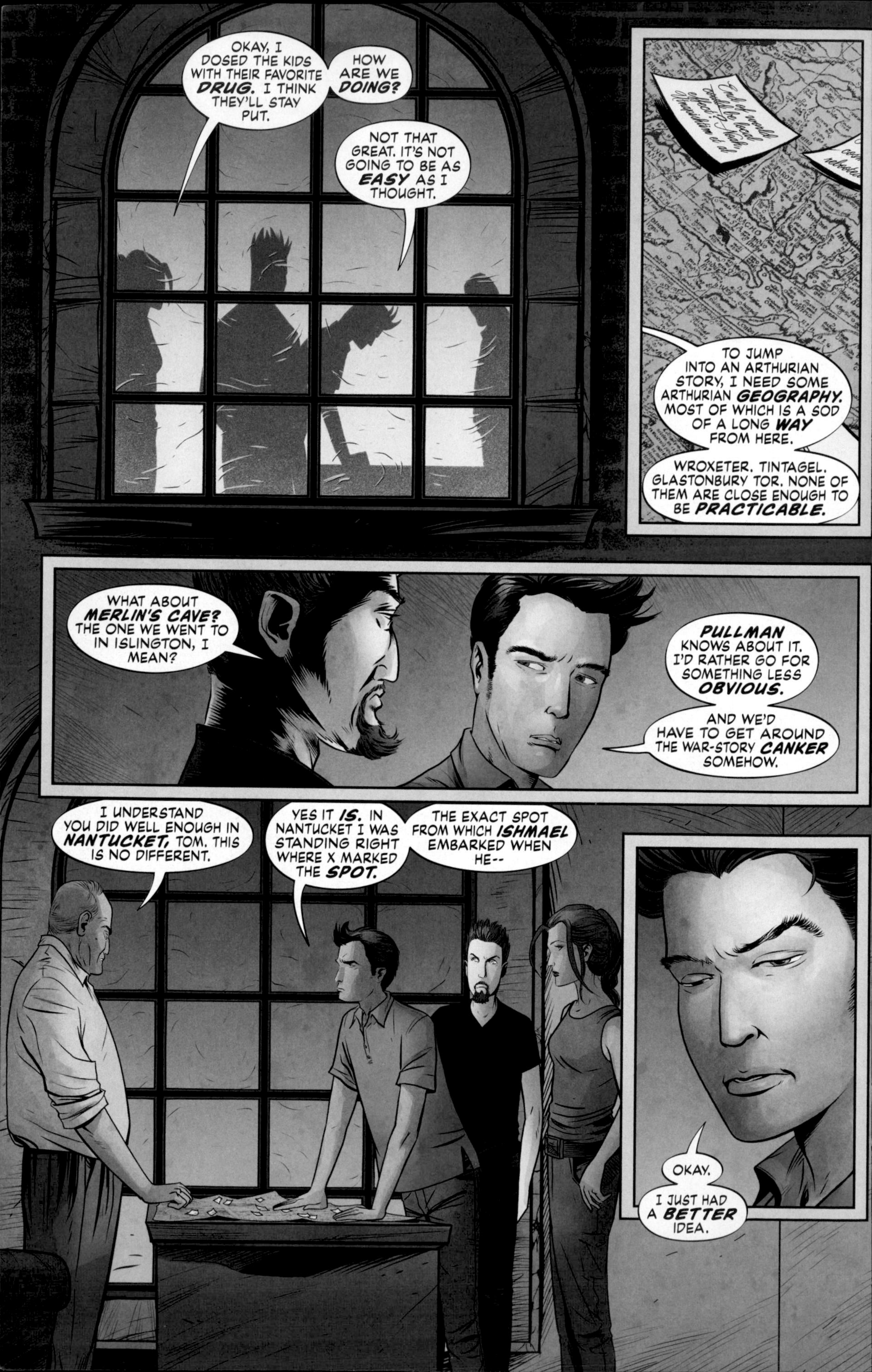
OKAY, I DOSED THE KIDS WITH THEIR FAVORITE DRUG. I THINK THEY'LL STAY PUT.
HOW ARE WE DOING?
NOT THAT GREAT. IT'S NOT GOING TO BE AS EASY AS I THOUGHT.
TO JUMP INTO AN ARTHURIAN STORY, I NEED SOME ARTHURIAN GEOGRAPHY. MOST OF WHICH IS A SOD OF A LONG WAY FROM HERE.
WROXETER. TINTAGEL. GLASTONBURY TOR. NONE OF THEM ARE CLOSE ENOUGH TO BE PRACTICABLE.
WHAT ABOUT MERLIN'S CAVE? THE ONE WE WENT TO IN ISLINGTON, I MEAN?
PULLMAN KNOWS ABOUT IT. I'D RATHER GO FOR SOMETHING LESS OBVIOUS.
AND WE'D HAVE TO GET AROUND THE WAR-STORY CANKER SOMEHOW.
I UNDERSTAND YOU DID WELL ENOUGH IN NANTUCKET, TOM. THIS IS NO DIFFERENT.
YES IT IS. IN NANTUCKET I WAS STANDING RIGHT WHERE X MARKED THE SPOT.
THE EXACT SPOT FROM WHICH ISHMAEL EMBARKED WHEN HE--
OKAY. I JUST HAD A BETTER IDEA.

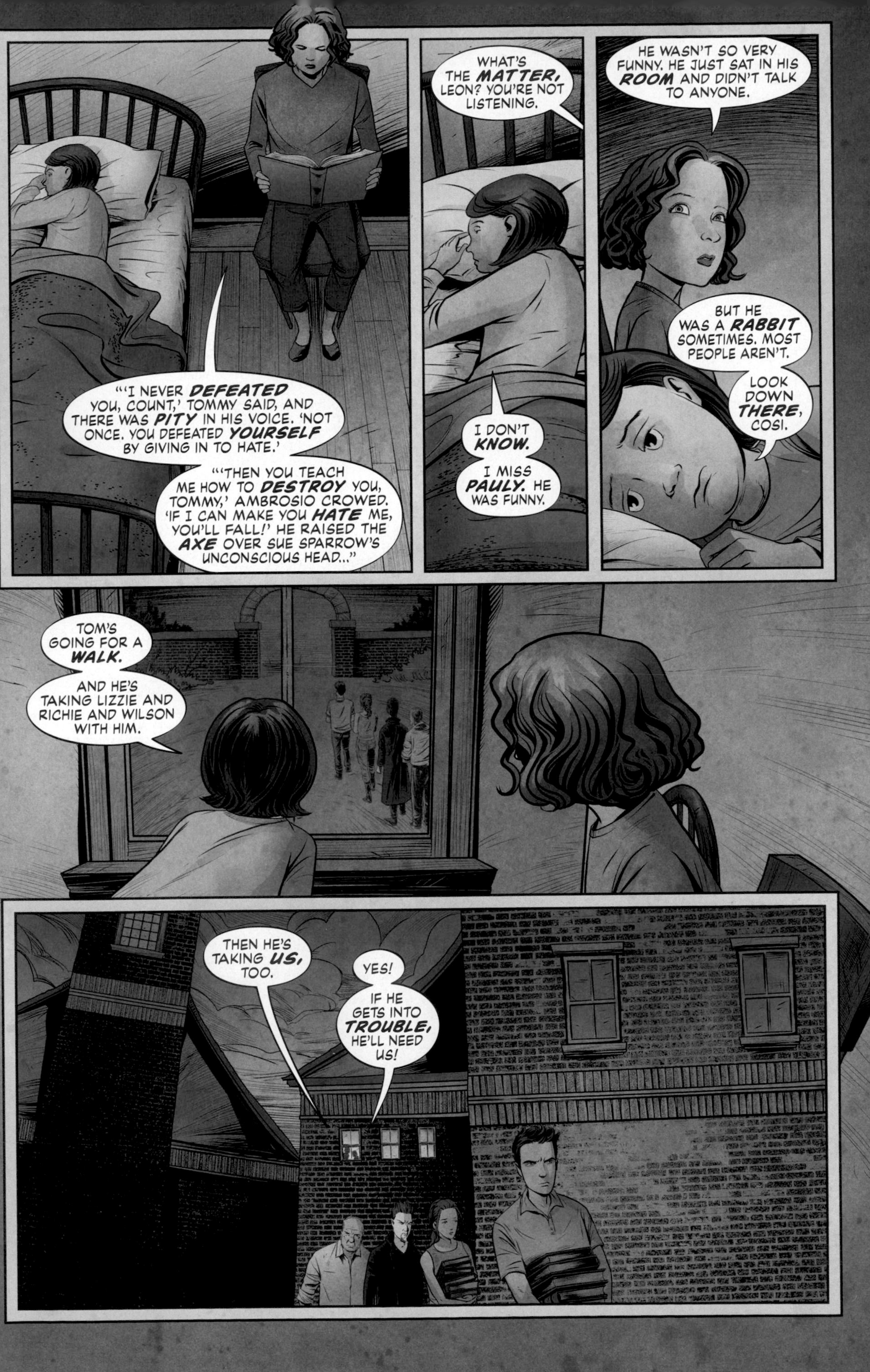
"'I NEVER DEFEATED YOU, COUNT,' TOMMY SAID, AND THERE WAS PITY IN HIS VOICE. 'NOT ONCE. YOU DEFEATED YOURSELF BY GIVING IN TO HATE.'
"'THEN YOU TEACH ME HOW TO DESTROY YOU, TOMMY,' AMBROSIO CROWED. 'IF I CAN MAKE YOU HATE ME, YOU'LL FALL!' HE RAISED THE AXE OVER SUE SPARROW'S UNCONSCIOUS HEAD..."
WHAT'S THE MATTER, LEON? YOU'RE NOT LISTENING.
I DON'T KNOW.
I MISS PAULY. HE WAS FUNNY.
HE WASN'T SO VERY FUNNY. HE JUST SAT IN HIS ROOM AND DIDN'T TALK TO ANYONE.
BUT HE WAS A RABBIT SOMETIMES. MOST PEOPLE AREN'T.
LOOK DOWN THERE, COSI.
TOM'S GOING FOR A WALK.
AND HE'S TAKING LIZZIE AND RICHIE AND WILSON WITH HIM.
THEN HE'S TAKING US, TOO.
YES!
IF HE GETS INTO TROUBLE, HE'LL NEED US!

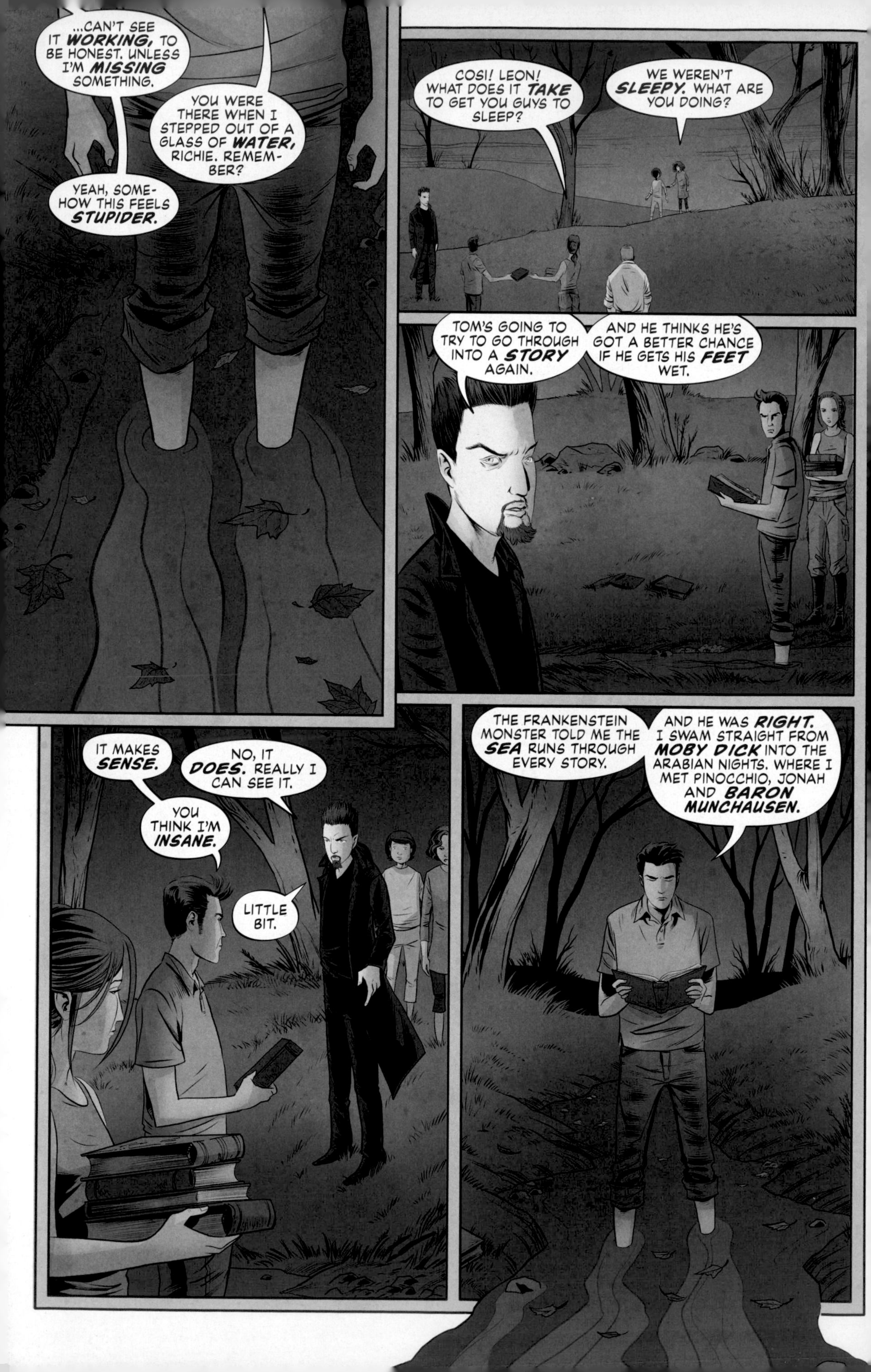
...CAN'T SEE IT WORKING, TO BE HONEST. UNLESS I'M MISSING SOMETHING.
YOU WERE THERE WHEN I STEPPED OUT OF A GLASS OF WATER, RICHIE. REMEMBER?
YEAH, SOMEHOW THIS FEELS STUPIDER.
COSI! LEON! WHAT DOES IT TAKE TO GET YOU GUYS TO SLEEP?
WE WEREN'T SLEEPY. WHAT ARE YOU DOING?
TOM'S GOING TO TRY TO GO THROUGH INTO A STORY AGAIN.
AND HE THINKS HE'S GOT A BETTER CHANCE IF HE GETS HIS FEET WET.
IT MAKES SENSE.
NO, IT DOES. REALLY I CAN SEE IT.
YOU THINK I'M INSANE.
LITTLE BIT.
THE FRANKENSTEIN MONSTER TOLD ME THE SEA RUNS THROUGH EVERY STORY.
AND HE WAS RIGHT. I SWAM STRAIGHT FROM MOBY DICK INTO THE ARABIAN NIGHTS. WHERE I MET PINOCCHIO, JONAH AND BARON MUNCHAUSEN.

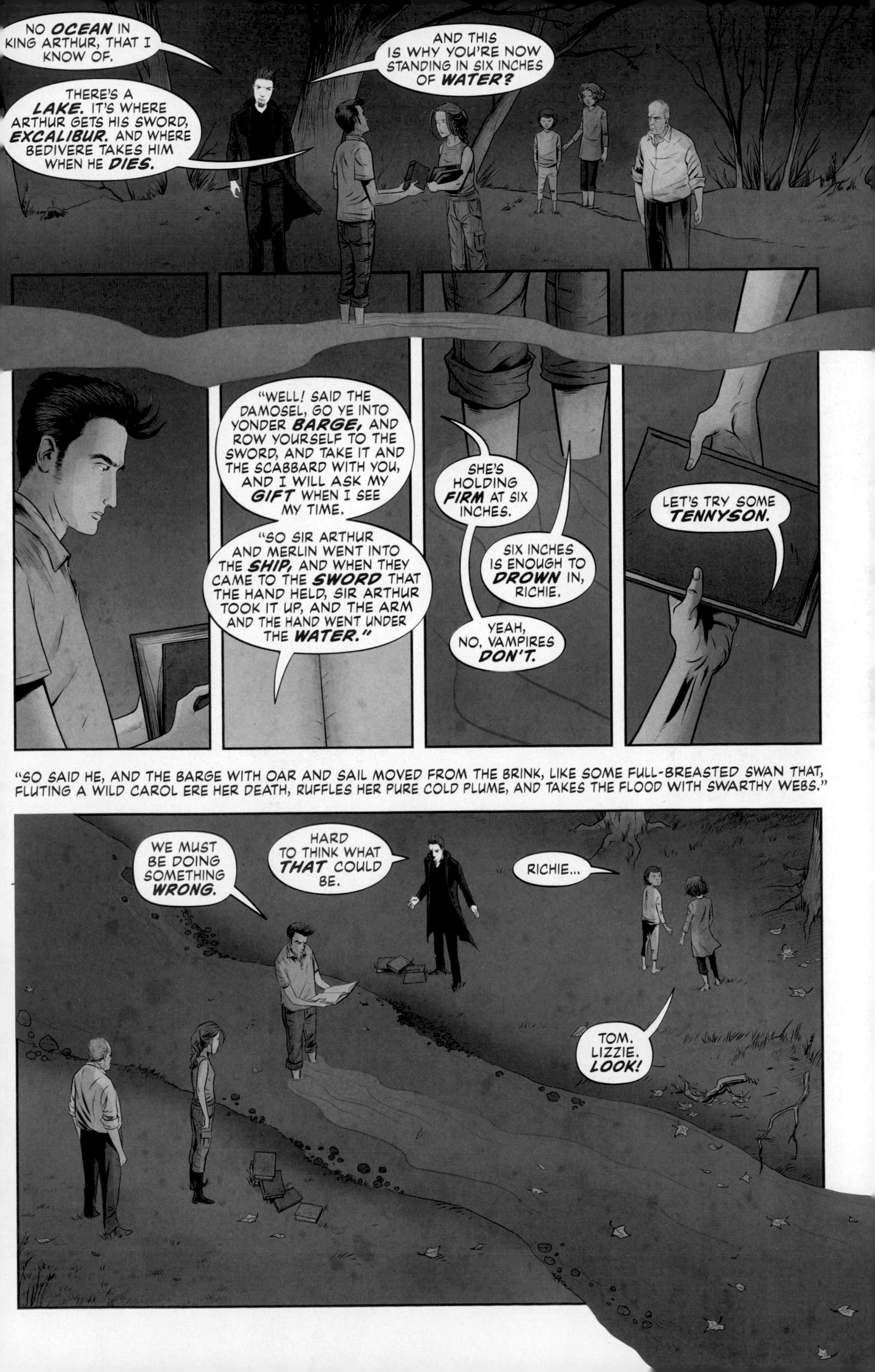

NO OCEAN IN KING ARTHUR, THAT I KNOW OF.
AND THIS IS WHY YOU'RE NOW STANDING IN SIX INCHES OF WATER?
THERE'S A LAKE. IT'S WHERE ARTHUR GETS HIS SWORD, EXCALIBUR. AND WHERE BEDIVERE TAKES HIM WHEN HE DIES.
"WELL! SAID THE DAMOSEL, GO YE INTO YONDER BARGE, AND ROW YOURSELF TO THE SWORD, AND TAKE IT AND THE SCABBARD WITH YOU, AND I WILL ASK MY GIFT WHEN I SEE MY TIME.
"SO SIR ARTHUR AND MERLIN WENT INTO THE SHIP, AND WHEN THEY CAME TO THE SWORD THAT THE HAND HELD, SIR ARTHUR TOOK IT UP, AND THE ARM AND THE HAND WENT UNDER THE WATER."
SHE'S HOLDING FIRM AT SIX INCHES.
SIX INCHES IS ENOUGH TO DROWN IN, RICHIE.
YEAH, NO, VAMPIRES DON'T.
LET'S TRY SOME TENNYSON.
"SO SAID HE, AND THE BARGE WITH OAR AND SAIL MOVED FROM THE BRINK, LIKE SOME FULL-BREASTED SWAN THAT, FLUTING A WILD CAROL ERE HER DEATH, RUFFLES HER PURE COLD PLUME, AND TAKES THE FLOOD WITH SWARTHY WEBS."
WE MUST BE DOING SOMETHING WRONG.
HARD TO THINK WHAT THAT COULD BE.
RICHIE...
TOM. LIZZIE. LOOK!

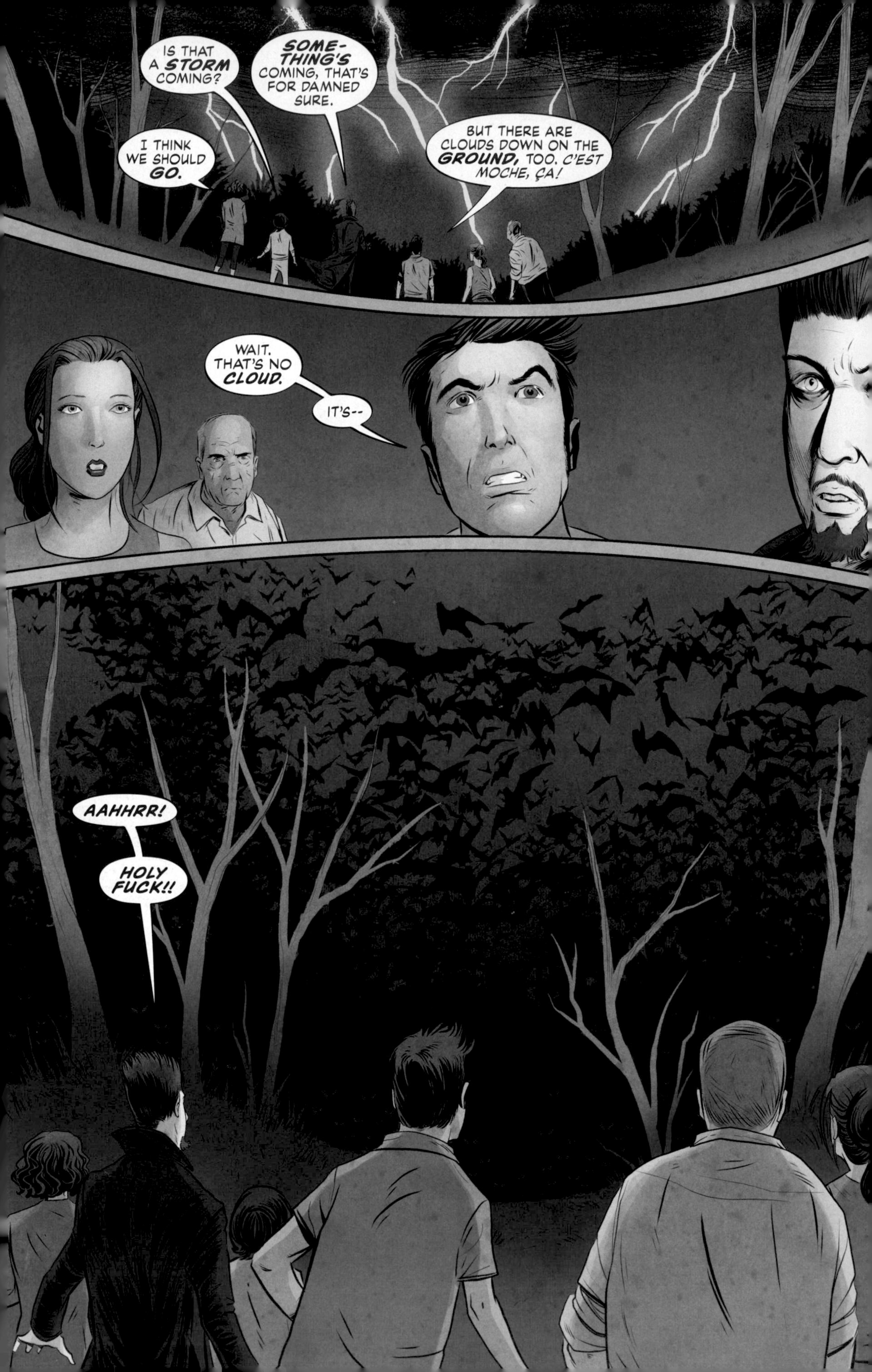
IS THAT A STORM COMING?
SOMETHING'S COMING, THAT'S FOR DAMNED SURE.
I THINK WE SHOULD GO.
BUT THERE ARE CLOUDS DOWN ON THE GROUND, TOO. C'EST MOCHE, ÇA!
WAIT. THAT'S NO CLOUD.
IT'S--
AAHHRR!
HOLY FUCK!!

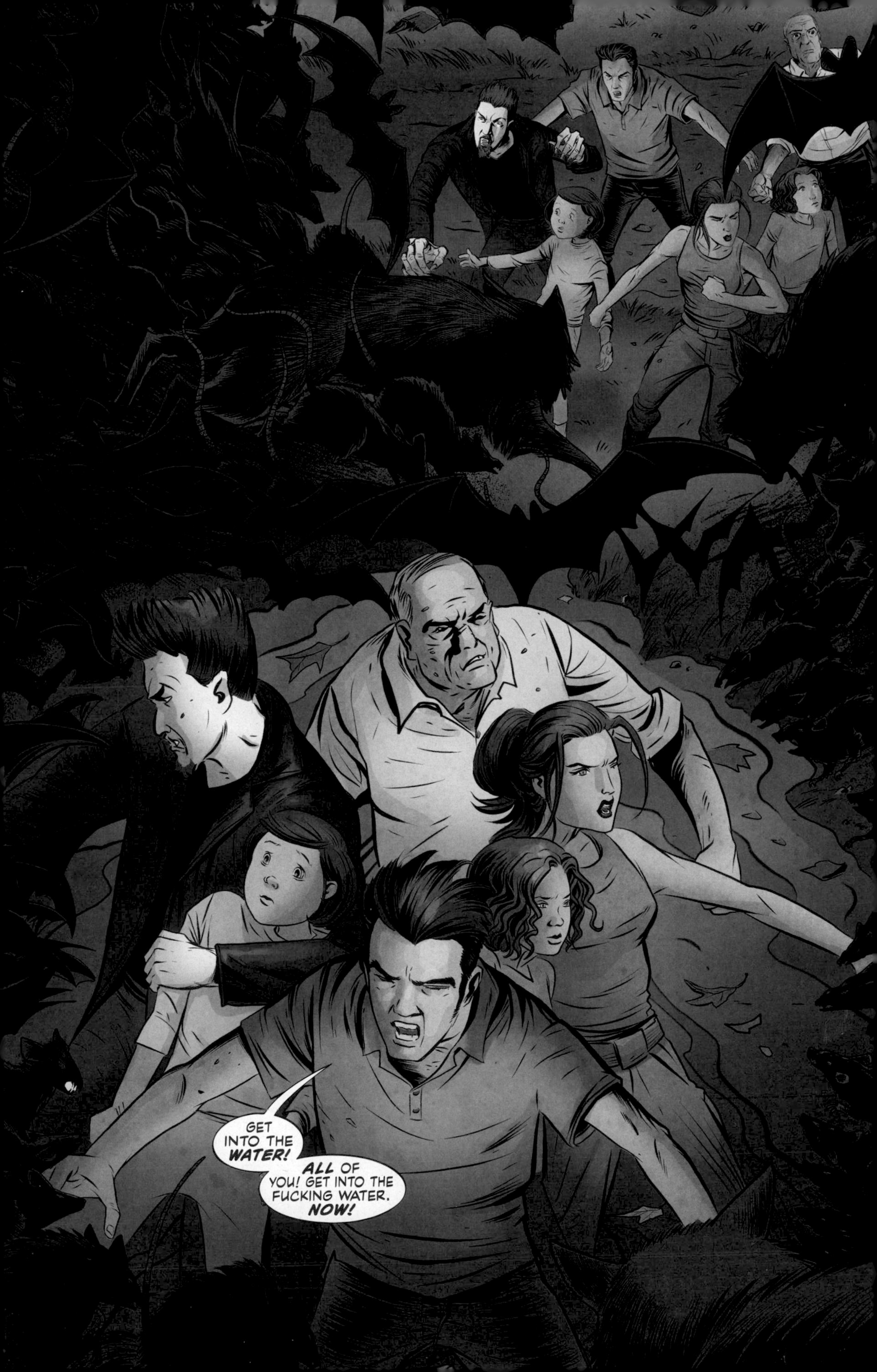
GET INTO THE WATER!
ALL OF YOU! GET INTO THE FUCKING WATER. NOW!

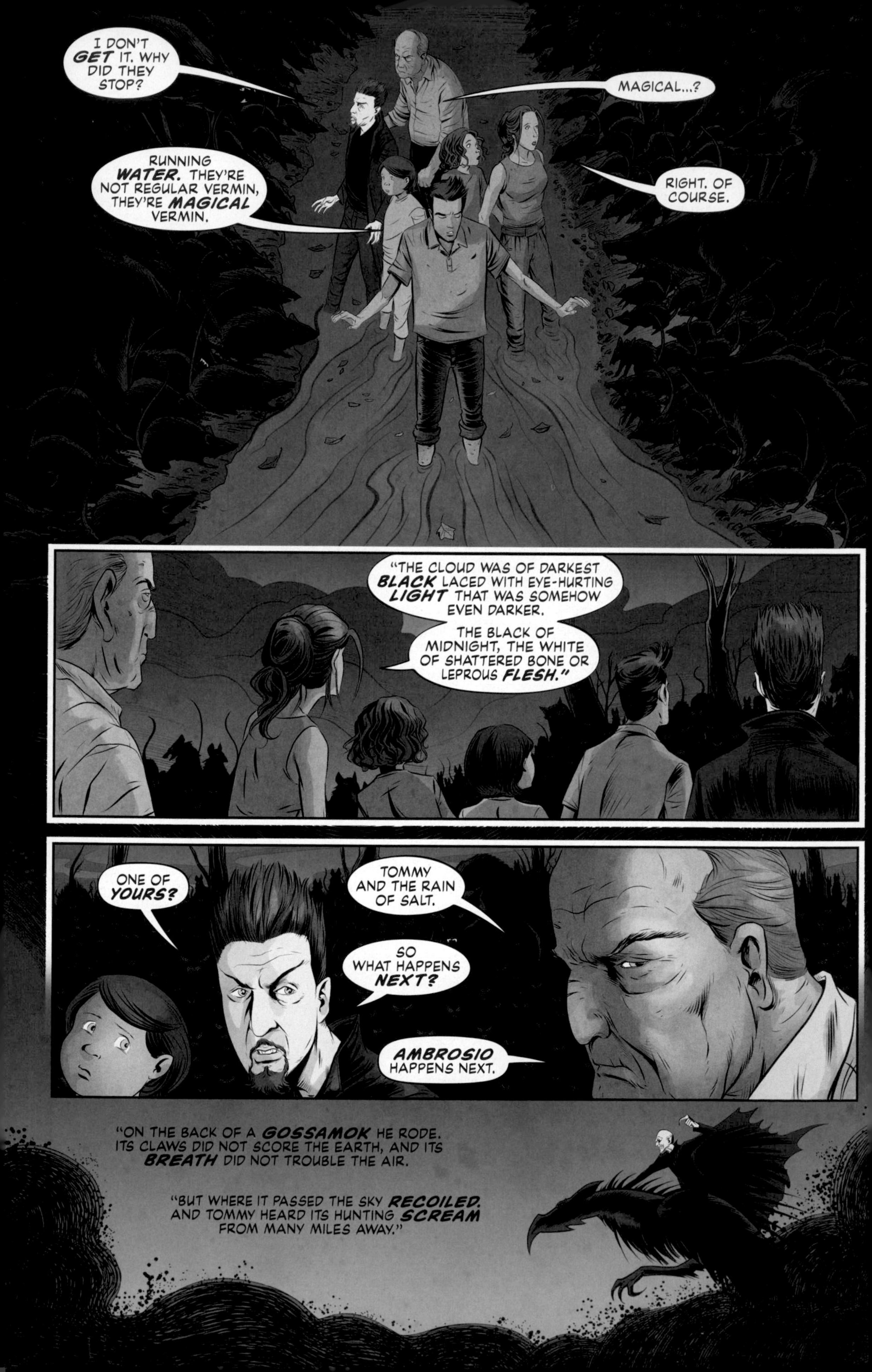
I DON'T GET IT. WHY DID THEY STOP?
MAGICAL...?
RUNNING WATER. THEY'RE NOT REGULAR VERMIN, THEY'RE MAGICAL VERMIN.
RIGHT. OF COURSE.
"THE CLOUD WAS OF DARKEST BLACK LACED WITH EYE-HURTING LIGHT THAT WAS SOMEHOW EVEN DARKER.
THE BLACK OF MIDNIGHT, THE WHITE OF SHATTERED BONE OR LEPROUS FLESH."
ONE OF YOURS?
TOMMY AND THE RAIN OF SALT.
SO WHAT HAPPENS NEXT?
AMBROSIO HAPPENS NEXT.
"ON THE BACK OF A GOSSAMOK HE RODE. ITS CLAWS DID NOT SCORE THE EARTH, AND ITS BREATH DID NOT TROUBLE THE AIR.
"BUT WHERE IT PASSED THE SKY RECOILED. AND TOMMY HEARD ITS HUNTING SCREAM FROM MANY MILES AWAY."

TOM, IF AMBROSIO SHOWS UP I'M FUCKED. HE'LL *BRAINWASH* ME LIKE HE DID LAST TIME.

I *KNOW*, RICHIE.

WE'VE GOT TO *RUN*.

WE CAN'T. IF WE RUN, THOSE THINGS WILL *EAT* US.

I NEED-- DAMN, I DON'T KNOW. A *BRANCH*. A FALLEN BRANCH.

YOU CAN'T *STAKE* HIM, MAN. HE'S WAY TOO FAST.

WHAT ABOUT *MAGIC?*

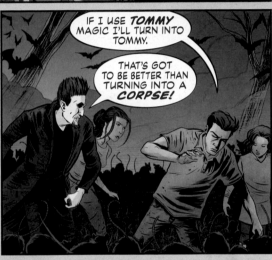

IF I USE *TOMMY* MAGIC I'LL TURN INTO TOMMY.

THAT'S GOT TO BE BETTER THAN TURNING INTO A *CORPSE!*

VOILÀ, TOM.

THANKS, LEON. THAT'S PERFECT.

SHIT! PERFECT FOR *WHAT?*

FOR THE *POSE*, MAINLY. I'D FEEL PRETTY RIDICULOUS DOING THIS WITH *EMPTY* HANDS.

GET BEHIND ME. I THINK I'VE *GOT* THIS.

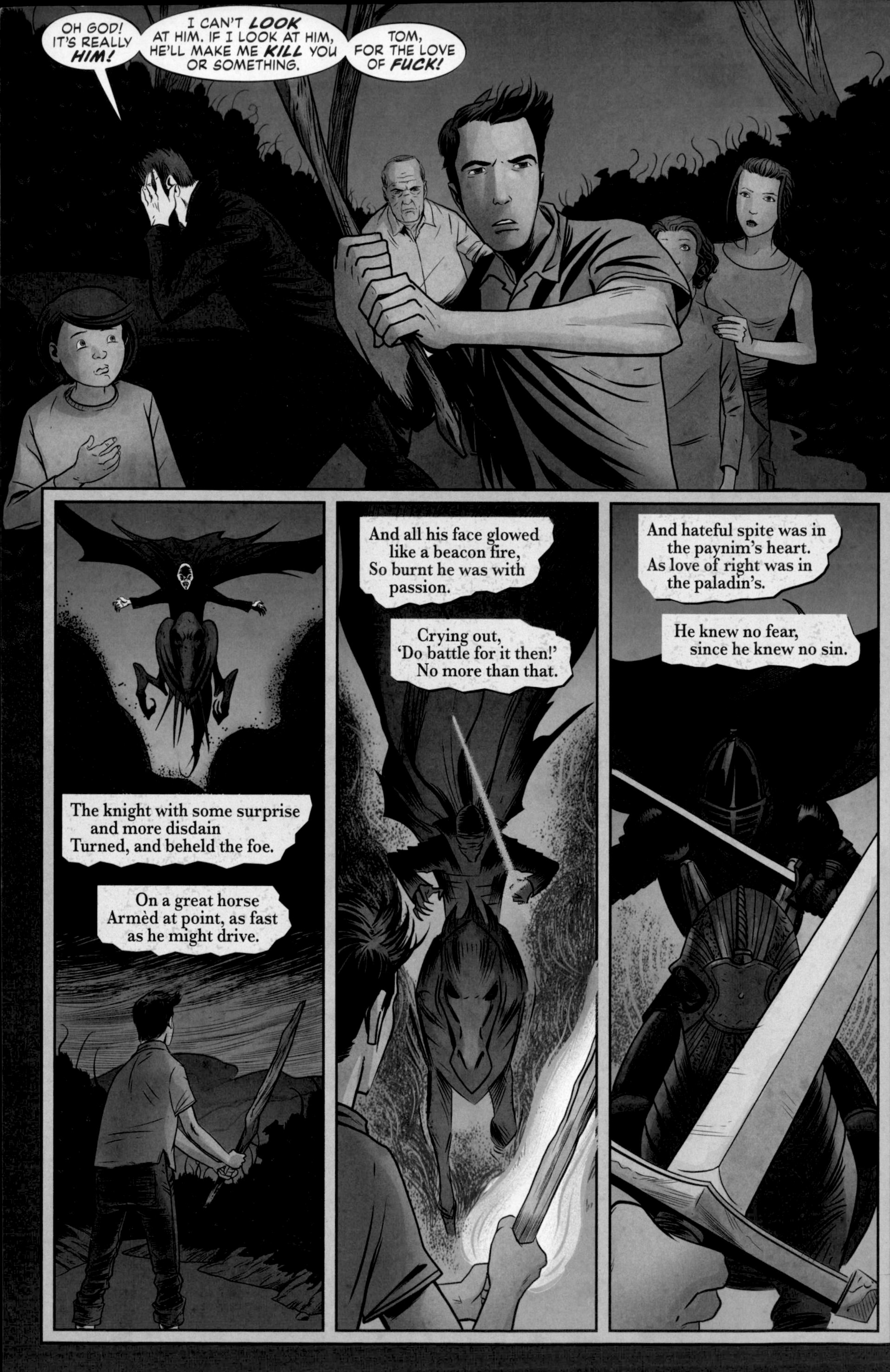
OH GOD! IT'S REALLY HIM!
I CAN'T LOOK AT HIM. IF I LOOK AT HIM, HE'LL MAKE ME KILL YOU OR SOMETHING.
TOM, FOR THE LOVE OF FUCK!
The knight with some surprise and more disdain Turned, and beheld the foe.
On a great horse Armèd at point, as fast as he might drive.
And all his face glowed like a beacon fire, So burnt he was with passion.
Crying out, 'Do battle for it then!' No more than that.
And hateful spite was in the paynim's heart. As love of right was in the paladin's.
He knew no fear, since he knew no sin.

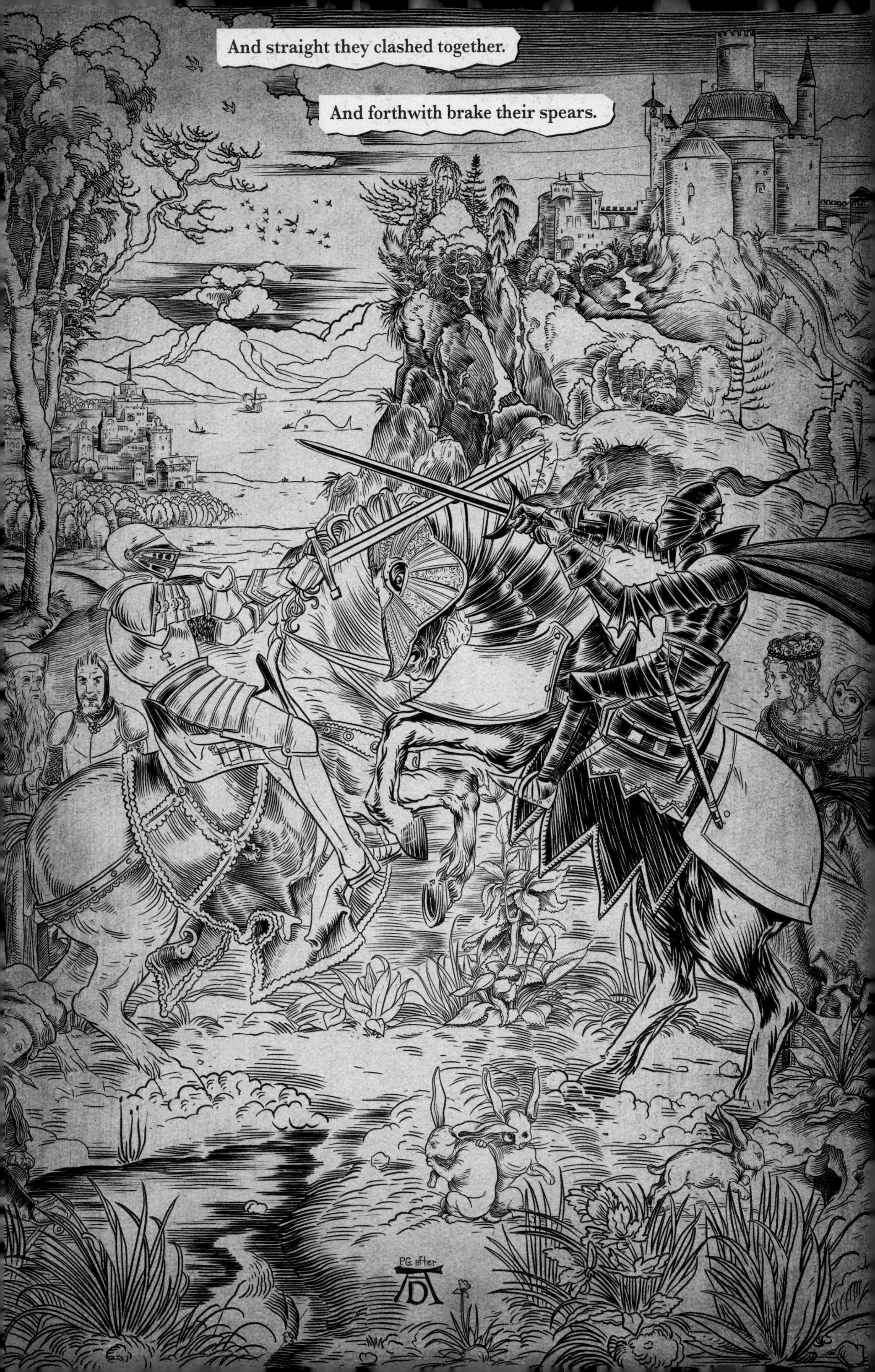
And straight they clashed together.
And forthwith brake their spears.
P.G. after

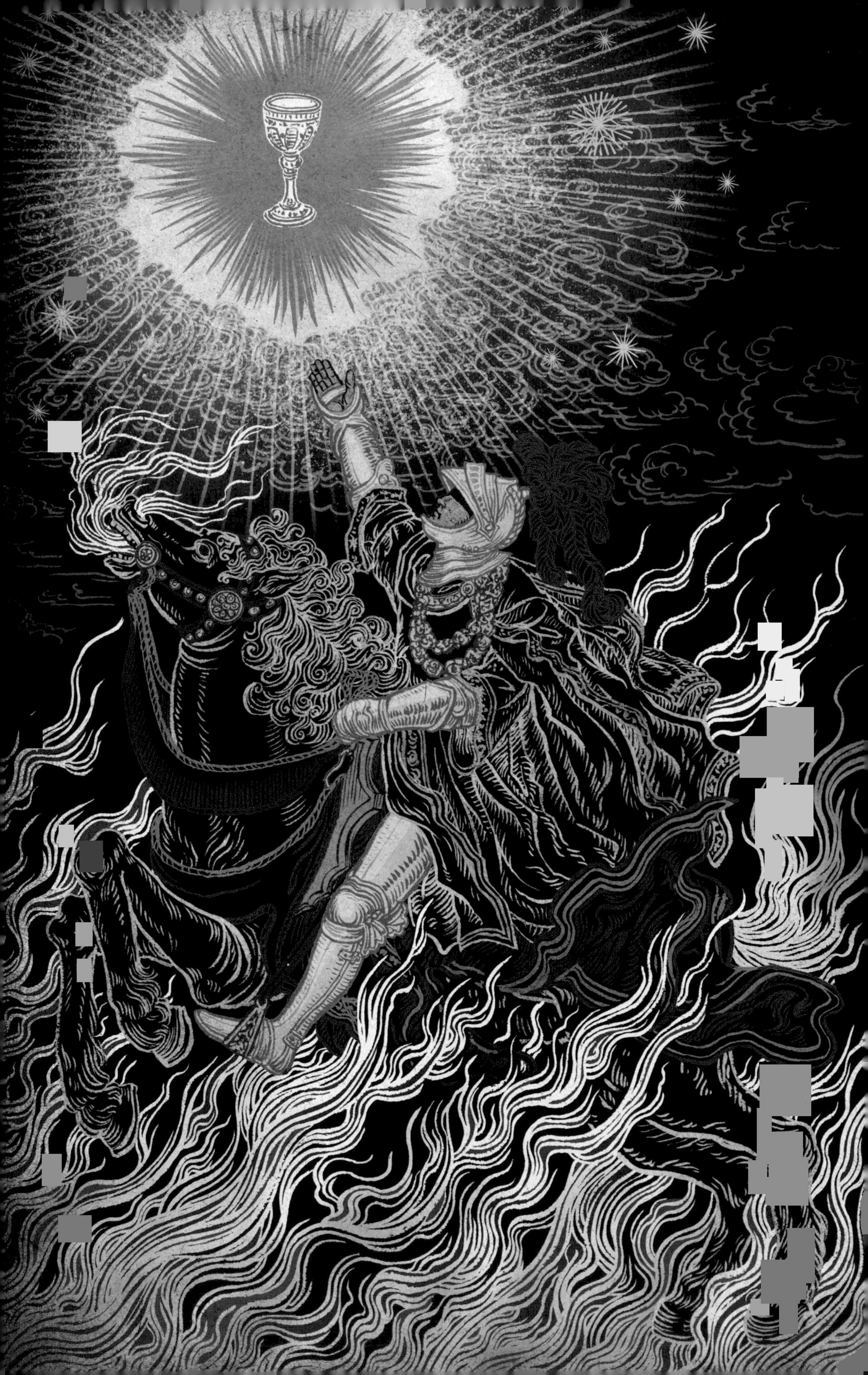

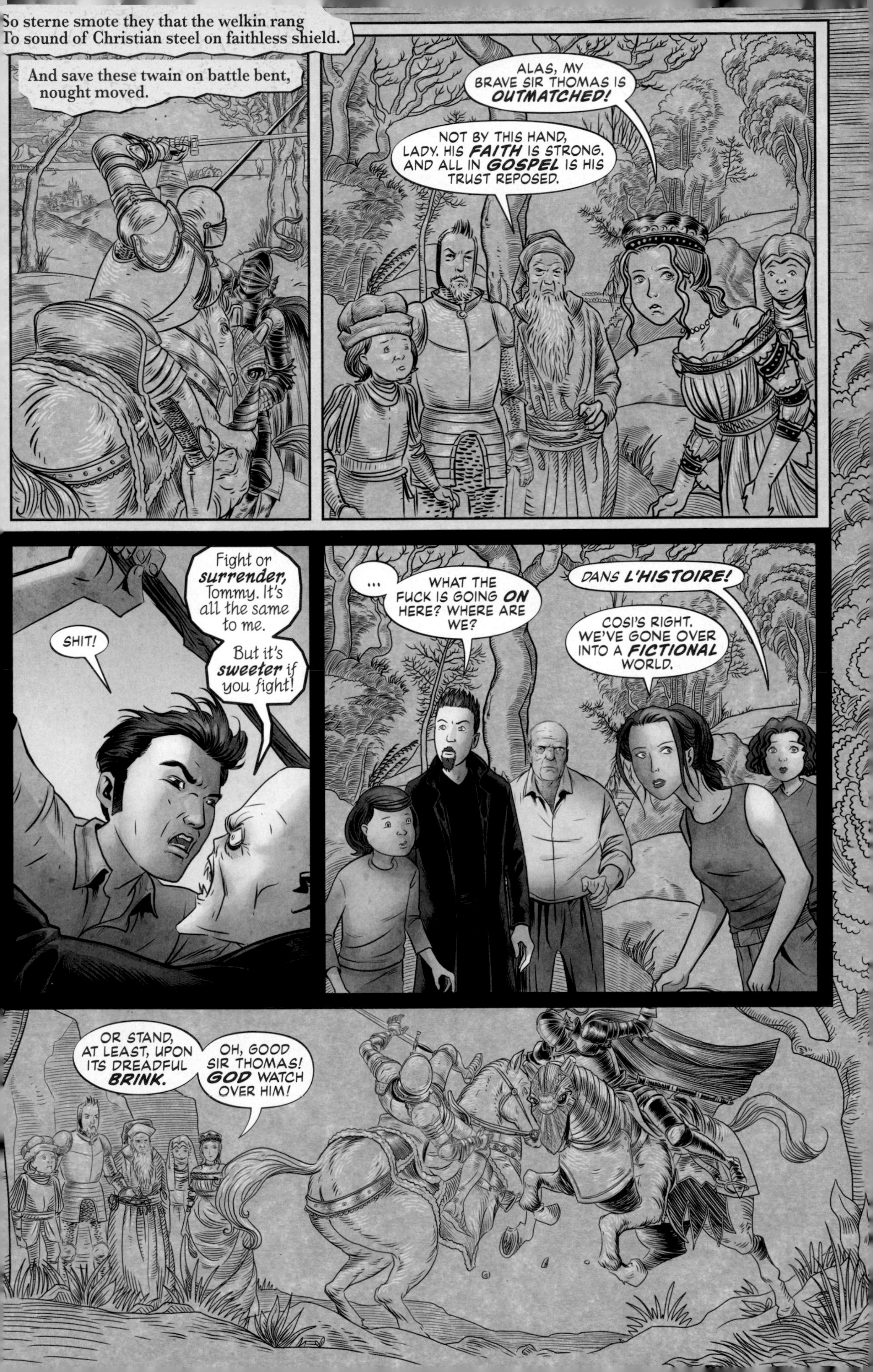

So sterne smote they that the welkin rang
To sound of Christian steel on faithless shield.
And save these twain on battle bent, nought moved.
ALAS, MY BRAVE SIR THOMAS IS OUTMATCHED!
NOT BY THIS HAND, LADY. HIS FAITH IS STRONG. AND ALL IN GOSPEL IS HIS TRUST REPOSED.
Fight or surrender, Tommy. It's all the same to me.
But it's sweeter if you fight!
SHIT!
...
WHAT THE FUCK IS GOING ON HERE? WHERE ARE WE?
DANS L'HISTOIRE!
COSI'S RIGHT. WE'VE GONE OVER INTO A FICTIONAL WORLD.
OR STAND, AT LEAST, UPON ITS DREADFUL BRINK.
OH, GOOD SIR THOMAS! GOD WATCH OVER HIM!

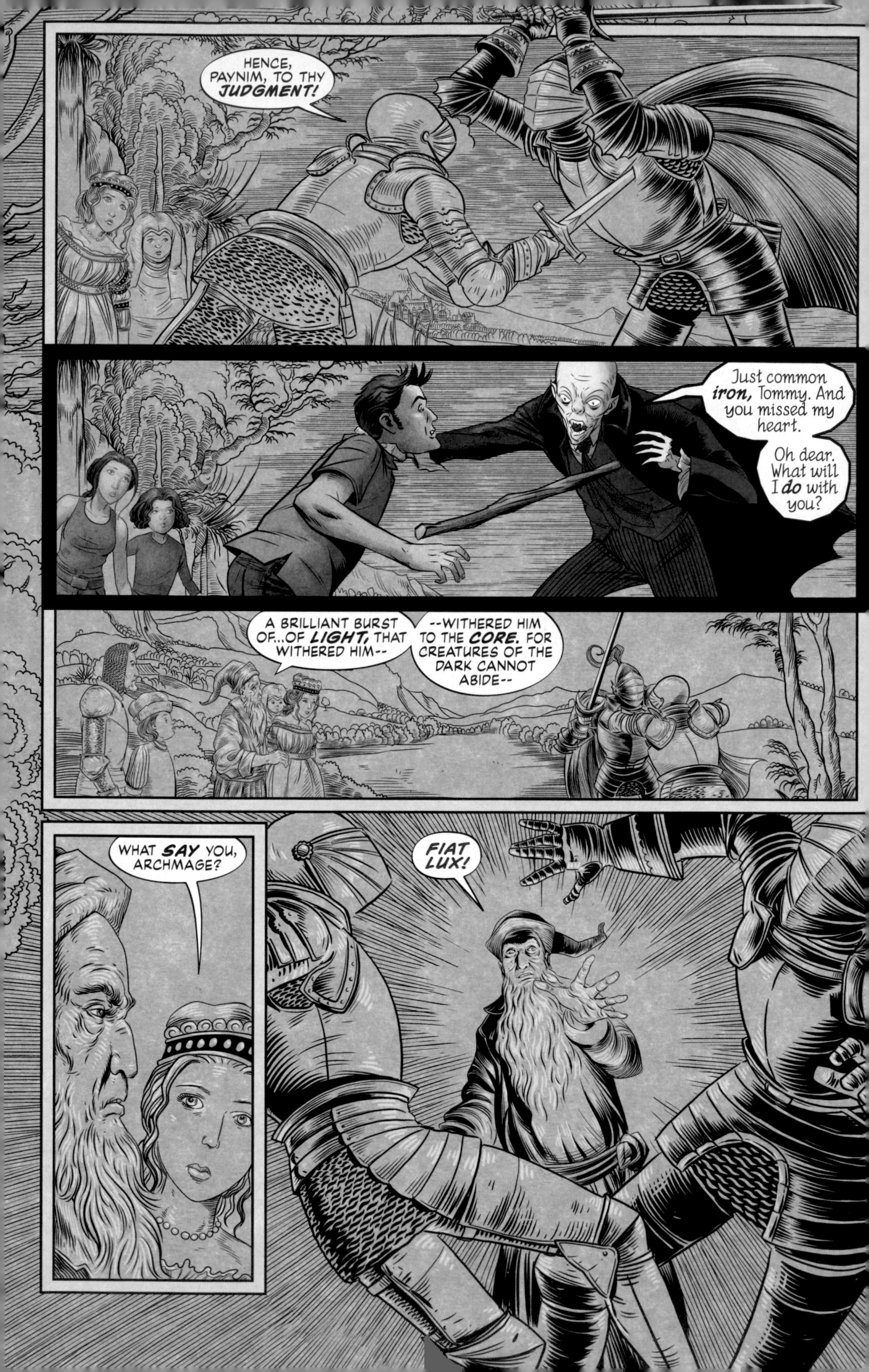
HENCE, PAYNIM, TO THY JUDGMENT!
Just common iron, Tommy. And you missed my heart.
Oh dear. What will I do with you?
A BRILLIANT BURST OF...OF LIGHT, THAT WITHERED HIM--
--WITHERED HIM TO THE CORE. FOR CREATURES OF THE DARK CANNOT ABIDE--
WHAT SAY YOU, ARCHMAGE?
FIAT LUX!

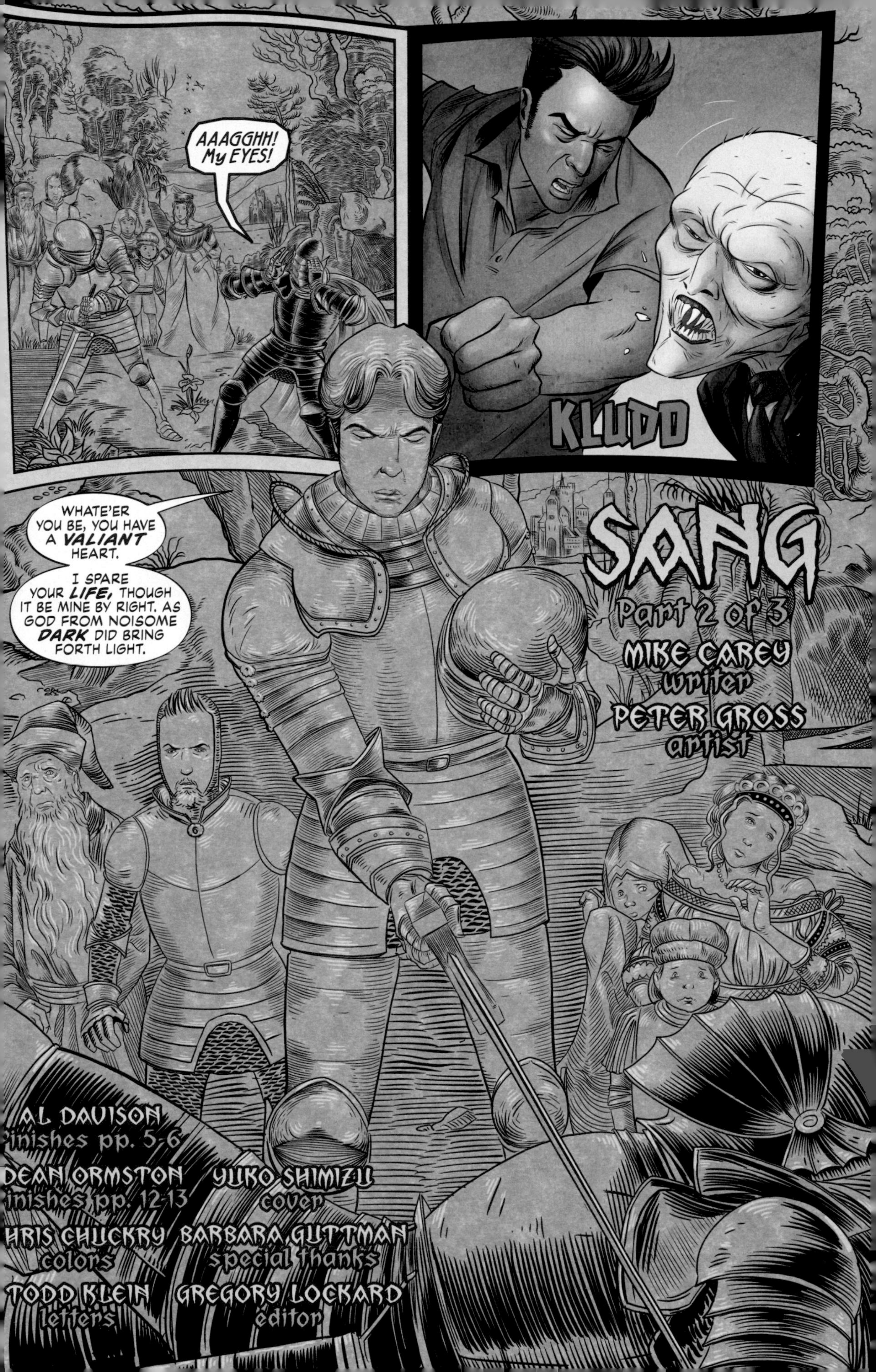
AAAGGHH! My EYES!
KLUDD
WHATE'ER YOU BE, YOU HAVE A VALIANT HEART.
I SPARE YOUR LIFE, THOUGH IT BE MINE BY RIGHT. AS GOD FROM NOISOME DARK DID BRING FORTH LIGHT.
SANG
Part 2 of 3
MIKE CAREY writer
PETER GROSS artist
AL DAVISON inishes pp. 5-6
DEAN ORMSTON inishes pp. 12-13
YUKO SHIMIZU cover
HRIS CHUCKRY colors
BARBARA GUTTMAN special thanks
TODD KLEIN letters
GREGORY LOCKARD editor

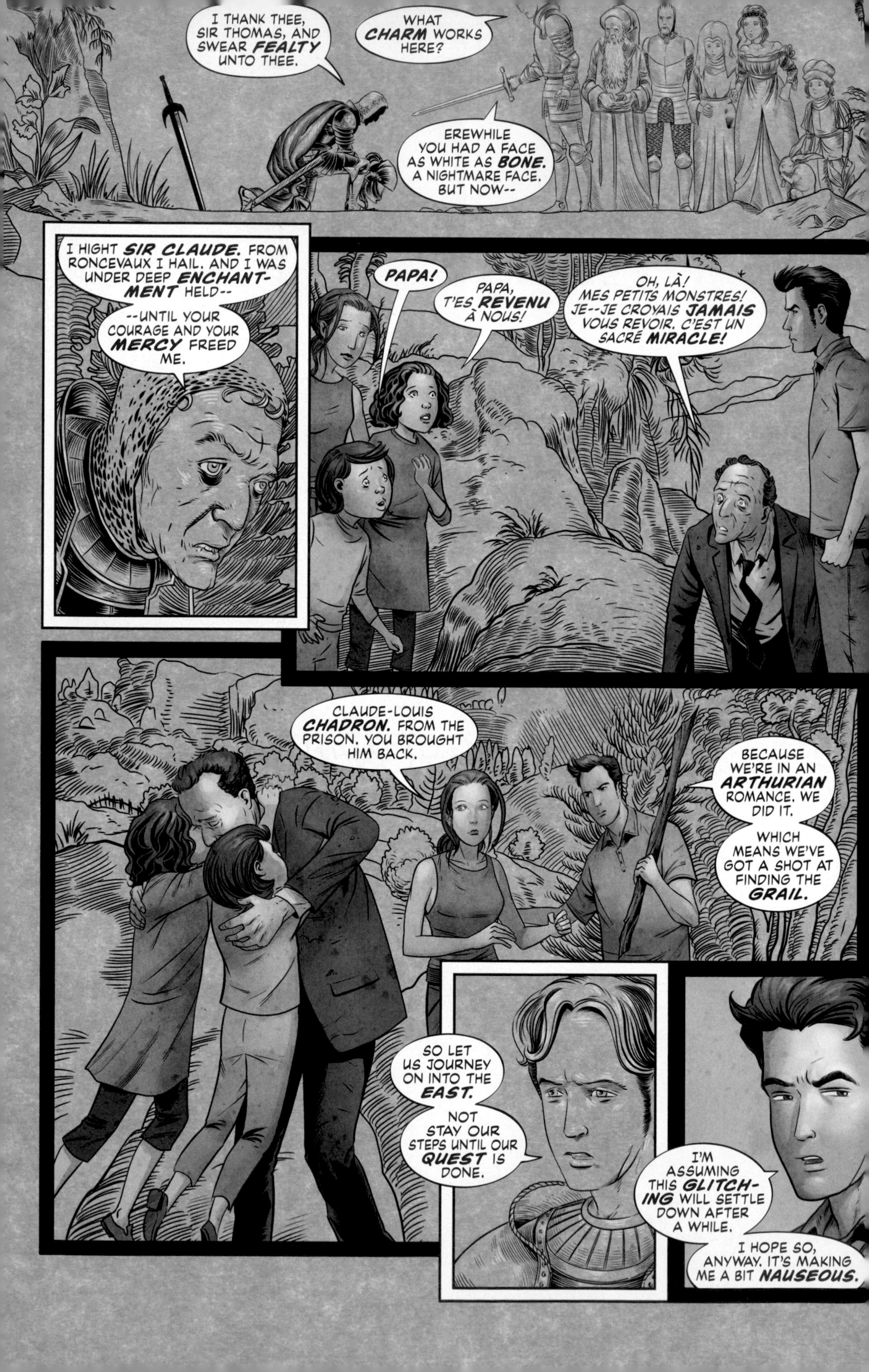
I THANK THEE, SIR THOMAS, AND SWEAR *FEALTY* UNTO THEE.
WHAT *CHARM* WORKS HERE?
EREWHILE YOU HAD A FACE AS WHITE AS *BONE*. A NIGHTMARE FACE. BUT NOW--
I HIGHT *SIR CLAUDE*. FROM RONCEVAUX I HAIL. AND I WAS UNDER DEEP *ENCHANT-MENT* HELD--
--UNTIL YOUR COURAGE AND YOUR *MERCY* FREED ME.
PAPA!
PAPA, T'ES *REVENU* À NOUS!
OH, LÀ! MES PETITS MONSTRES! JE--JE CROYAIS *JAMAIS* VOUS REVOIR. C'EST UN SACRÉ *MIRACLE!*
CLAUDE-LOUIS *CHADRON*. FROM THE PRISON. YOU BROUGHT HIM BACK.
BECAUSE WE'RE IN AN *ARTHURIAN* ROMANCE. WE DID IT.
WHICH MEANS WE'VE GOT A SHOT AT FINDING THE *GRAIL*.
SO LET US JOURNEY ON INTO THE *EAST*.
NOT STAY OUR STEPS UNTIL OUR *QUEST* IS DONE.
I'M ASSUMING THIS *GLITCH-ING* WILL SETTLE DOWN AFTER A WHILE.
I HOPE SO, ANYWAY. IT'S MAKING ME A BIT *NAUSEOUS*.

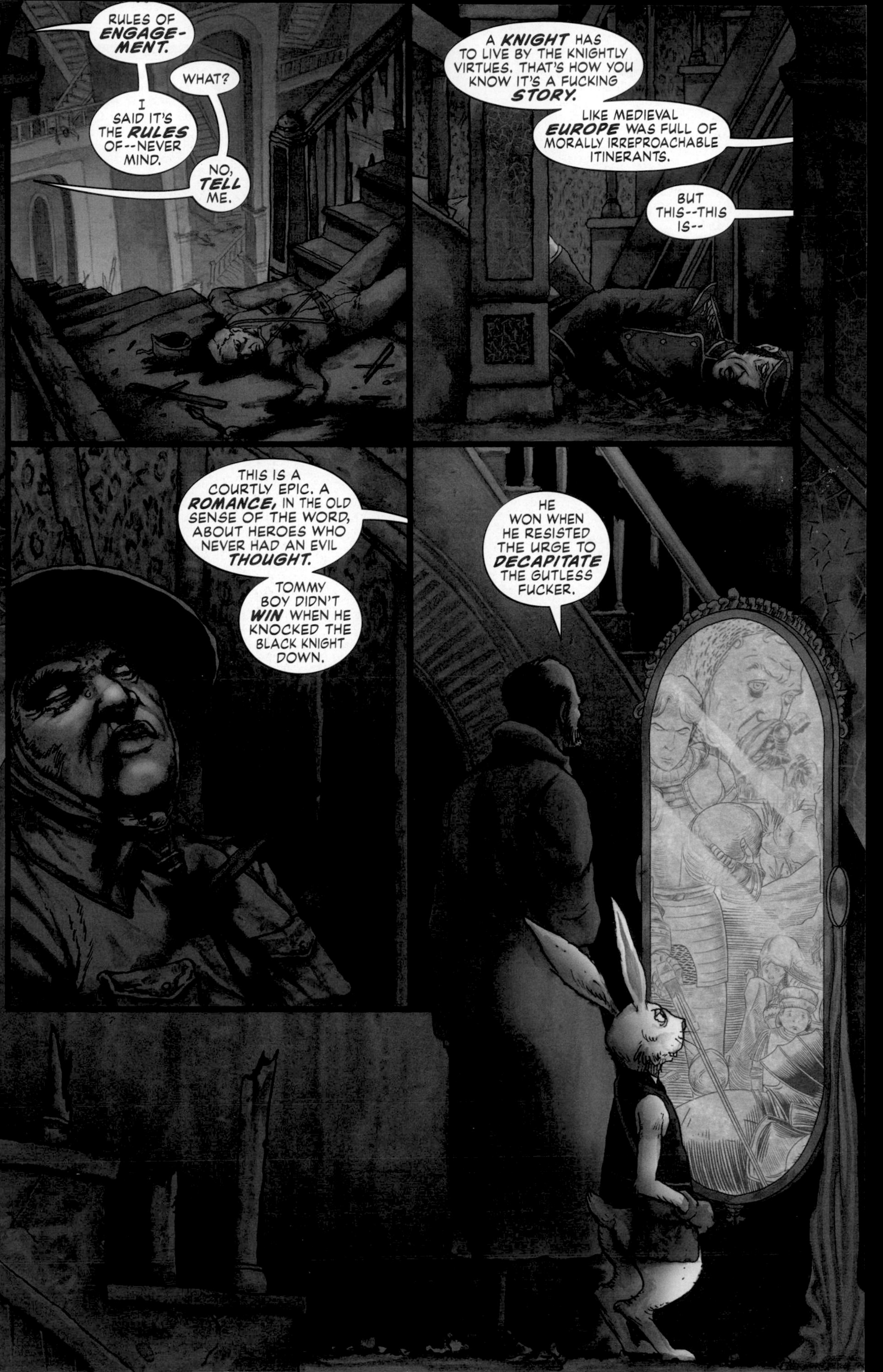

RULES OF ENGAGEMENT.
WHAT?
I SAID IT'S THE RULES OF--NEVER MIND.
NO, TELL ME.
A KNIGHT HAS TO LIVE BY THE KNIGHTLY VIRTUES. THAT'S HOW YOU KNOW IT'S A FUCKING STORY.
LIKE MEDIEVAL EUROPE WAS FULL OF MORALLY IRREPROACHABLE ITINERANTS.
BUT THIS--THIS IS--
THIS IS A COURTLY EPIC. A ROMANCE, IN THE OLD SENSE OF THE WORD, ABOUT HEROES WHO NEVER HAD AN EVIL THOUGHT.
TOMMY BOY DIDN'T WIN WHEN HE KNOCKED THE BLACK KNIGHT DOWN.
HE WON WHEN HE RESISTED THE URGE TO DECAPITATE THE GUTLESS FUCKER.

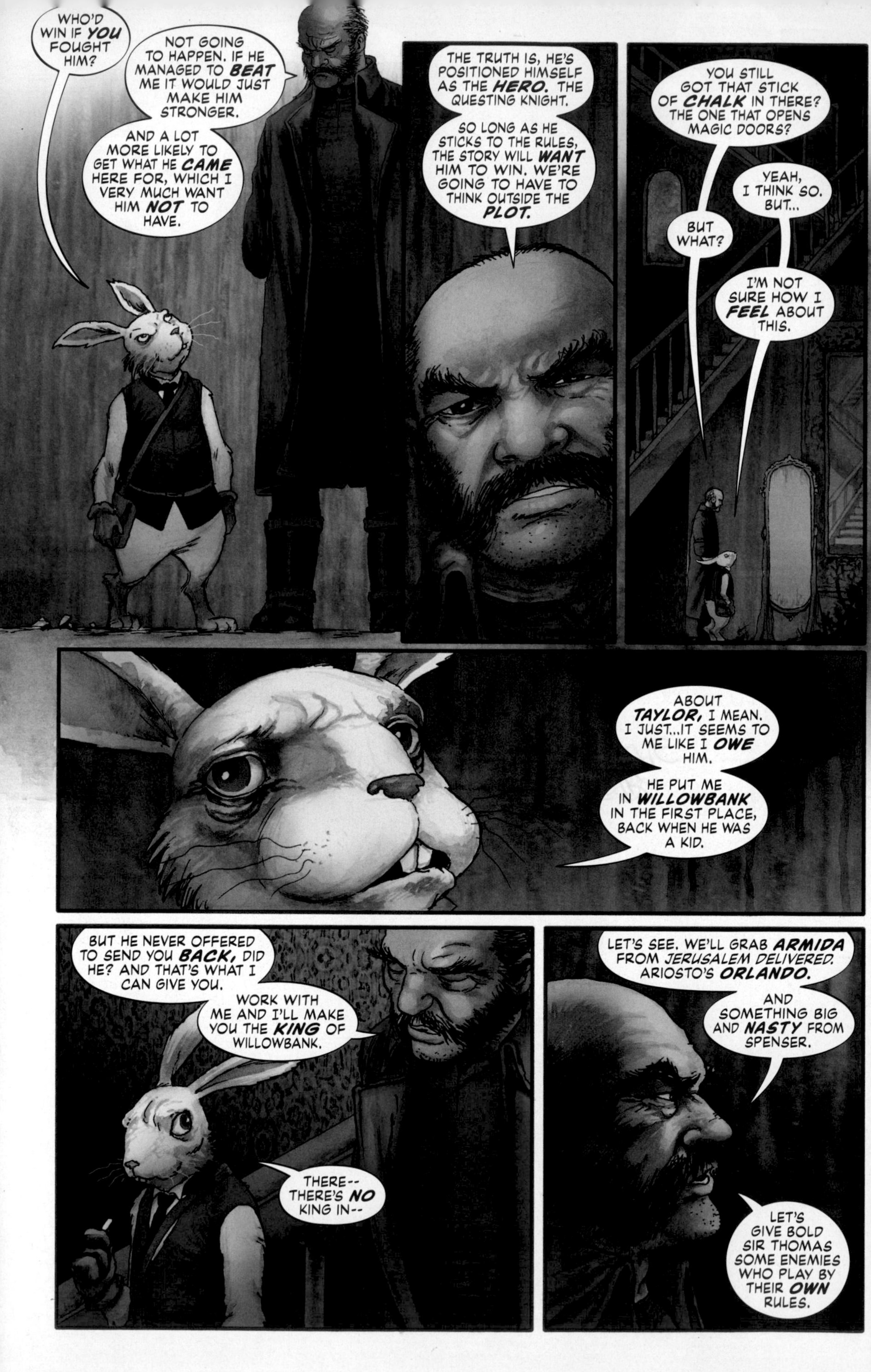
WHO'D WIN IF *YOU* FOUGHT HIM?
NOT GOING TO HAPPEN. IF HE MANAGED TO *BEAT* ME IT WOULD JUST MAKE HIM STRONGER.
AND A LOT MORE LIKELY TO GET WHAT HE *CAME* HERE FOR, WHICH I VERY MUCH WANT HIM *NOT* TO HAVE.
THE TRUTH IS, HE'S POSITIONED HIMSELF AS THE *HERO.* THE QUESTING KNIGHT.
SO LONG AS HE STICKS TO THE RULES, THE STORY WILL *WANT* HIM TO WIN. WE'RE GOING TO HAVE TO THINK OUTSIDE THE *PLOT.*
YOU STILL GOT THAT STICK OF *CHALK* IN THERE? THE ONE THAT OPENS MAGIC DOORS?
YEAH, I THINK SO. BUT...
BUT WHAT?
I'M NOT SURE HOW I *FEEL* ABOUT THIS.
ABOUT *TAYLOR,* I MEAN. I JUST...IT SEEMS TO ME LIKE I *OWE* HIM.
HE PUT ME IN *WILLOWBANK* IN THE FIRST PLACE, BACK WHEN HE WAS A KID.
BUT HE NEVER OFFERED TO SEND YOU *BACK,* DID HE? AND THAT'S WHAT I CAN GIVE YOU.
WORK WITH ME AND I'LL MAKE YOU THE *KING* OF WILLOWBANK.
THERE-- THERE'S *NO* KING IN--
LET'S SEE. WE'LL GRAB *ARMIDA* FROM *JERUSALEM DELIVERED.* ARIOSTO'S *ORLANDO.*
AND SOMETHING BIG AND *NASTY* FROM SPENSER.
LET'S GIVE BOLD SIR THOMAS SOME ENEMIES WHO PLAY BY THEIR *OWN* RULES.

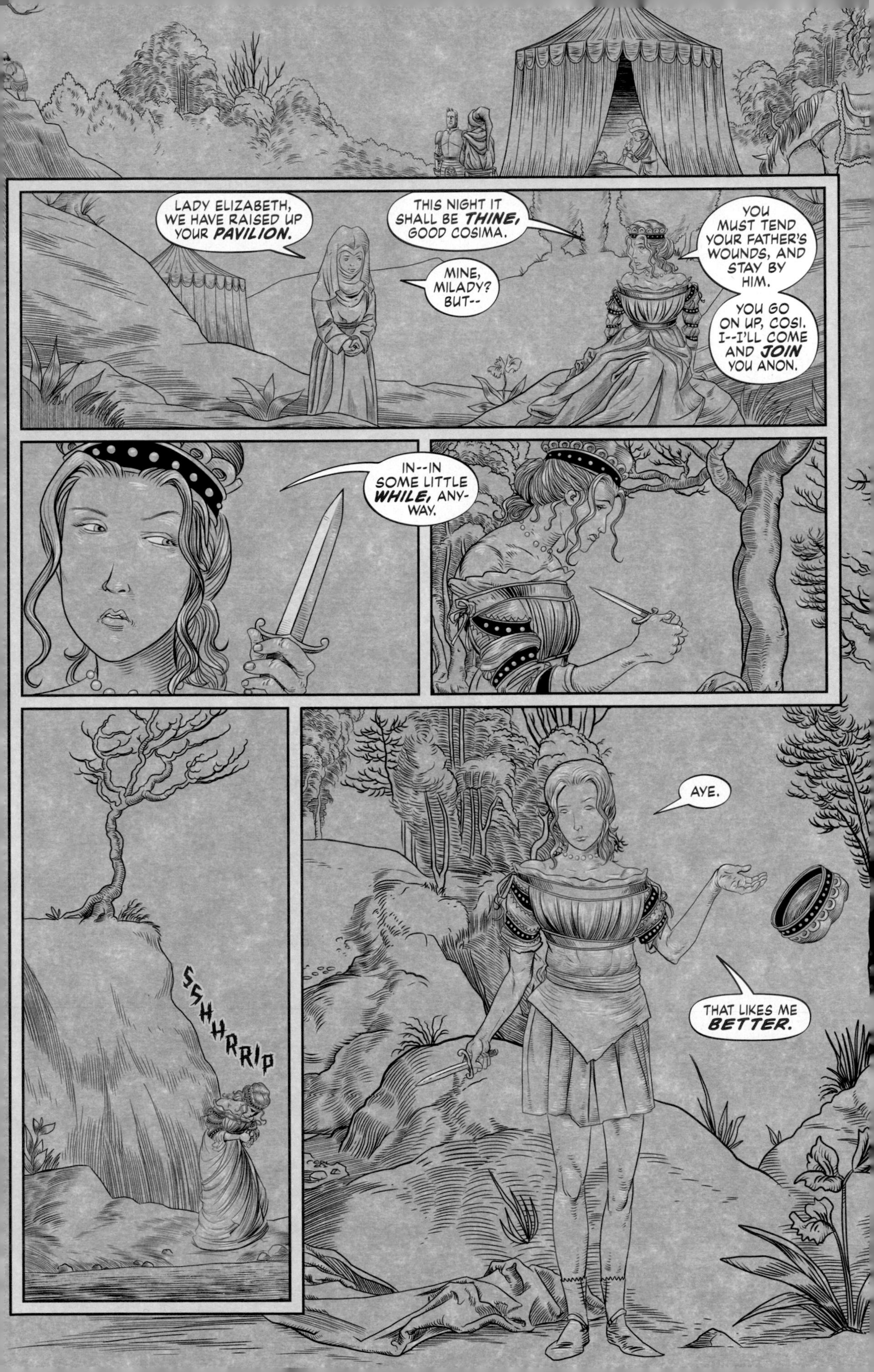
LADY ELIZABETH, WE HAVE RAISED UP YOUR **PAVILION.**
THIS NIGHT IT SHALL BE **THINE,** GOOD COSIMA.
MINE, MILADY? BUT--
YOU MUST TEND YOUR FATHER'S WOUNDS, AND STAY BY HIM.
YOU GO ON UP, COSI. I--I'LL COME AND **JOIN** YOU ANON.
IN--IN SOME LITTLE **WHILE,** ANY-WAY.
SSHHRRIP
AYE.
THAT LIKES ME **BETTER.**

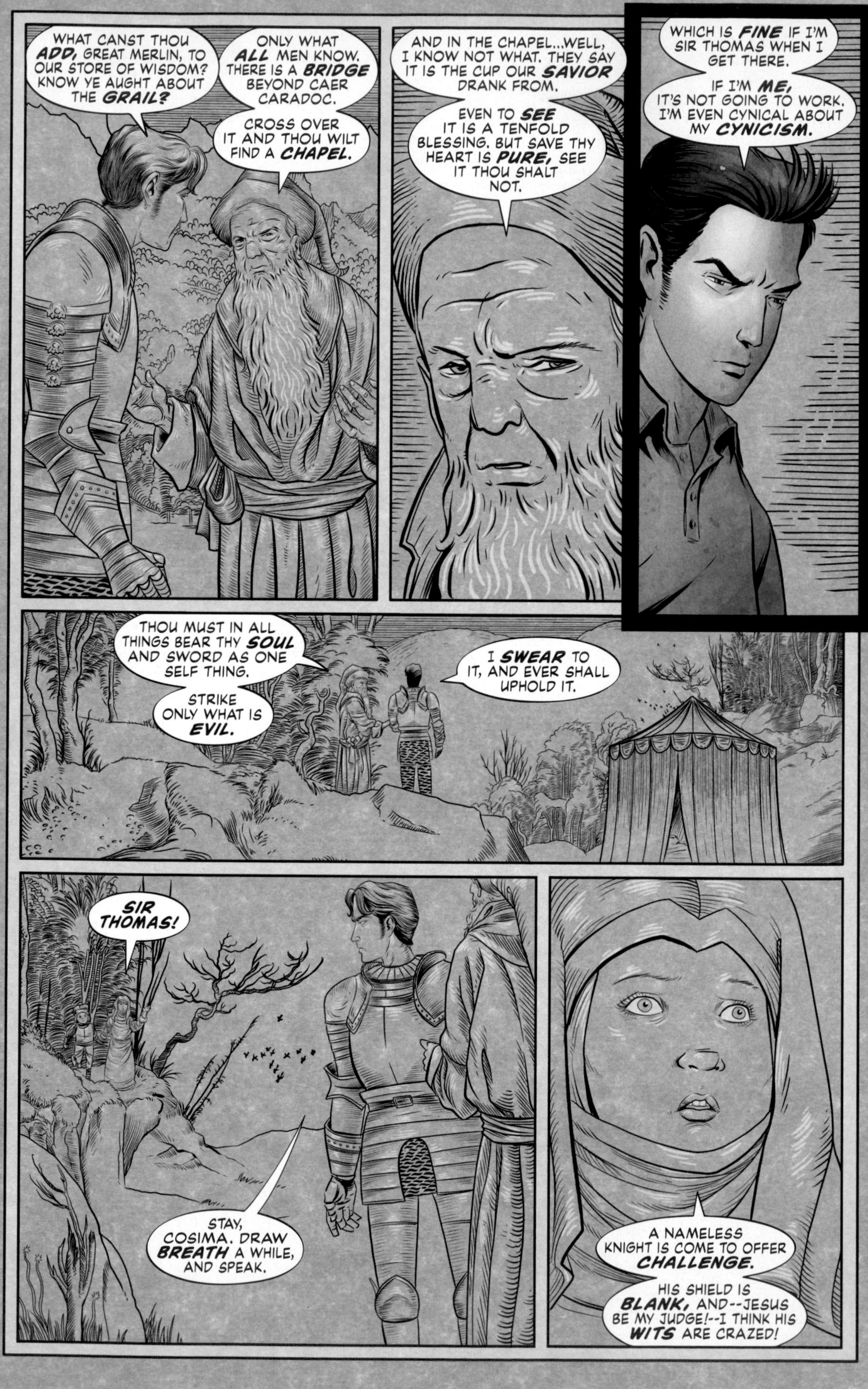

WHAT CANST THOU ADD, GREAT MERLIN, TO OUR STORE OF WISDOM? KNOW YE AUGHT ABOUT THE GRAIL?
ONLY WHAT ALL MEN KNOW. THERE IS A BRIDGE BEYOND CAER CARADOC.
CROSS OVER IT AND THOU WILT FIND A CHAPEL.
AND IN THE CHAPEL...WELL, I KNOW NOT WHAT. THEY SAY IT IS THE CUP OUR SAVIOR DRANK FROM.
EVEN TO SEE IT IS A TENFOLD BLESSING. BUT SAVE THY HEART IS PURE, SEE IT THOU SHALT NOT.
WHICH IS FINE IF I'M SIR THOMAS WHEN I GET THERE.
IF I'M ME, IT'S NOT GOING TO WORK. I'M EVEN CYNICAL ABOUT MY CYNICISM.
THOU MUST IN ALL THINGS BEAR THY SOUL AND SWORD AS ONE SELF THING.
STRIKE ONLY WHAT IS EVIL.
I SWEAR TO IT, AND EVER SHALL UPHOLD IT.
SIR THOMAS!
STAY, COSIMA. DRAW BREATH A WHILE, AND SPEAK.
A NAMELESS KNIGHT IS COME TO OFFER CHALLENGE.
HIS SHIELD IS BLANK, AND--JESUS BE MY JUDGE!--I THINK HIS WITS ARE CRAZED!

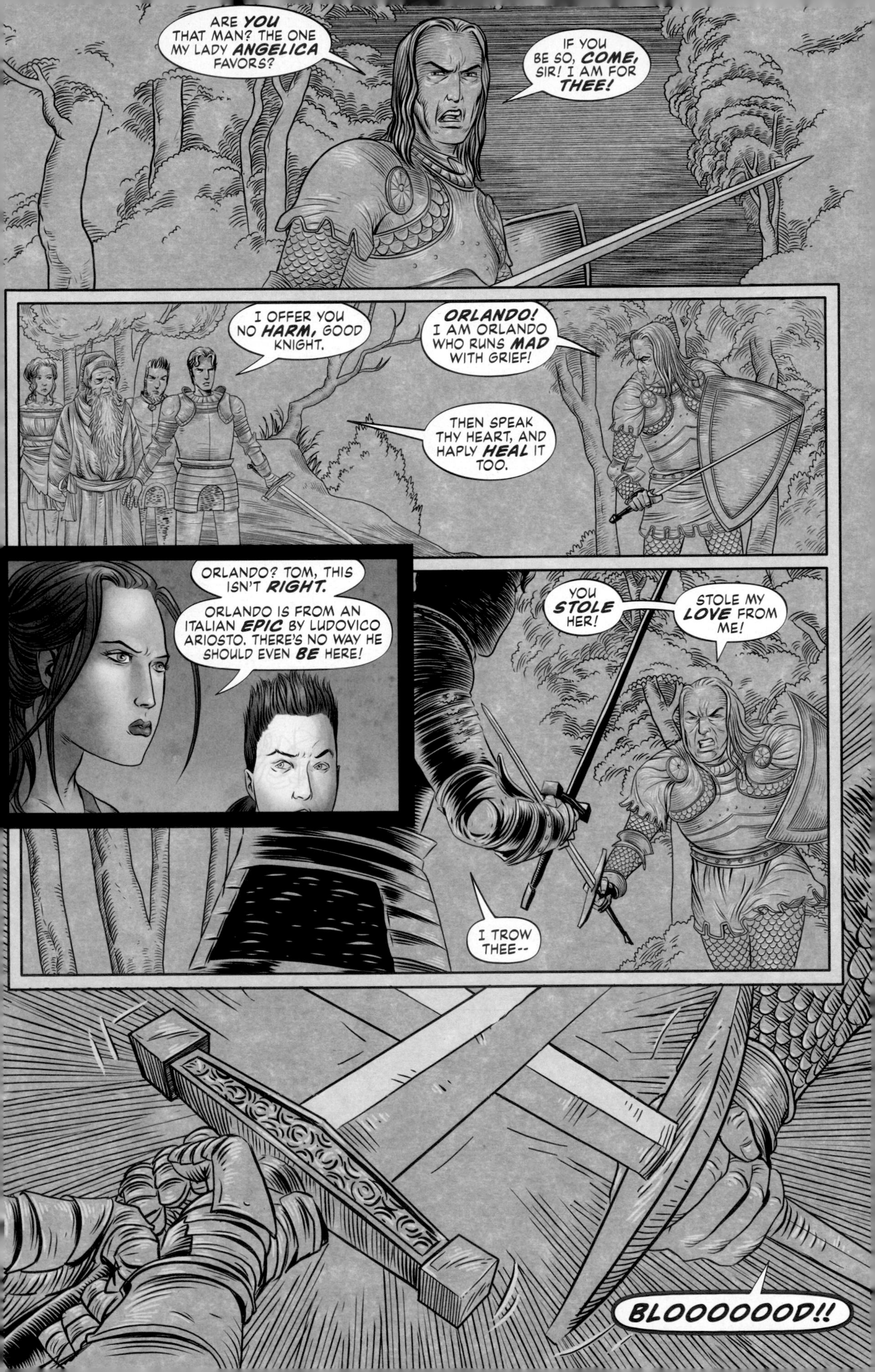
ARE YOU THAT MAN? THE ONE MY LADY ANGELICA FAVORS?
IF YOU BE SO, COME, SIR! I AM FOR THEE!
I OFFER YOU NO HARM, GOOD KNIGHT.
ORLANDO! I AM ORLANDO WHO RUNS MAD WITH GRIEF!
THEN SPEAK THY HEART, AND HAPLY HEAL IT TOO.
ORLANDO? TOM, THIS ISN'T RIGHT.
ORLANDO IS FROM AN ITALIAN EPIC BY LUDOVICO ARIOSTO. THERE'S NO WAY HE SHOULD EVEN BE HERE!
YOU STOLE HER!
STOLE MY LOVE FROM ME!
I TROW THEE--
BLOOOOOOD!!

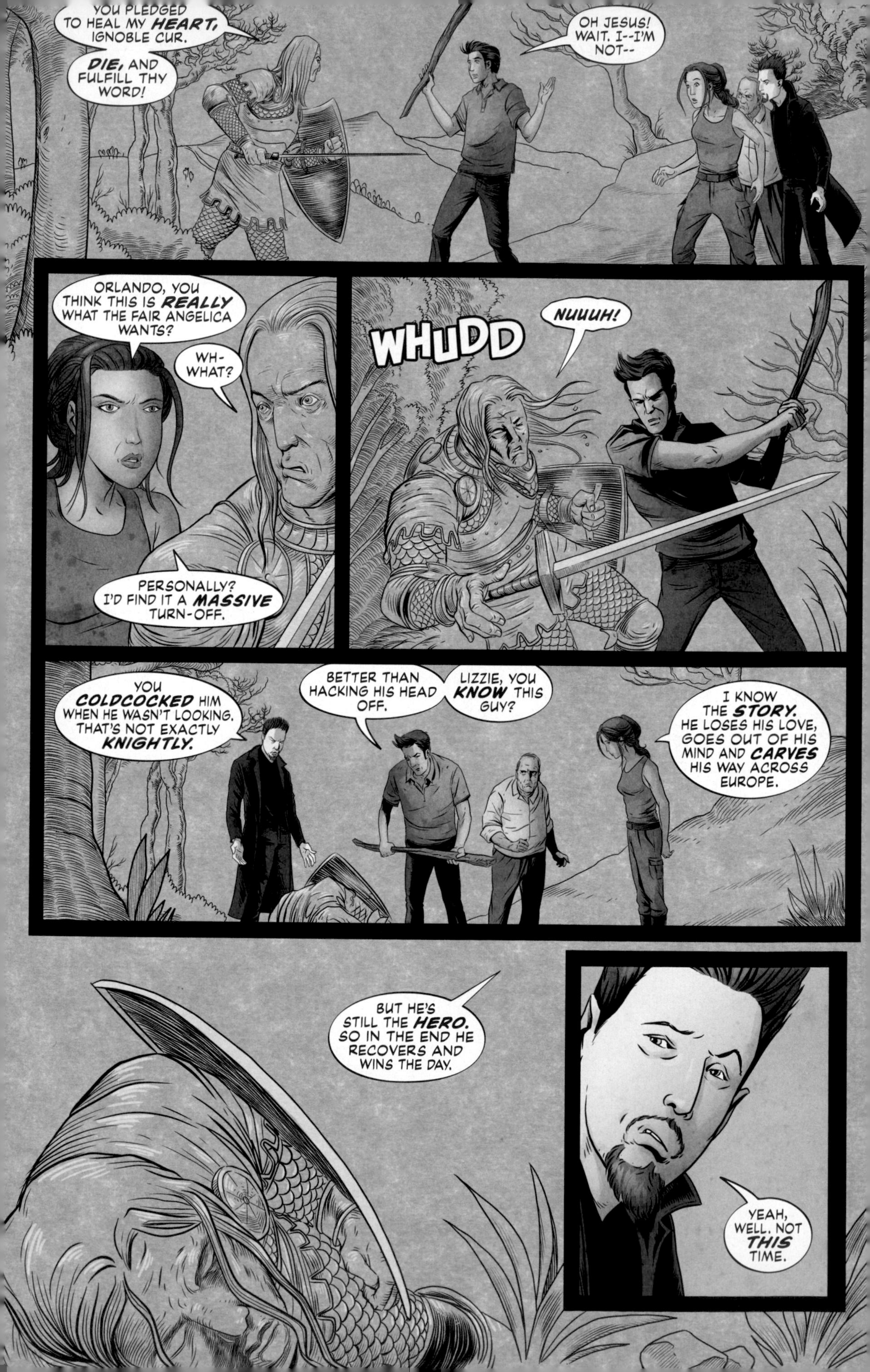
YOU PLEDGED TO HEAL MY HEART, IGNOBLE CUR.
DIE, AND FULFILL THY WORD!
OH JESUS! WAIT. I--I'M NOT--
ORLANDO, YOU THINK THIS IS REALLY WHAT THE FAIR ANGELICA WANTS?
WH-WHAT?
PERSONALLY? I'D FIND IT A MASSIVE TURN-OFF.
NUUUH!
WHUDD
YOU COLDCOCKED HIM WHEN HE WASN'T LOOKING. THAT'S NOT EXACTLY KNIGHTLY.
BETTER THAN HACKING HIS HEAD OFF.
LIZZIE, YOU KNOW THIS GUY?
I KNOW THE STORY. HE LOSES HIS LOVE, GOES OUT OF HIS MIND AND CARVES HIS WAY ACROSS EUROPE.
BUT HE'S STILL THE HERO. SO IN THE END HE RECOVERS AND WINS THE DAY.
YEAH, WELL. NOT THIS TIME.

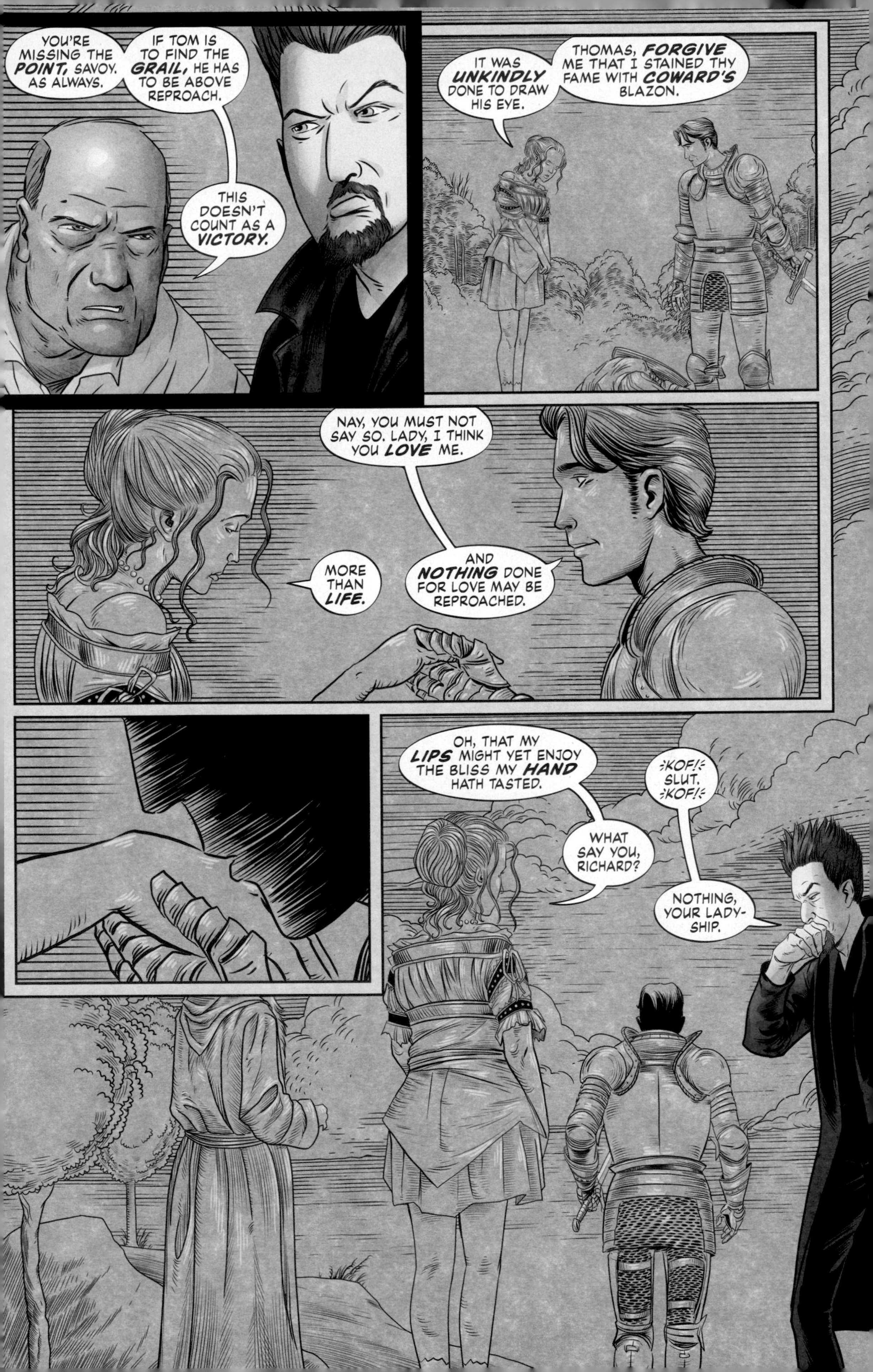
YOU'RE MISSING THE POINT, SAVOY. AS ALWAYS.
IF TOM IS TO FIND THE GRAIL, HE HAS TO BE ABOVE REPROACH.
THIS DOESN'T COUNT AS A VICTORY.
IT WAS UNKINDLY DONE TO DRAW HIS EYE.
THOMAS, FORGIVE ME THAT I STAINED THY FAME WITH COWARD'S BLAZON.
NAY, YOU MUST NOT SAY SO. LADY, I THINK YOU LOVE ME.
MORE THAN LIFE.
AND NOTHING DONE FOR LOVE MAY BE REPROACHED.
OH, THAT MY LIPS MIGHT YET ENJOY THE BLISS MY HAND HATH TASTED.
WHAT SAY YOU, RICHARD?
KOF! SLUT. KOF!
NOTHING, YOUR LADYSHIP.

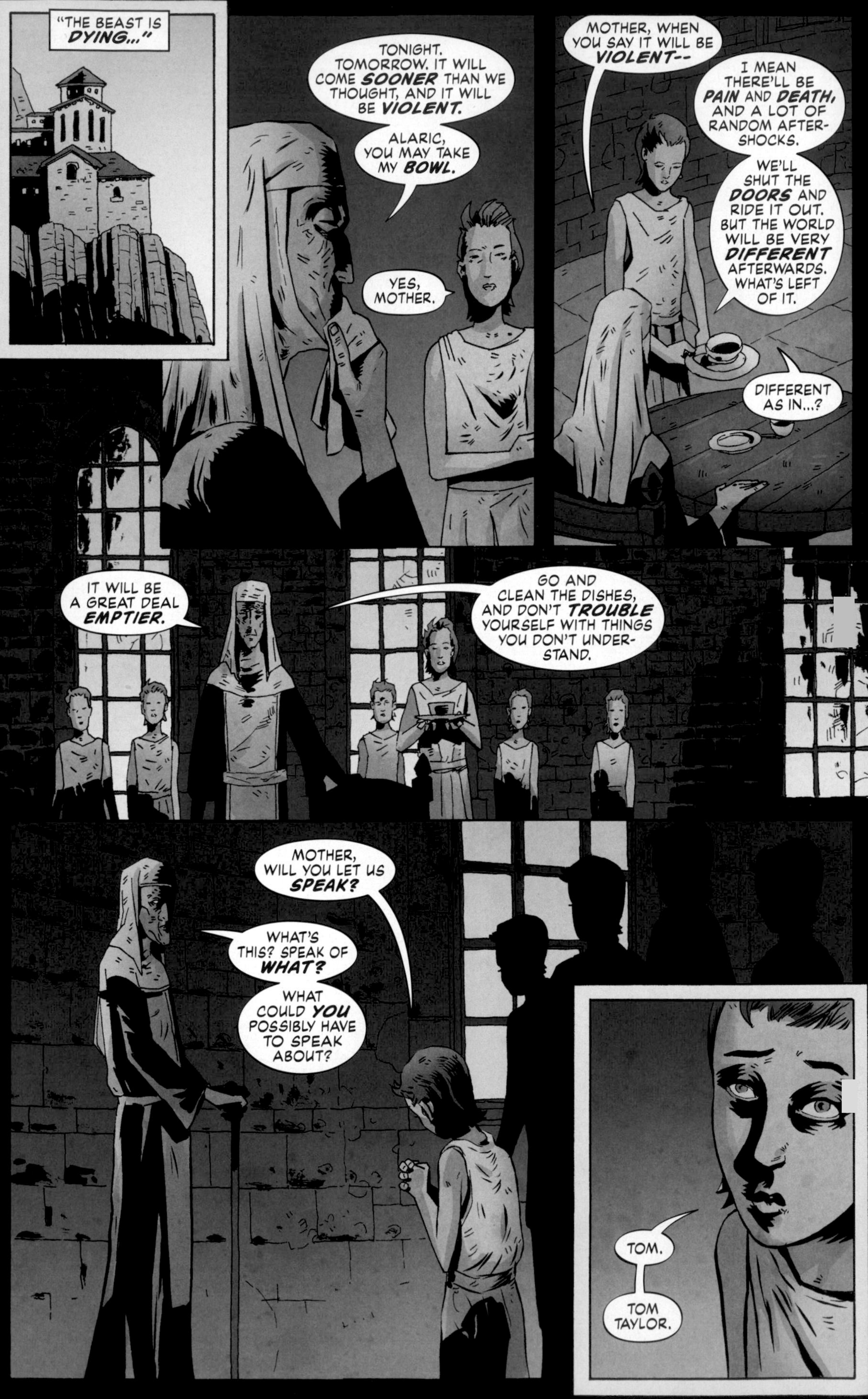
"THE BEAST IS DYING..."
TONIGHT. TOMORROW. IT WILL COME SOONER THAN WE THOUGHT, AND IT WILL BE VIOLENT.
ALARIC, YOU MAY TAKE MY BOWL.
YES, MOTHER.
MOTHER, WHEN YOU SAY IT WILL BE VIOLENT--
I MEAN THERE'LL BE PAIN AND DEATH, AND A LOT OF RANDOM AFTER-SHOCKS.
WE'LL SHUT THE DOORS AND RIDE IT OUT. BUT THE WORLD WILL BE VERY DIFFERENT AFTERWARDS. WHAT'S LEFT OF IT.
DIFFERENT AS IN...?
IT WILL BE A GREAT DEAL EMPTIER.
GO AND CLEAN THE DISHES, AND DON'T TROUBLE YOURSELF WITH THINGS YOU DON'T UNDER-STAND.
MOTHER, WILL YOU LET US SPEAK?
WHAT'S THIS? SPEAK OF WHAT?
WHAT COULD YOU POSSIBLY HAVE TO SPEAK ABOUT?
TOM.
TOM TAYLOR.

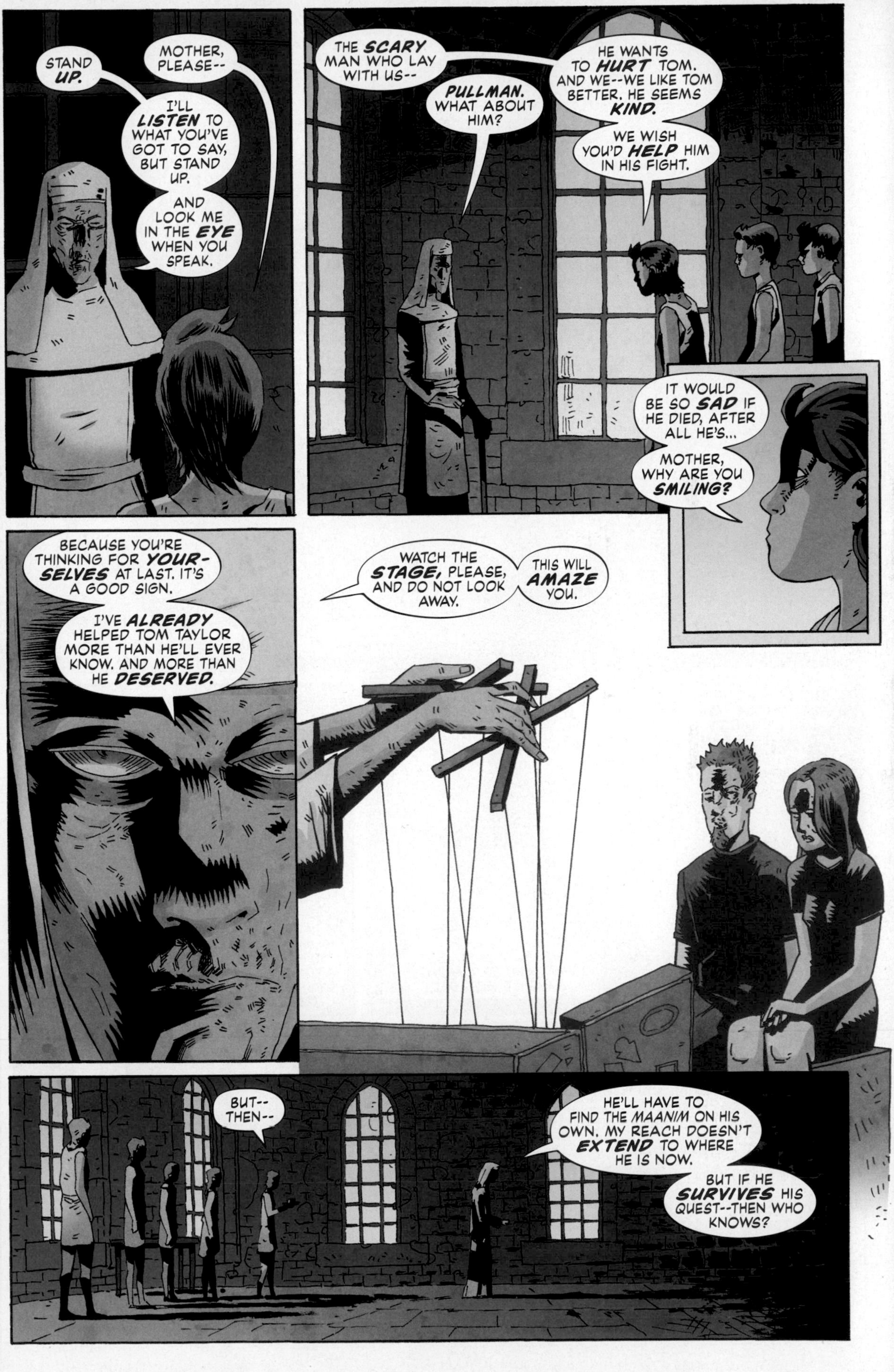
STAND *UP.*
MOTHER, PLEASE--
I'LL *LISTEN* TO WHAT YOU'VE GOT TO SAY, BUT STAND UP.
AND LOOK ME IN THE *EYE* WHEN YOU SPEAK.
THE *SCARY* MAN WHO LAY WITH US--
PULLMAN. WHAT ABOUT HIM?
HE WANTS TO *HURT* TOM. AND WE--WE LIKE TOM BETTER. HE SEEMS *KIND.*
WE WISH YOU'D *HELP* HIM IN HIS FIGHT.
IT WOULD BE SO *SAD* IF HE DIED, AFTER ALL HE'S...
MOTHER, WHY ARE YOU *SMILING?*
BECAUSE YOU'RE THINKING FOR *YOUR-SELVES* AT LAST. IT'S A GOOD SIGN.
I'VE *ALREADY* HELPED TOM TAYLOR MORE THAN HE'LL EVER KNOW. AND MORE THAN HE *DESERVED.*
WATCH THE *STAGE,* PLEASE, AND DO NOT LOOK AWAY.
THIS WILL *AMAZE* YOU.
BUT-- THEN--
HE'LL HAVE TO FIND THE *MAANIM* ON HIS OWN. MY REACH DOESN'T *EXTEND* TO WHERE HE IS NOW.
BUT IF HE *SURVIVES* HIS QUEST--THEN WHO KNOWS?

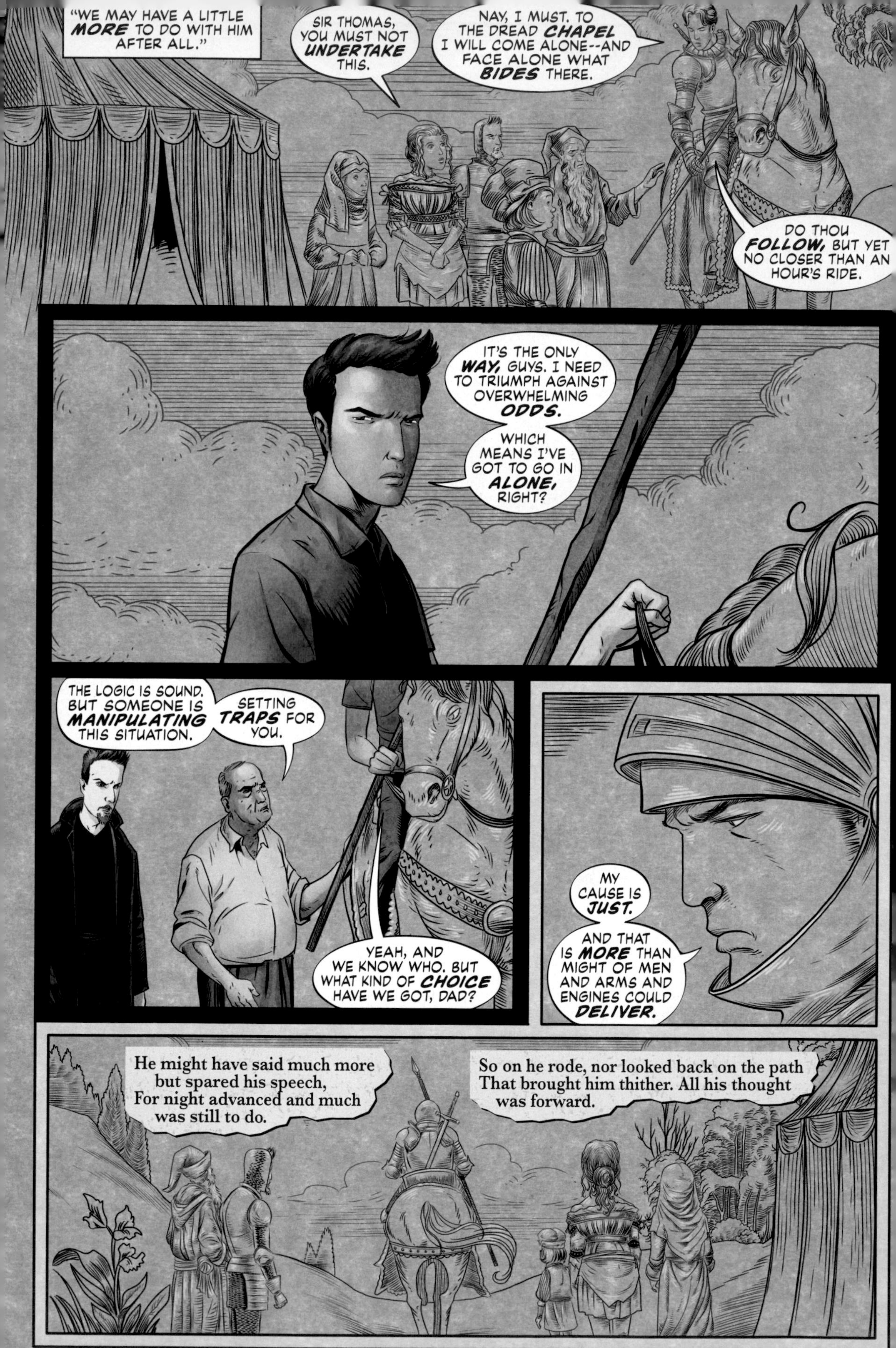
"WE MAY HAVE A LITTLE MORE TO DO WITH HIM AFTER ALL."
SIR THOMAS, YOU MUST NOT UNDERTAKE THIS.
NAY, I MUST. TO THE DREAD CHAPEL I WILL COME ALONE--AND FACE ALONE WHAT BIDES THERE.
DO THOU FOLLOW, BUT YET NO CLOSER THAN AN HOUR'S RIDE.
IT'S THE ONLY WAY, GUYS. I NEED TO TRIUMPH AGAINST OVERWHELMING ODDS.
WHICH MEANS I'VE GOT TO GO IN ALONE, RIGHT?
THE LOGIC IS SOUND. BUT SOMEONE IS MANIPULATING THIS SITUATION.
SETTING TRAPS FOR YOU.
YEAH, AND WE KNOW WHO. BUT WHAT KIND OF CHOICE HAVE WE GOT, DAD?
MY CAUSE IS JUST.
AND THAT IS MORE THAN MIGHT OF MEN AND ARMS AND ENGINES COULD DELIVER.
He might have said much more but spared his speech, For night advanced and much was still to do.
So on he rode, nor looked back on the path That brought him thither. All his thought was forward.

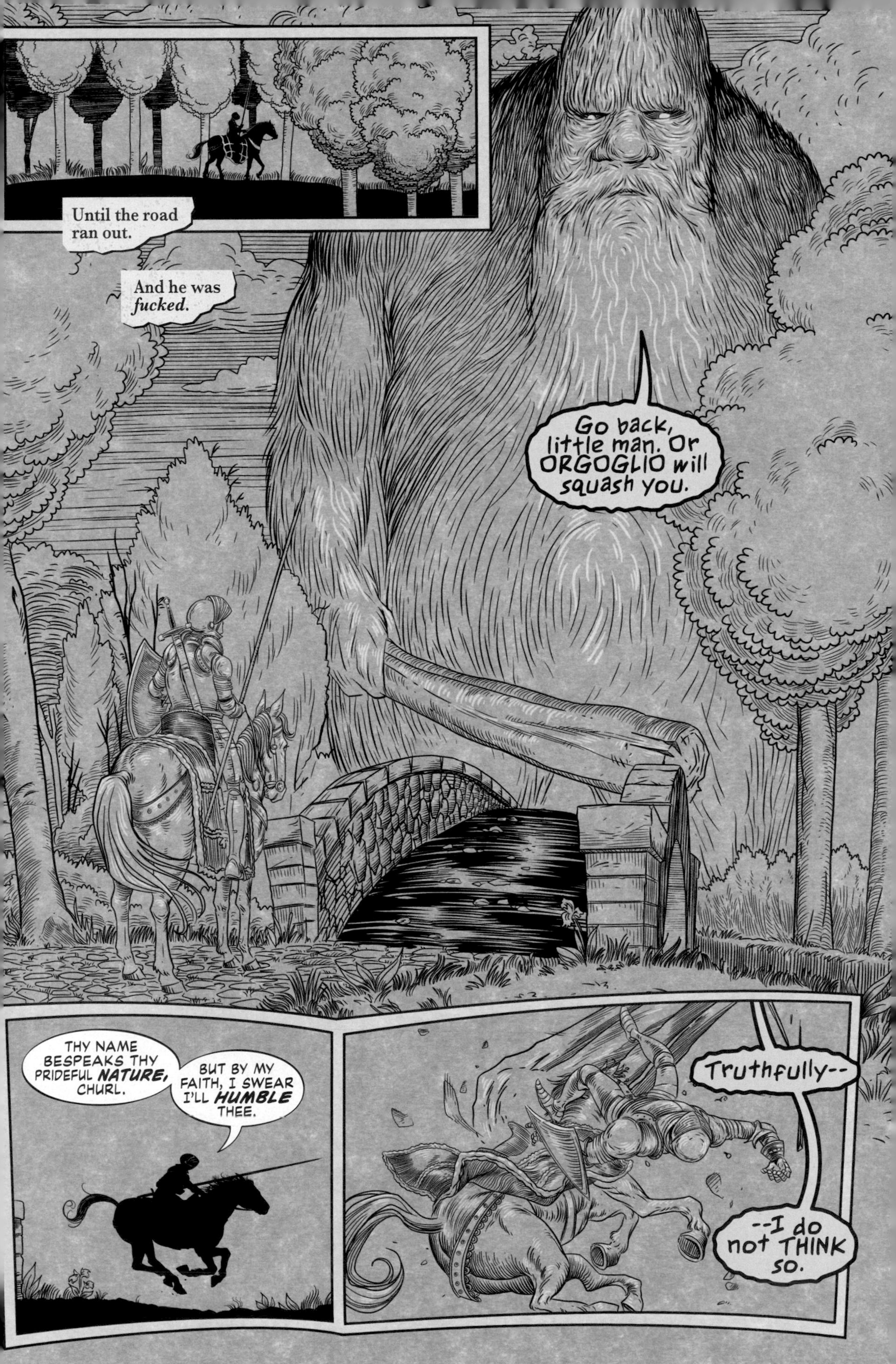
Until the road ran out.
And he was *fucked*.
Go back, little man. Or ORGOGLIO will squash you.
THY NAME BESPEAKS THY PRIDEFUL ***NATURE,*** CHURL.
BUT BY MY FAITH, I SWEAR I'LL ***HUMBLE*** THEE.
Truthfully--
--I do not THINK so.

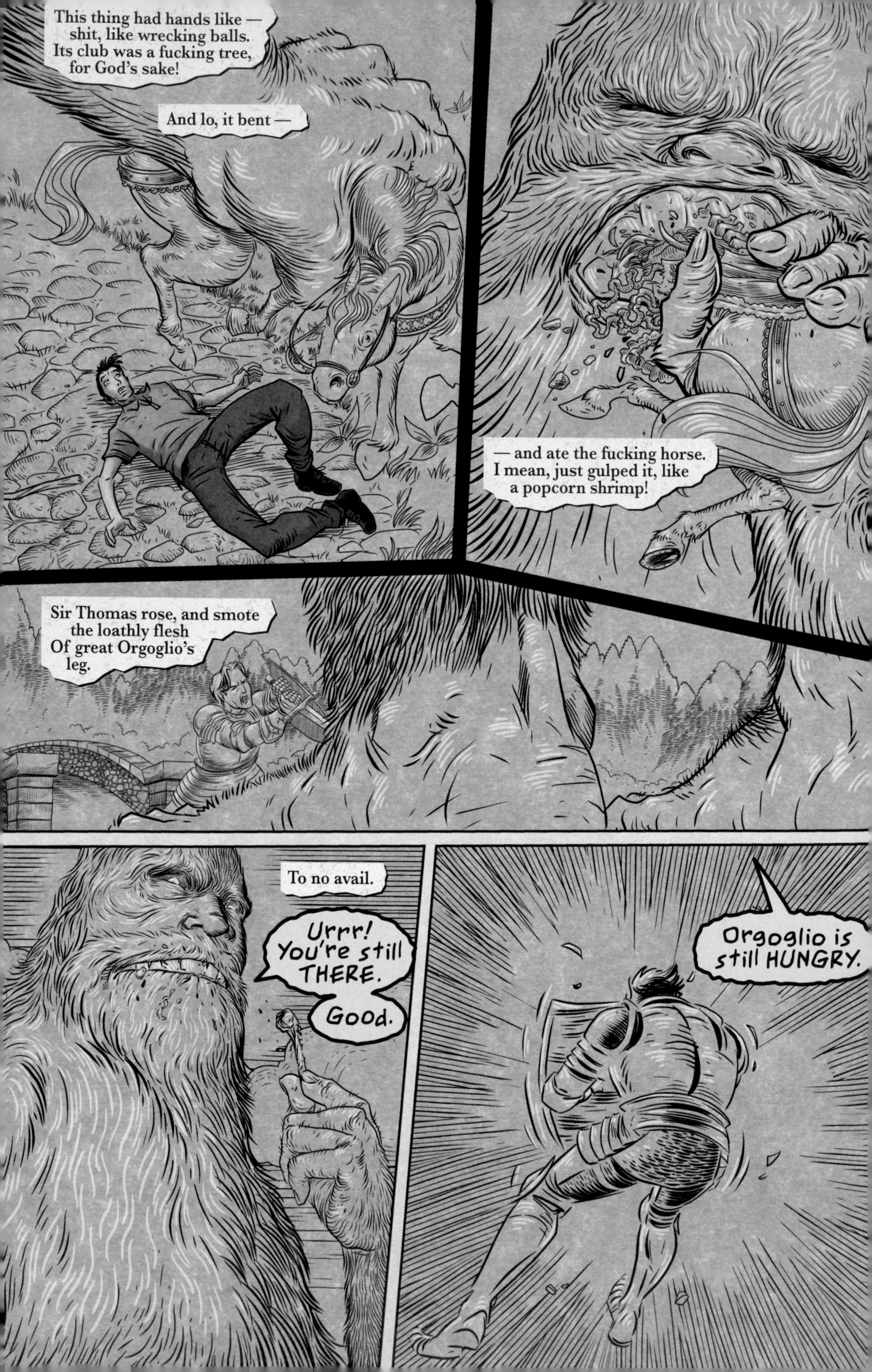
This thing had hands like — shit, like wrecking balls. Its club was a fucking tree, for God's sake!
And lo, it bent —
— and ate the fucking horse. I mean, just gulped it, like a popcorn shrimp!
Sir Thomas rose, and smote the loathly flesh Of great Orgoglio's leg.
To no avail.
Urrr! You're still THERE.
Good.
Orgoglio is still HUNGRY.

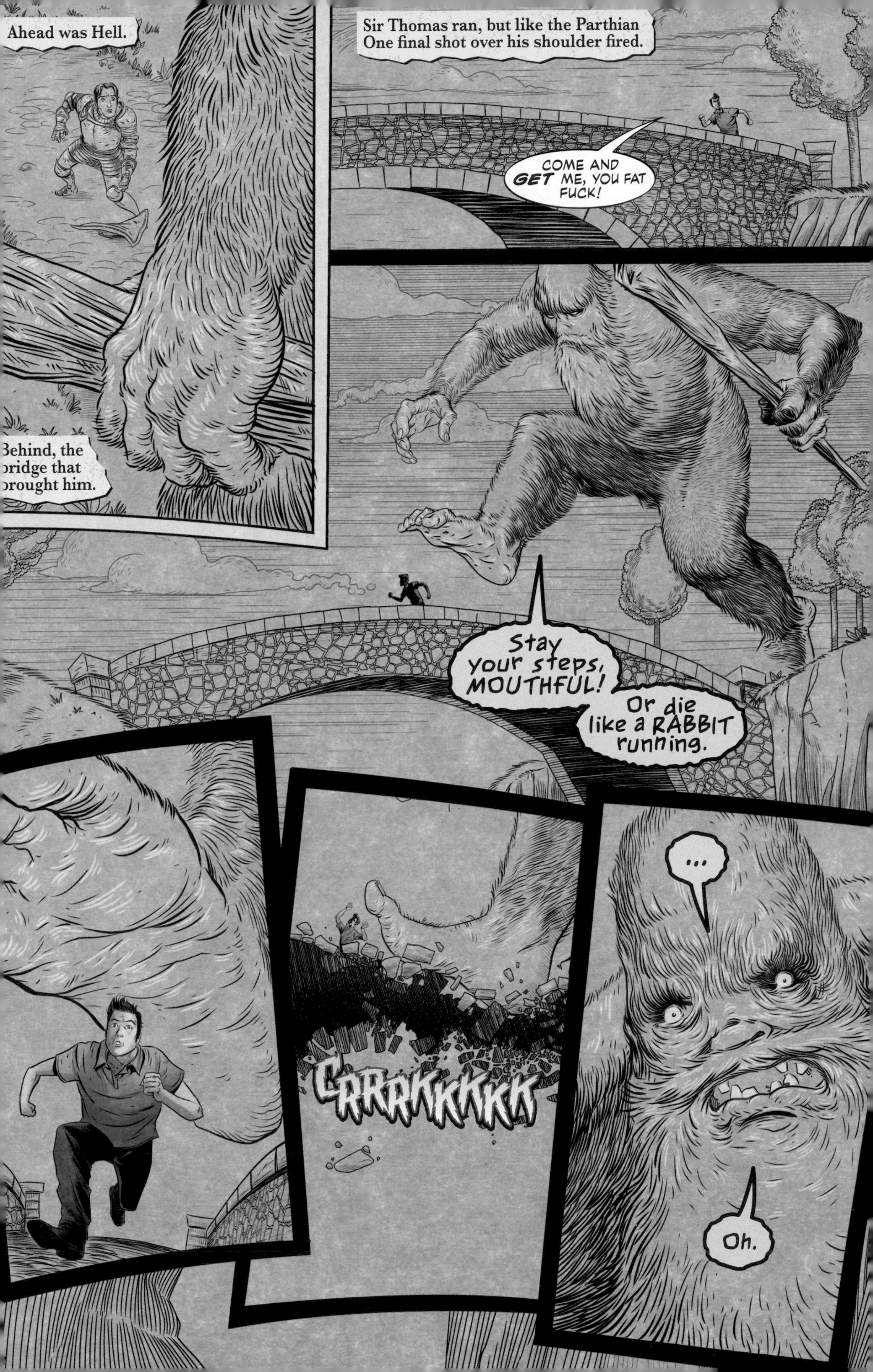
Ahead was Hell.
Behind, the bridge that brought him.
Sir Thomas ran, but like the Parthian One final shot over his shoulder fired.
COME AND GET ME, YOU FAT FUCK!
Stay your steps, MOUTHFUL!
Or die like a RABBIT running.
CRRRKKKKK
...
Oh.

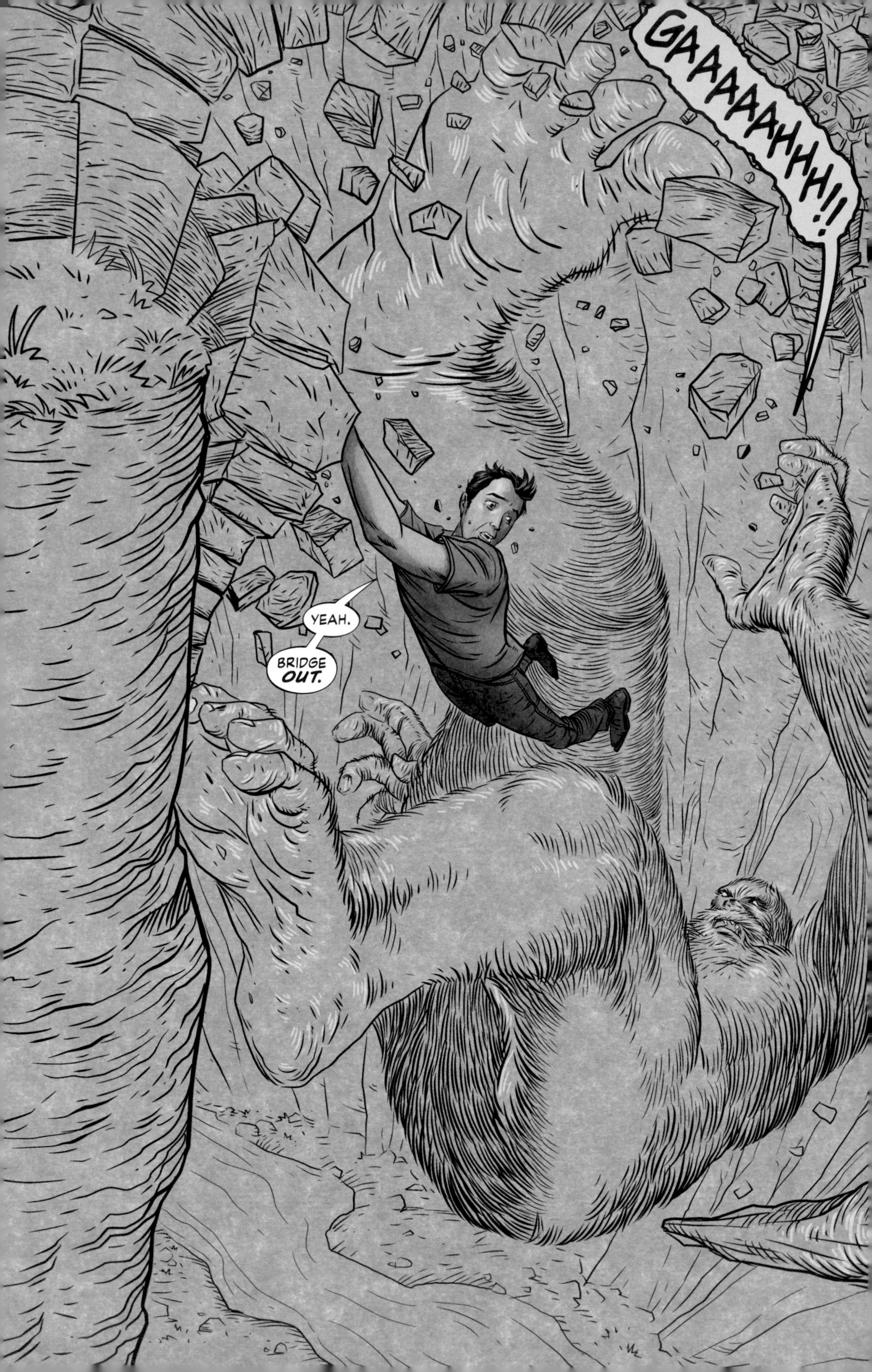
GAAAAAHHH!!
YEAH.
BRIDGE OUT.

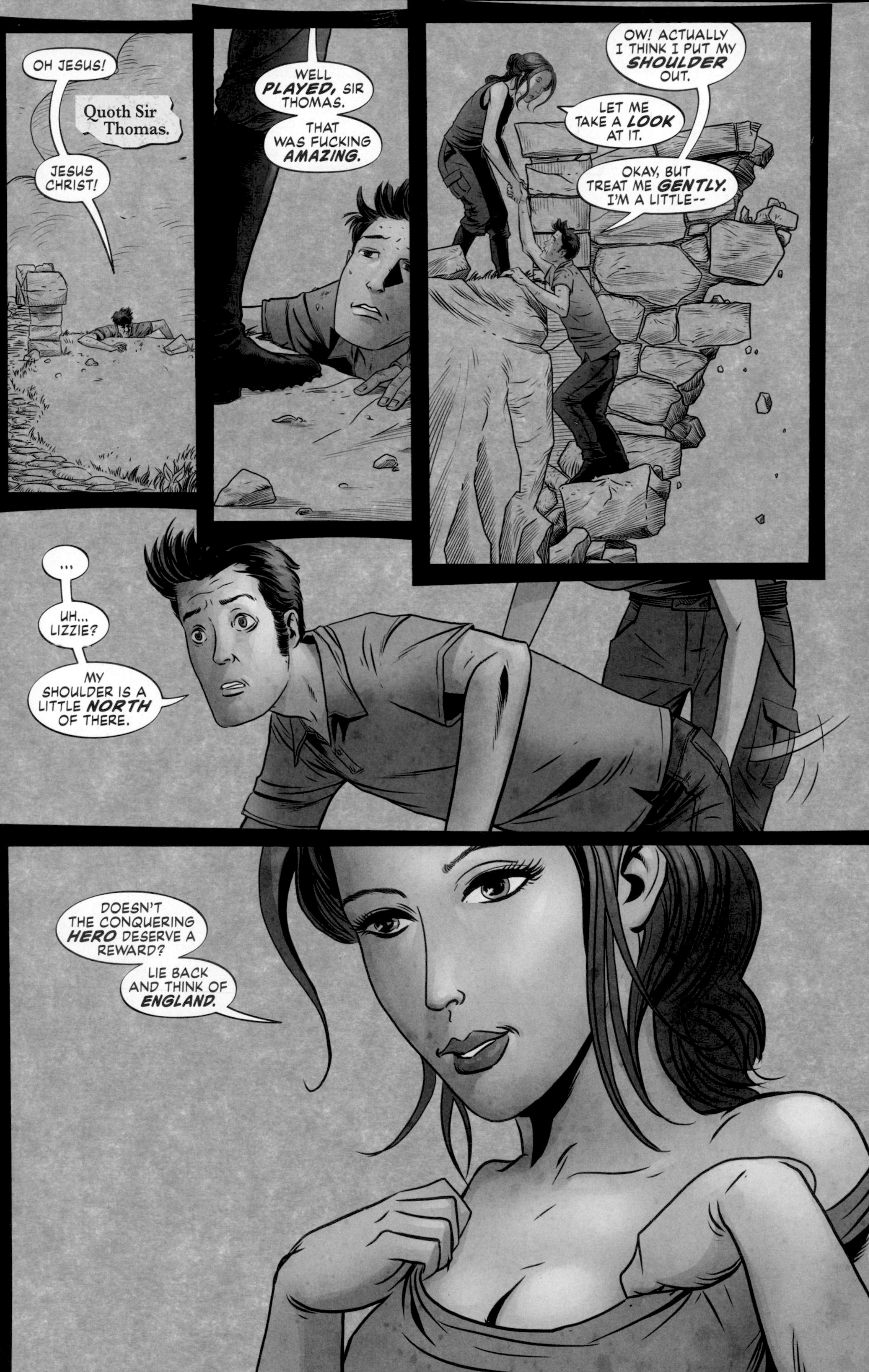
OH JESUS!
Quoth Sir Thomas.
JESUS CHRIST!
WELL PLAYED, SIR THOMAS.
THAT WAS FUCKING AMAZING.
OW! ACTUALLY I THINK I PUT MY SHOULDER OUT.
LET ME TAKE A LOOK AT IT.
OKAY, BUT TREAT ME GENTLY. I'M A LITTLE--
...
UH... LIZZIE?
MY SHOULDER IS A LITTLE NORTH OF THERE.
DOESN'T THE CONQUERING HERO DESERVE A REWARD?
LIE BACK AND THINK OF ENGLAND.

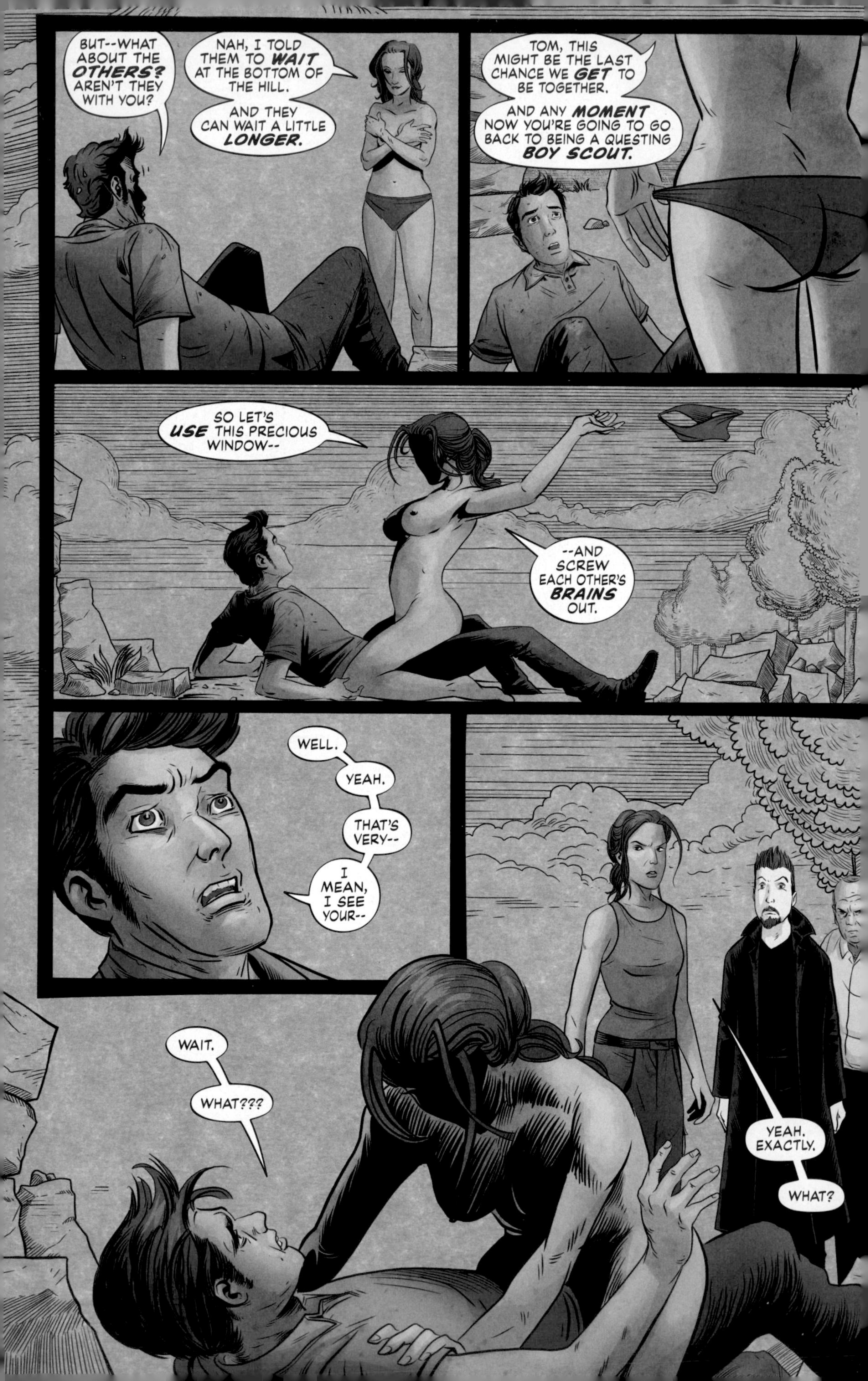
BUT--WHAT ABOUT THE OTHERS? AREN'T THEY WITH YOU?
NAH, I TOLD THEM TO WAIT AT THE BOTTOM OF THE HILL.
AND THEY CAN WAIT A LITTLE LONGER.
TOM, THIS MIGHT BE THE LAST CHANCE WE GET TO BE TOGETHER.
AND ANY MOMENT NOW YOU'RE GOING TO GO BACK TO BEING A QUESTING BOY SCOUT.
SO LET'S USE THIS PRECIOUS WINDOW--
--AND SCREW EACH OTHER'S BRAINS OUT.
WELL.
YEAH.
THAT'S VERY--
I MEAN, I SEE YOUR--
WAIT.
WHAT???
YEAH. EXACTLY.
WHAT?

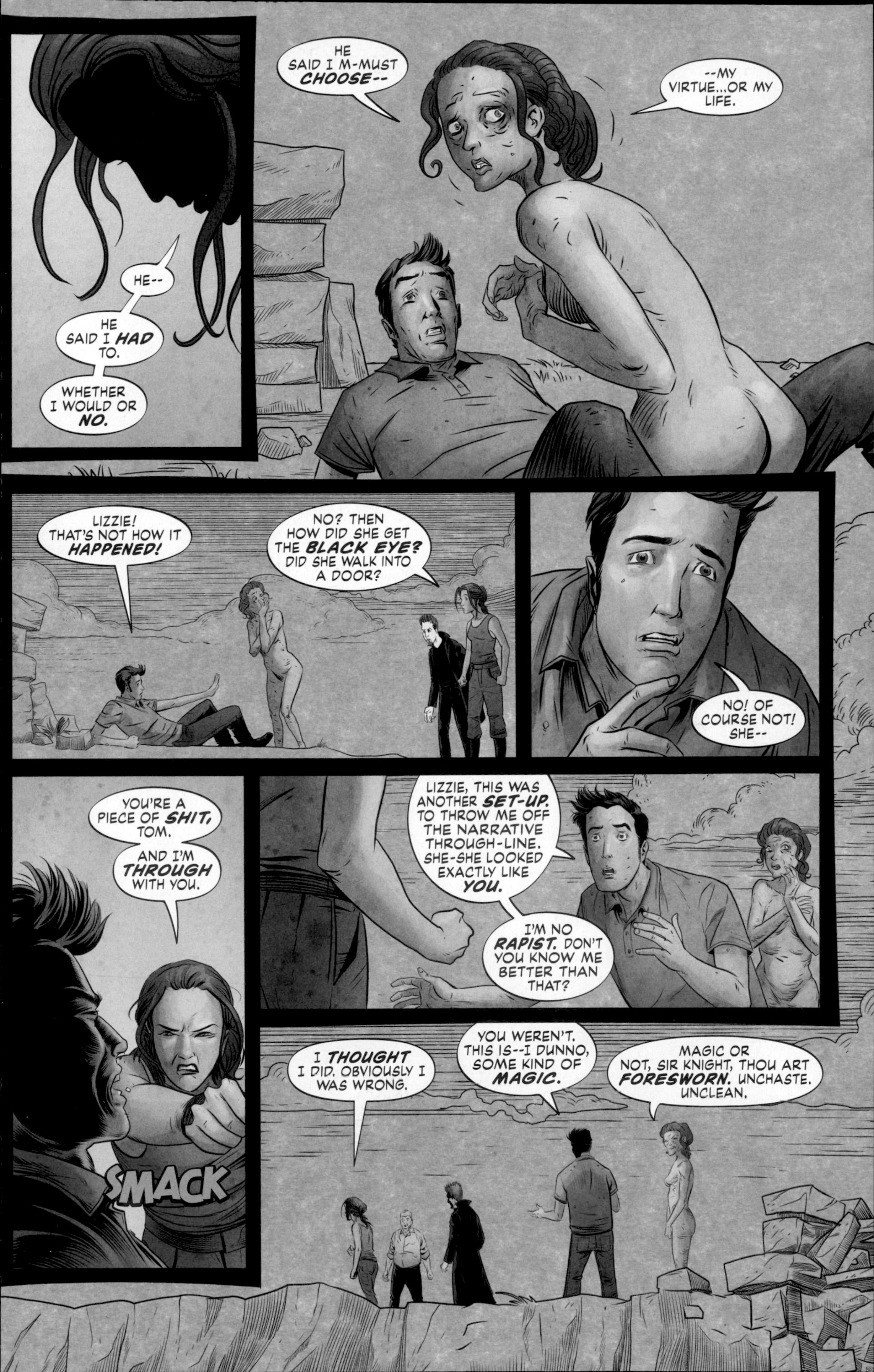
HE SAID I M-MUST CHOOSE--
--MY VIRTUE...OR MY LIFE.
HE--
HE SAID I HAD TO.
WHETHER I WOULD OR NO.
LIZZIE! THAT'S NOT HOW IT HAPPENED!
NO? THEN HOW DID SHE GET THE BLACK EYE? DID SHE WALK INTO A DOOR?
NO! OF COURSE NOT! SHE--
YOU'RE A PIECE OF SHIT, TOM.
AND I'M THROUGH WITH YOU.
SMACK
LIZZIE, THIS WAS ANOTHER SET-UP. TO THROW ME OFF THE NARRATIVE THROUGH-LINE. SHE-SHE LOOKED EXACTLY LIKE YOU.
I'M NO RAPIST. DON'T YOU KNOW ME BETTER THAN THAT?
I THOUGHT I DID. OBVIOUSLY I WAS WRONG.
YOU WEREN'T. THIS IS--I DUNNO, SOME KIND OF MAGIC.
MAGIC OR NOT, SIR KNIGHT, THOU ART FORESWORN. UNCHASTE. UNCLEAN.

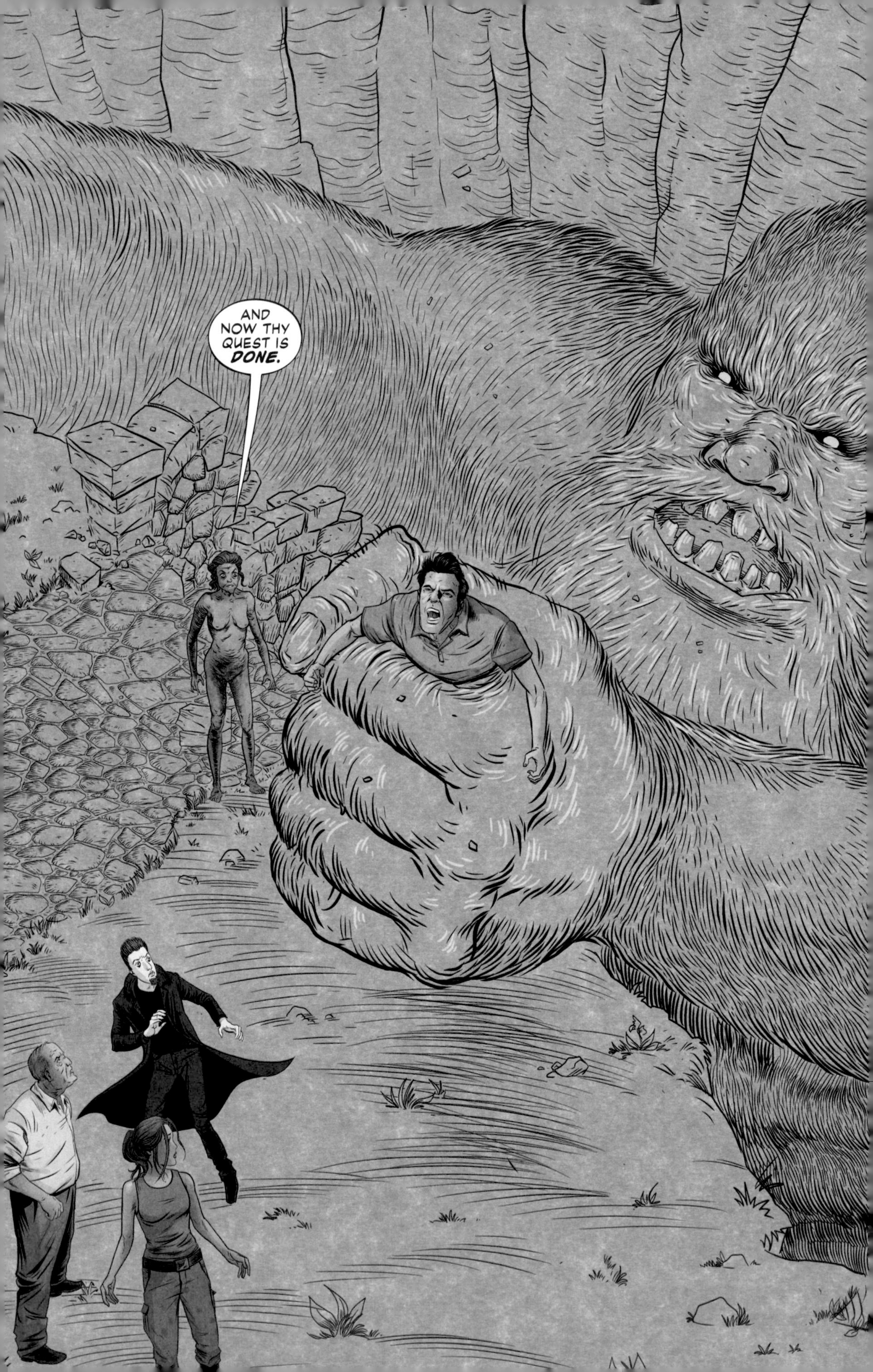
AND NOW THY QUEST IS **DONE.**

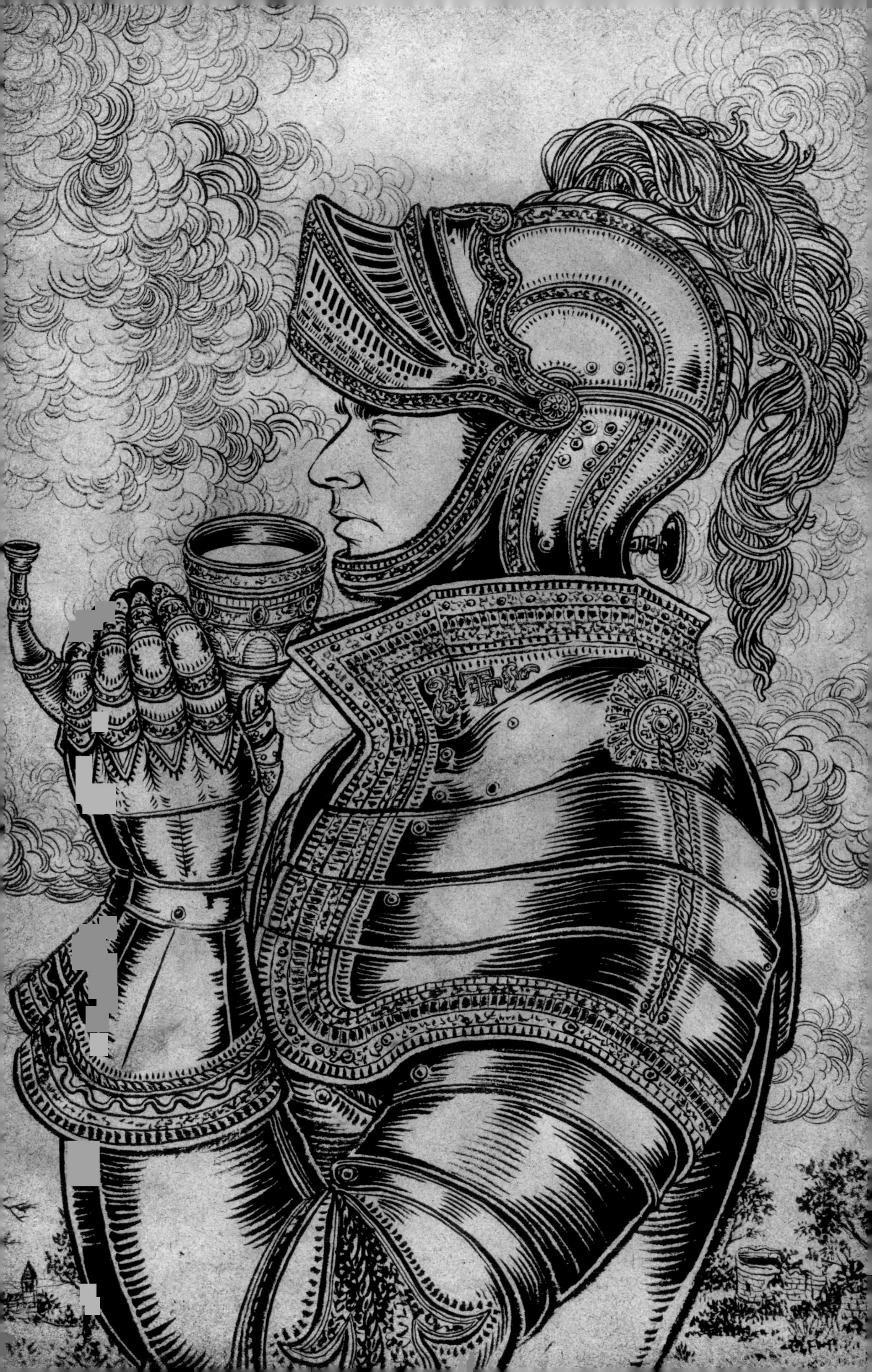

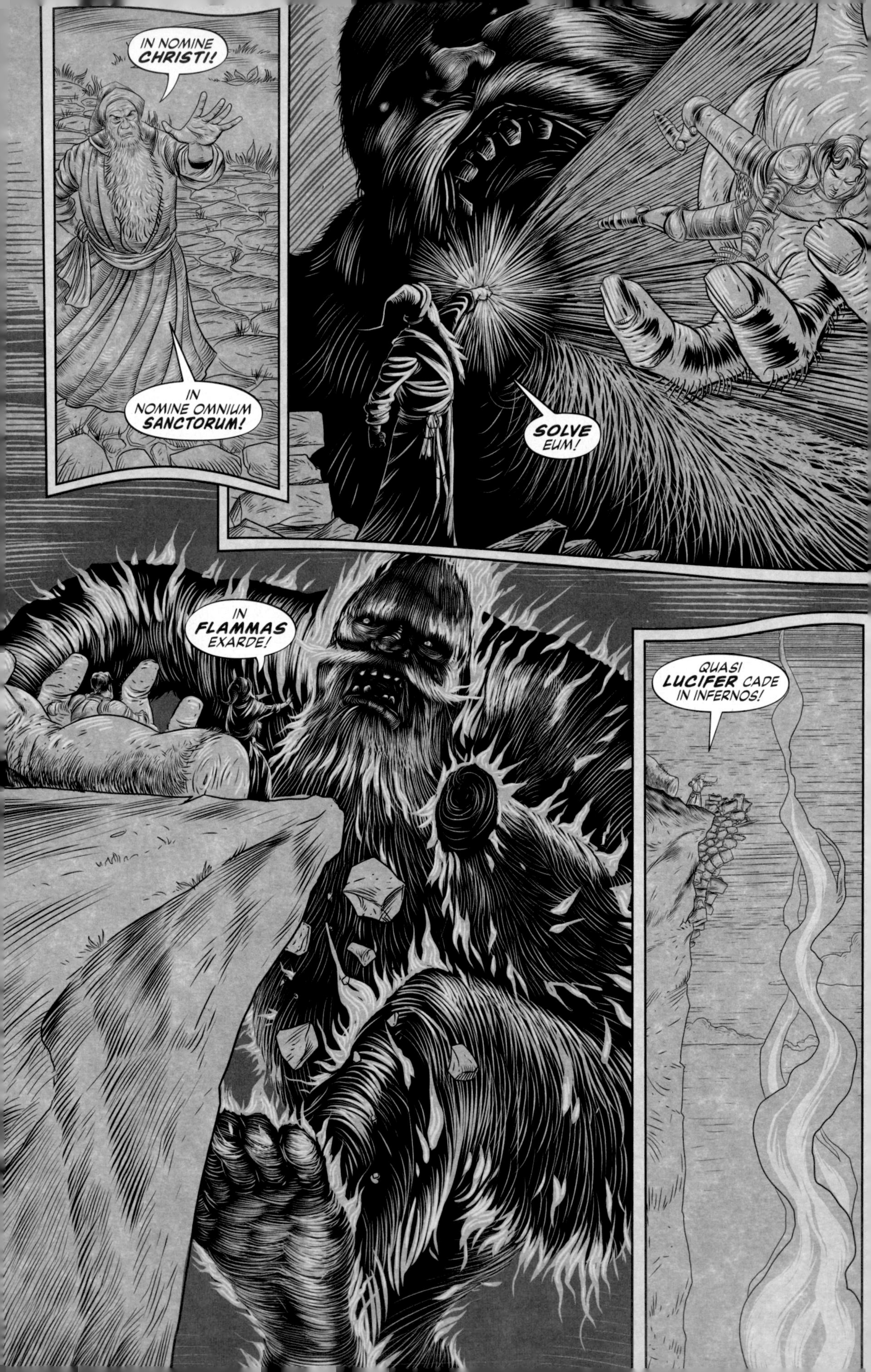
IN NOMINE CHRISTI!
IN NOMINE OMNIUM SANCTORUM!
SOLVE EUM!
IN FLAMMAS EXARDE!
QUASI LUCIFER CADE IN INFERNOS!

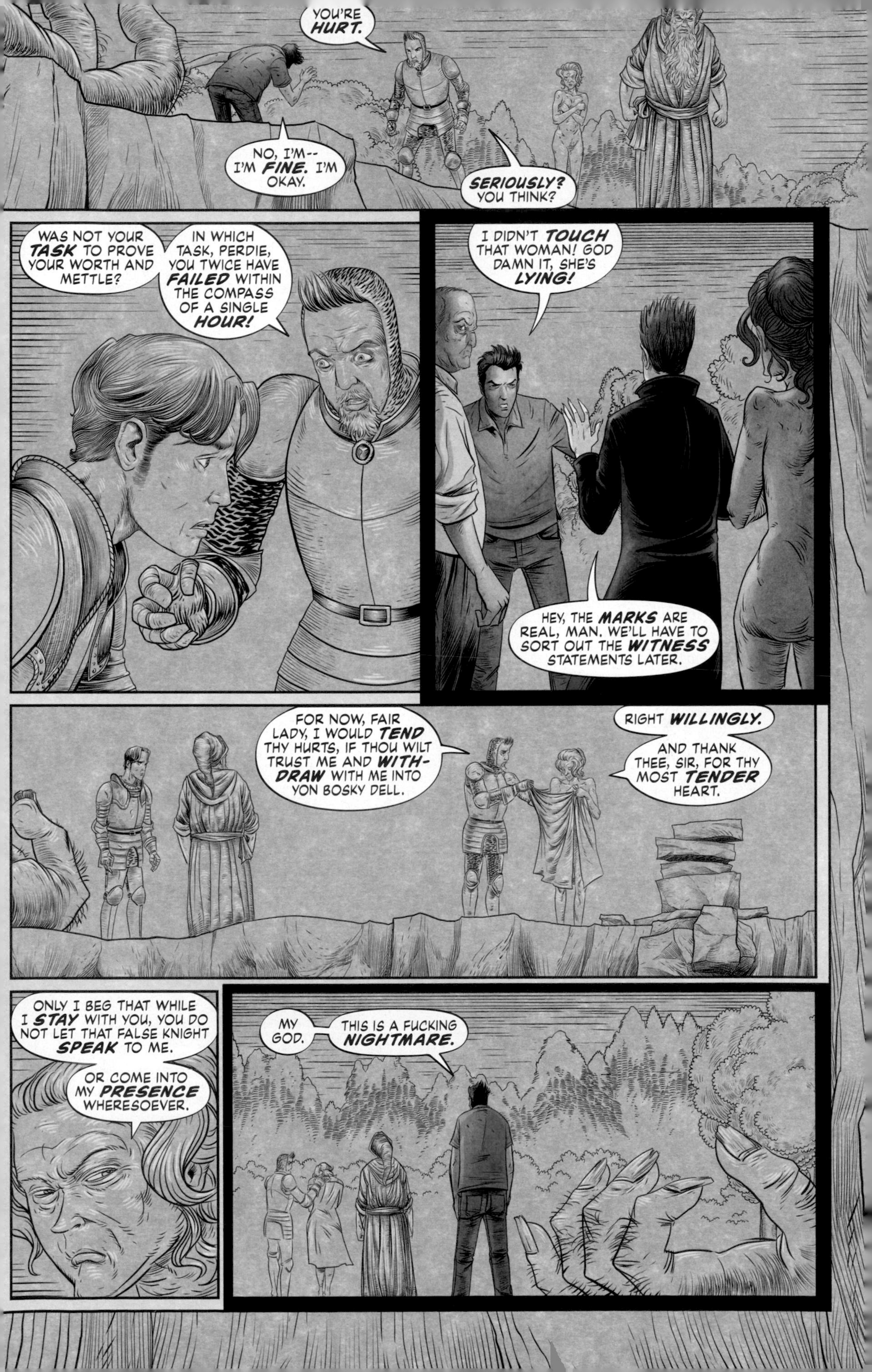
YOU'RE HURT.
NO, I'M-- I'M FINE. I'M OKAY.
SERIOUSLY? YOU THINK?
WAS NOT YOUR TASK TO PROVE YOUR WORTH AND METTLE?
IN WHICH TASK, PERDIE, YOU TWICE HAVE FAILED WITHIN THE COMPASS OF A SINGLE HOUR!
I DIDN'T TOUCH THAT WOMAN! GOD DAMN IT, SHE'S LYING!
HEY, THE MARKS ARE REAL, MAN. WE'LL HAVE TO SORT OUT THE WITNESS STATEMENTS LATER.
FOR NOW, FAIR LADY, I WOULD TEND THY HURTS, IF THOU WILT TRUST ME AND WITH-DRAW WITH ME INTO YON BOSKY DELL.
RIGHT WILLINGLY.
AND THANK THEE, SIR, FOR THY MOST TENDER HEART.
ONLY I BEG THAT WHILE I STAY WITH YOU, YOU DO NOT LET THAT FALSE KNIGHT SPEAK TO ME.
OR COME INTO MY PRESENCE WHERESOEVER.
MY GOD.
THIS IS A FUCKING NIGHTMARE.

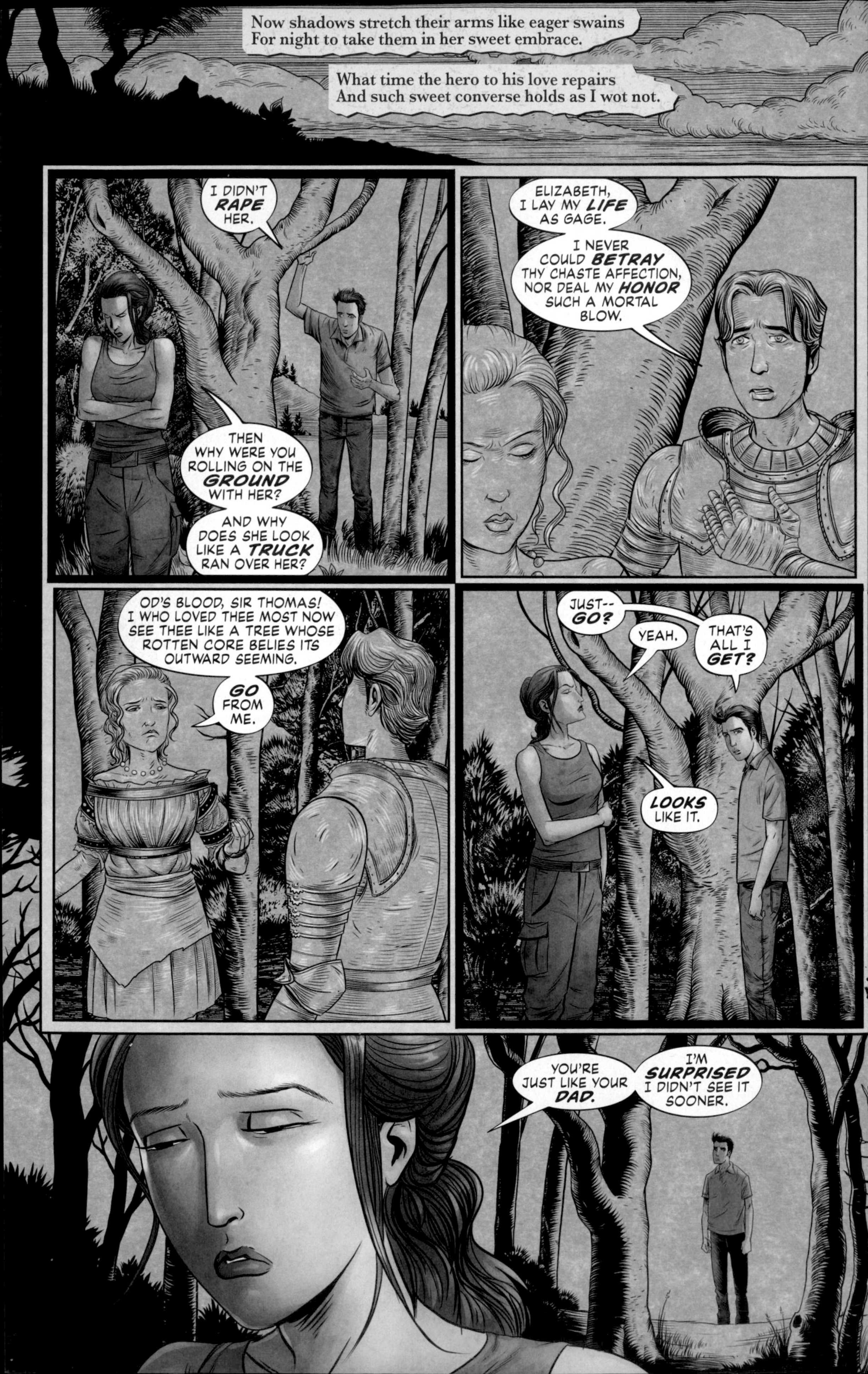
Now shadows stretch their arms like eager swains
For night to take them in her sweet embrace.
What time the hero to his love repairs
And such sweet converse holds as I wot not.
I DIDN'T RAPE HER.
THEN WHY WERE YOU ROLLING ON THE GROUND WITH HER?
AND WHY DOES SHE LOOK LIKE A TRUCK RAN OVER HER?
ELIZABETH, I LAY MY LIFE AS GAGE.
I NEVER COULD BETRAY THY CHASTE AFFECTION, NOR DEAL MY HONOR SUCH A MORTAL BLOW.
OD'S BLOOD, SIR THOMAS! I WHO LOVED THEE MOST NOW SEE THEE LIKE A TREE WHOSE ROTTEN CORE BELIES ITS OUTWARD SEEMING.
GO FROM ME.
JUST-- GO?
YEAH.
THAT'S ALL I GET?
LOOKS LIKE IT.
YOU'RE JUST LIKE YOUR DAD.
I'M SURPRISED I DIDN'T SEE IT SOONER.

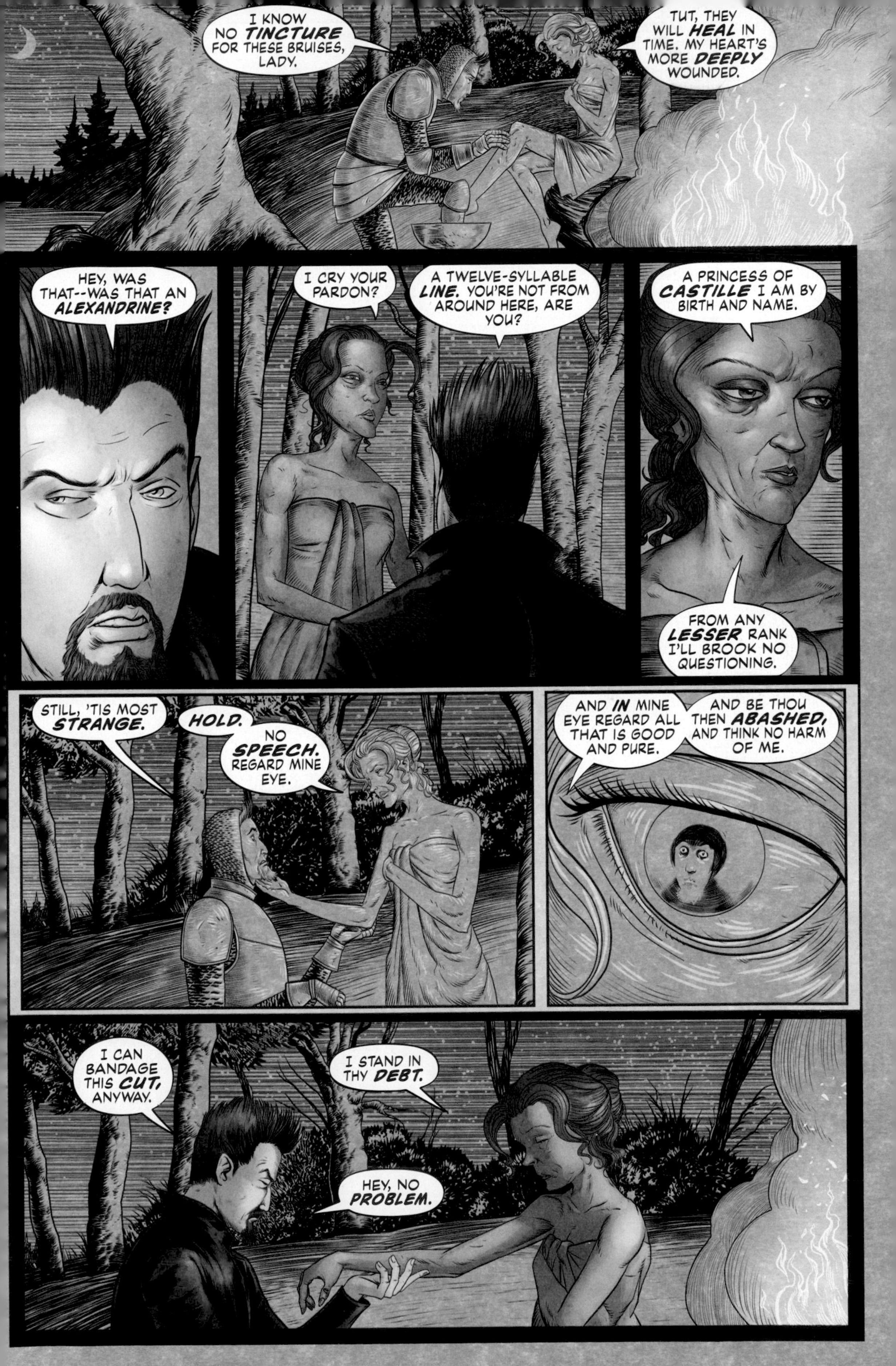
I KNOW NO TINCTURE FOR THESE BRUISES, LADY.
TUT, THEY WILL HEAL IN TIME. MY HEART'S MORE DEEPLY WOUNDED.
HEY, WAS THAT--WAS THAT AN ALEXANDRINE?
I CRY YOUR PARDON?
A TWELVE-SYLLABLE LINE. YOU'RE NOT FROM AROUND HERE, ARE YOU?
A PRINCESS OF CASTILLE I AM BY BIRTH AND NAME.
FROM ANY LESSER RANK I'LL BROOK NO QUESTIONING.
STILL, 'TIS MOST STRANGE.
HOLD.
NO SPEECH. REGARD MINE EYE.
AND IN MINE EYE REGARD ALL THAT IS GOOD AND PURE.
AND BE THOU THEN ABASHED, AND THINK NO HARM OF ME.
I CAN BANDAGE THIS CUT, ANYWAY.
I STAND IN THY DEBT.
HEY, NO PROBLEM.

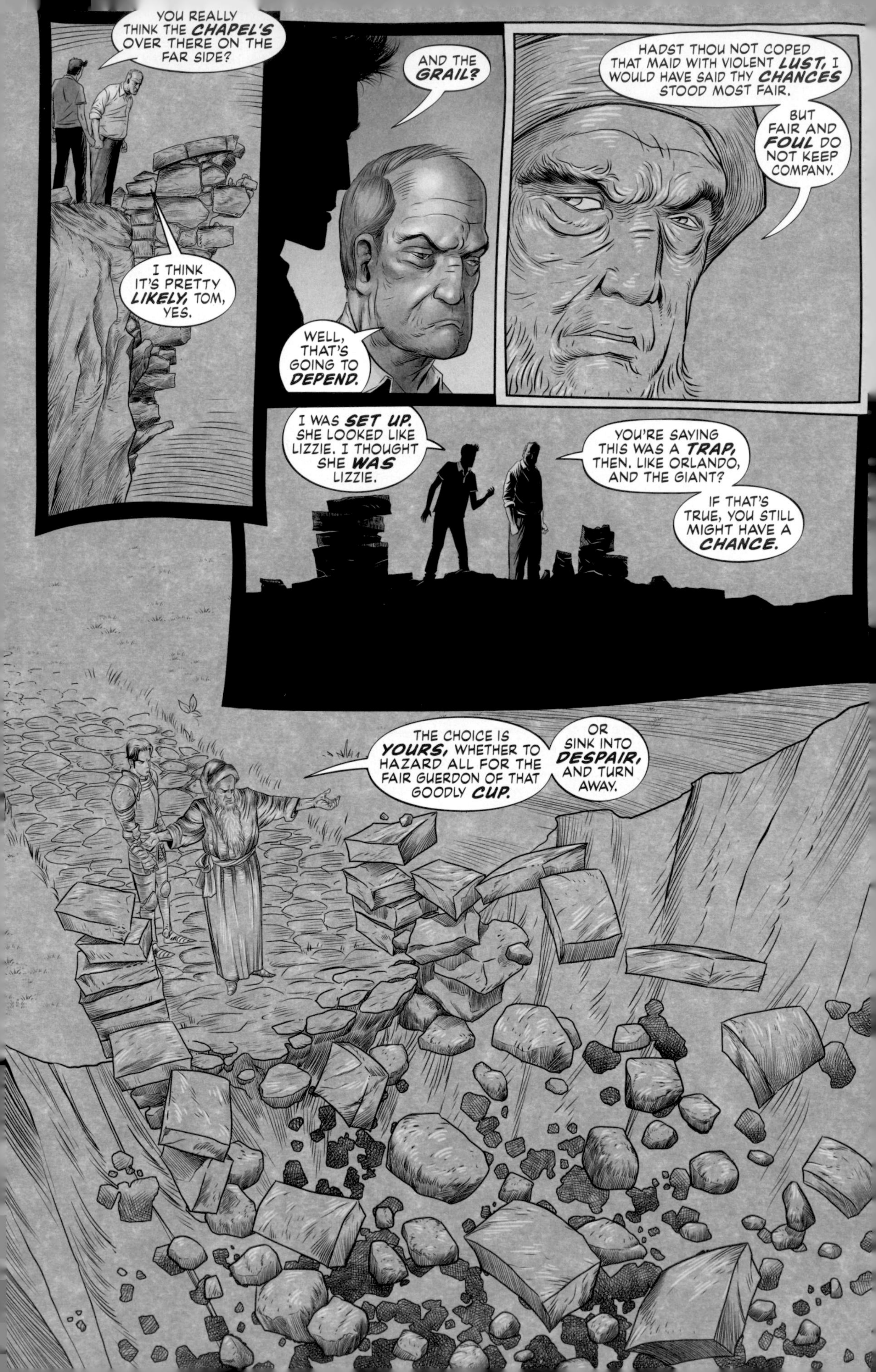
YOU REALLY THINK THE CHAPEL'S OVER THERE ON THE FAR SIDE?
I THINK IT'S PRETTY LIKELY, TOM, YES.
AND THE GRAIL?
WELL, THAT'S GOING TO DEPEND.
HADST THOU NOT COPED THAT MAID WITH VIOLENT LUST, I WOULD HAVE SAID THY CHANCES STOOD MOST FAIR.
BUT FAIR AND FOUL DO NOT KEEP COMPANY.
I WAS SET UP. SHE LOOKED LIKE LIZZIE. I THOUGHT SHE WAS LIZZIE.
YOU'RE SAYING THIS WAS A TRAP, THEN. LIKE ORLANDO, AND THE GIANT?
IF THAT'S TRUE, YOU STILL MIGHT HAVE A CHANCE.
THE CHOICE IS YOURS, WHETHER TO HAZARD ALL FOR THE FAIR GUERDON OF THAT GOODLY CUP.
OR SINK INTO DESPAIR, AND TURN AWAY.

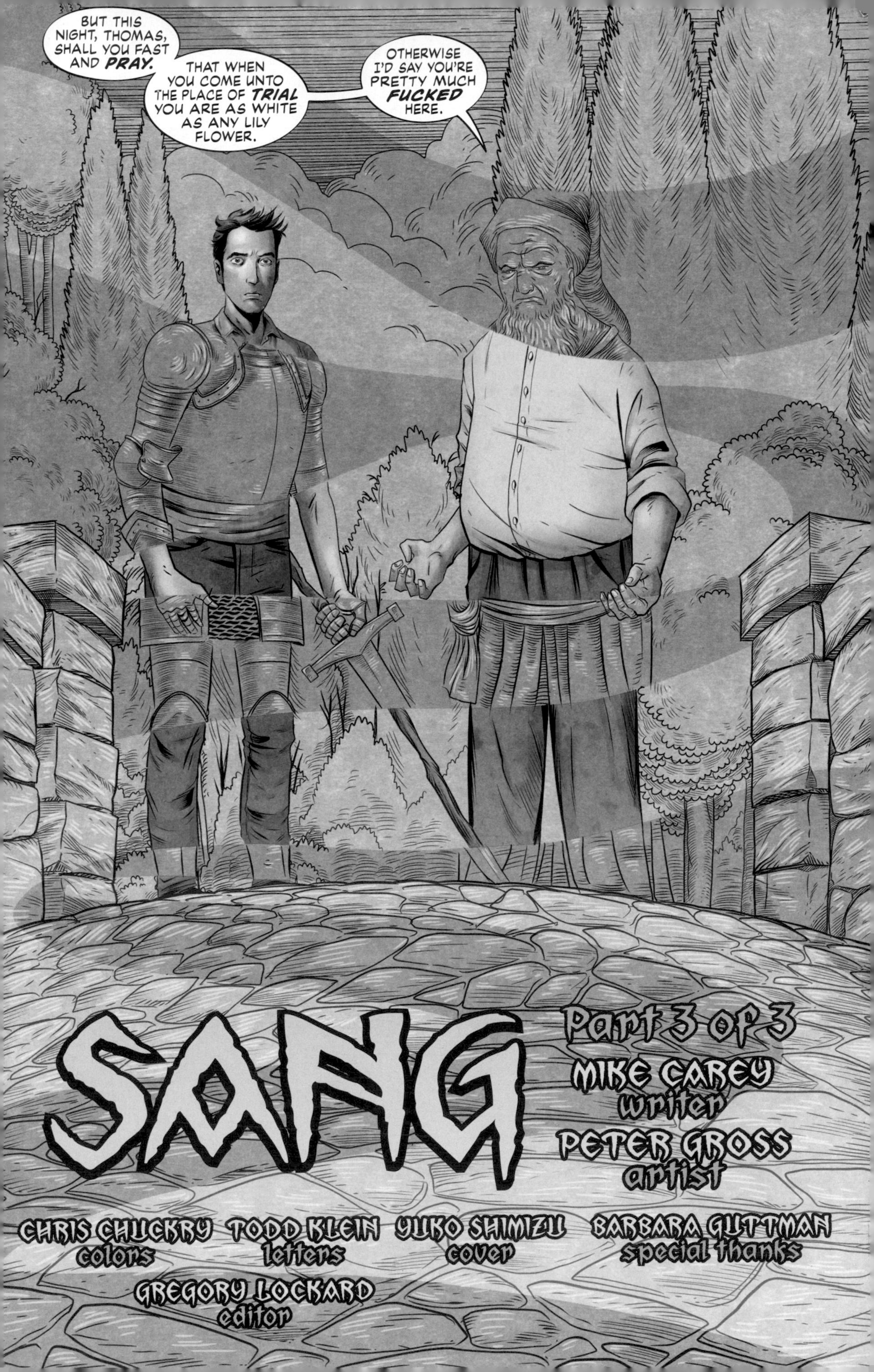
BUT THIS NIGHT, THOMAS, SHALL YOU FAST AND PRAY.
THAT WHEN YOU COME UNTO THE PLACE OF TRIAL YOU ARE AS WHITE AS ANY LILY FLOWER.
OTHERWISE I'D SAY YOU'RE PRETTY MUCH FUCKED HERE.
SANG
Part 3 of 3
MIKE CAREY writer
PETER GROSS artist
CHRIS CHUCKRY colors
TODD KLEIN letters
YUKO SHIMIZU cover
BARBARA GUTTMAN special thanks
GREGORY LOCKARD editor

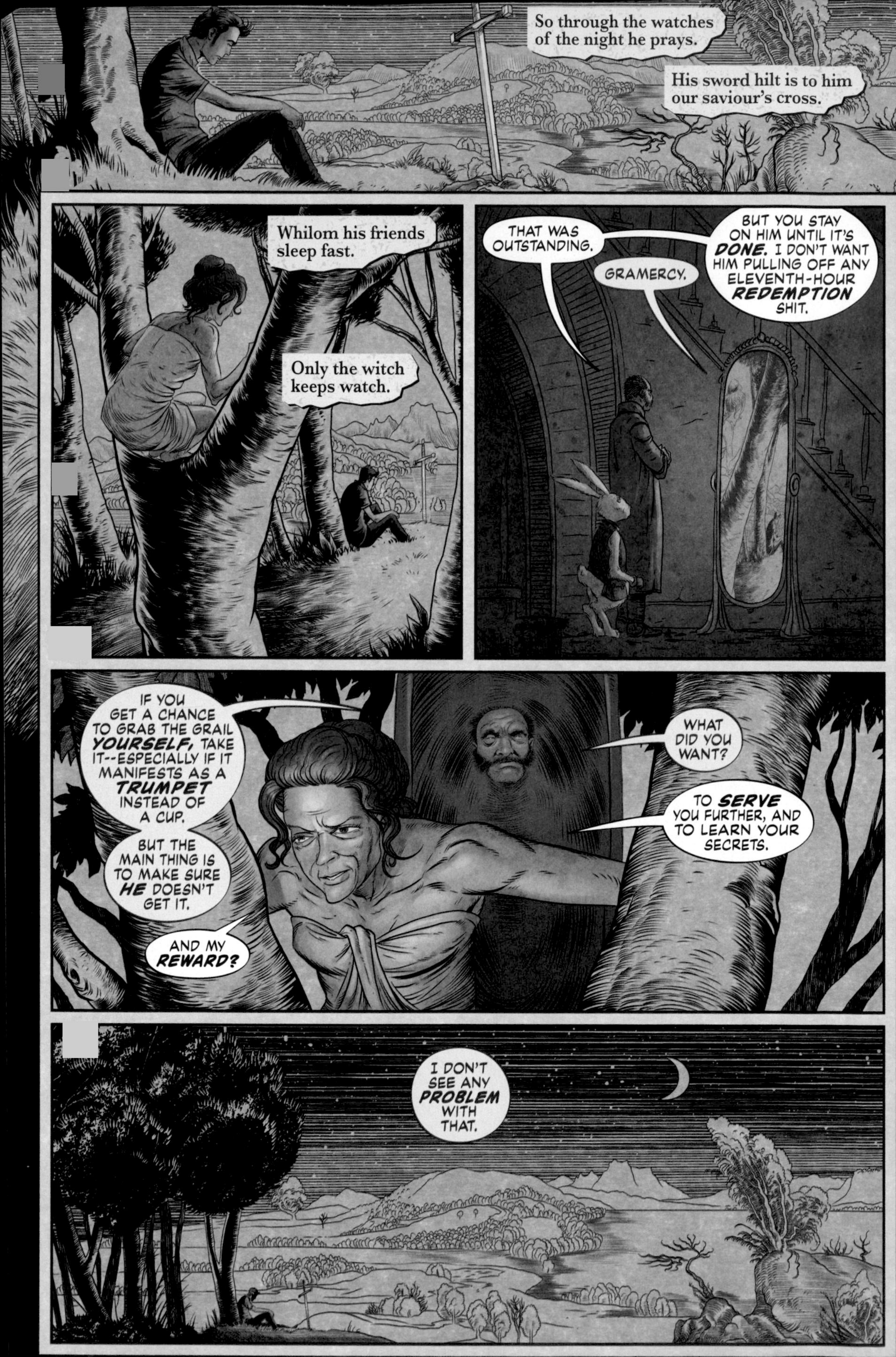
So through the watches of the night he prays.
His sword hilt is to him our saviour's cross.
Whilom his friends sleep fast.
Only the witch keeps watch.
THAT WAS OUTSTANDING.
BUT YOU STAY ON HIM UNTIL IT'S DONE. I DON'T WANT HIM PULLING OFF ANY ELEVENTH-HOUR REDEMPTION SHIT.
GRAMERCY.
IF YOU GET A CHANCE TO GRAB THE GRAIL YOURSELF, TAKE IT--ESPECIALLY IF IT MANIFESTS AS A TRUMPET INSTEAD OF A CUP.
BUT THE MAIN THING IS TO MAKE SURE HE DOESN'T GET IT.
AND MY REWARD?
WHAT DID YOU WANT?
TO SERVE YOU FURTHER, AND TO LEARN YOUR SECRETS.
I DON'T SEE ANY PROBLEM WITH THAT.

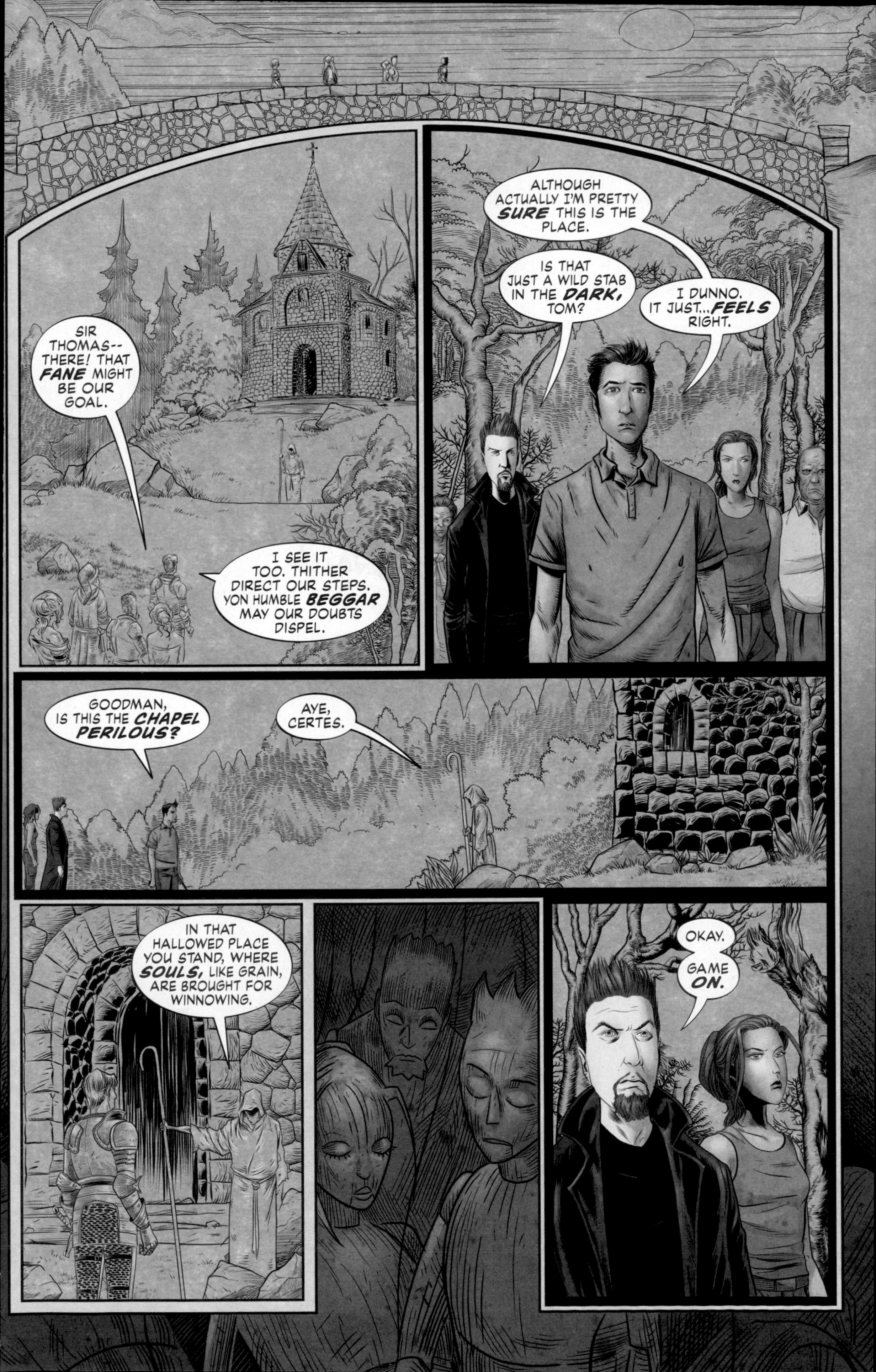
SIR THOMAS-- THERE! THAT FANE MIGHT BE OUR GOAL.
I SEE IT TOO. THITHER DIRECT OUR STEPS. YON HUMBLE BEGGAR MAY OUR DOUBTS DISPEL.
ALTHOUGH ACTUALLY I'M PRETTY SURE THIS IS THE PLACE.
IS THAT JUST A WILD STAB IN THE DARK, TOM?
I DUNNO. IT JUST...FEELS RIGHT.
GOODMAN, IS THIS THE CHAPEL PERILOUS?
AYE, CERTES.
IN THAT HALLOWED PLACE YOU STAND, WHERE SOULS, LIKE GRAIN, ARE BROUGHT FOR WINNOWING.
OKAY.
GAME ON.

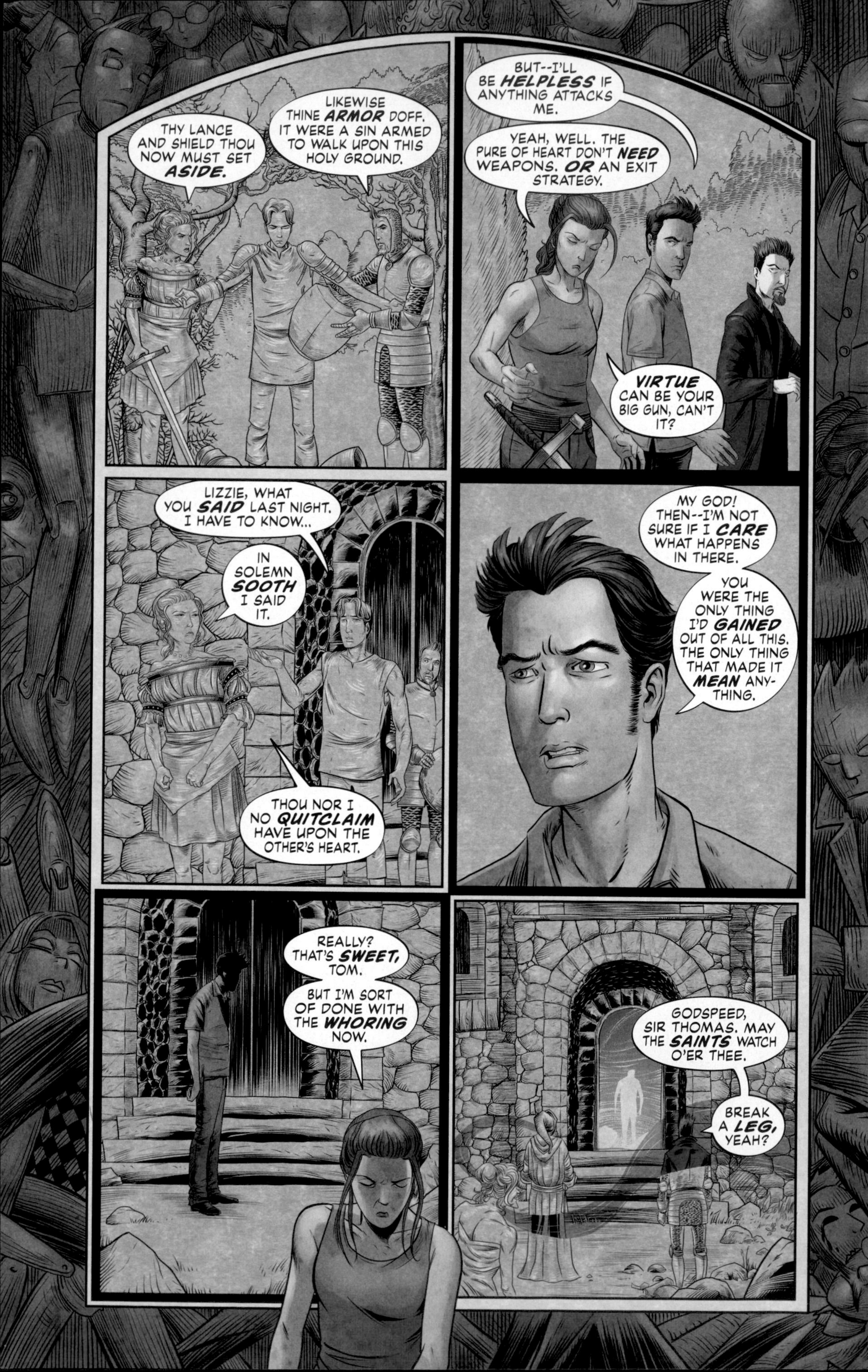
THY LANCE AND SHIELD THOU NOW MUST SET ASIDE.
LIKEWISE THINE ARMOR DOFF. IT WERE A SIN ARMED TO WALK UPON THIS HOLY GROUND.
BUT--I'LL BE HELPLESS IF ANYTHING ATTACKS ME.
YEAH, WELL. THE PURE OF HEART DON'T NEED WEAPONS. OR AN EXIT STRATEGY.
VIRTUE CAN BE YOUR BIG GUN, CAN'T IT?
LIZZIE, WHAT YOU SAID LAST NIGHT. I HAVE TO KNOW...
IN SOLEMN SOOTH I SAID IT.
THOU NOR I NO QUITCLAIM HAVE UPON THE OTHER'S HEART.
MY GOD! THEN--I'M NOT SURE IF I CARE WHAT HAPPENS IN THERE.
YOU WERE THE ONLY THING I'D GAINED OUT OF ALL THIS. THE ONLY THING THAT MADE IT MEAN ANY-THING.
REALLY? THAT'S SWEET, TOM.
BUT I'M SORT OF DONE WITH THE WHORING NOW.
GODSPEED, SIR THOMAS. MAY THE SAINTS WATCH O'ER THEE.
BREAK A LEG, YEAH?

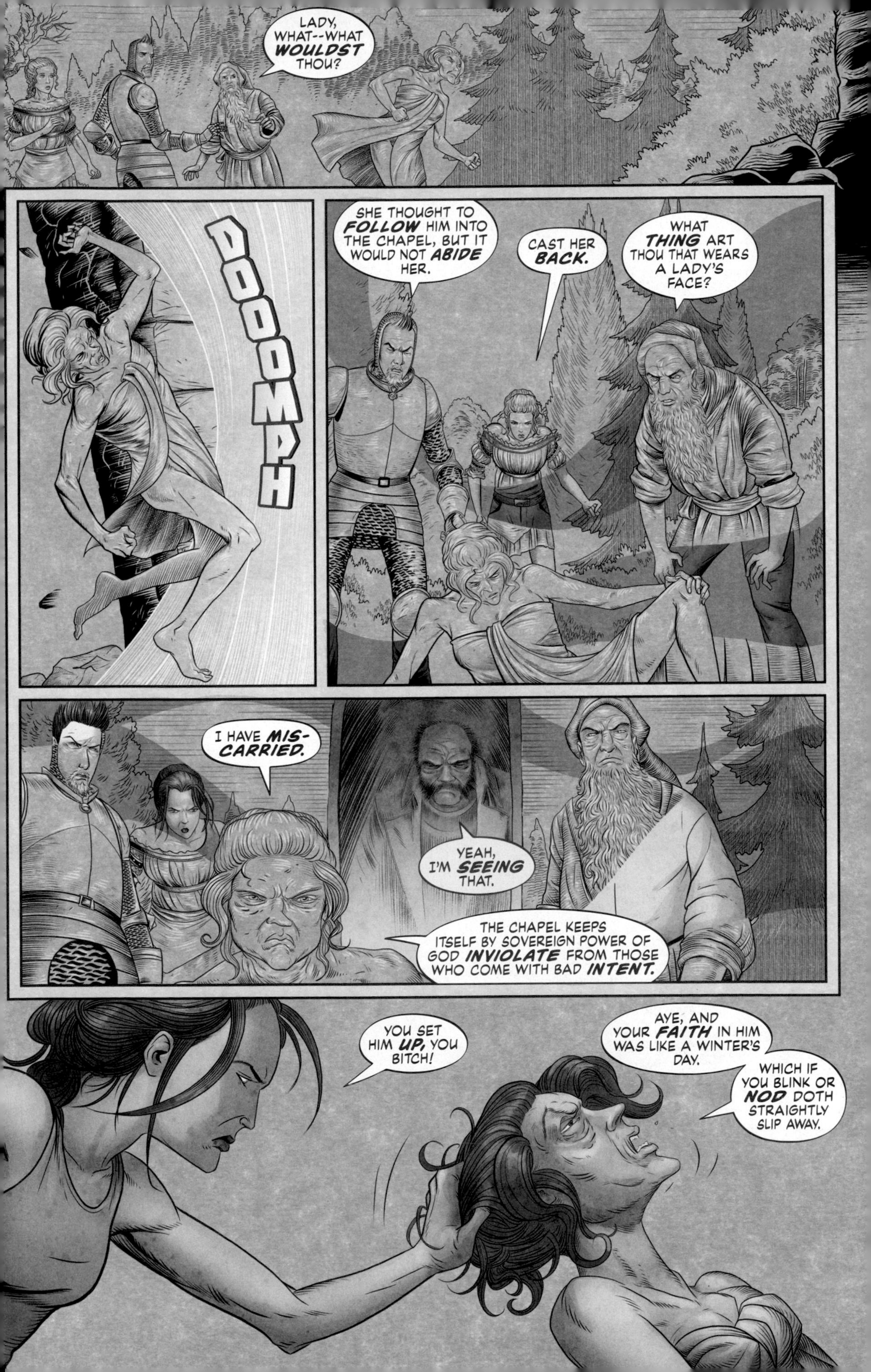
LADY, WHAT--WHAT WOULDST THOU?
DOOOMPH
SHE THOUGHT TO FOLLOW HIM INTO THE CHAPEL, BUT IT WOULD NOT ABIDE HER.
CAST HER BACK.
WHAT THING ART THOU THAT WEARS A LADY'S FACE?
I HAVE MIS-CARRIED.
YEAH, I'M SEEING THAT.
THE CHAPEL KEEPS ITSELF BY SOVEREIGN POWER OF GOD INVIOLATE FROM THOSE WHO COME WITH BAD INTENT.
YOU SET HIM UP, YOU BITCH!
AYE, AND YOUR FAITH IN HIM WAS LIKE A WINTER'S DAY.
WHICH IF YOU BLINK OR NOD DOTH STRAIGHTLY SLIP AWAY.

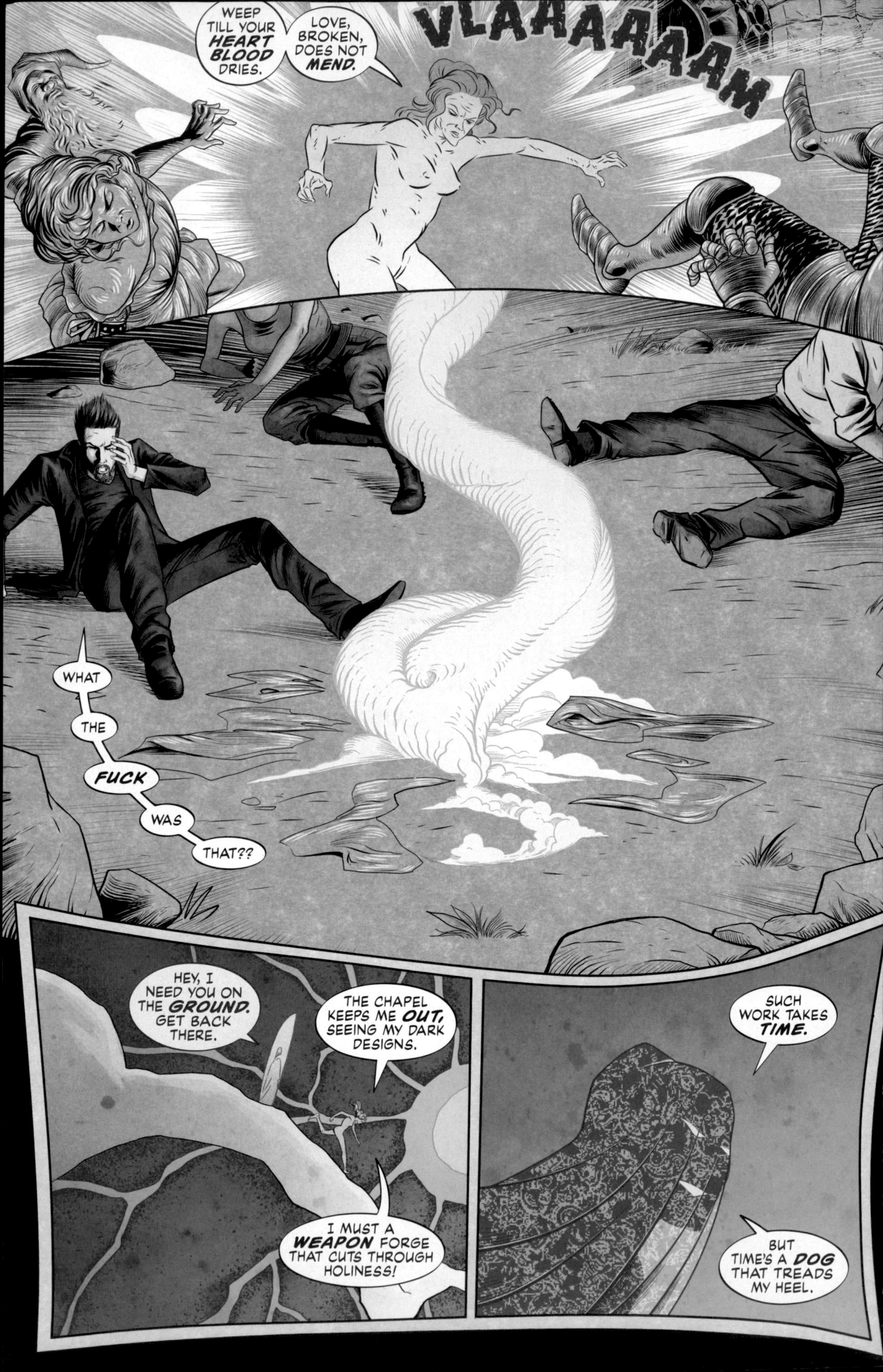
WEEP TILL YOUR HEART BLOOD DRIES.
LOVE, BROKEN, DOES NOT MEND.
VLAAAAAAAM
WHAT THE FUCK WAS THAT??
HEY, I NEED YOU ON THE GROUND. GET BACK THERE.
THE CHAPEL KEEPS ME OUT, SEEING MY DARK DESIGNS.
I MUST A WEAPON FORGE THAT CUTS THROUGH HOLINESS!
SUCH WORK TAKES TIME.
BUT TIME'S A DOG THAT TREADS MY HEEL.

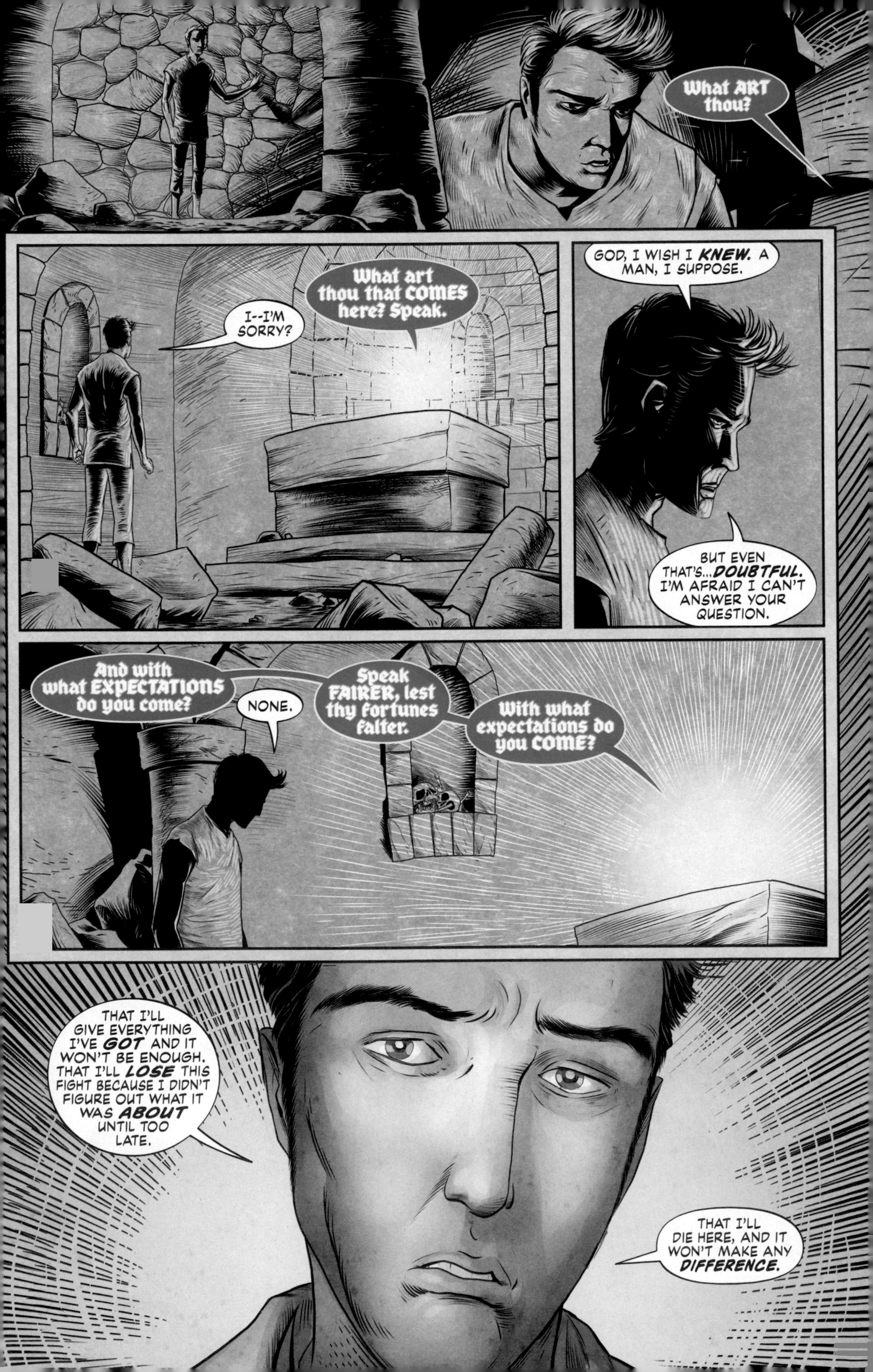
What ART thou?
I--I'M SORRY?
What art thou that COMES here? Speak.
GOD, I WISH I KNEW. A MAN, I SUPPOSE.
BUT EVEN THAT'S...DOUBTFUL. I'M AFRAID I CAN'T ANSWER YOUR QUESTION.
And with what EXPECTATIONS do you come?
NONE.
Speak FAIRER, lest thy fortunes falter.
With what expectations do you COME?
THAT I'LL GIVE EVERYTHING I'VE GOT AND IT WON'T BE ENOUGH. THAT I'LL LOSE THIS FIGHT BECAUSE I DIDN'T FIGURE OUT WHAT IT WAS ABOUT UNTIL TOO LATE.
THAT I'LL DIE HERE, AND IT WON'T MAKE ANY DIFFERENCE.

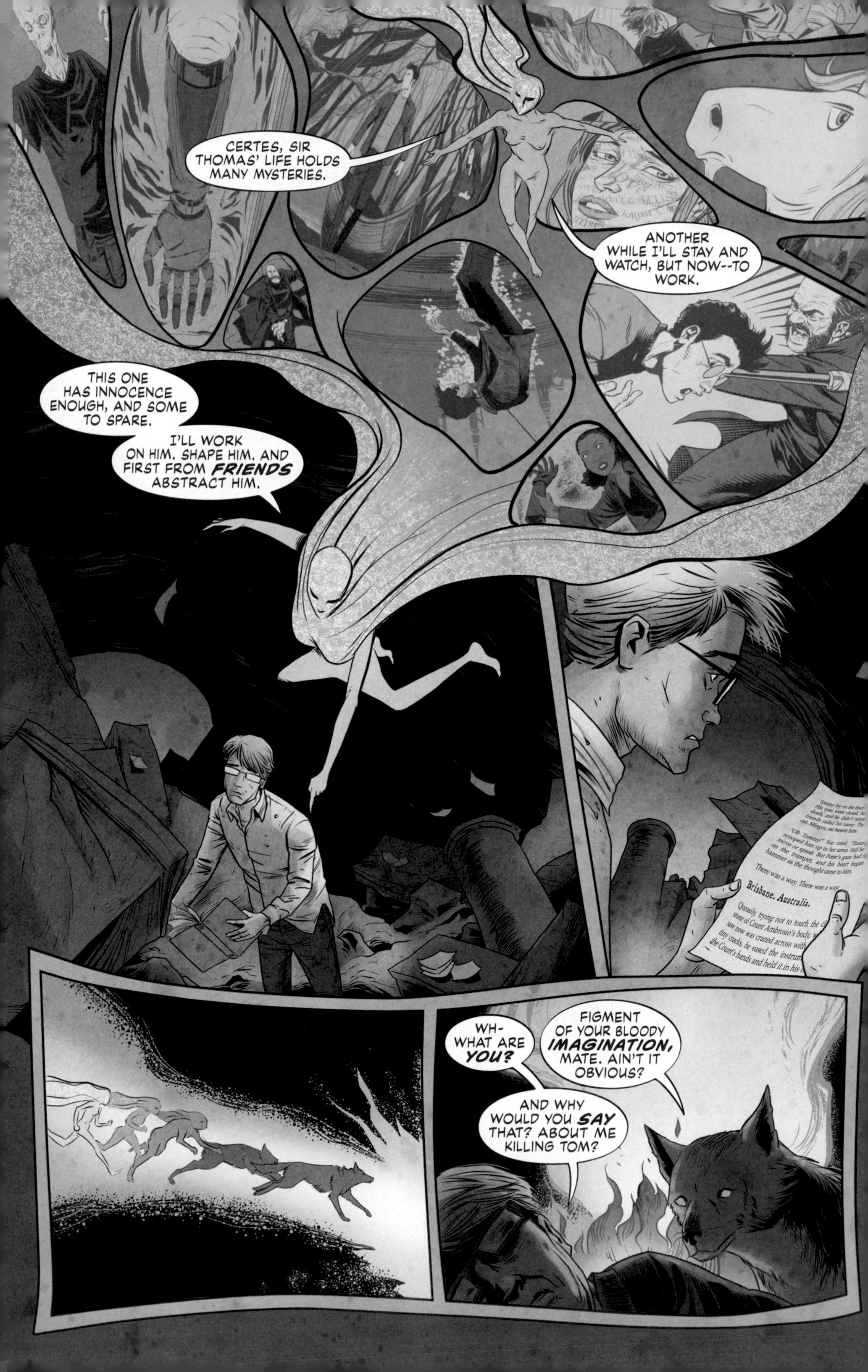
CERTES, SIR THOMAS' LIFE HOLDS MANY MYSTERIES.
ANOTHER WHILE I'LL STAY AND WATCH, BUT NOW--TO WORK.
THIS ONE HAS INNOCENCE ENOUGH, AND SOME TO SPARE.
I'LL WORK ON HIM. SHAPE HIM. AND FIRST FROM FRIENDS ABSTRACT HIM.
Brisbane, Australia.
WH- WHAT ARE YOU?
FIGMENT OF YOUR BLOODY IMAGINATION, MATE. AIN'T IT OBVIOUS?
AND WHY WOULD YOU SAY THAT? ABOUT ME KILLING TOM?

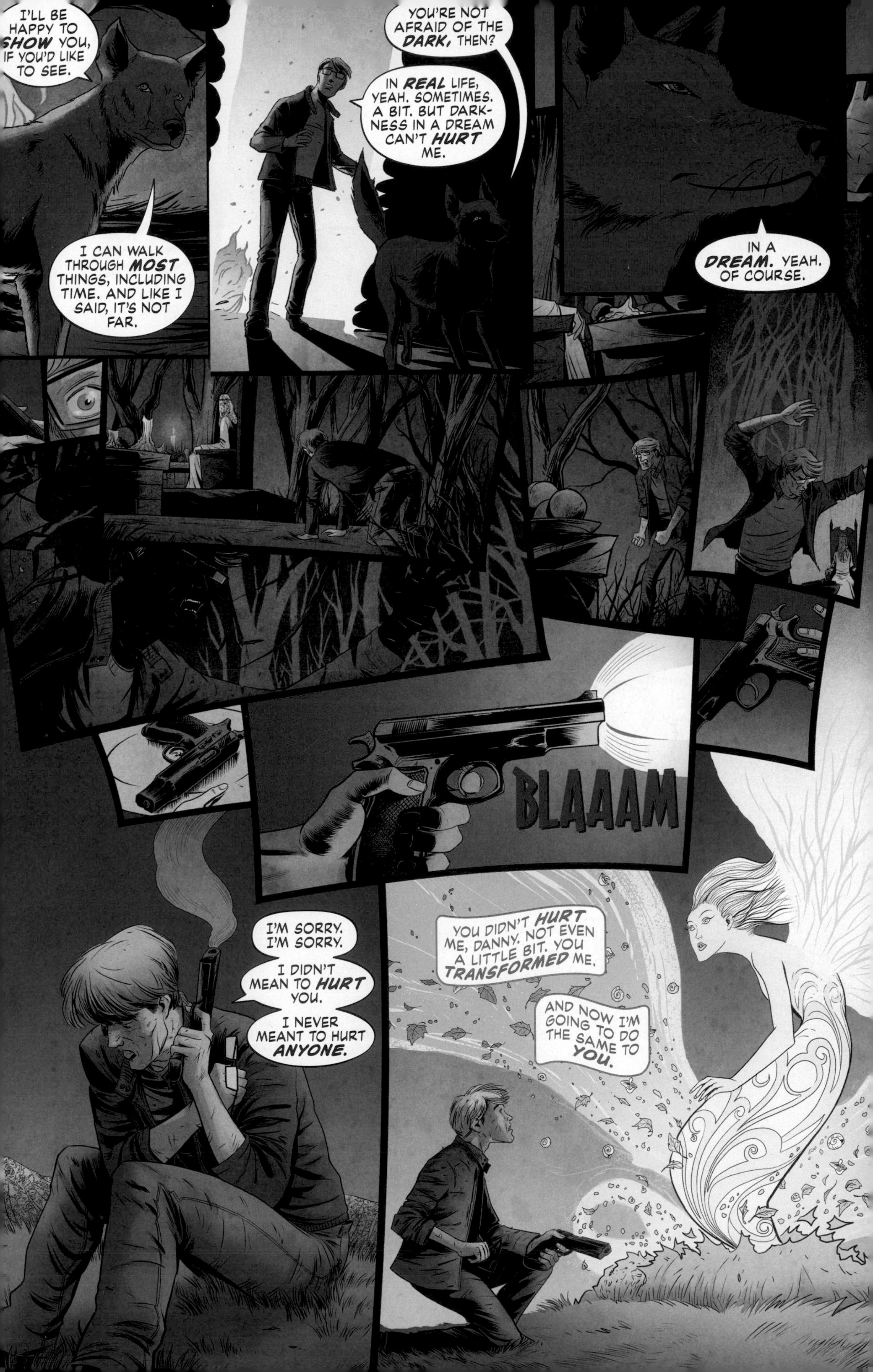
I'LL BE HAPPY TO SHOW YOU, IF YOU'D LIKE TO SEE.
I CAN WALK THROUGH MOST THINGS, INCLUDING TIME. AND LIKE I SAID, IT'S NOT FAR.
YOU'RE NOT AFRAID OF THE DARK, THEN?
IN REAL LIFE, YEAH. SOMETIMES. A BIT. BUT DARKNESS IN A DREAM CAN'T HURT ME.
IN A DREAM. YEAH. OF COURSE.
BLAAAM
I'M SORRY. I'M SORRY.
I DIDN'T MEAN TO HURT YOU.
I NEVER MEANT TO HURT ANYONE.
YOU DIDN'T HURT ME, DANNY. NOT EVEN A LITTLE BIT. YOU TRANSFORMED ME.
AND NOW I'M GOING TO DO THE SAME TO YOU.

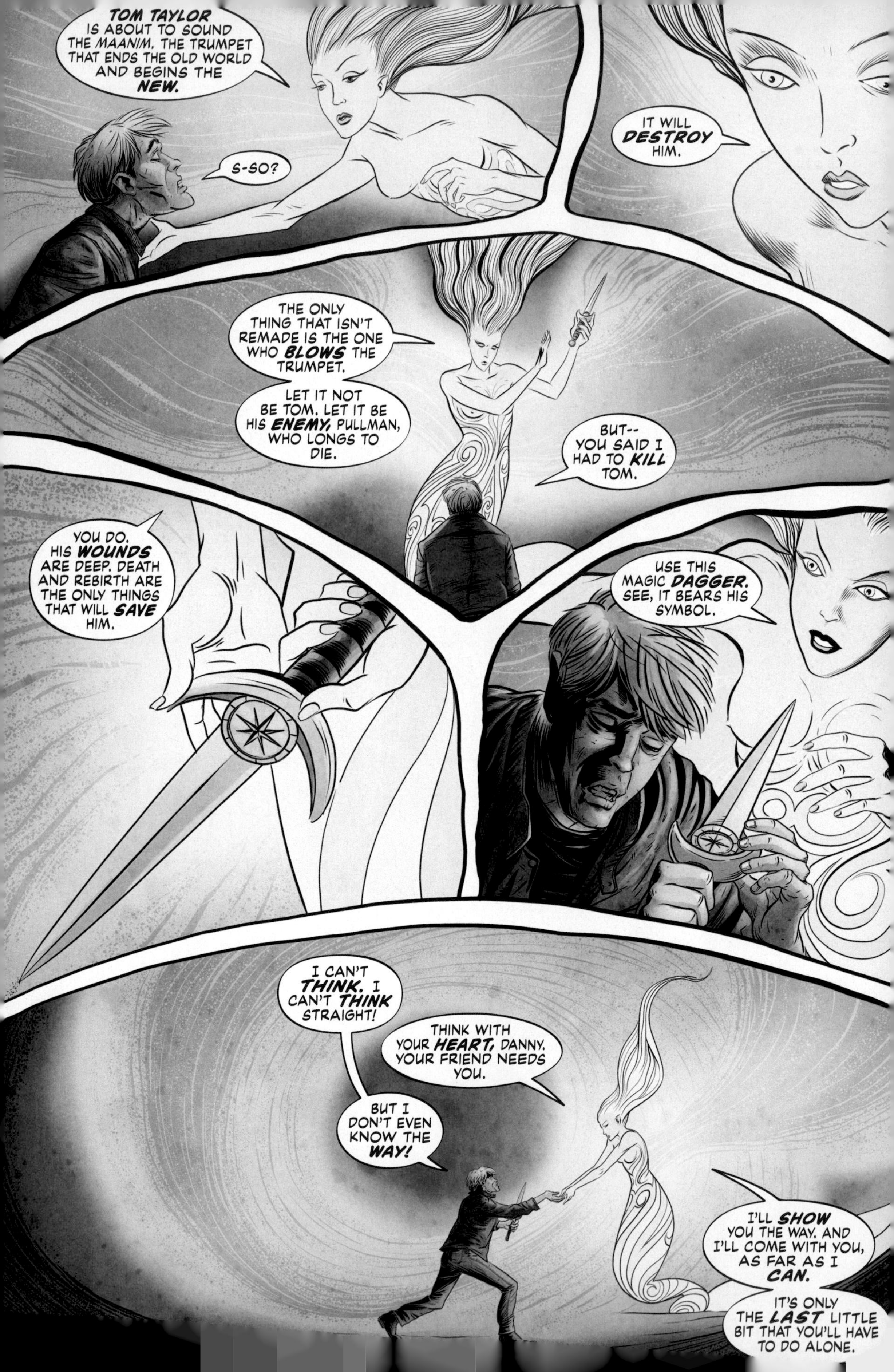
TOM TAYLOR IS ABOUT TO SOUND THE MAANIM, THE TRUMPET THAT ENDS THE OLD WORLD AND BEGINS THE NEW.
S-SO?
IT WILL DESTROY HIM.
THE ONLY THING THAT ISN'T REMADE IS THE ONE WHO BLOWS THE TRUMPET.
LET IT NOT BE TOM. LET IT BE HIS ENEMY, PULLMAN, WHO LONGS TO DIE.
BUT-- YOU SAID I HAD TO KILL TOM.
YOU DO. HIS WOUNDS ARE DEEP. DEATH AND REBIRTH ARE THE ONLY THINGS THAT WILL SAVE HIM.
USE THIS MAGIC DAGGER. SEE, IT BEARS HIS SYMBOL.
I CAN'T THINK. I CAN'T THINK STRAIGHT!
THINK WITH YOUR HEART, DANNY. YOUR FRIEND NEEDS YOU.
BUT I DON'T EVEN KNOW THE WAY!
I'LL SHOW YOU THE WAY. AND I'LL COME WITH YOU, AS FAR AS I CAN.
IT'S ONLY THE LAST LITTLE BIT THAT YOU'LL HAVE TO DO ALONE.

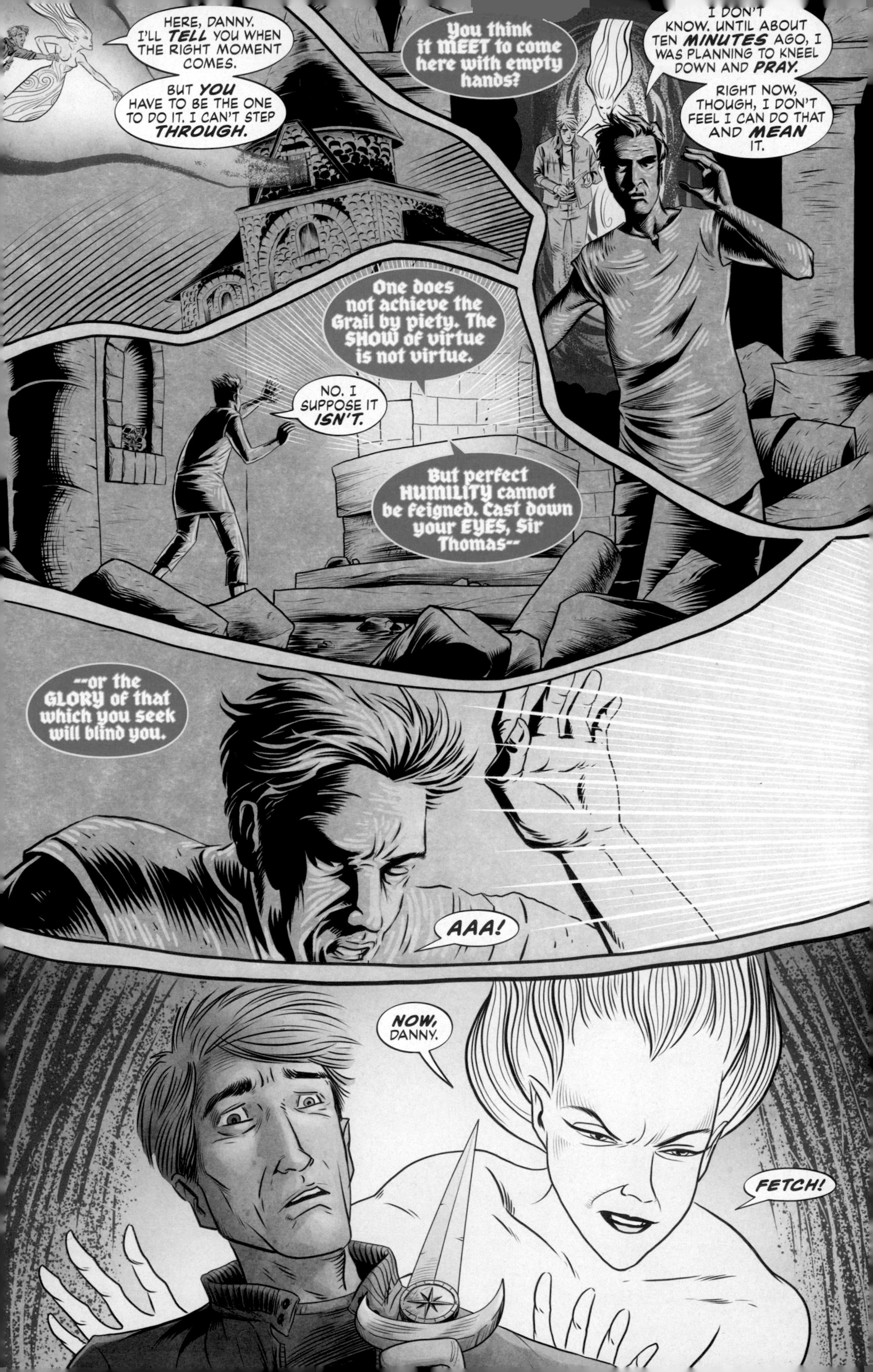

HERE, DANNY. I'LL TELL YOU WHEN THE RIGHT MOMENT COMES.
BUT YOU HAVE TO BE THE ONE TO DO IT. I CAN'T STEP THROUGH.
You think it MEET to come here with empty hands?
I DON'T KNOW. UNTIL ABOUT TEN MINUTES AGO, I WAS PLANNING TO KNEEL DOWN AND PRAY.
RIGHT NOW, THOUGH, I DON'T FEEL I CAN DO THAT AND MEAN IT.
One does not achieve the Grail by piety. The SHOW of virtue is not virtue.
NO. I SUPPOSE IT ISN'T.
But perfect HUMILITY cannot be feigned. Cast down your EYES, Sir Thomas--
--or the GLORY of that which you seek will blind you.
AAA!
NOW, DANNY.
FETCH!

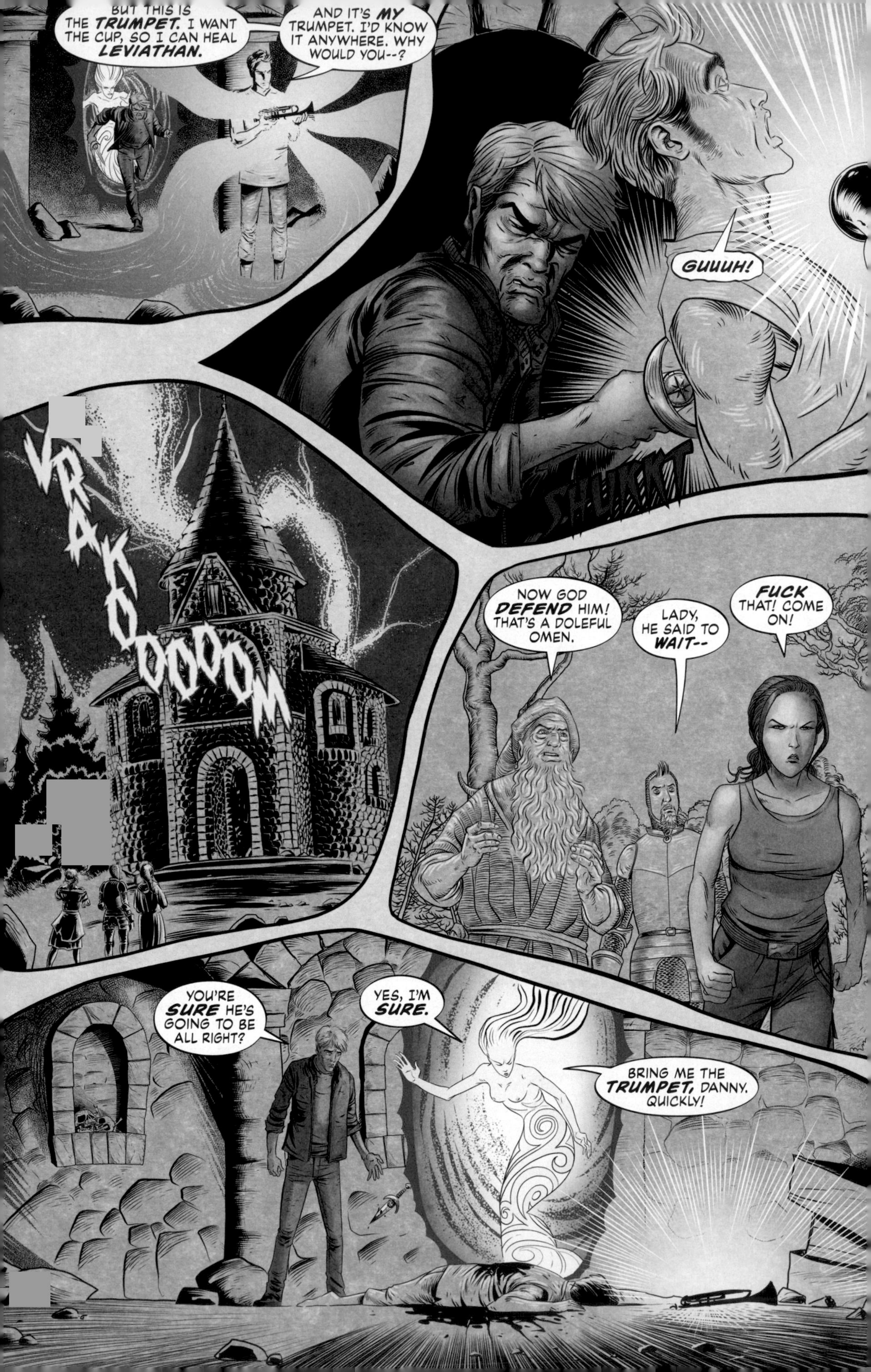
BUT THIS IS THE TRUMPET. I WANT THE CUP, SO I CAN HEAL LEVIATHAN.
AND IT'S MY TRUMPET. I'D KNOW IT ANYWHERE. WHY WOULD YOU--?
GUUUH!
SHUKKT
VRAKOOOOOOM
NOW GOD DEFEND HIM! THAT'S A DOLEFUL OMEN.
LADY, HE SAID TO WAIT--
FUCK THAT! COME ON!
YOU'RE SURE HE'S GOING TO BE ALL RIGHT?
YES, I'M SURE.
BRING ME THE TRUMPET, DANNY. QUICKLY!

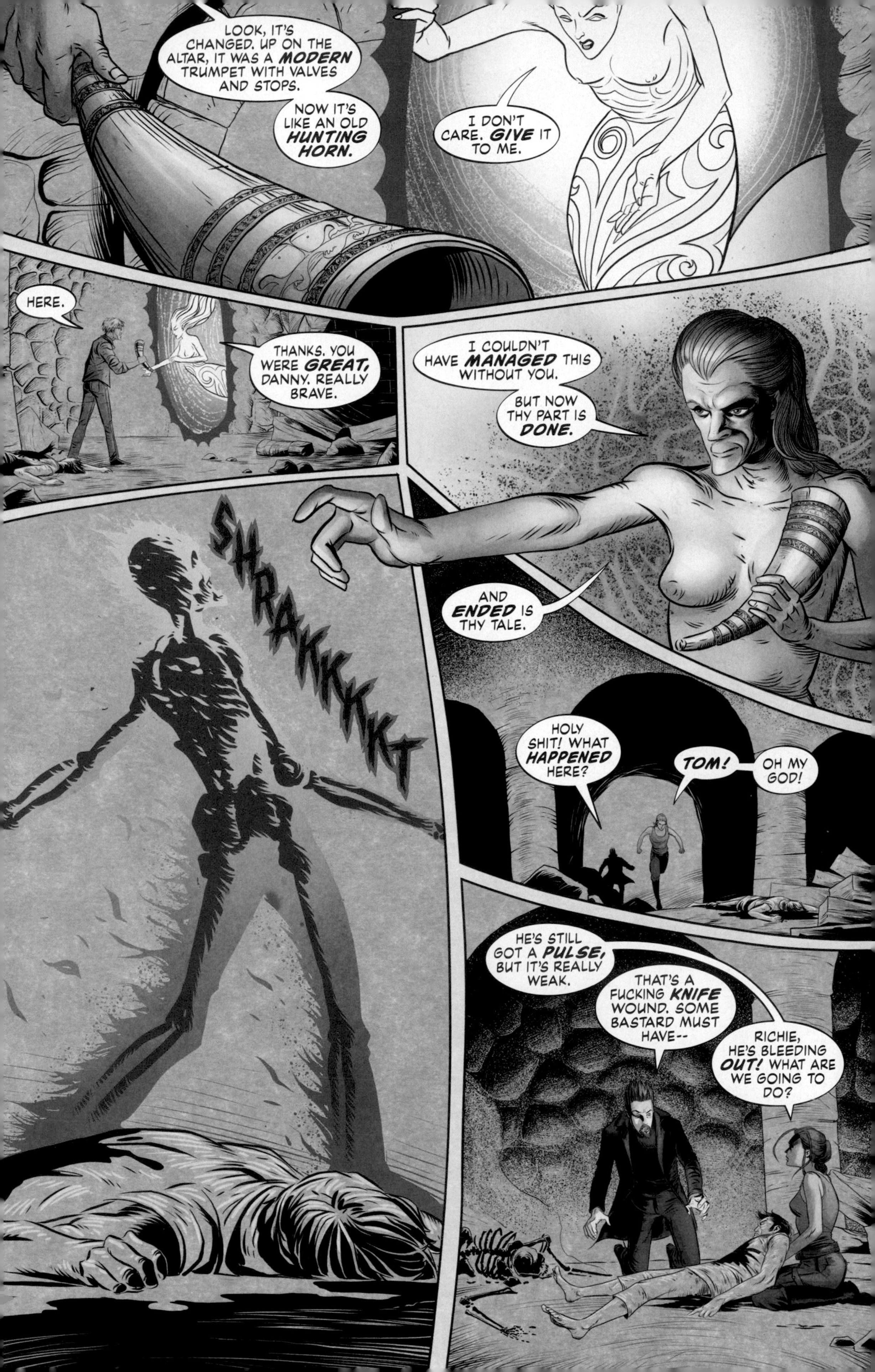
LOOK, IT'S CHANGED. UP ON THE ALTAR, IT WAS A MODERN TRUMPET WITH VALVES AND STOPS.
NOW IT'S LIKE AN OLD HUNTING HORN.
I DON'T CARE. GIVE IT TO ME.
HERE.
THANKS. YOU WERE GREAT, DANNY. REALLY BRAVE.
I COULDN'T HAVE MANAGED THIS WITHOUT YOU.
BUT NOW THY PART IS DONE.
AND ENDED IS THY TALE.
SHRAKKKKKT
HOLY SHIT! WHAT HAPPENED HERE?
TOM!
OH MY GOD!
HE'S STILL GOT A PULSE, BUT IT'S REALLY WEAK.
THAT'S A FUCKING KNIFE WOUND. SOME BASTARD MUST HAVE--
RICHIE, HE'S BLEEDING OUT! WHAT ARE WE GOING TO DO?

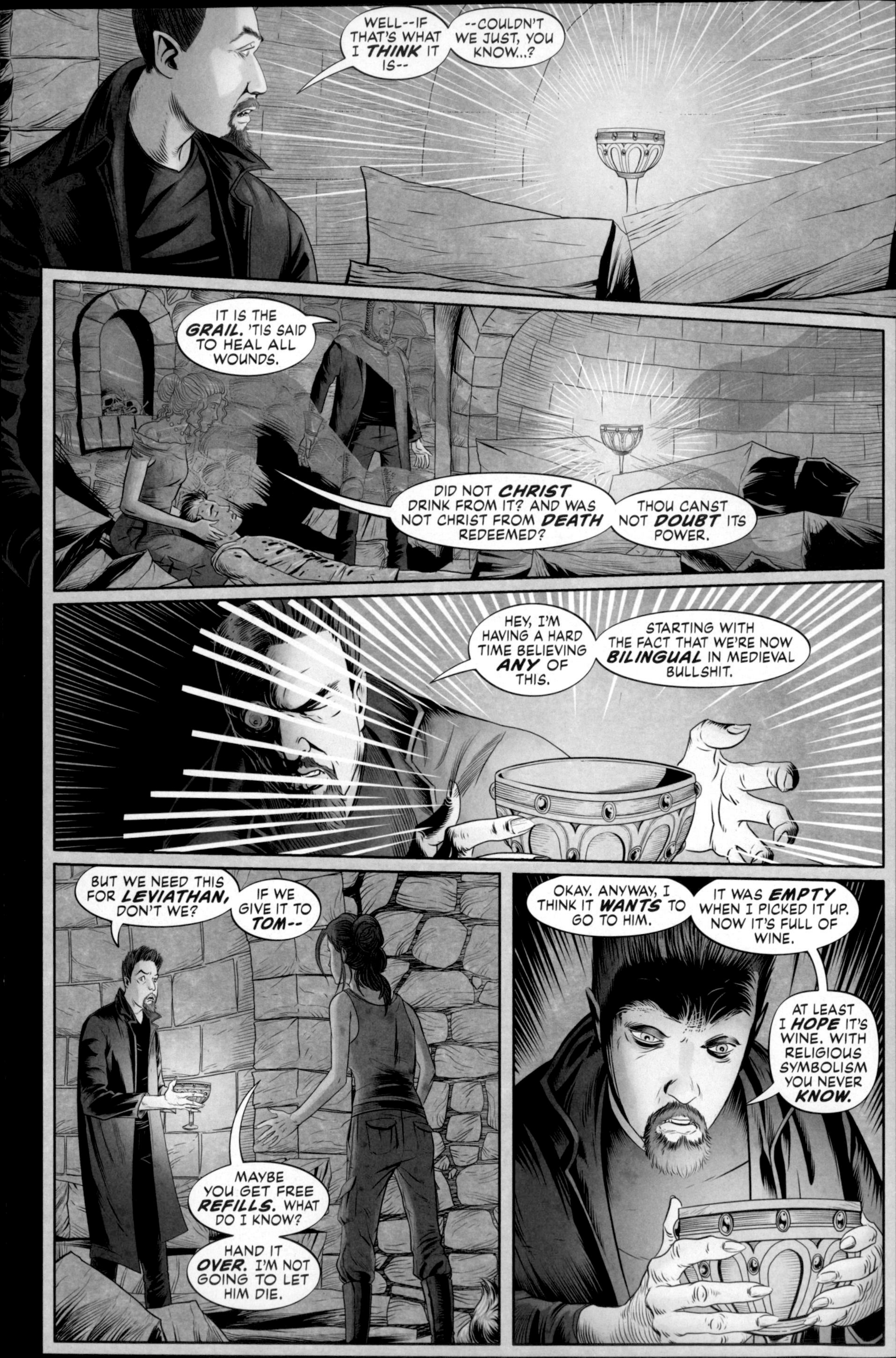
WELL--IF THAT'S WHAT I THINK IT IS--
--COULDN'T WE JUST, YOU KNOW...?
IT IS THE GRAIL. 'TIS SAID TO HEAL ALL WOUNDS.
DID NOT CHRIST DRINK FROM IT? AND WAS NOT CHRIST FROM DEATH REDEEMED?
THOU CANST NOT DOUBT ITS POWER.
HEY, I'M HAVING A HARD TIME BELIEVING ANY OF THIS.
STARTING WITH THE FACT THAT WE'RE NOW BILINGUAL IN MEDIEVAL BULLSHIT.
BUT WE NEED THIS FOR LEVIATHAN, DON'T WE?
IF WE GIVE IT TO TOM--
MAYBE YOU GET FREE REFILLS. WHAT DO I KNOW?
HAND IT OVER. I'M NOT GOING TO LET HIM DIE.
OKAY. ANYWAY, I THINK IT WANTS TO GO TO HIM.
IT WAS EMPTY WHEN I PICKED IT UP. NOW IT'S FULL OF WINE.
AT LEAST I HOPE IT'S WINE. WITH RELIGIOUS SYMBOLISM YOU NEVER KNOW.

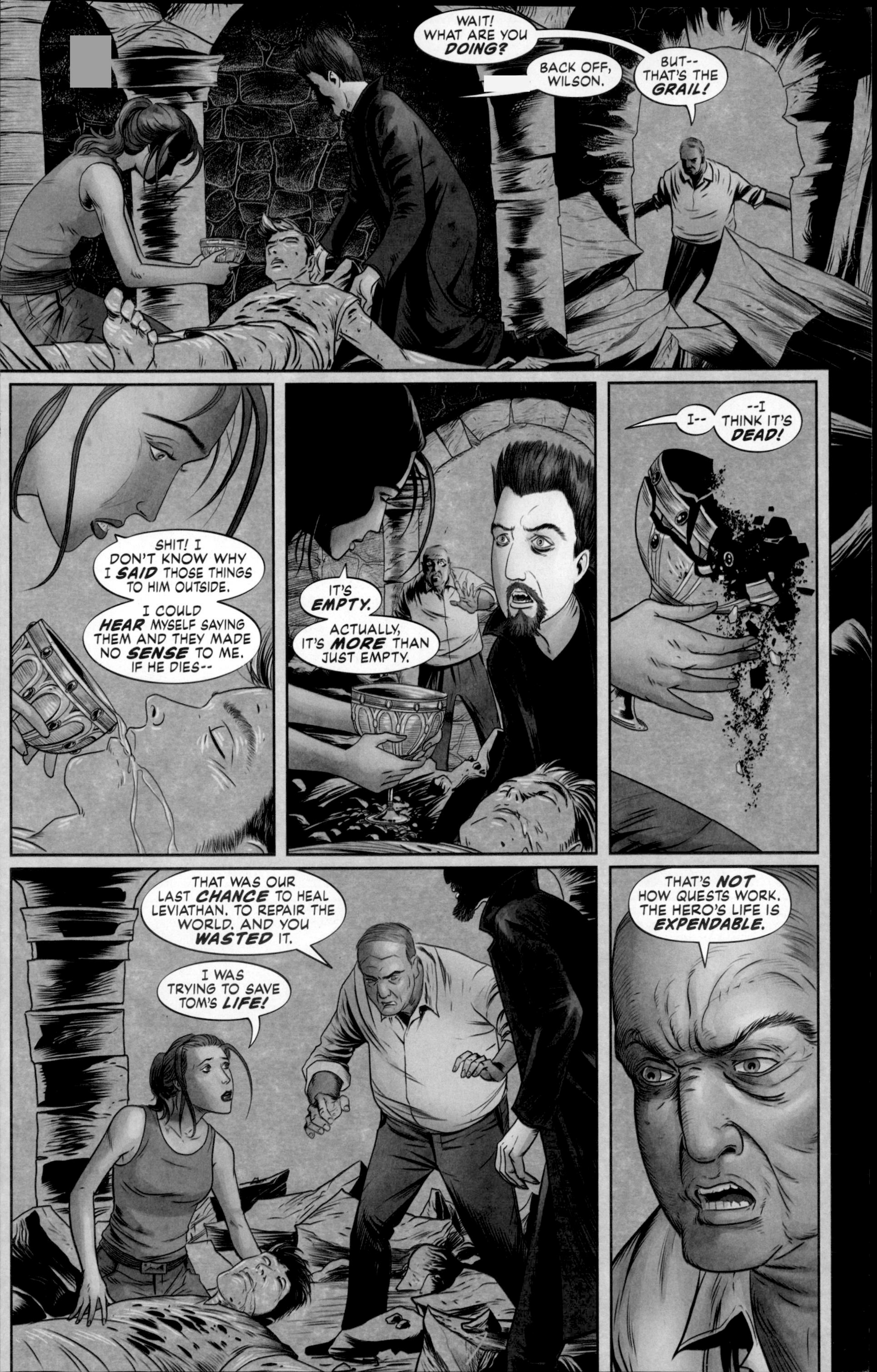
WAIT! WHAT ARE YOU DOING?
BACK OFF, WILSON.
BUT-- THAT'S THE GRAIL!
SHIT! I DON'T KNOW WHY I SAID THOSE THINGS TO HIM OUTSIDE.
I COULD HEAR MYSELF SAYING THEM AND THEY MADE NO SENSE TO ME. IF HE DIES--
IT'S EMPTY.
ACTUALLY, IT'S MORE THAN JUST EMPTY.
I--
--I THINK IT'S DEAD!
THAT WAS OUR LAST CHANCE TO HEAL LEVIATHAN. TO REPAIR THE WORLD. AND YOU WASTED IT.
I WAS TRYING TO SAVE TOM'S LIFE!
THAT'S NOT HOW QUESTS WORK. THE HERO'S LIFE IS EXPENDABLE.

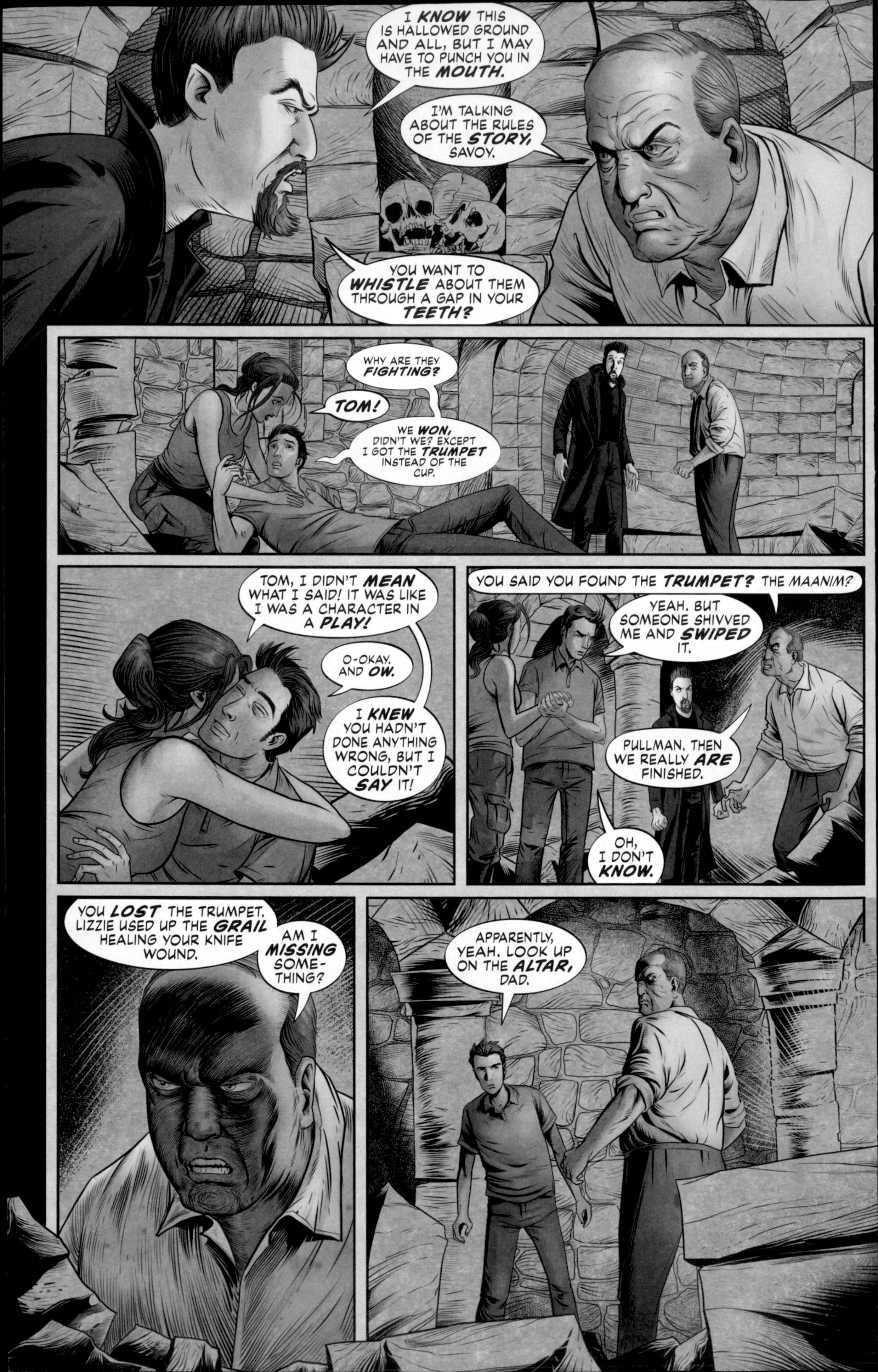
I KNOW THIS IS HALLOWED GROUND AND ALL, BUT I MAY HAVE TO PUNCH YOU IN THE MOUTH.
I'M TALKING ABOUT THE RULES OF THE STORY, SAVOY.
YOU WANT TO WHISTLE ABOUT THEM THROUGH A GAP IN YOUR TEETH?
WHY ARE THEY FIGHTING?
TOM!
WE WON, DIDN'T WE? EXCEPT I GOT THE TRUMPET INSTEAD OF THE CUP.
TOM, I DIDN'T MEAN WHAT I SAID! IT WAS LIKE I WAS A CHARACTER IN A PLAY!
O-OKAY. AND OW.
I KNEW YOU HADN'T DONE ANYTHING WRONG, BUT I COULDN'T SAY IT!
YOU SAID YOU FOUND THE TRUMPET? THE MAANIM?
YEAH. BUT SOMEONE SHIVVED ME AND SWIPED IT.
PULLMAN. THEN WE REALLY ARE FINISHED.
OH, I DON'T KNOW.
YOU LOST THE TRUMPET. LIZZIE USED UP THE GRAIL HEALING YOUR KNIFE WOUND.
AM I MISSING SOME-THING?
APPARENTLY, YEAH. LOOK UP ON THE ALTAR, DAD.

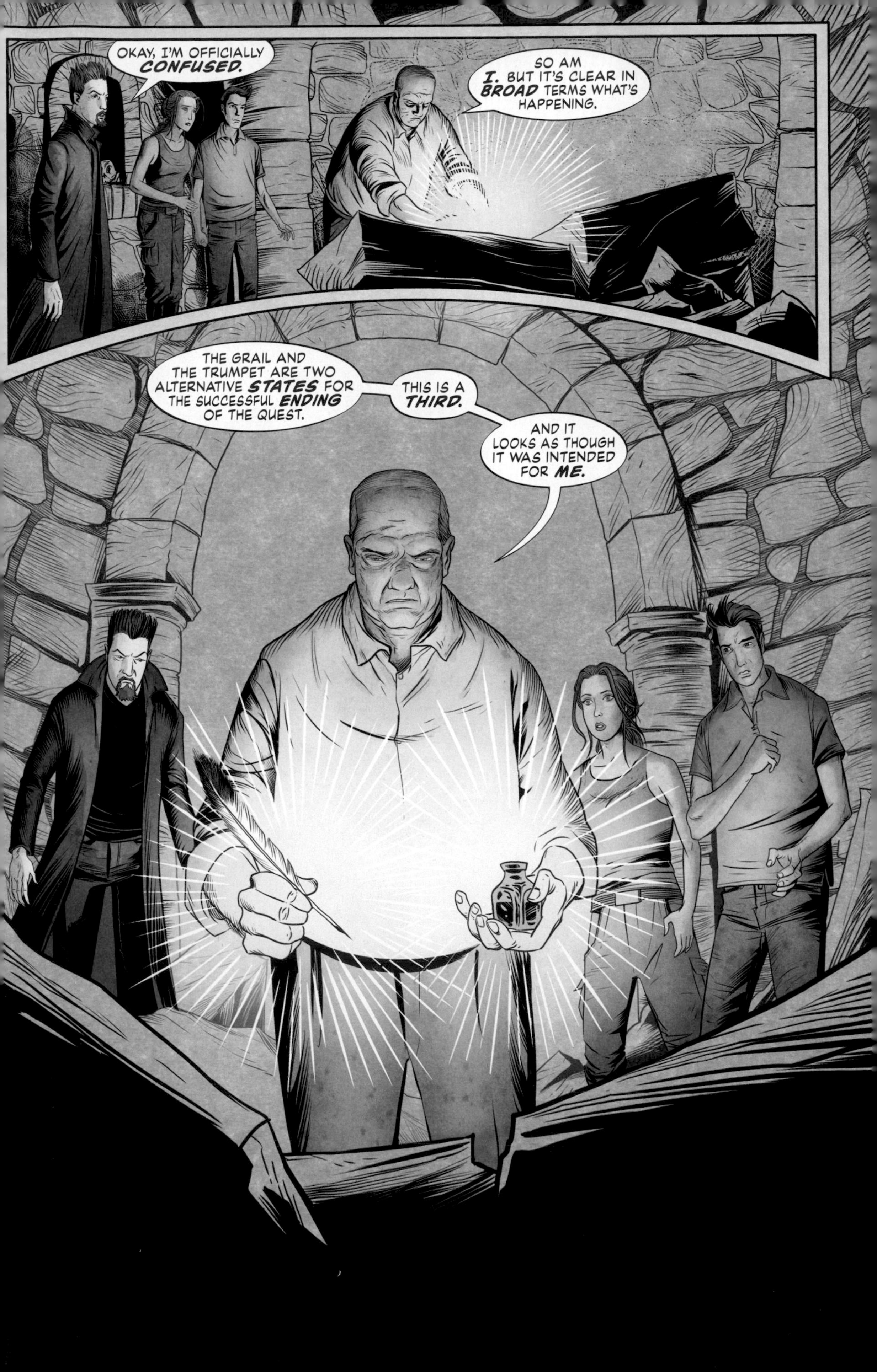
OKAY, I'M OFFICIALLY CONFUSED.
SO AM I. BUT IT'S CLEAR IN BROAD TERMS WHAT'S HAPPENING.
THE GRAIL AND THE TRUMPET ARE TWO ALTERNATIVE STATES FOR THE SUCCESSFUL ENDING OF THE QUEST.
THIS IS A THIRD.
AND IT LOOKS AS THOUGH IT WAS INTENDED FOR ME.

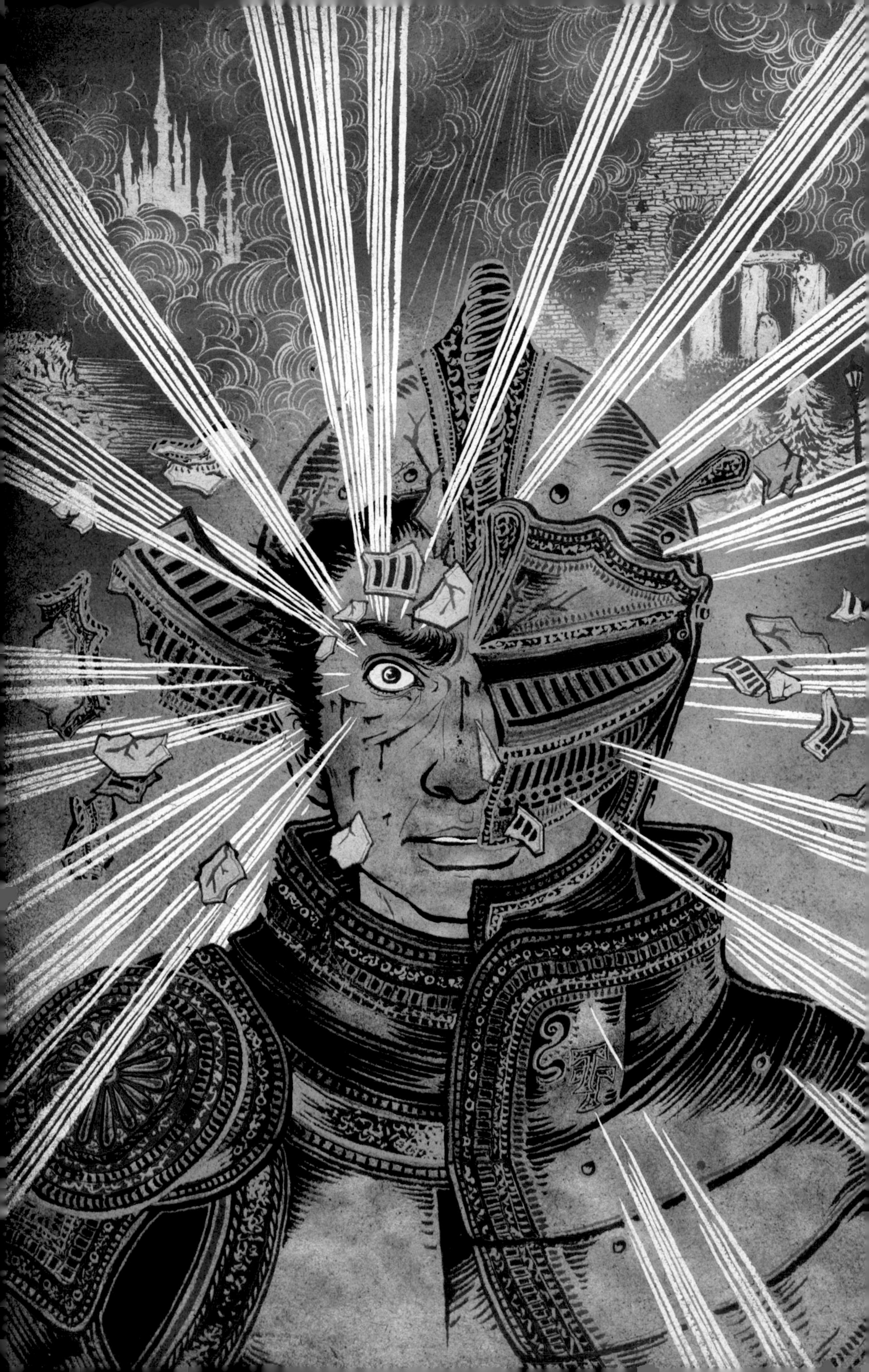

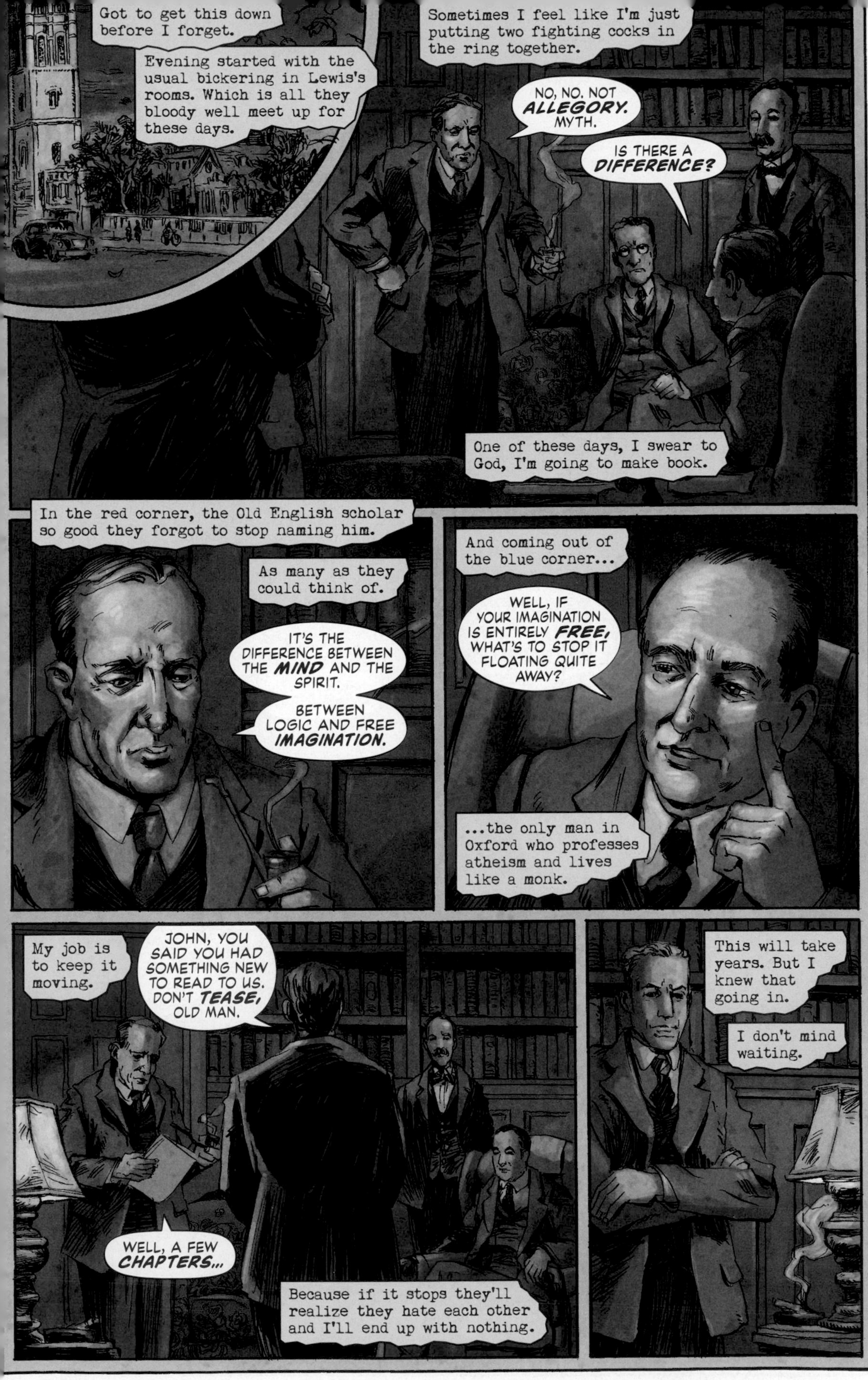
Got to get this down before I forget.
Evening started with the usual bickering in Lewis's rooms. Which is all they bloody well meet up for these days.
Sometimes I feel like I'm just putting two fighting cocks in the ring together.
NO, NO. NOT *ALLEGORY.* MYTH.
IS THERE A *DIFFERENCE?*
One of these days, I swear to God, I'm going to make book.
In the red corner, the Old English scholar so good they forgot to stop naming him.
As many as they could think of.
IT'S THE DIFFERENCE BETWEEN THE *MIND* AND THE SPIRIT.
BETWEEN LOGIC AND FREE *IMAGINATION.*
And coming out of the blue corner...
WELL, IF YOUR IMAGINATION IS ENTIRELY *FREE,* WHAT'S TO STOP IT FLOATING QUITE AWAY?
...the only man in Oxford who professes atheism and lives like a monk.
My job is to keep it moving.
JOHN, YOU SAID YOU HAD SOMETHING NEW TO READ TO US. DON'T *TEASE,* OLD MAN.
WELL, A FEW *CHAPTERS...*
Because if it stops they'll realize they hate each other and I'll end up with nothing.
This will take years. But I knew that going in.
I don't mind waiting.

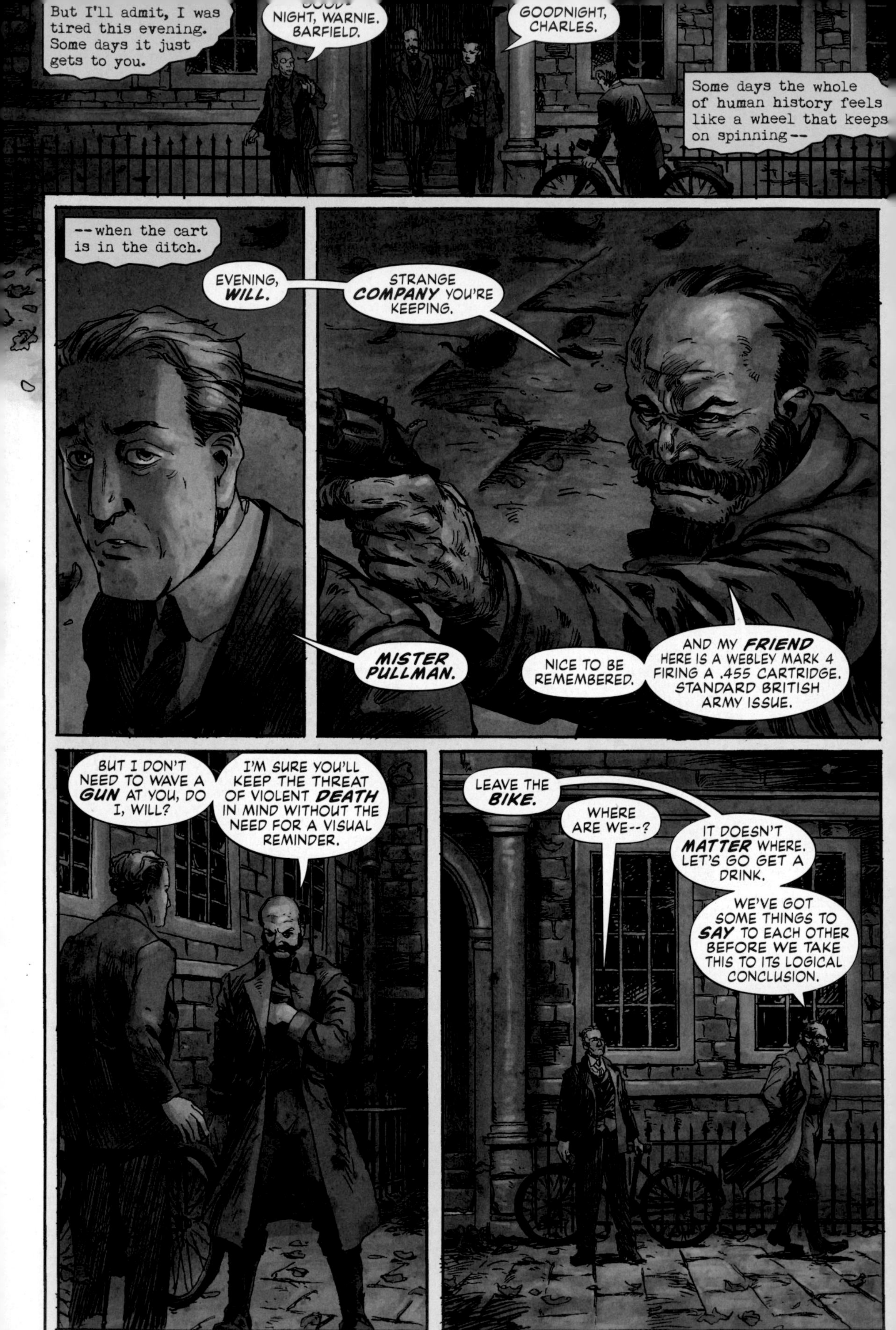
But I'll admit, I was tired this evening. Some days it just gets to you.
NIGHT, WARNIE. BARFIELD.
GOODNIGHT, CHARLES.
Some days the whole of human history feels like a wheel that keeps on spinning--
--when the cart is in the ditch.
EVENING, WILL.
STRANGE COMPANY YOU'RE KEEPING.
MISTER PULLMAN.
NICE TO BE REMEMBERED.
AND MY FRIEND HERE IS A WEBLEY MARK 4 FIRING A .455 CARTRIDGE. STANDARD BRITISH ARMY ISSUE.
BUT I DON'T NEED TO WAVE A GUN AT YOU, DO I, WILL?
I'M SURE YOU'LL KEEP THE THREAT OF VIOLENT DEATH IN MIND WITHOUT THE NEED FOR A VISUAL REMINDER.
LEAVE THE BIKE.
WHERE ARE WE--?
IT DOESN'T MATTER WHERE. LET'S GO GET A DRINK.
WE'VE GOT SOME THINGS TO SAY TO EACH OTHER BEFORE WE TAKE THIS TO ITS LOGICAL CONCLUSION.

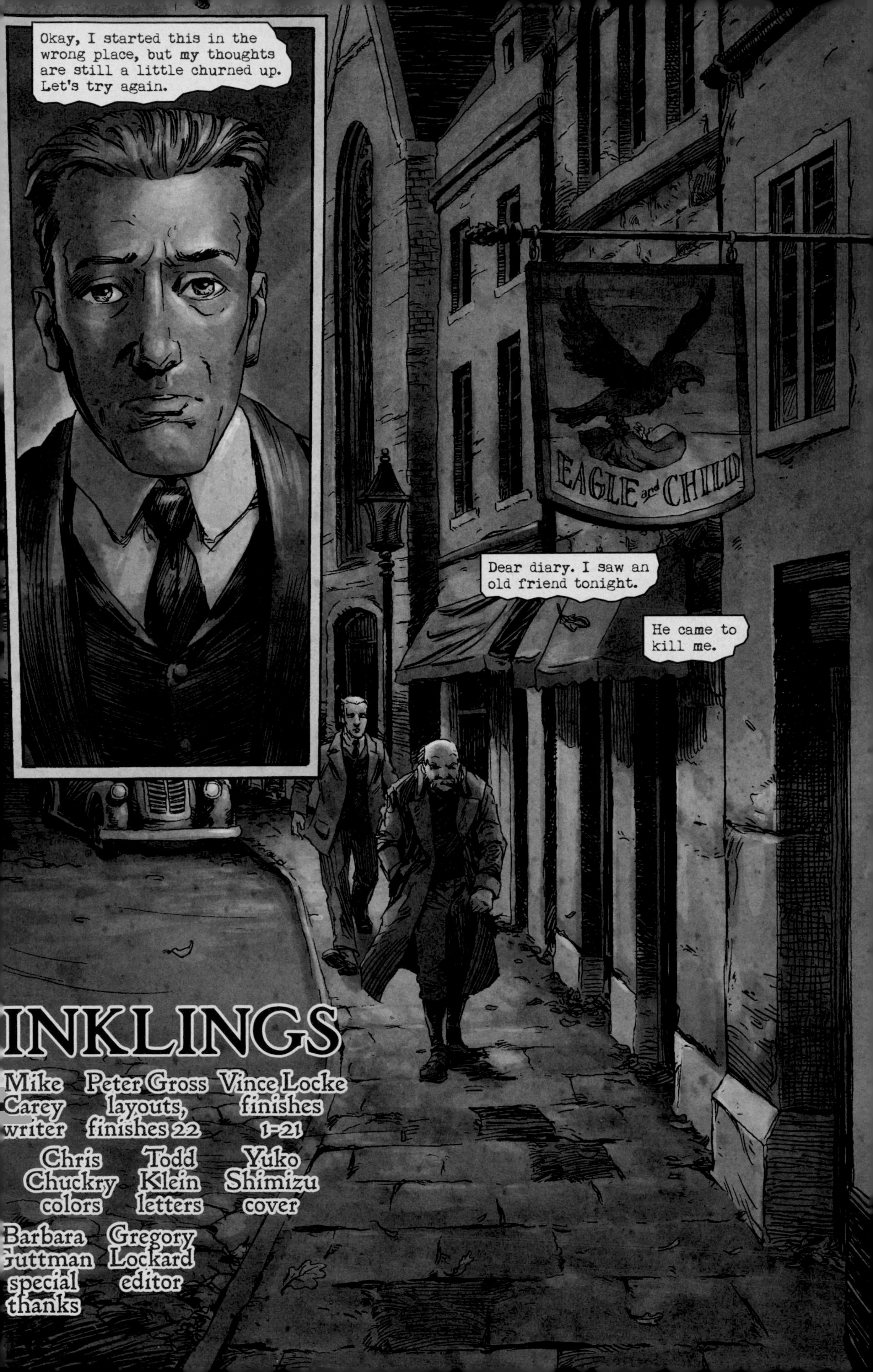

Okay, I started this in the wrong place, but my thoughts are still a little churned up. Let's try again.
EAGLE and CHILD
Dear diary. I saw an old friend tonight.
He came to kill me.
INKLINGS
Mike Carey writer
Peter Gross layouts, finishes 22
Vince Locke finishes 1-21
Chris Chuckry colors
Todd Klein letters
Yuko Shimizu cover
Barbara Guttman special thanks
Gregory Lockard editor

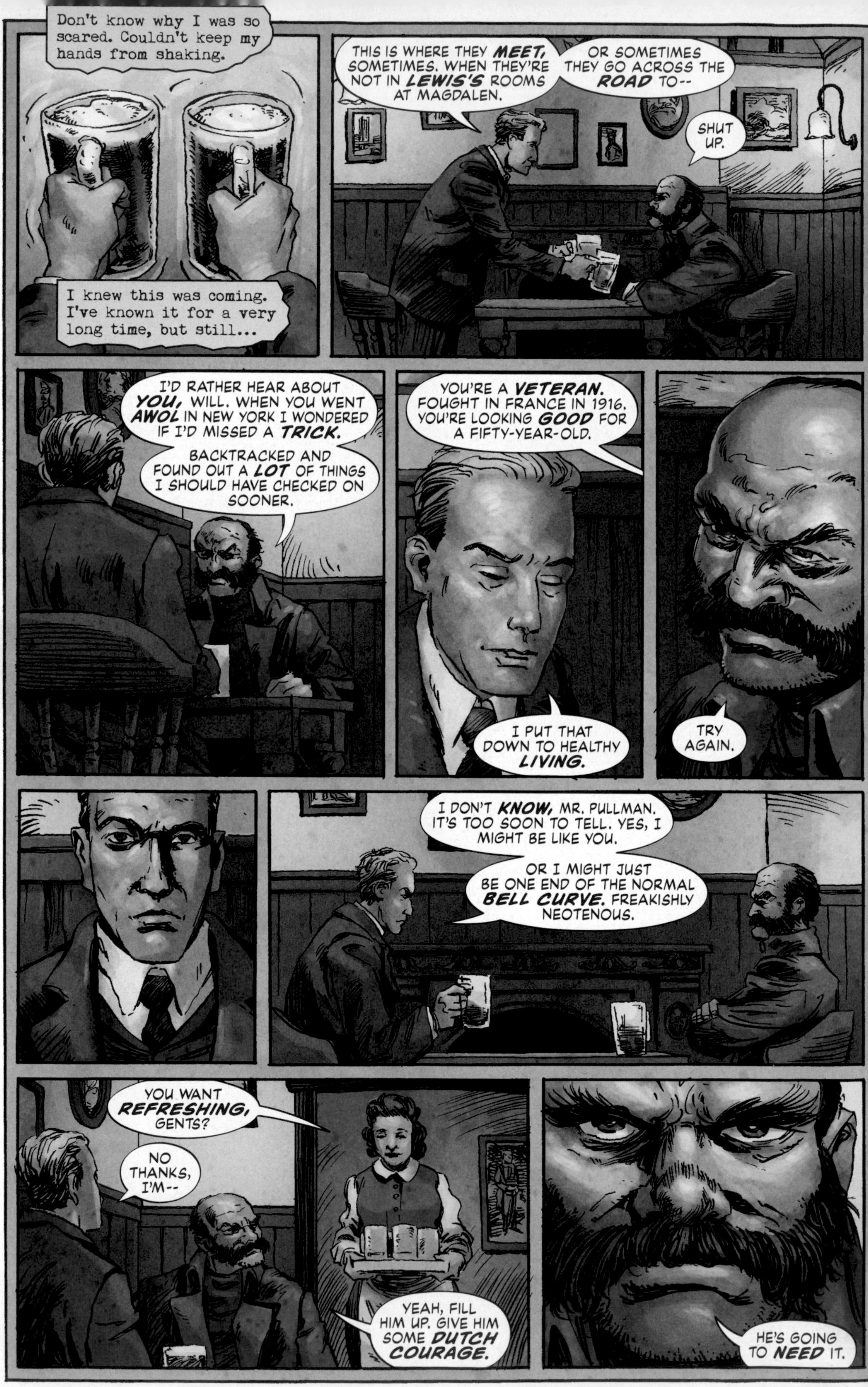
Don't know why I was so scared. Couldn't keep my hands from shaking.
I knew this was coming. I've known it for a very long time, but still...
THIS IS WHERE THEY MEET, SOMETIMES. WHEN THEY'RE NOT IN LEWIS'S ROOMS AT MAGDALEN.
OR SOMETIMES THEY GO ACROSS THE ROAD TO--
SHUT UP.
I'D RATHER HEAR ABOUT YOU, WILL. WHEN YOU WENT AWOL IN NEW YORK I WONDERED IF I'D MISSED A TRICK.
BACKTRACKED AND FOUND OUT A LOT OF THINGS I SHOULD HAVE CHECKED ON SOONER.
YOU'RE A VETERAN. FOUGHT IN FRANCE IN 1916. YOU'RE LOOKING GOOD FOR A FIFTY-YEAR-OLD.
I PUT THAT DOWN TO HEALTHY LIVING.
TRY AGAIN.
I DON'T KNOW, MR. PULLMAN. IT'S TOO SOON TO TELL. YES, I MIGHT BE LIKE YOU.
OR I MIGHT JUST BE ONE END OF THE NORMAL BELL CURVE. FREAKISHLY NEOTENOUS.
YOU WANT REFRESHING, GENTS?
NO THANKS, I'M--
YEAH, FILL HIM UP. GIVE HIM SOME DUTCH COURAGE.
HE'S GOING TO NEED IT.

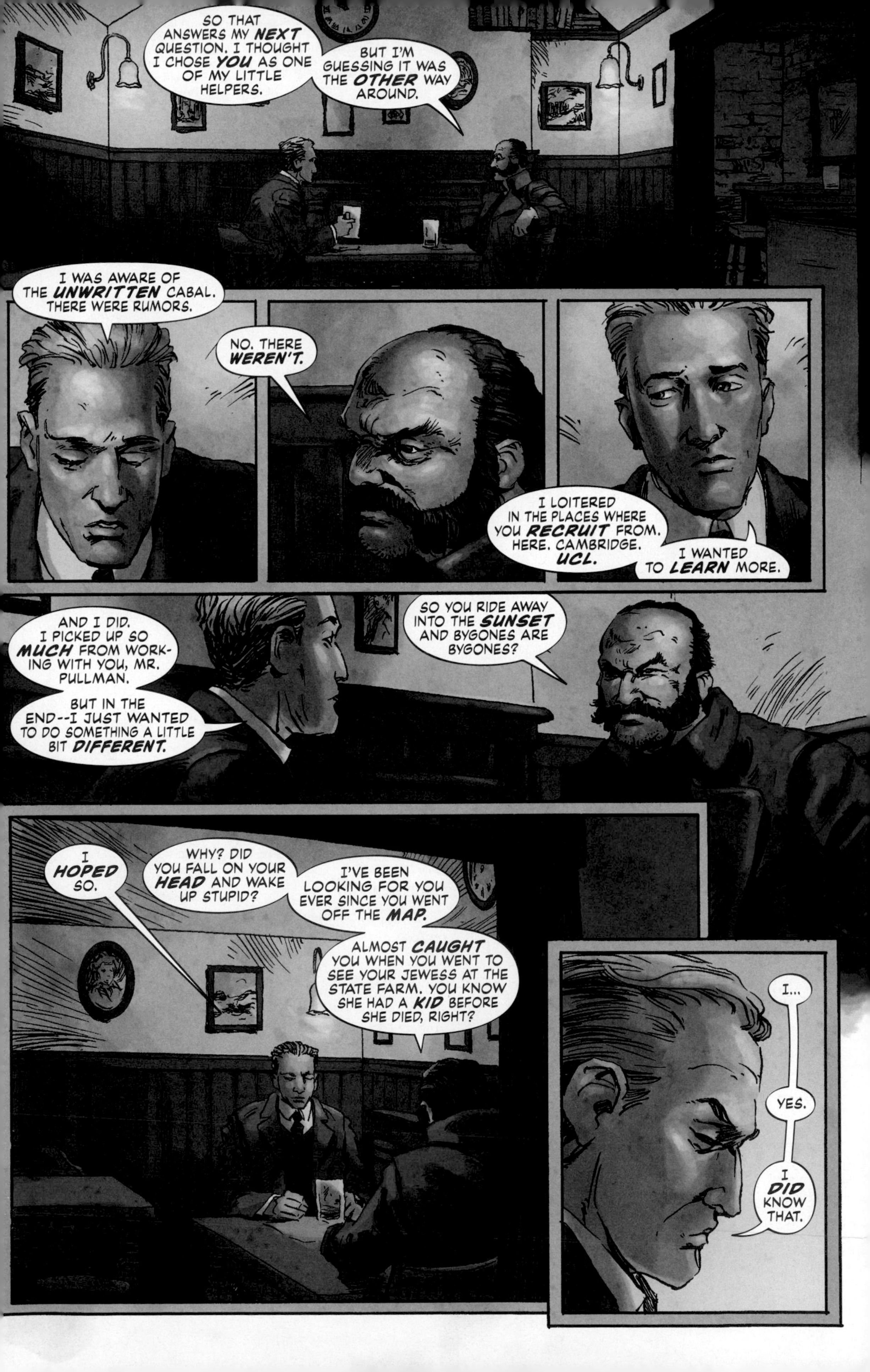
SO THAT ANSWERS MY NEXT QUESTION. I THOUGHT I CHOSE YOU AS ONE OF MY LITTLE HELPERS.
BUT I'M GUESSING IT WAS THE OTHER WAY AROUND.
I WAS AWARE OF THE UNWRITTEN CABAL. THERE WERE RUMORS.
NO. THERE WEREN'T.
I LOITERED IN THE PLACES WHERE YOU RECRUIT FROM. HERE. CAMBRIDGE. UCL.
I WANTED TO LEARN MORE.
AND I DID. I PICKED UP SO MUCH FROM WORKING WITH YOU, MR. PULLMAN.
BUT IN THE END--I JUST WANTED TO DO SOMETHING A LITTLE BIT DIFFERENT.
SO YOU RIDE AWAY INTO THE SUNSET AND BYGONES ARE BYGONES?
I HOPED SO.
WHY? DID YOU FALL ON YOUR HEAD AND WAKE UP STUPID?
I'VE BEEN LOOKING FOR YOU EVER SINCE YOU WENT OFF THE MAP.
ALMOST CAUGHT YOU WHEN YOU WENT TO SEE YOUR JEWESS AT THE STATE FARM. YOU KNOW SHE HAD A KID BEFORE SHE DIED, RIGHT?
I...
YES.
I DID KNOW THAT.

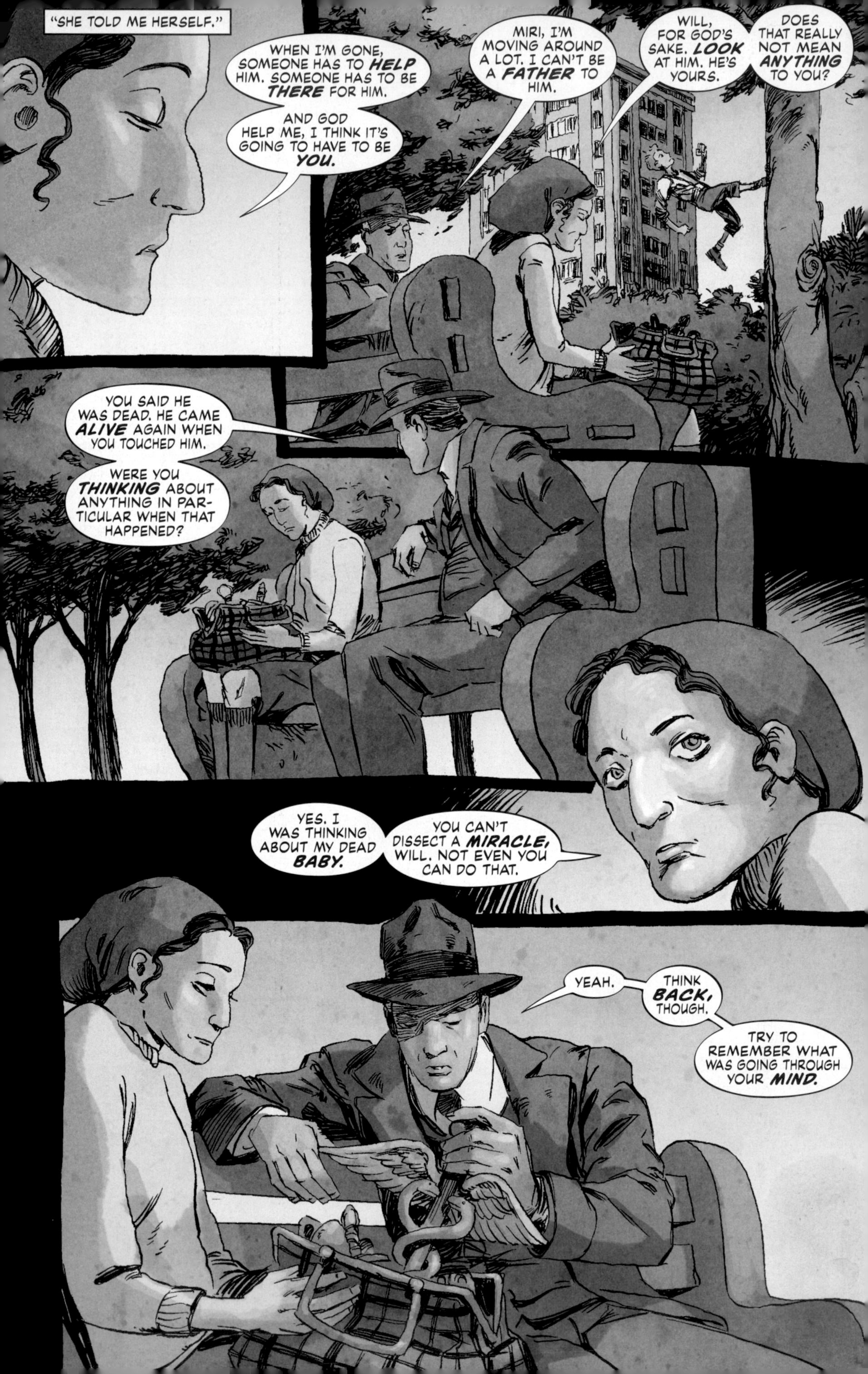
"SHE TOLD ME HERSELF."
WHEN I'M GONE, SOMEONE HAS TO HELP HIM. SOMEONE HAS TO BE THERE FOR HIM.
AND GOD HELP ME, I THINK IT'S GOING TO HAVE TO BE YOU.
MIRI, I'M MOVING AROUND A LOT. I CAN'T BE A FATHER TO HIM.
WILL, FOR GOD'S SAKE. LOOK AT HIM. HE'S YOURS.
DOES THAT REALLY NOT MEAN ANYTHING TO YOU?
YOU SAID HE WAS DEAD. HE CAME ALIVE AGAIN WHEN YOU TOUCHED HIM.
WERE YOU THINKING ABOUT ANYTHING IN PARTICULAR WHEN THAT HAPPENED?
YES. I WAS THINKING ABOUT MY DEAD BABY.
YOU CAN'T DISSECT A MIRACLE, WILL. NOT EVEN YOU CAN DO THAT.
YEAH.
THINK BACK, THOUGH.
TRY TO REMEMBER WHAT WAS GOING THROUGH YOUR MIND.

I'M NOT *LYING* TO YOU.

NO, I'M PRETTY SURE YOU'RE NOT. BUT YOU'RE HOLDING SOMETHING *BACK*. SPIT IT OUT.

YOU'RE NOT BEING *FRANK* WITH ME, ARE YOU, WILL?

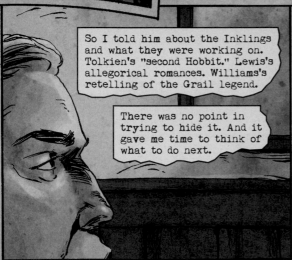

So I told him about the Inklings and what they were working on. Tolkien's "second Hobbit." Lewis's allegorical romances. Williams's retelling of the Grail legend.

There was no point in trying to hide it. And it gave me time to think of what to do next.

SO THEY'RE ALL WORKING ON MODERN *MYTHS*. WHAT A COINCIDENCE.

I PLANTED SOME OF THE SEEDS. MADE SOME OF THE *INTRODUCTIONS*.

I'LL *BET* YOU DID.

YOU TALKED TO ME ONCE ABOUT *MESSIAHS*. YOU SAID THEY GREW IN SOIL OF *POVERTY* AND MISERY AND DISPOSSESSION.

I WONDERED IF I COULD TAKE CUTTINGS FROM *OLD* MESSIAHS AND GROW A NEW ONE.

YOU WONDERED THAT?

YES.

DID YOU WONDER HOW *FAR* YOU'D GET BEFORE I CAME AROUND AND BLEW YOUR BRAINS OUT?

NOT REALLY.

BUT I'LL ADMIT I WAS HOPING FOR A BIT *LONGER*.

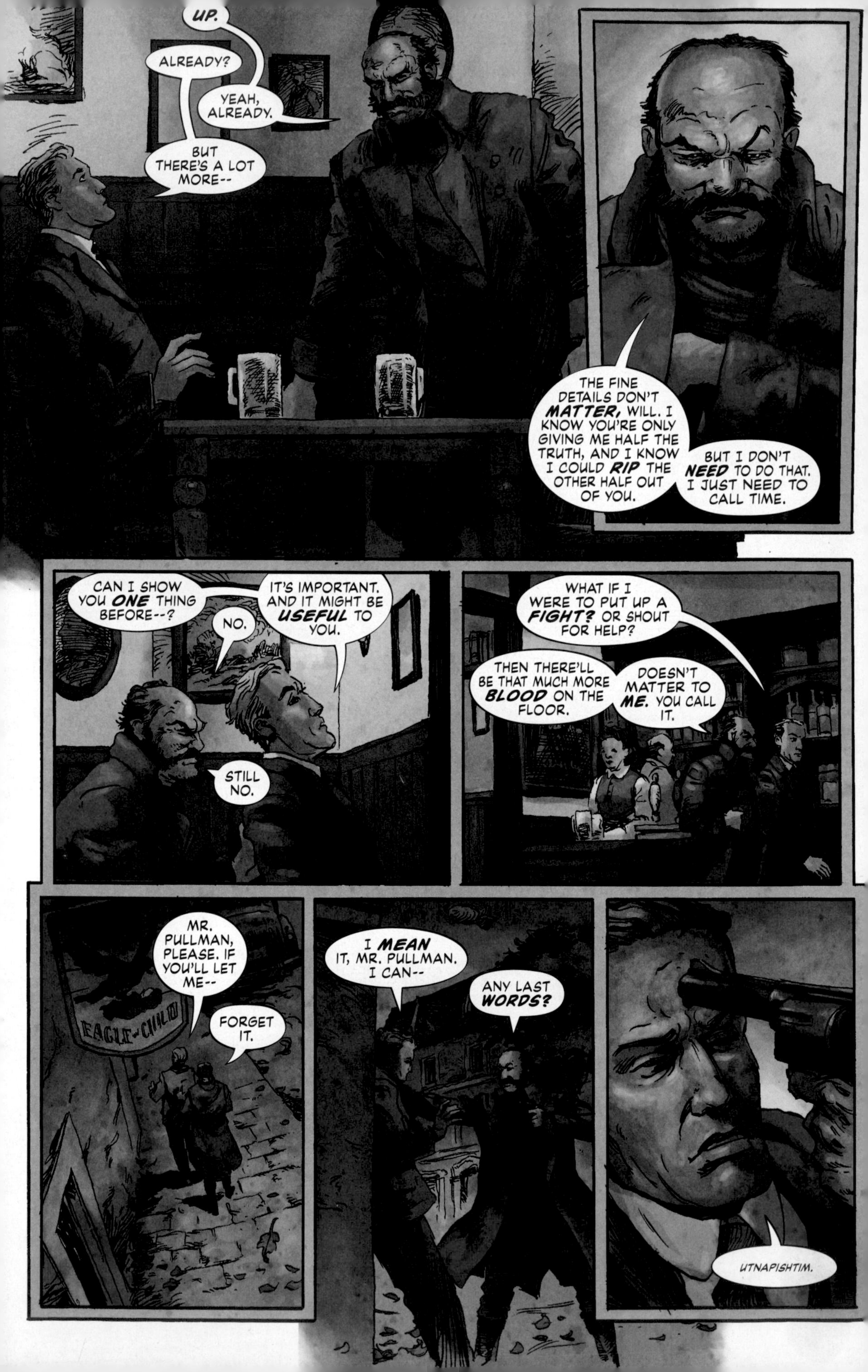
UP.
ALREADY?
YEAH, ALREADY.
BUT THERE'S A LOT MORE--
THE FINE DETAILS DON'T MATTER, WILL. I KNOW YOU'RE ONLY GIVING ME HALF THE TRUTH, AND I KNOW I COULD RIP THE OTHER HALF OUT OF YOU.
BUT I DON'T NEED TO DO THAT. I JUST NEED TO CALL TIME.
CAN I SHOW YOU ONE THING BEFORE--?
NO.
IT'S IMPORTANT. AND IT MIGHT BE USEFUL TO YOU.
STILL NO.
WHAT IF I WERE TO PUT UP A FIGHT? OR SHOUT FOR HELP?
THEN THERE'LL BE THAT MUCH MORE BLOOD ON THE FLOOR.
DOESN'T MATTER TO ME. YOU CALL IT.
MR. PULLMAN, PLEASE. IF YOU'LL LET ME--
FORGET IT.
EAGLE-CHILD
I MEAN IT, MR. PULLMAN. I CAN--
ANY LAST WORDS?
UTNAPISHTIM.

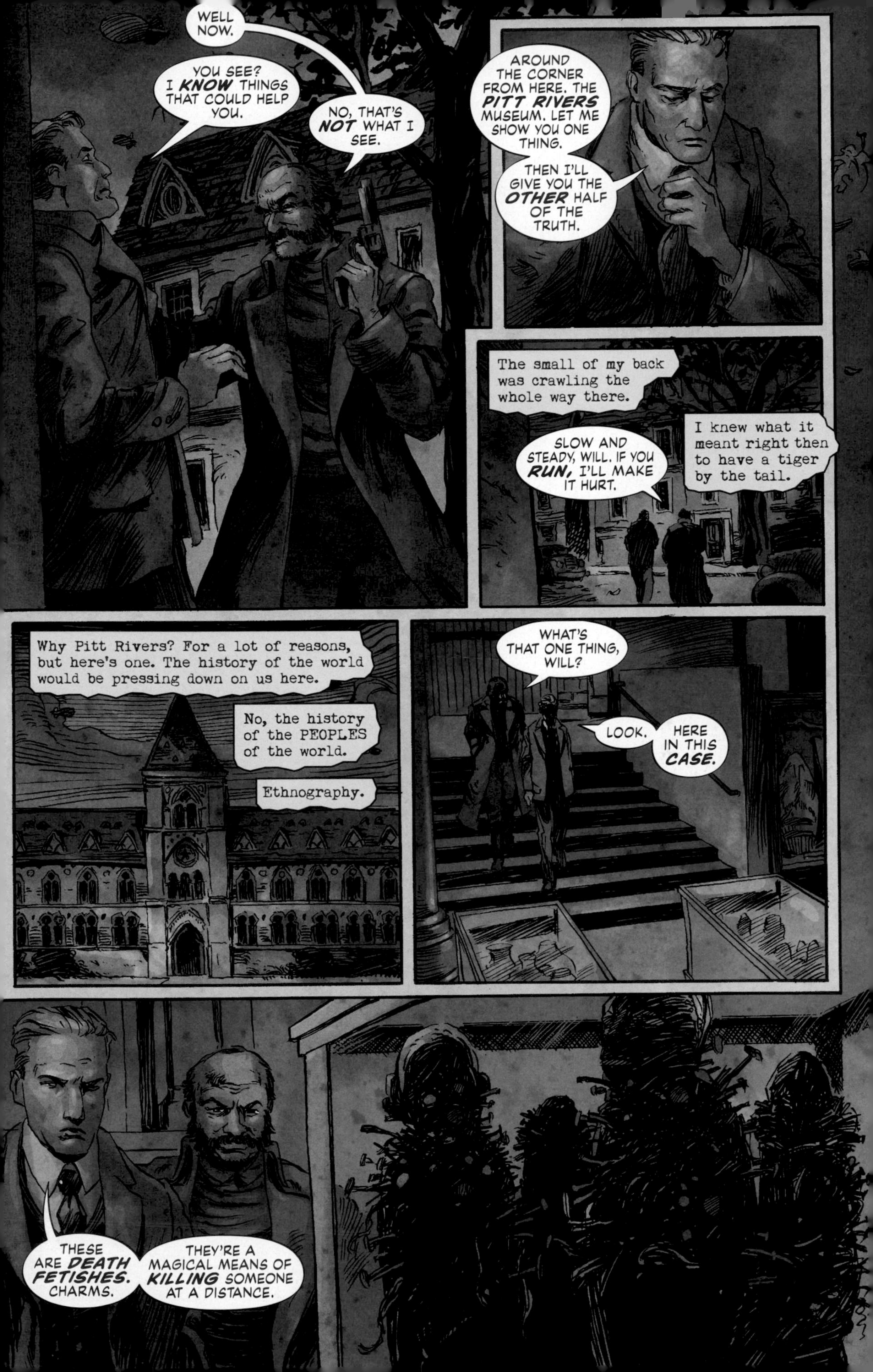
WELL NOW.
YOU SEE? I KNOW THINGS THAT COULD HELP YOU.
NO, THAT'S NOT WHAT I SEE.
AROUND THE CORNER FROM HERE. THE PITT RIVERS MUSEUM. LET ME SHOW YOU ONE THING.
THEN I'LL GIVE YOU THE OTHER HALF OF THE TRUTH.
The small of my back was crawling the whole way there.
SLOW AND STEADY, WILL. IF YOU RUN, I'LL MAKE IT HURT.
I knew what it meant right then to have a tiger by the tail.
Why Pitt Rivers? For a lot of reasons, but here's one. The history of the world would be pressing down on us here.
No, the history of the PEOPLES of the world.
Ethnography.
WHAT'S THAT ONE THING, WILL?
LOOK.
HERE IN THIS CASE.
THESE ARE DEATH FETISHES. CHARMS.
THEY'RE A MAGICAL MEANS OF KILLING SOMEONE AT A DISTANCE.

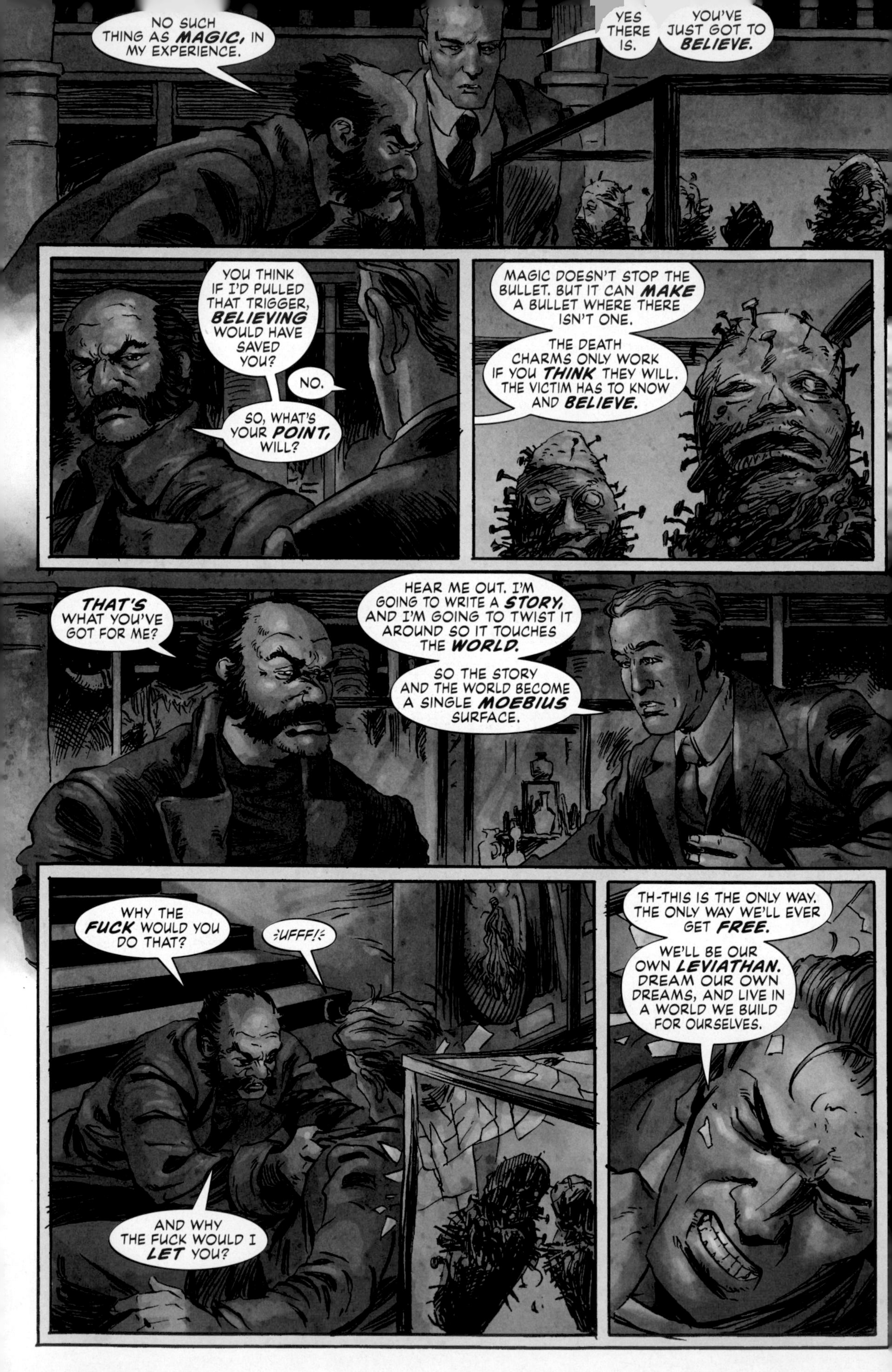
NO SUCH THING AS MAGIC, IN MY EXPERIENCE.
YES THERE IS.
YOU'VE JUST GOT TO BELIEVE.
YOU THINK IF I'D PULLED THAT TRIGGER, BELIEVING WOULD HAVE SAVED YOU?
NO.
SO, WHAT'S YOUR POINT, WILL?
MAGIC DOESN'T STOP THE BULLET. BUT IT CAN MAKE A BULLET WHERE THERE ISN'T ONE.
THE DEATH CHARMS ONLY WORK IF YOU THINK THEY WILL. THE VICTIM HAS TO KNOW AND BELIEVE.
THAT'S WHAT YOU'VE GOT FOR ME?
HEAR ME OUT. I'M GOING TO WRITE A STORY, AND I'M GOING TO TWIST IT AROUND SO IT TOUCHES THE WORLD.
SO THE STORY AND THE WORLD BECOME A SINGLE MOEBIUS SURFACE.
WHY THE FUCK WOULD YOU DO THAT?
UFFF!
AND WHY THE FUCK WOULD I LET YOU?
TH-THIS IS THE ONLY WAY. THE ONLY WAY WE'LL EVER GET FREE.
WE'LL BE OUR OWN LEVIATHAN. DREAM OUR OWN DREAMS, AND LIVE IN A WORLD WE BUILD FOR OURSELVES.

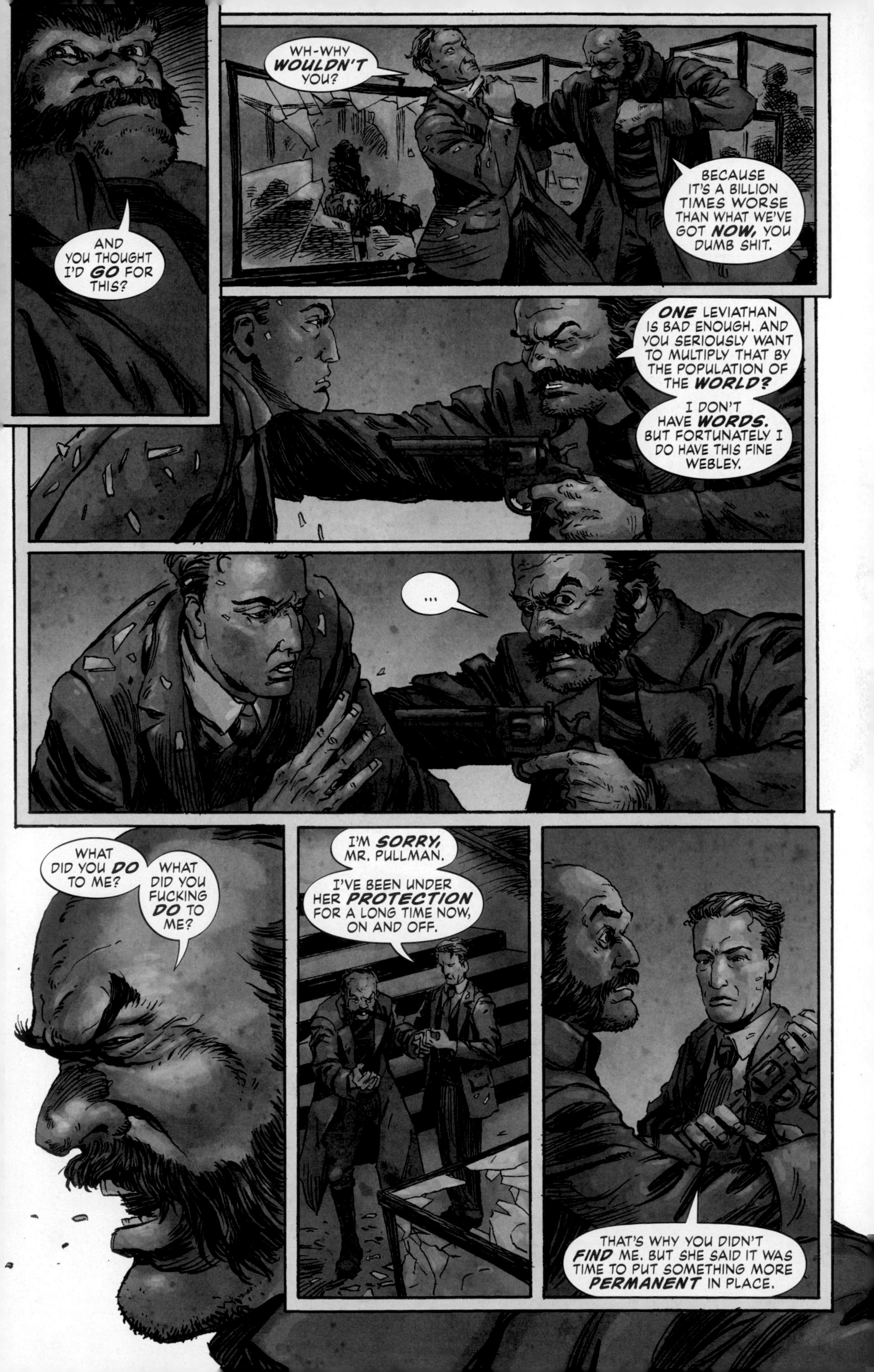

AND YOU THOUGHT I'D GO FOR THIS?
WH-WHY WOULDN'T YOU?
BECAUSE IT'S A BILLION TIMES WORSE THAN WHAT WE'VE GOT NOW, YOU DUMB SHIT.
ONE LEVIATHAN IS BAD ENOUGH. AND YOU SERIOUSLY WANT TO MULTIPLY THAT BY THE POPULATION OF THE WORLD?
I DON'T HAVE WORDS. BUT FORTUNATELY I DO HAVE THIS FINE WEBLEY.
...
WHAT DID YOU DO TO ME?
WHAT DID YOU FUCKING DO TO ME?
I'M SORRY, MR. PULLMAN.
I'VE BEEN UNDER HER PROTECTION FOR A LONG TIME NOW, ON AND OFF.
THAT'S WHY YOU DIDN'T FIND ME. BUT SHE SAID IT WAS TIME TO PUT SOMETHING MORE PERMANENT IN PLACE.

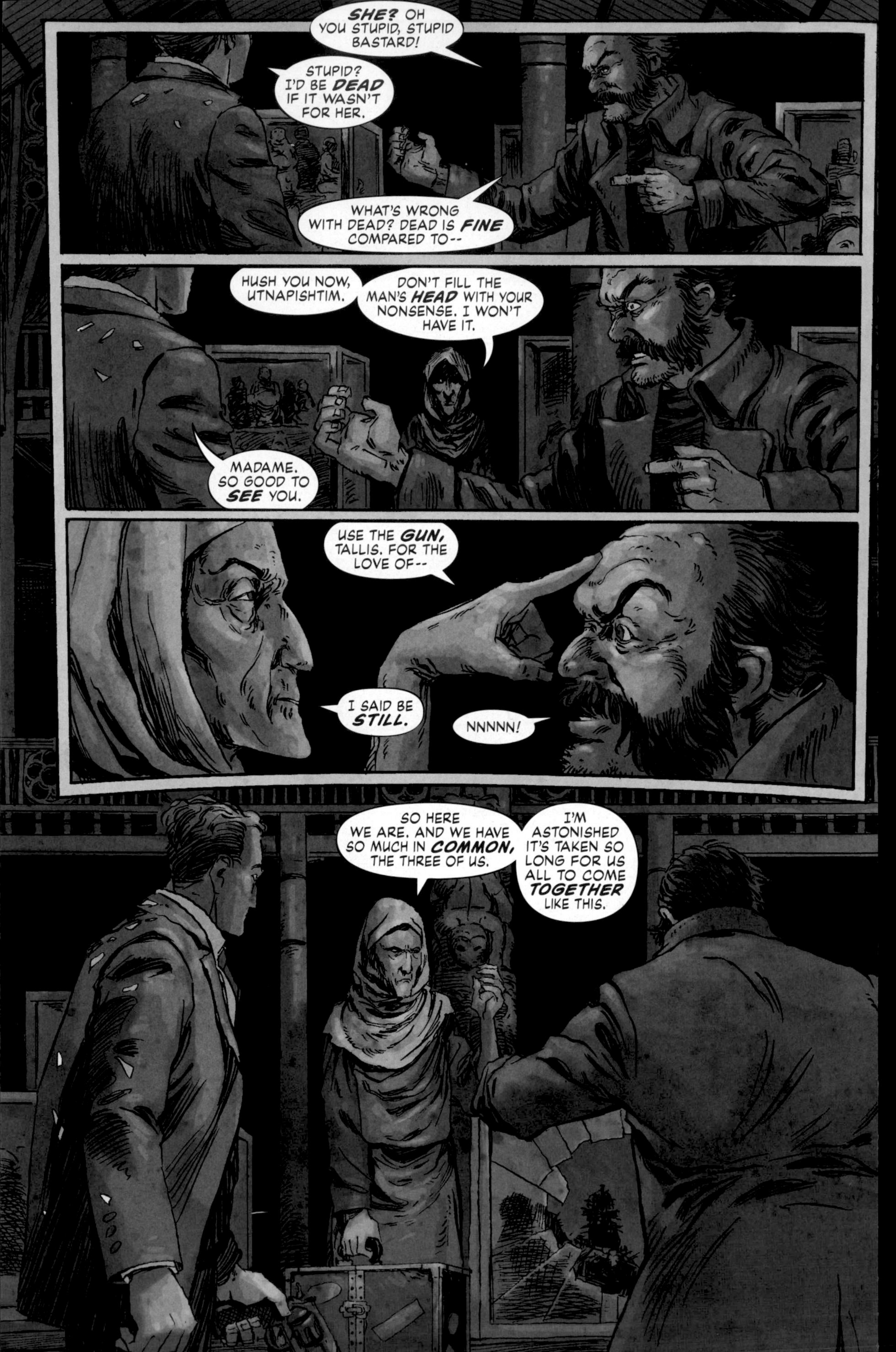
SHE? OH YOU STUPID, STUPID BASTARD!
STUPID? I'D BE DEAD IF IT WASN'T FOR HER.
WHAT'S WRONG WITH DEAD? DEAD IS FINE COMPARED TO--
HUSH YOU NOW, UTNAPISHTIM.
DON'T FILL THE MAN'S HEAD WITH YOUR NONSENSE. I WON'T HAVE IT.
MADAME. SO GOOD TO SEE YOU.
USE THE GUN, TALLIS. FOR THE LOVE OF--
I SAID BE STILL.
NNNNN!
SO HERE WE ARE. AND WE HAVE SO MUCH IN COMMON, THE THREE OF US.
I'M ASTONISHED IT'S TAKEN SO LONG FOR US ALL TO COME TOGETHER LIKE THIS.

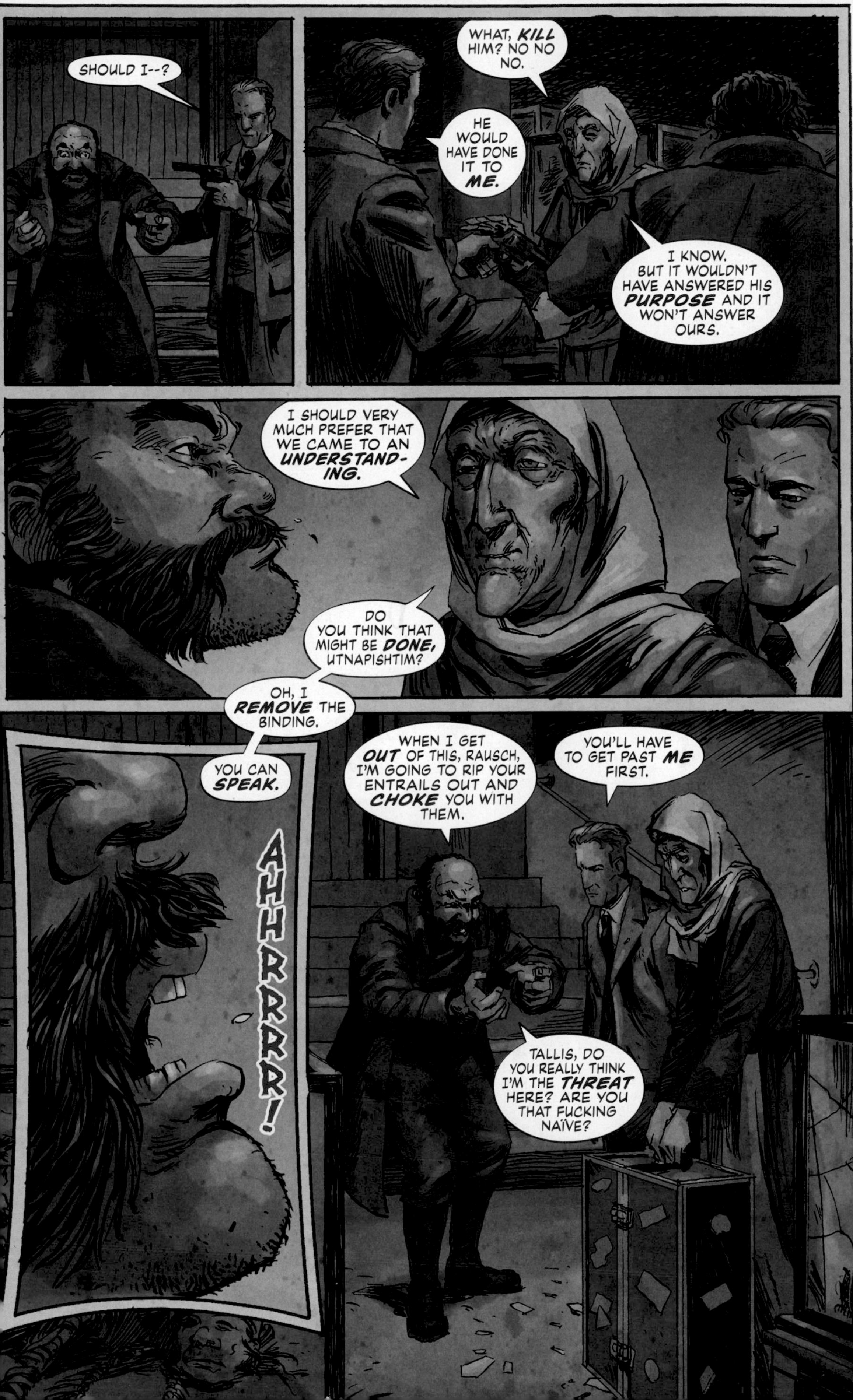

SHOULD I--?
WHAT, KILL HIM? NO NO NO.
HE WOULD HAVE DONE IT TO ME.
I KNOW. BUT IT WOULDN'T HAVE ANSWERED HIS PURPOSE AND IT WON'T ANSWER OURS.
I SHOULD VERY MUCH PREFER THAT WE CAME TO AN UNDERSTANDING.
DO YOU THINK THAT MIGHT BE DONE, UTNAPISHTIM?
OH, I REMOVE THE BINDING.
YOU CAN SPEAK.
AHHRRRRR!
WHEN I GET OUT OF THIS, RAUSCH, I'M GOING TO RIP YOUR ENTRAILS OUT AND CHOKE YOU WITH THEM.
YOU'LL HAVE TO GET PAST ME FIRST.
TALLIS, DO YOU REALLY THINK I'M THE THREAT HERE? ARE YOU THAT FUCKING NAÏVE?

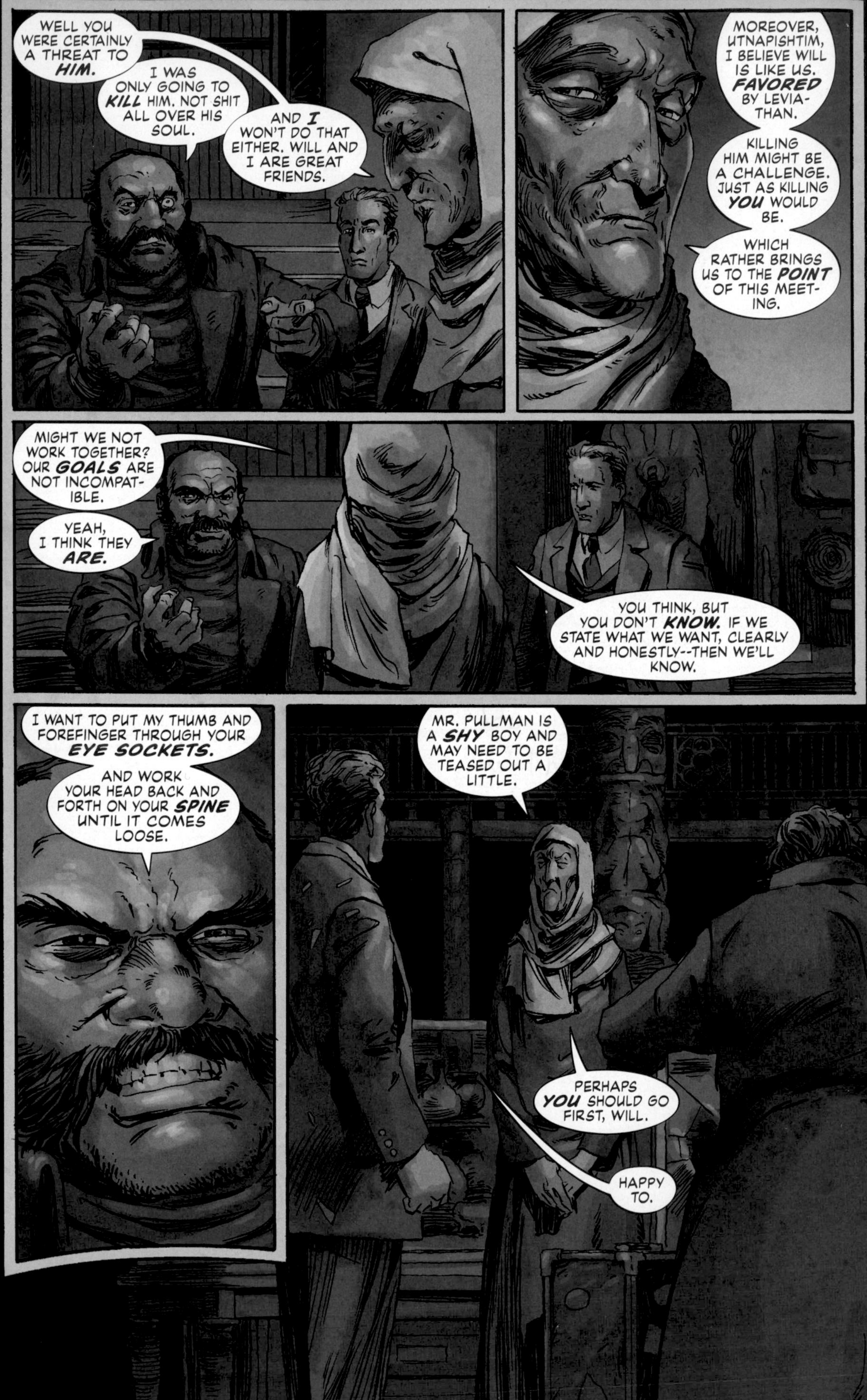
WELL YOU WERE CERTAINLY A THREAT TO HIM.
I WAS ONLY GOING TO KILL HIM. NOT SHIT ALL OVER HIS SOUL.
AND I WON'T DO THAT EITHER. WILL AND I ARE GREAT FRIENDS.
MOREOVER, UTNAPISHTIM, I BELIEVE WILL IS LIKE US. FAVORED BY LEVIA-THAN.
KILLING HIM MIGHT BE A CHALLENGE. JUST AS KILLING YOU WOULD BE.
WHICH RATHER BRINGS US TO THE POINT OF THIS MEET-ING.
MIGHT WE NOT WORK TOGETHER? OUR GOALS ARE NOT INCOMPAT-IBLE.
YEAH, I THINK THEY ARE.
YOU THINK, BUT YOU DON'T KNOW. IF WE STATE WHAT WE WANT, CLEARLY AND HONESTLY--THEN WE'LL KNOW.
I WANT TO PUT MY THUMB AND FOREFINGER THROUGH YOUR EYE SOCKETS.
AND WORK YOUR HEAD BACK AND FORTH ON YOUR SPINE UNTIL IT COMES LOOSE.
MR. PULLMAN IS A SHY BOY AND MAY NEED TO BE TEASED OUT A LITTLE.
PERHAPS YOU SHOULD GO FIRST, WILL.
HAPPY TO.

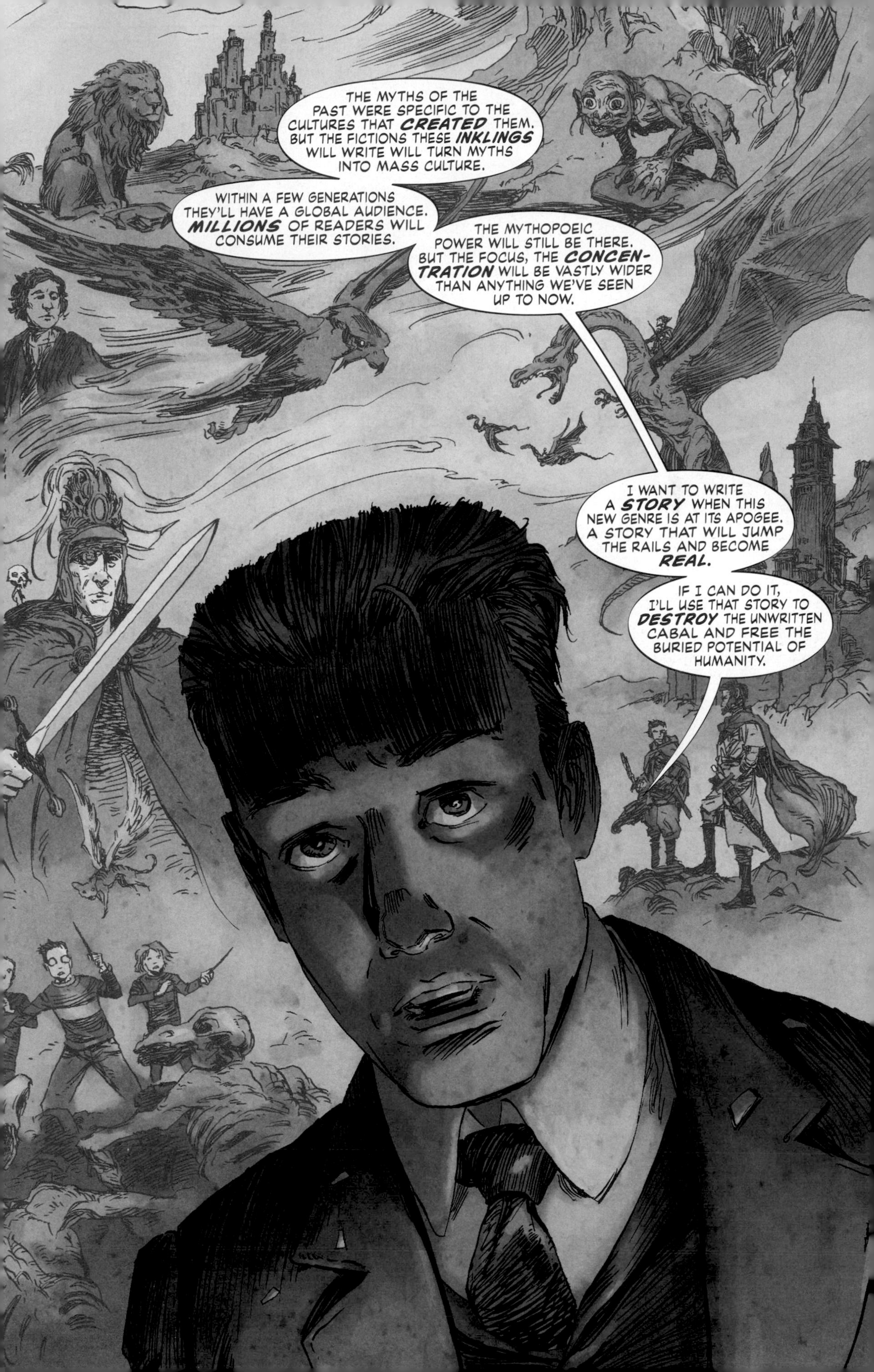
THE MYTHS OF THE PAST WERE SPECIFIC TO THE CULTURES THAT CREATED THEM. BUT THE FICTIONS THESE INKLINGS WILL WRITE WILL TURN MYTHS INTO MASS CULTURE.
WITHIN A FEW GENERATIONS THEY'LL HAVE A GLOBAL AUDIENCE. MILLIONS OF READERS WILL CONSUME THEIR STORIES.
THE MYTHOPOEIC POWER WILL STILL BE THERE. BUT THE FOCUS, THE CONCENTRATION WILL BE VASTLY WIDER THAN ANYTHING WE'VE SEEN UP TO NOW.
I WANT TO WRITE A STORY WHEN THIS NEW GENRE IS AT ITS APOGEE. A STORY THAT WILL JUMP THE RAILS AND BECOME REAL.
IF I CAN DO IT, I'LL USE THAT STORY TO DESTROY THE UNWRITTEN CABAL AND FREE THE BURIED POTENTIAL OF HUMANITY.

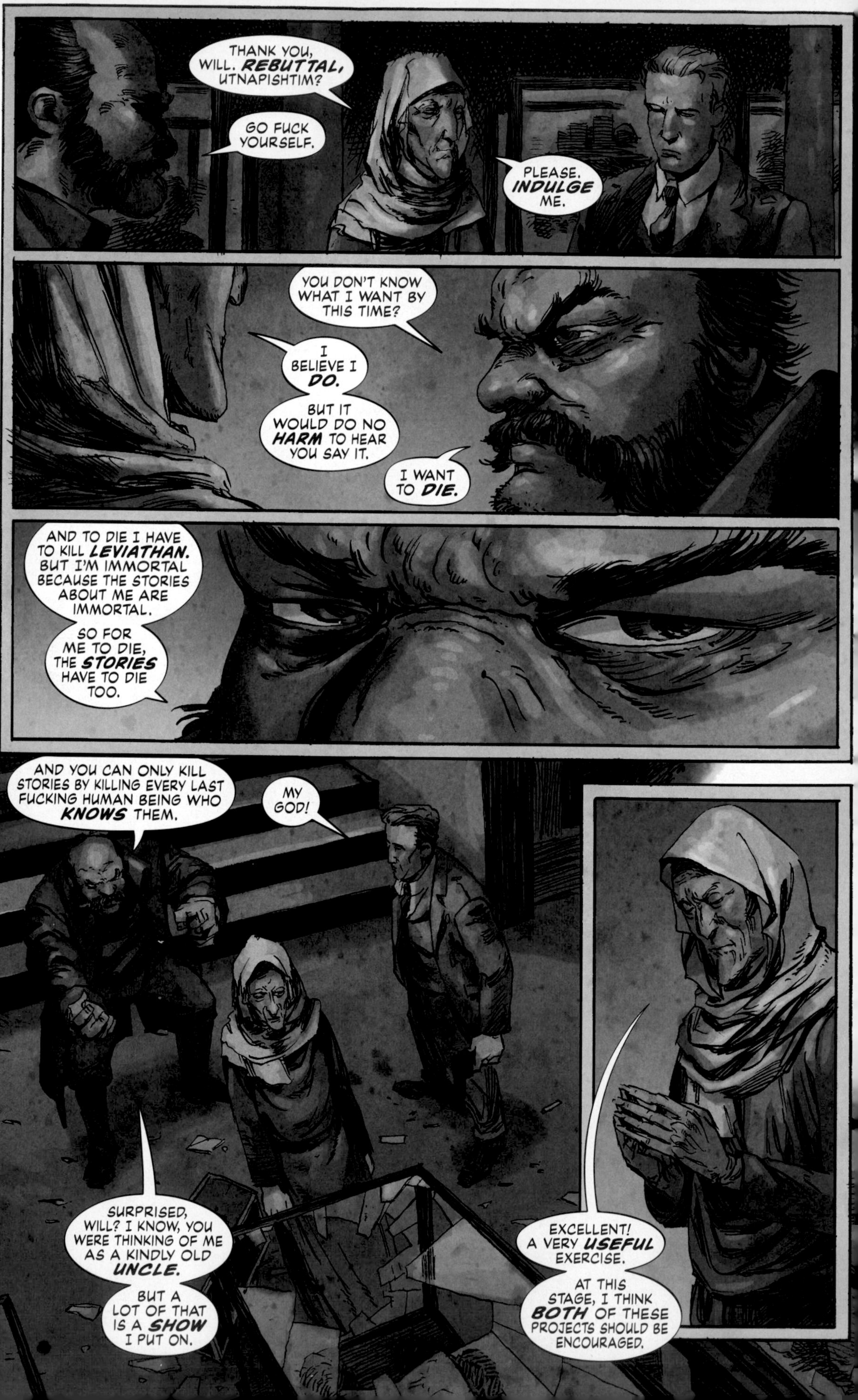
THANK YOU, WILL. REBUTTAL, UTNAPISHTIM?
GO FUCK YOURSELF.
PLEASE. INDULGE ME.
YOU DON'T KNOW WHAT I WANT BY THIS TIME?
I BELIEVE I DO.
BUT IT WOULD DO NO HARM TO HEAR YOU SAY IT.
I WANT TO DIE.
AND TO DIE I HAVE TO KILL LEVIATHAN. BUT I'M IMMORTAL BECAUSE THE STORIES ABOUT ME ARE IMMORTAL.
SO FOR ME TO DIE, THE STORIES HAVE TO DIE TOO.
AND YOU CAN ONLY KILL STORIES BY KILLING EVERY LAST FUCKING HUMAN BEING WHO KNOWS THEM.
MY GOD!
SURPRISED, WILL? I KNOW, YOU WERE THINKING OF ME AS A KINDLY OLD UNCLE.
BUT A LOT OF THAT IS A SHOW I PUT ON.
EXCELLENT! A VERY USEFUL EXERCISE.
AT THIS STAGE, I THINK BOTH OF THESE PROJECTS SHOULD BE ENCOURAGED.

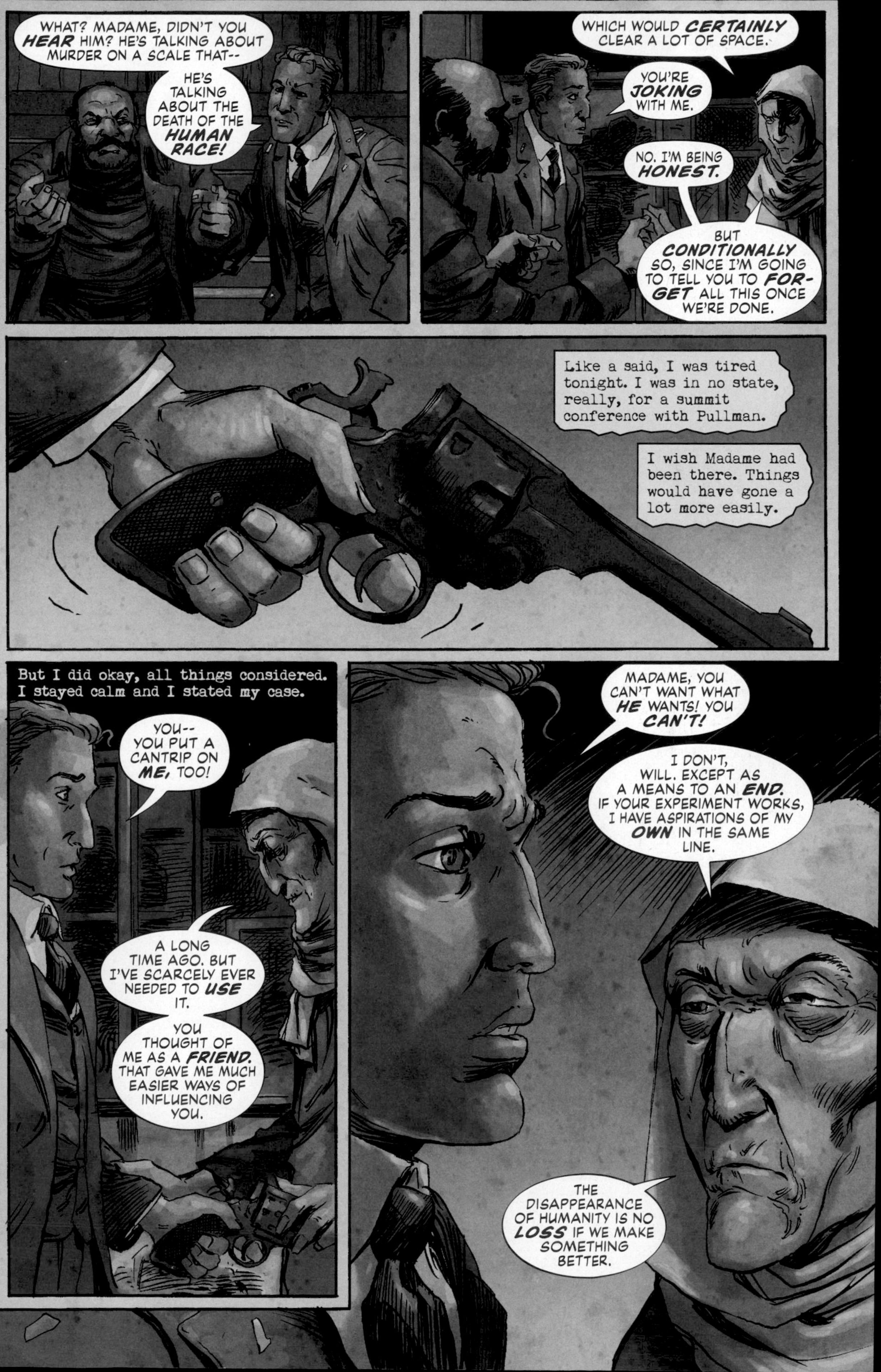
WHAT? MADAME, DIDN'T YOU HEAR HIM? HE'S TALKING ABOUT MURDER ON A SCALE THAT--
HE'S TALKING ABOUT THE DEATH OF THE HUMAN RACE!
WHICH WOULD CERTAINLY CLEAR A LOT OF SPACE.
YOU'RE JOKING WITH ME.
NO. I'M BEING HONEST.
BUT CONDITIONALLY SO, SINCE I'M GOING TO TELL YOU TO FOR-GET ALL THIS ONCE WE'RE DONE.
Like a said, I was tired tonight. I was in no state, really, for a summit conference with Pullman.
I wish Madame had been there. Things would have gone a lot more easily.
But I did okay, all things considered. I stayed calm and I stated my case.
YOU-- YOU PUT A CANTRIP ON ME, TOO!
A LONG TIME AGO. BUT I'VE SCARCELY EVER NEEDED TO USE IT.
YOU THOUGHT OF ME AS A FRIEND. THAT GAVE ME MUCH EASIER WAYS OF INFLUENCING YOU.
MADAME, YOU CAN'T WANT WHAT HE WANTS! YOU CAN'T!
I DON'T, WILL. EXCEPT AS A MEANS TO AN END. IF YOUR EXPERIMENT WORKS, I HAVE ASPIRATIONS OF MY OWN IN THE SAME LINE.
THE DISAPPEARANCE OF HUMANITY IS NO LOSS IF WE MAKE SOMETHING BETTER.

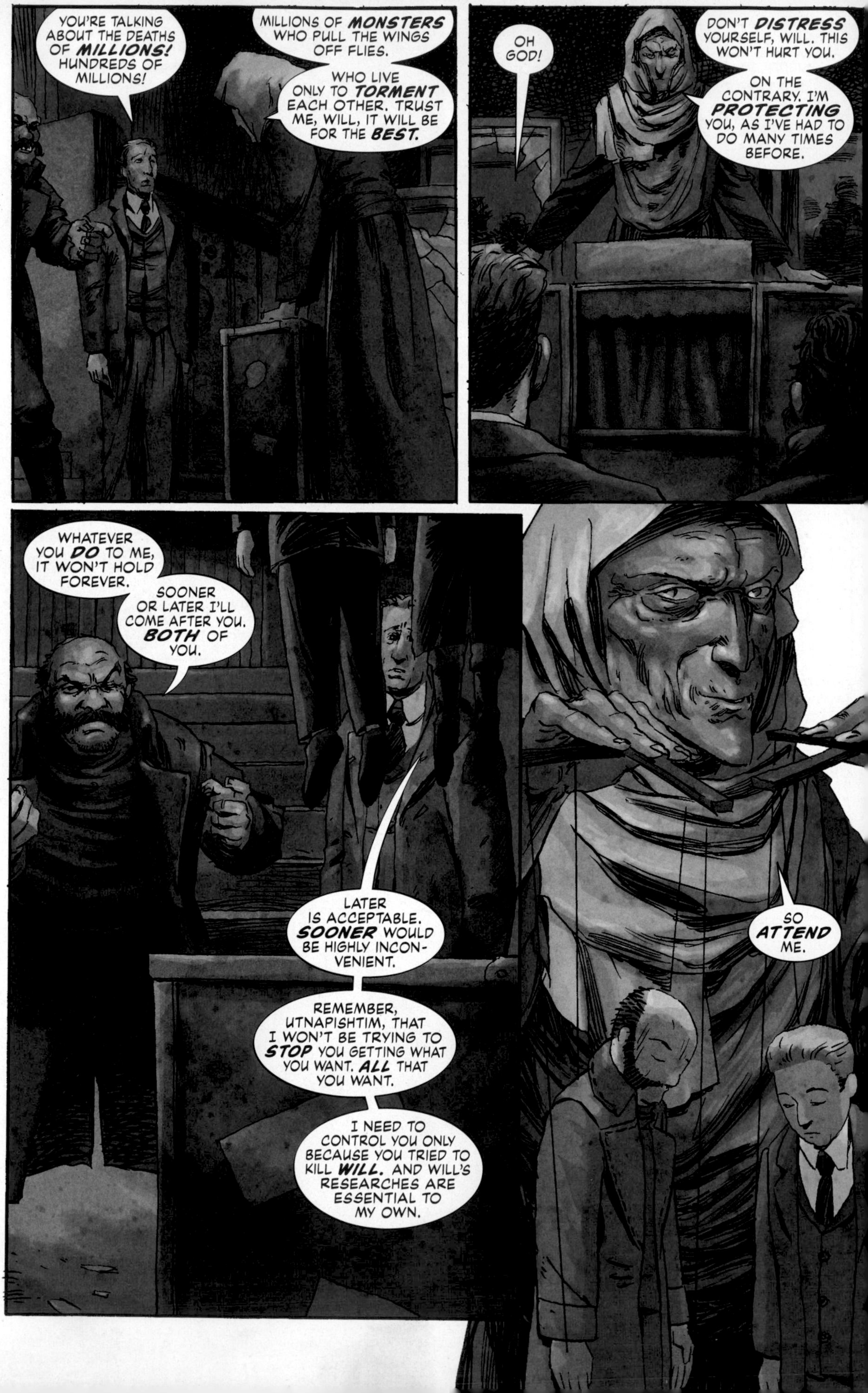
YOU'RE TALKING ABOUT THE DEATHS OF MILLIONS! HUNDREDS OF MILLIONS!
MILLIONS OF MONSTERS WHO PULL THE WINGS OFF FLIES.
WHO LIVE ONLY TO TORMENT EACH OTHER. TRUST ME, WILL, IT WILL BE FOR THE BEST.
OH GOD!
DON'T DISTRESS YOURSELF, WILL. THIS WON'T HURT YOU.
ON THE CONTRARY. I'M PROTECTING YOU, AS I'VE HAD TO DO MANY TIMES BEFORE.
WHATEVER YOU DO TO ME, IT WON'T HOLD FOREVER.
SOONER OR LATER I'LL COME AFTER YOU. BOTH OF YOU.
LATER IS ACCEPTABLE. SOONER WOULD BE HIGHLY INCON-VENIENT.
REMEMBER, UTNAPISHTIM, THAT I WON'T BE TRYING TO STOP YOU GETTING WHAT YOU WANT. ALL THAT YOU WANT.
I NEED TO CONTROL YOU ONLY BECAUSE YOU TRIED TO KILL WILL. AND WILL'S RESEARCHES ARE ESSENTIAL TO MY OWN.
SO ATTEND ME.

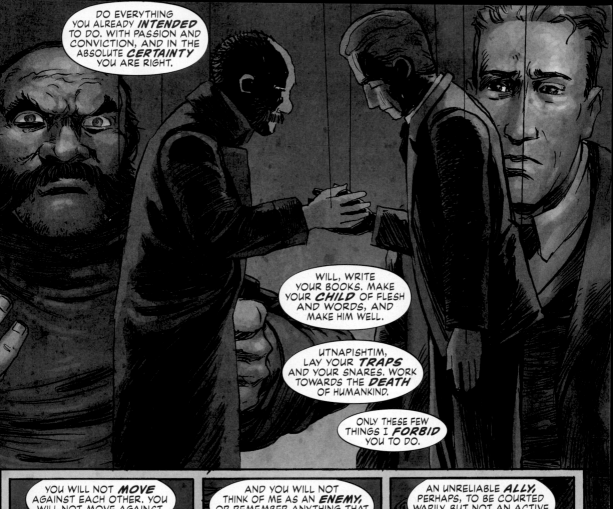

DO EVERYTHING YOU ALREADY *INTENDED* TO DO. WITH PASSION AND CONVICTION, AND IN THE ABSOLUTE *CERTAINTY* YOU ARE RIGHT.

WILL, WRITE YOUR BOOKS. MAKE YOUR *CHILD* OF FLESH AND WORDS, AND MAKE HIM WELL.

UTNAPISHTIM, LAY YOUR *TRAPS* AND YOUR SNARES. WORK TOWARDS THE *DEATH* OF HUMANKIND.

ONLY THESE FEW THINGS I *FORBID* YOU TO DO.

YOU WILL NOT *MOVE* AGAINST EACH OTHER. YOU WILL NOT MOVE AGAINST *ME*.

AND YOU WILL NOT THINK OF ME AS AN *ENEMY*, OR REMEMBER ANYTHING THAT MIGHT MAKE YOU THINK THAT.

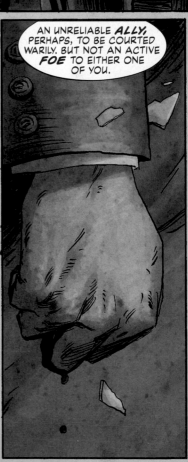

AN UNRELIABLE *ALLY*, PERHAPS, TO BE COURTED WARILY. BUT NOT AN ACTIVE *FOE* TO EITHER ONE OF YOU.

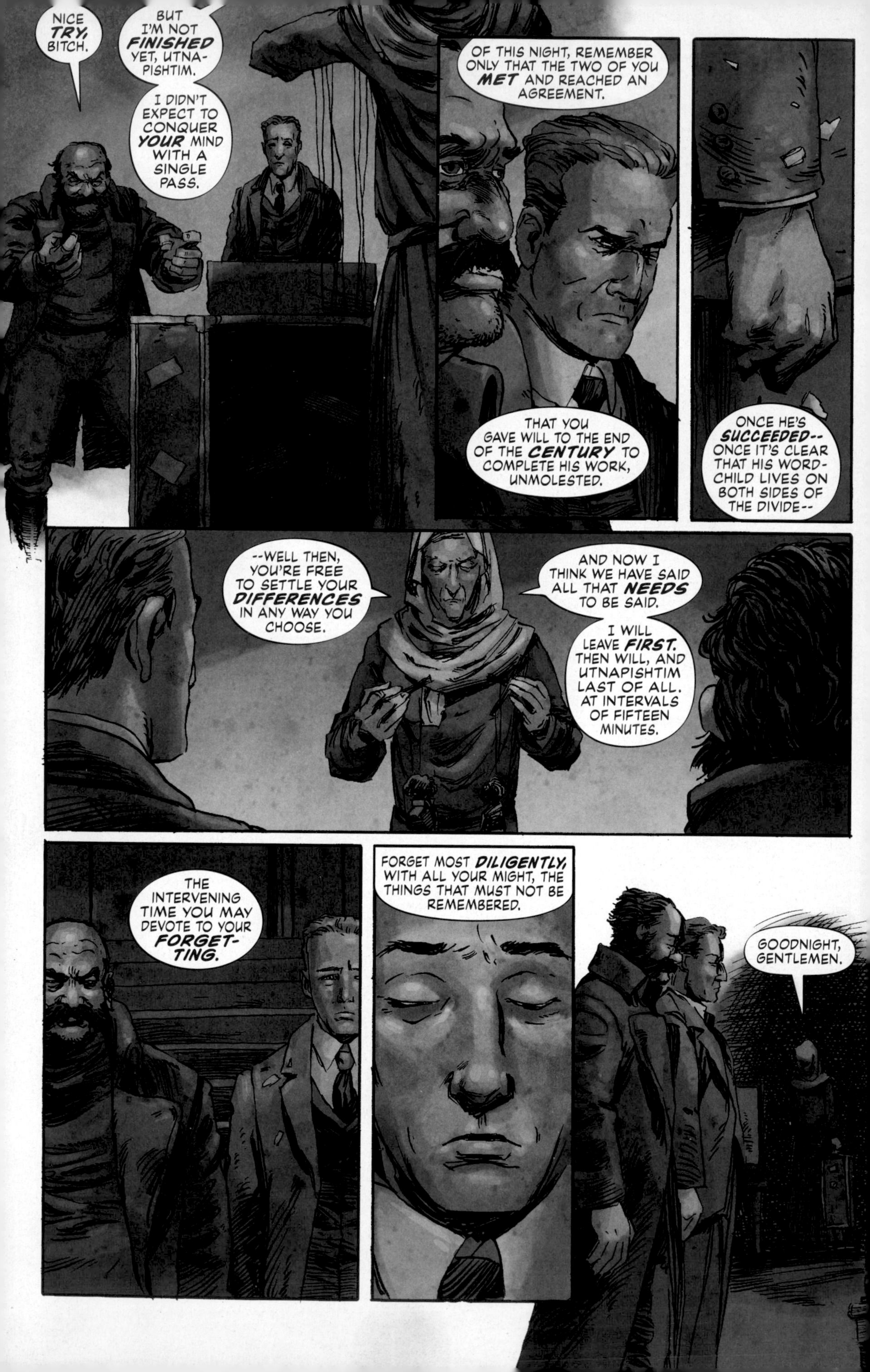
NICE TRY, BITCH.
BUT I'M NOT FINISHED YET, UTNA-PISHTIM.
I DIDN'T EXPECT TO CONQUER YOUR MIND WITH A SINGLE PASS.
OF THIS NIGHT, REMEMBER ONLY THAT THE TWO OF YOU MET AND REACHED AN AGREEMENT.
THAT YOU GAVE WILL TO THE END OF THE CENTURY TO COMPLETE HIS WORK, UNMOLESTED.
ONCE HE'S SUCCEEDED-- ONCE IT'S CLEAR THAT HIS WORD-CHILD LIVES ON BOTH SIDES OF THE DIVIDE--
--WELL THEN, YOU'RE FREE TO SETTLE YOUR DIFFERENCES IN ANY WAY YOU CHOOSE.
AND NOW I THINK WE HAVE SAID ALL THAT NEEDS TO BE SAID.
I WILL LEAVE FIRST. THEN WILL, AND UTNAPISHTIM LAST OF ALL. AT INTERVALS OF FIFTEEN MINUTES.
THE INTERVENING TIME YOU MAY DEVOTE TO YOUR FORGET-TING.
FORGET MOST DILIGENTLY, WITH ALL YOUR MIGHT, THE THINGS THAT MUST NOT BE REMEMBERED.
GOODNIGHT, GENTLEMEN.

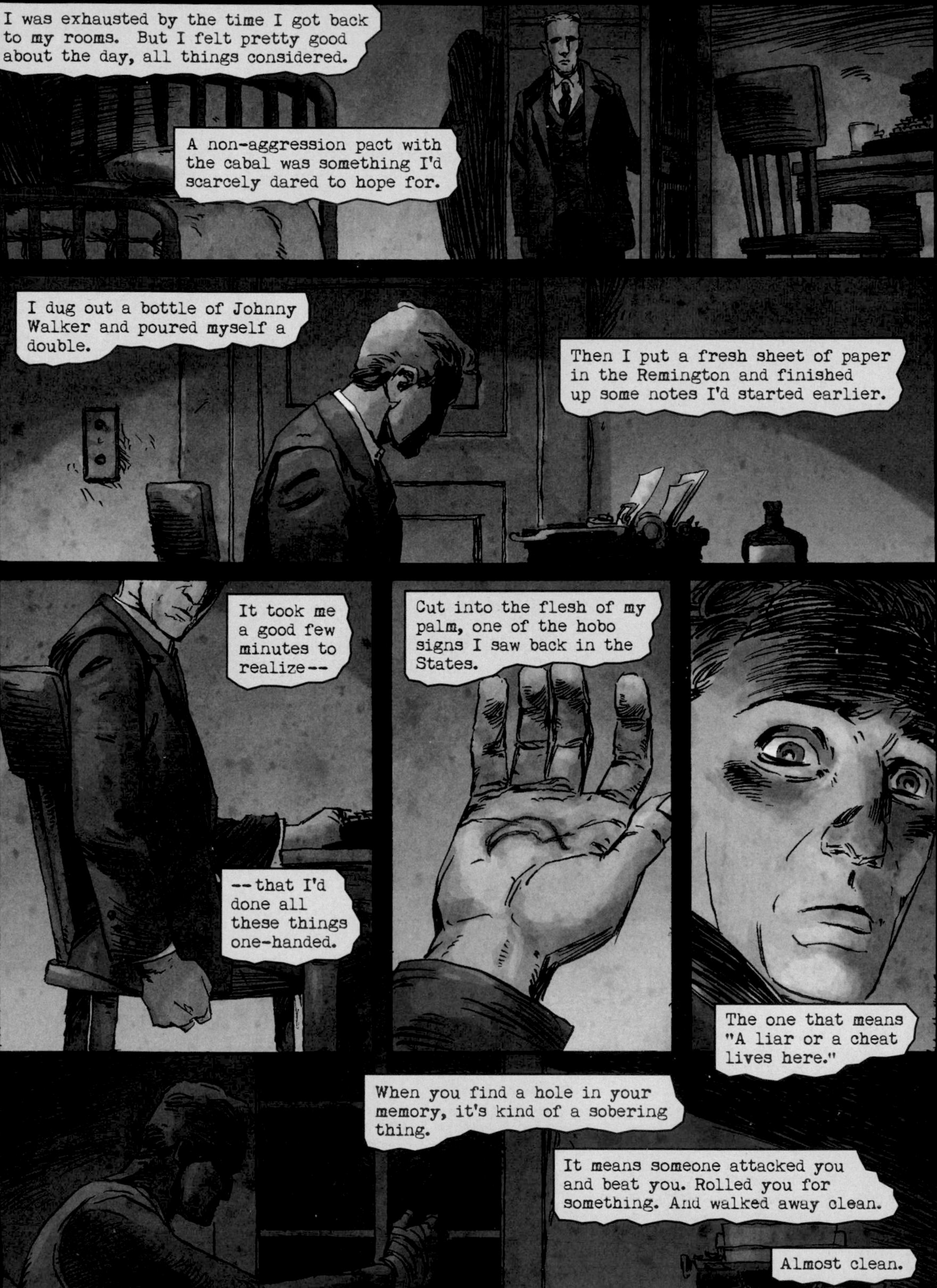
I was exhausted by the time I got back to my rooms. But I felt pretty good about the day, all things considered.
A non-aggression pact with the cabal was something I'd scarcely dared to hope for.
I dug out a bottle of Johnny Walker and poured myself a double.
Then I put a fresh sheet of paper in the Remington and finished up some notes I'd started earlier.
It took me a good few minutes to realize--
--that I'd done all these things one-handed.
Cut into the flesh of my palm, one of the hobo signs I saw back in the States.
The one that means "A liar or a cheat lives here."
When you find a hole in your memory, it's kind of a sobering thing.
It means someone attacked you and beat you. Rolled you for something. And walked away clean.
Almost clean.

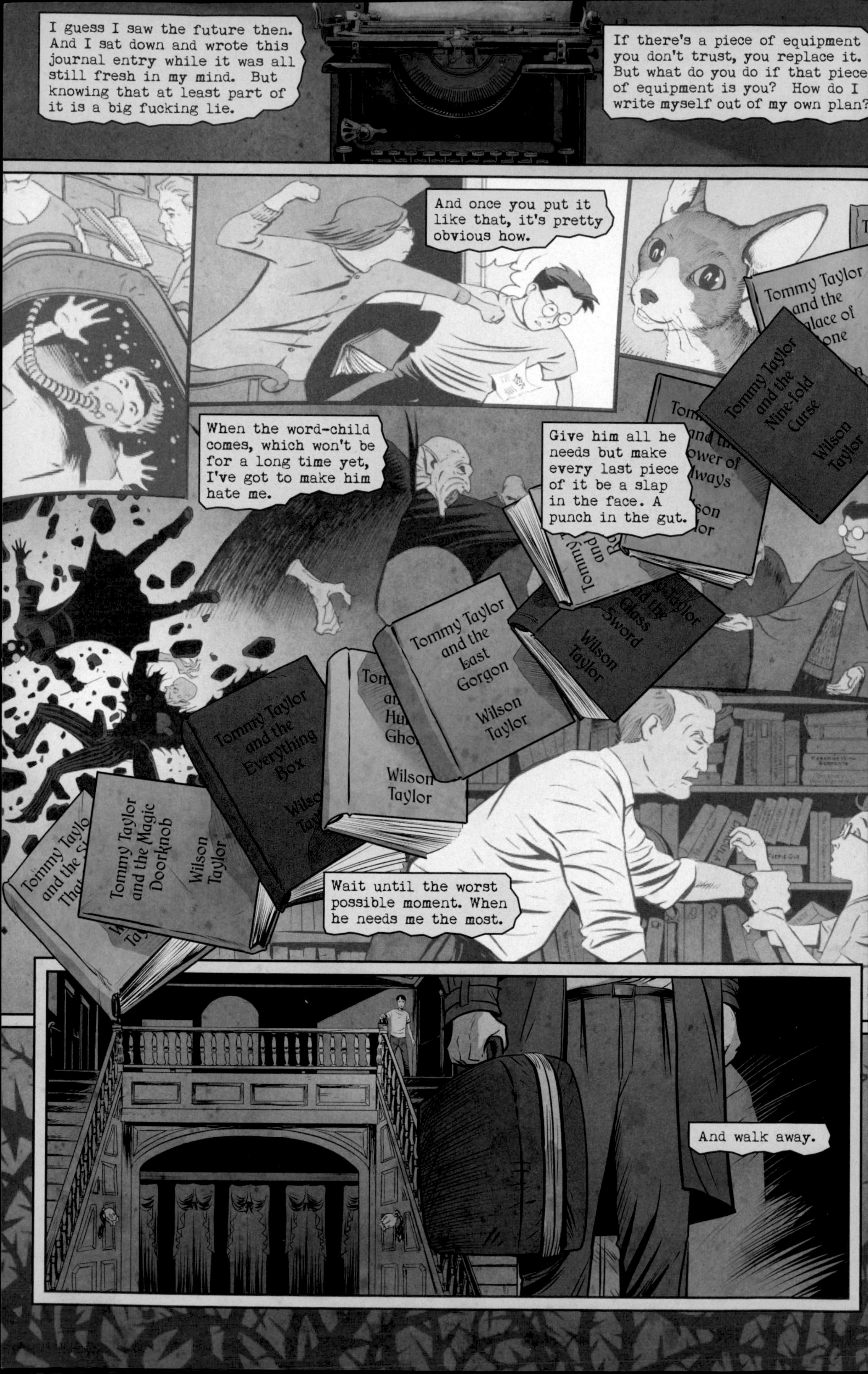

I guess I saw the future then. And I sat down and wrote this journal entry while it was all still fresh in my mind. But knowing that at least part of it is a big fucking lie.
If there's a piece of equipment you don't trust, you replace it. But what do you do if that piece of equipment is you? How do I write myself out of my own plan?
And once you put it like that, it's pretty obvious how.
When the word-child comes, which won't be for a long time yet, I've got to make him hate me.
Give him all he needs but make every last piece of it be a slap in the face. A punch in the gut.
Tommy Taylor and the Nine-fold Curse Wilson Taylor
Tommy Taylor and the Last Gorgon Wilson Taylor
Tommy Taylor and the Everything Box Wilson Taylor
Tommy Taylor and the Magic Doorknob Wilson Taylor
Wait until the worst possible moment. When he needs me the most.
And walk away.

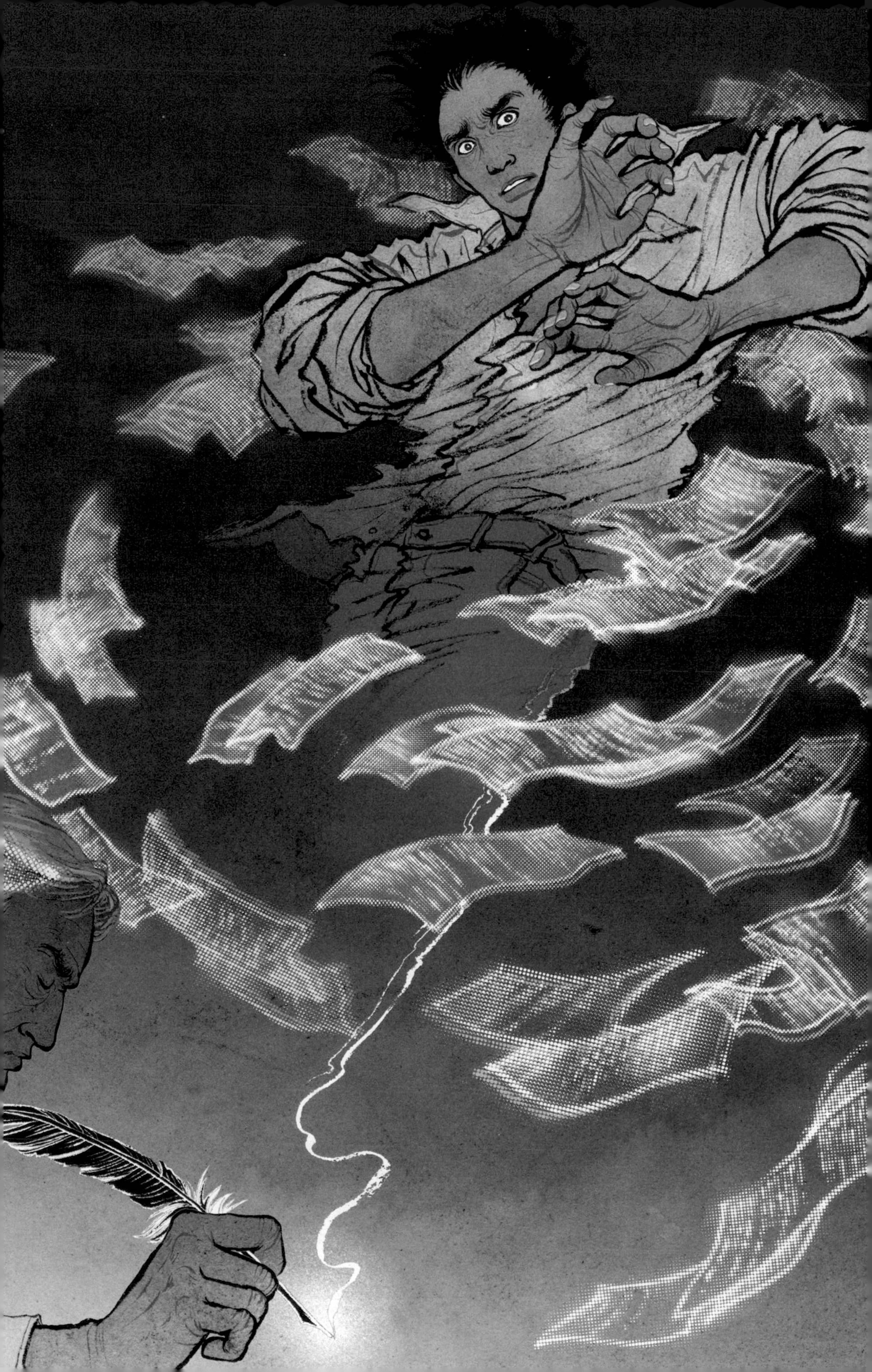

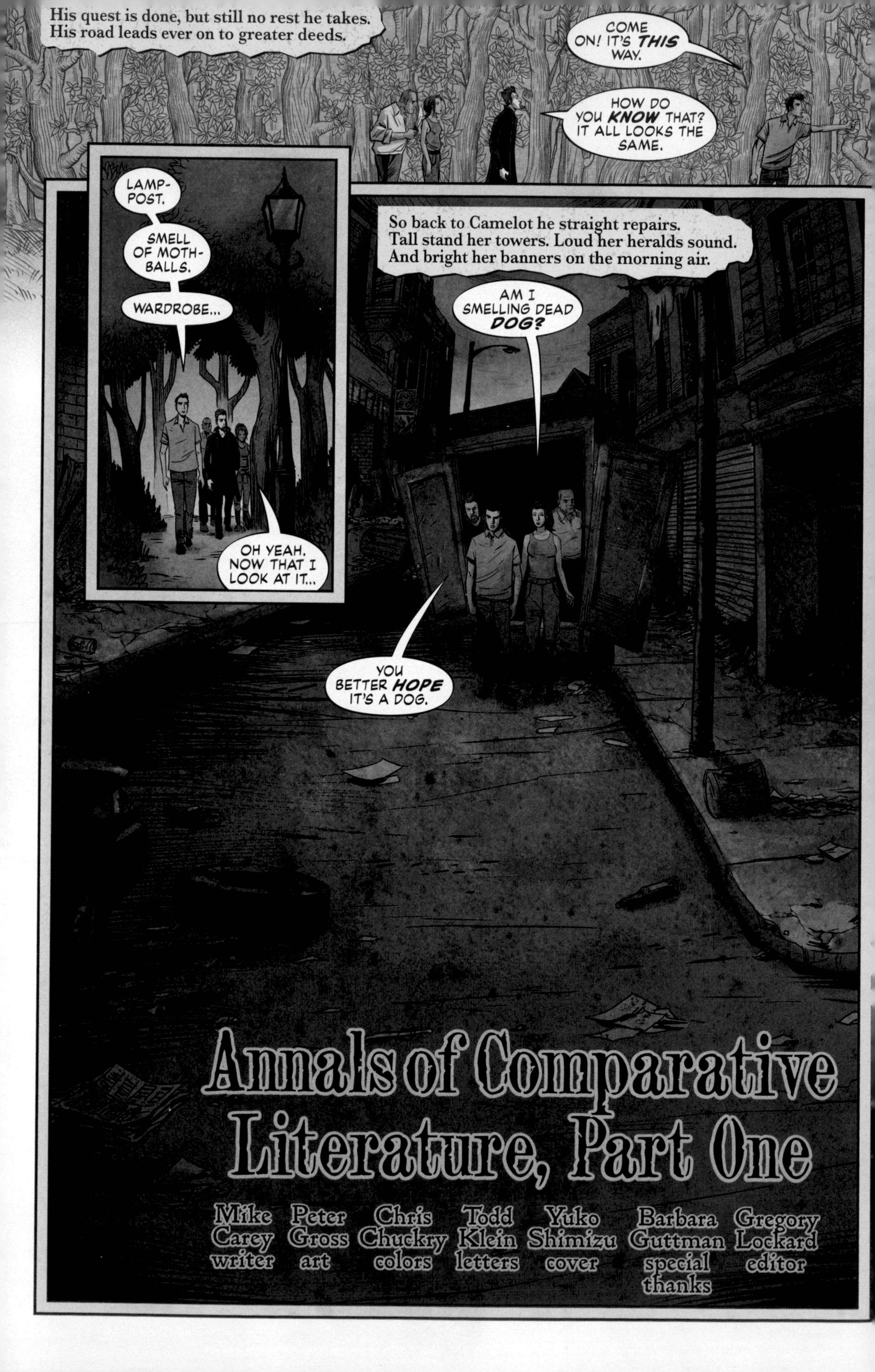

His quest is done, but still no rest he takes.
His road leads ever on to greater deeds.
COME ON! IT'S THIS WAY.
HOW DO YOU KNOW THAT? IT ALL LOOKS THE SAME.
LAMP-POST.
SMELL OF MOTH-BALLS.
WARDROBE...
OH YEAH. NOW THAT I LOOK AT IT...
So back to Camelot he straight repairs.
Tall stand her towers. Loud her heralds sound.
And bright her banners on the morning air.
AM I SMELLING DEAD DOG?
YOU BETTER HOPE IT'S A DOG.
Annals of Comparative Literature, Part One
Mike Carey writer
Peter Gross art
Chris Chuckry colors
Todd Klein letters
Yuko Shimizu cover
Barbara Guttman special thanks
Gregory Lockard editor

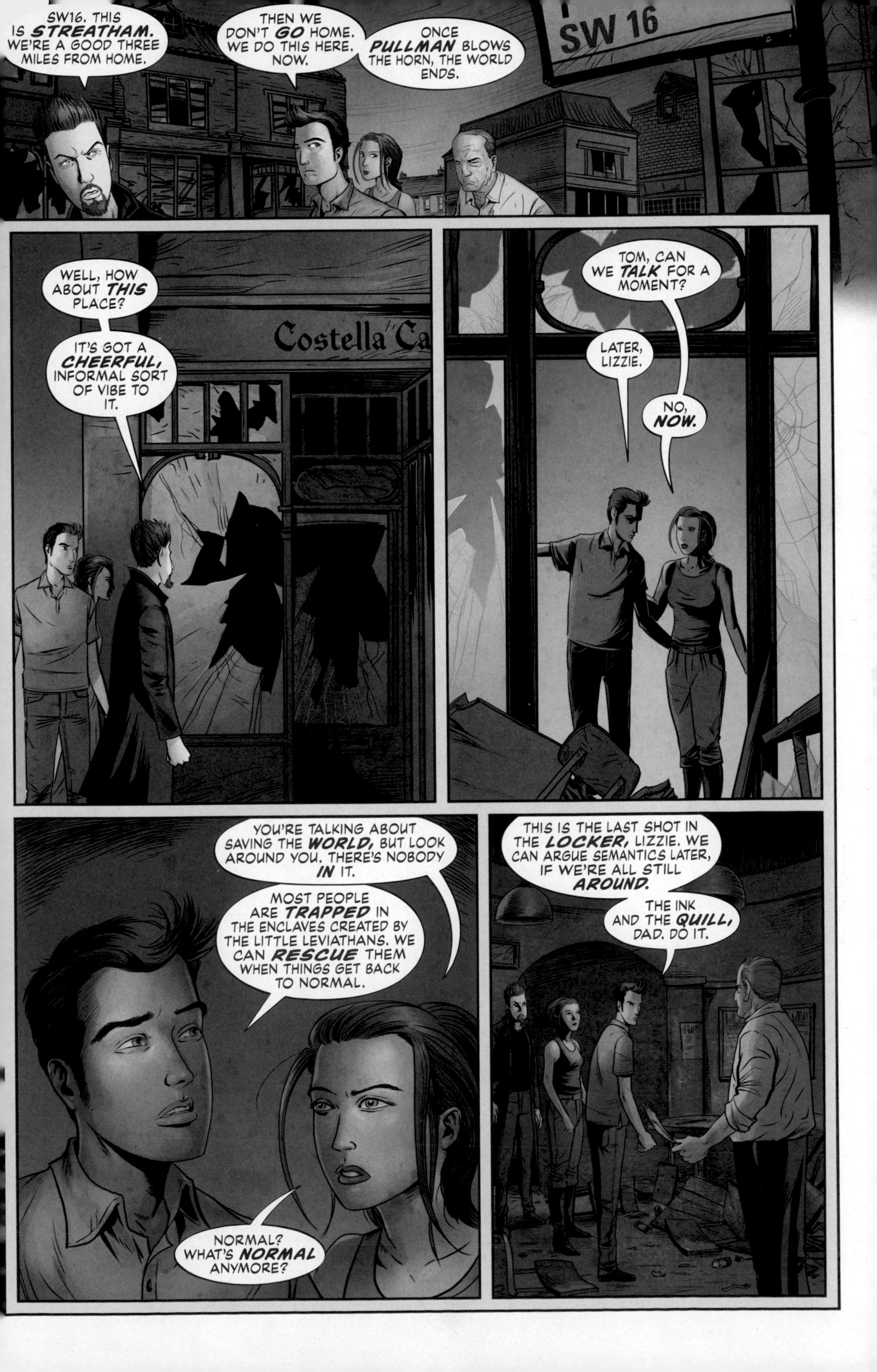
SW16. THIS IS STREATHAM. WE'RE A GOOD THREE MILES FROM HOME.
THEN WE DON'T GO HOME. WE DO THIS HERE. NOW.
ONCE PULLMAN BLOWS THE HORN, THE WORLD ENDS.
SW 16
WELL, HOW ABOUT THIS PLACE?
IT'S GOT A CHEERFUL, INFORMAL SORT OF VIBE TO IT.
Costella Ca
TOM, CAN WE TALK FOR A MOMENT?
LATER, LIZZIE.
NO, NOW.
YOU'RE TALKING ABOUT SAVING THE WORLD, BUT LOOK AROUND YOU. THERE'S NOBODY IN IT.
MOST PEOPLE ARE TRAPPED IN THE ENCLAVES CREATED BY THE LITTLE LEVIATHANS. WE CAN RESCUE THEM WHEN THINGS GET BACK TO NORMAL.
NORMAL? WHAT'S NORMAL ANYMORE?
THIS IS THE LAST SHOT IN THE LOCKER, LIZZIE. WE CAN ARGUE SEMANTICS LATER, IF WE'RE ALL STILL AROUND.
THE INK AND THE QUILL, DAD. DO IT.

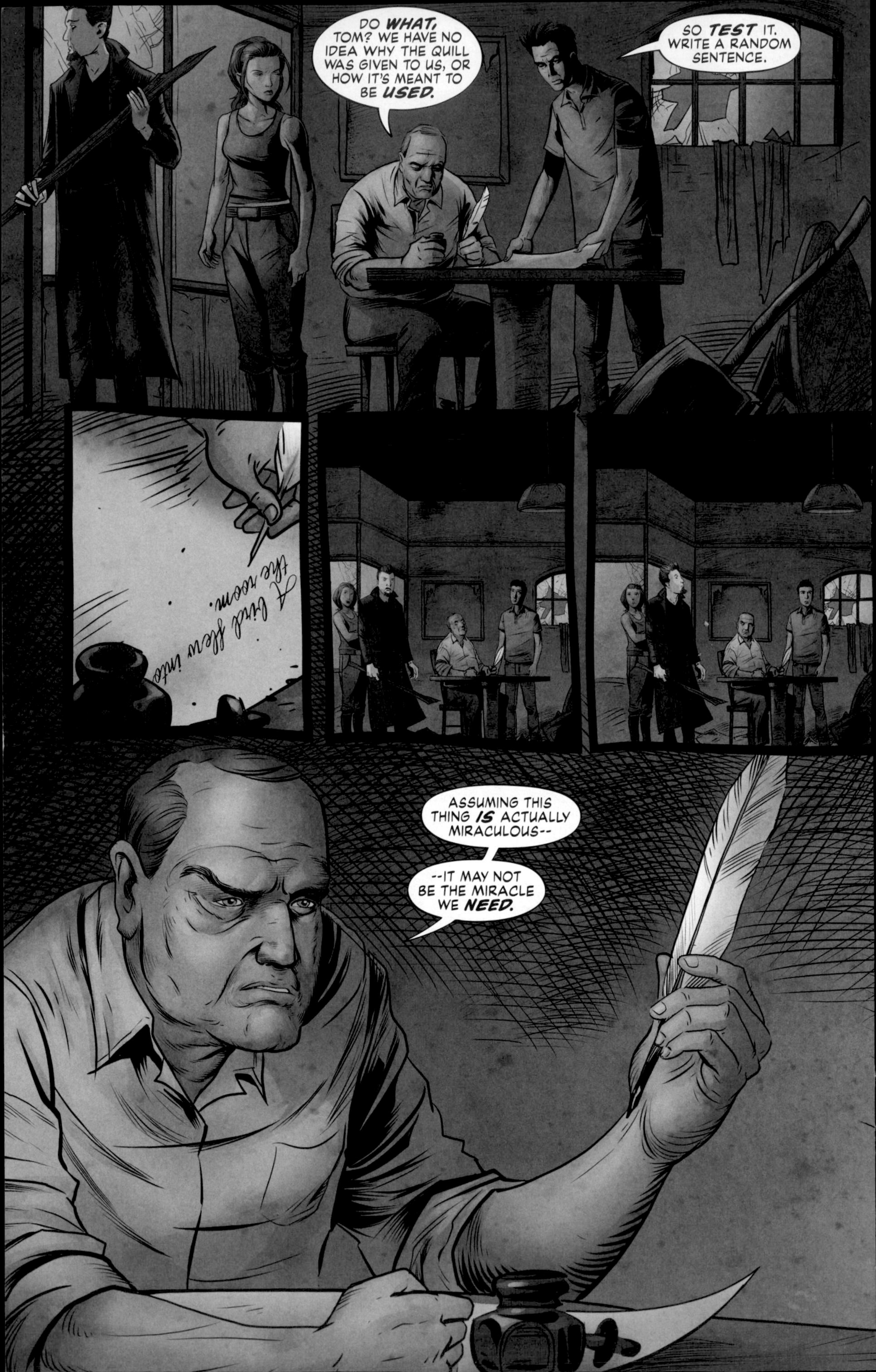
DO WHAT, TOM? WE HAVE NO IDEA WHY THE QUILL WAS GIVEN TO US, OR HOW IT'S MEANT TO BE USED.
SO TEST IT. WRITE A RANDOM SENTENCE.
A bird flew into the room.
ASSUMING THIS THING IS ACTUALLY MIRACULOUS--
--IT MAY NOT BE THE MIRACLE WE NEED.

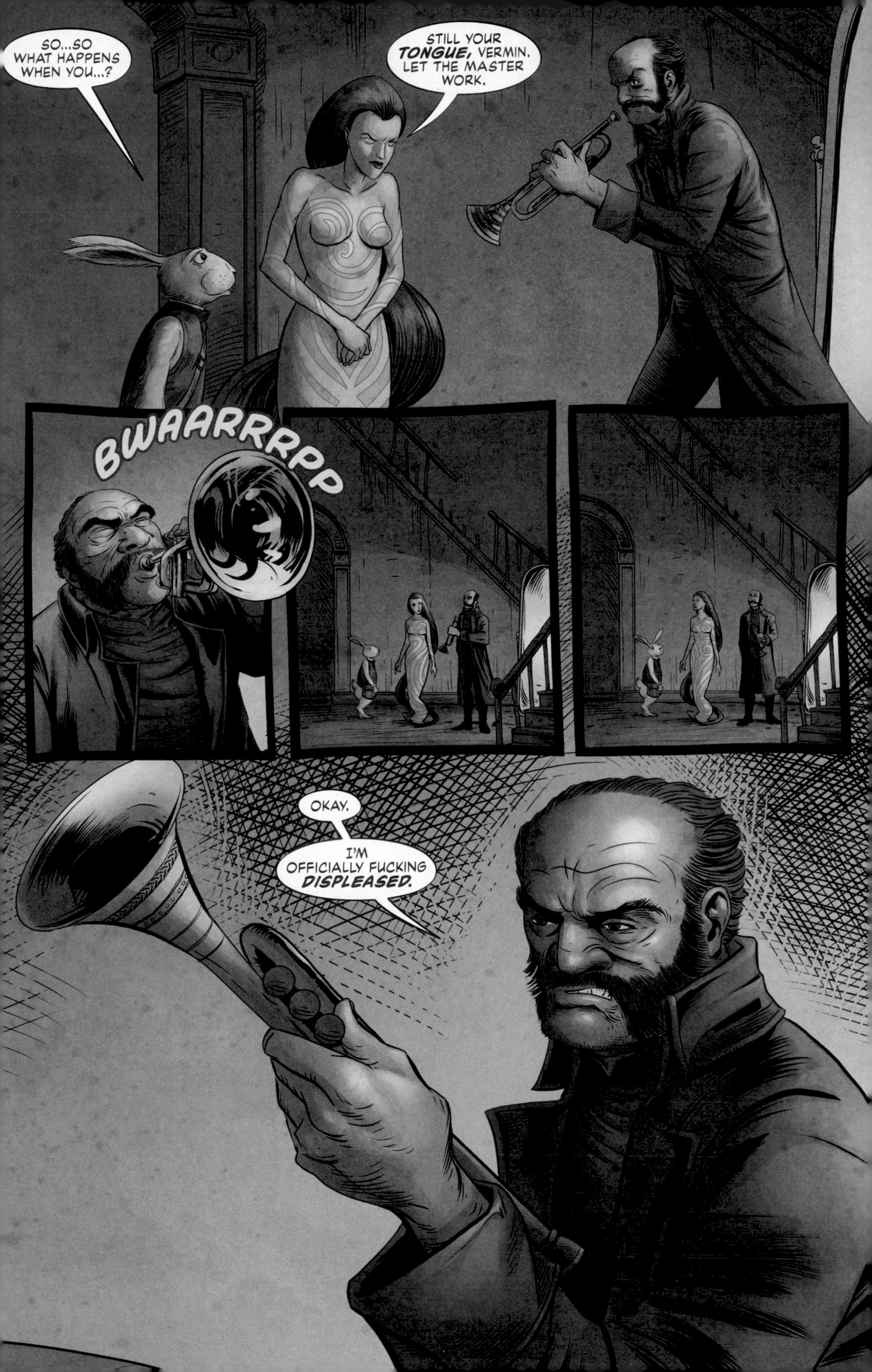
SO...SO WHAT HAPPENS WHEN YOU...?
STILL YOUR TONGUE, VERMIN. LET THE MASTER WORK.
BWAARRRPP
OKAY.
I'M OFFICIALLY FUCKING DISPLEASED.

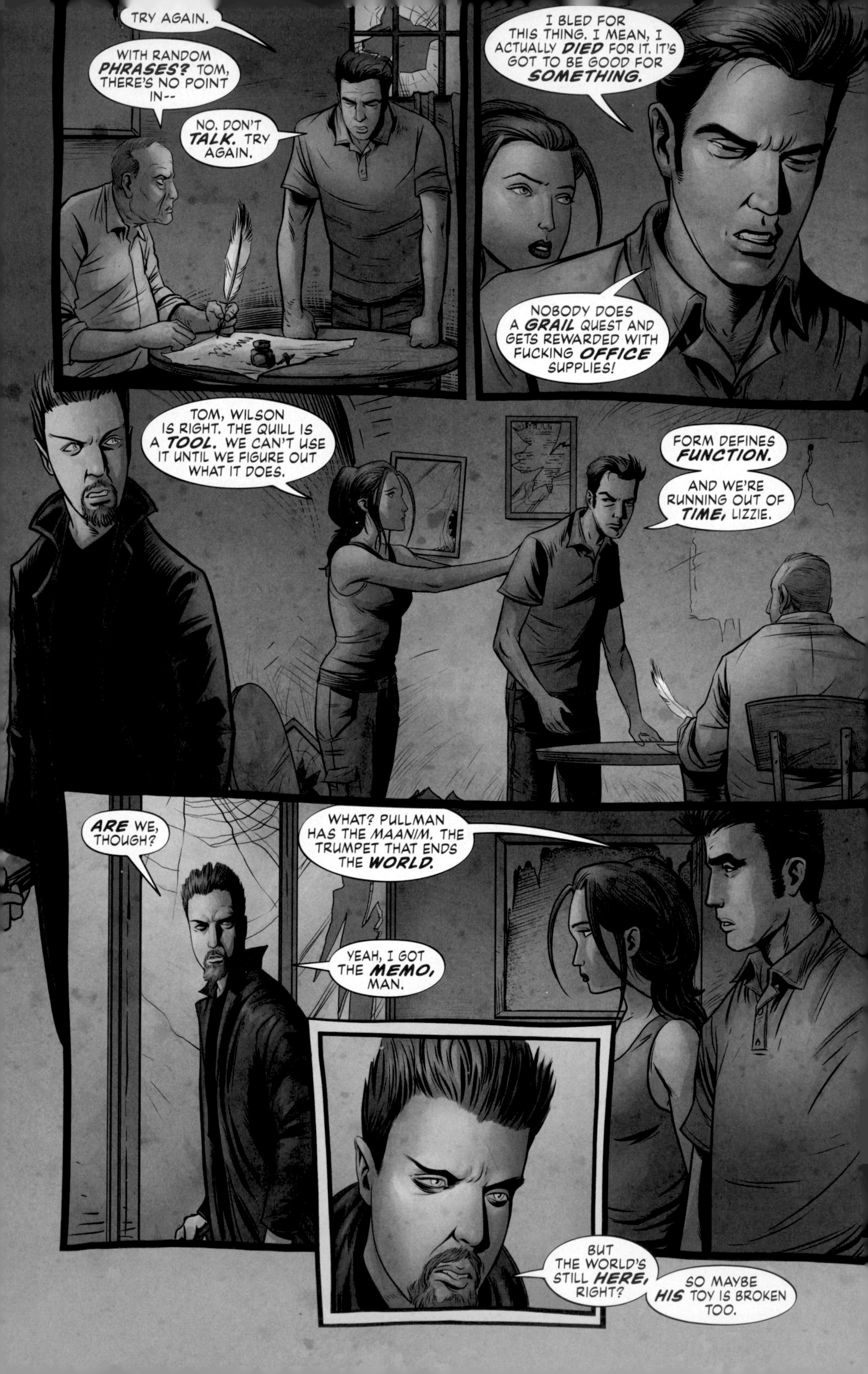
TRY AGAIN.
WITH RANDOM PHRASES? TOM, THERE'S NO POINT IN--
NO. DON'T TALK. TRY AGAIN.
I BLED FOR THIS THING. I MEAN, I ACTUALLY DIED FOR IT. IT'S GOT TO BE GOOD FOR SOMETHING.
NOBODY DOES A GRAIL QUEST AND GETS REWARDED WITH FUCKING OFFICE SUPPLIES!
TOM, WILSON IS RIGHT. THE QUILL IS A TOOL. WE CAN'T USE IT UNTIL WE FIGURE OUT WHAT IT DOES.
FORM DEFINES FUNCTION.
AND WE'RE RUNNING OUT OF TIME, LIZZIE.
ARE WE, THOUGH?
WHAT? PULLMAN HAS THE MAANIM. THE TRUMPET THAT ENDS THE WORLD.
YEAH, I GOT THE MEMO, MAN.
BUT THE WORLD'S STILL HERE, RIGHT?
SO MAYBE HIS TOY IS BROKEN TOO.

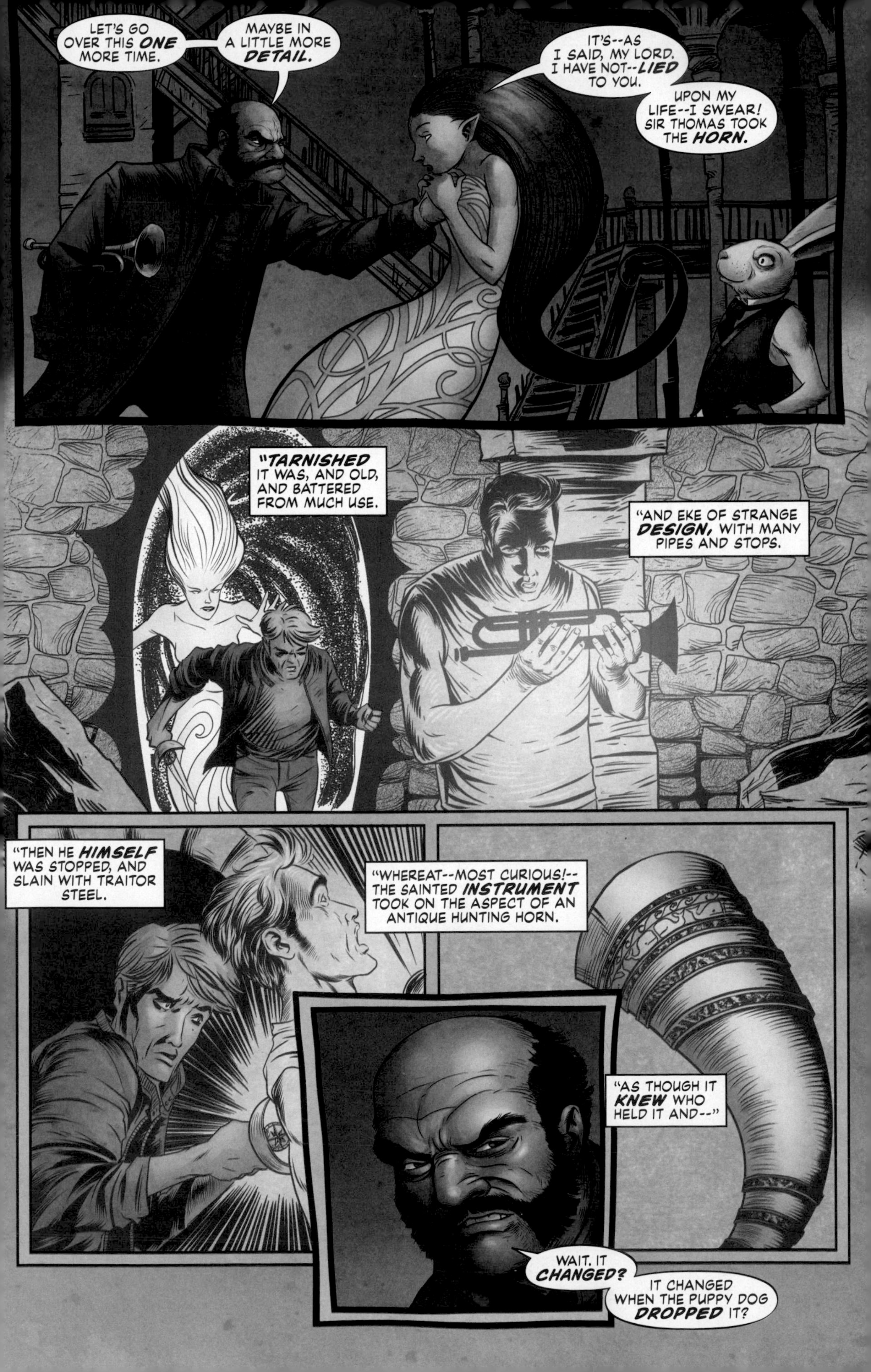
LET'S GO OVER THIS ONE MORE TIME.
MAYBE IN A LITTLE MORE DETAIL.
IT'S--AS I SAID, MY LORD. I HAVE NOT--LIED TO YOU.
UPON MY LIFE--I SWEAR! SIR THOMAS TOOK THE HORN.
"TARNISHED IT WAS, AND OLD, AND BATTERED FROM MUCH USE.
"AND EKE OF STRANGE DESIGN, WITH MANY PIPES AND STOPS.
"THEN HE HIMSELF WAS STOPPED, AND SLAIN WITH TRAITOR STEEL.
"WHEREAT--MOST CURIOUS!--THE SAINTED INSTRUMENT TOOK ON THE ASPECT OF AN ANTIQUE HUNTING HORN.
"AS THOUGH IT KNEW WHO HELD IT AND--"
WAIT. IT CHANGED?
IT CHANGED WHEN THE PUPPY DOG DROPPED IT?

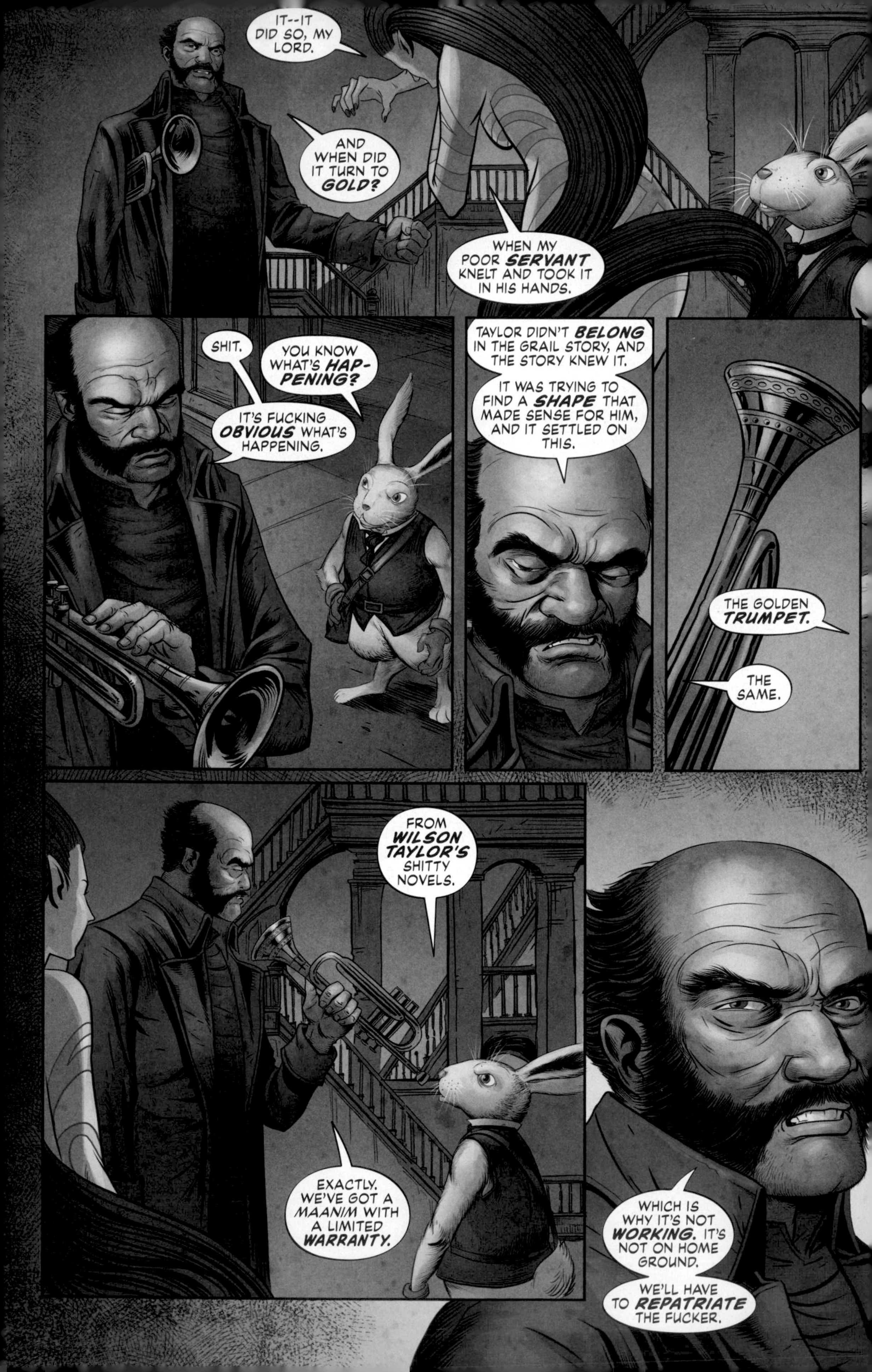
IT--IT DID SO, MY LORD.
AND WHEN DID IT TURN TO GOLD?
WHEN MY POOR SERVANT KNELT AND TOOK IT IN HIS HANDS.
SHIT.
YOU KNOW WHAT'S HAP-PENING?
IT'S FUCKING OBVIOUS WHAT'S HAPPENING.
TAYLOR DIDN'T BELONG IN THE GRAIL STORY, AND THE STORY KNEW IT.
IT WAS TRYING TO FIND A SHAPE THAT MADE SENSE FOR HIM, AND IT SETTLED ON THIS.
THE GOLDEN TRUMPET.
THE SAME.
FROM WILSON TAYLOR'S SHITTY NOVELS.
EXACTLY. WE'VE GOT A MAANIM WITH A LIMITED WARRANTY.
WHICH IS WHY IT'S NOT WORKING. IT'S NOT ON HOME GROUND.
WE'LL HAVE TO REPATRIATE THE FUCKER.

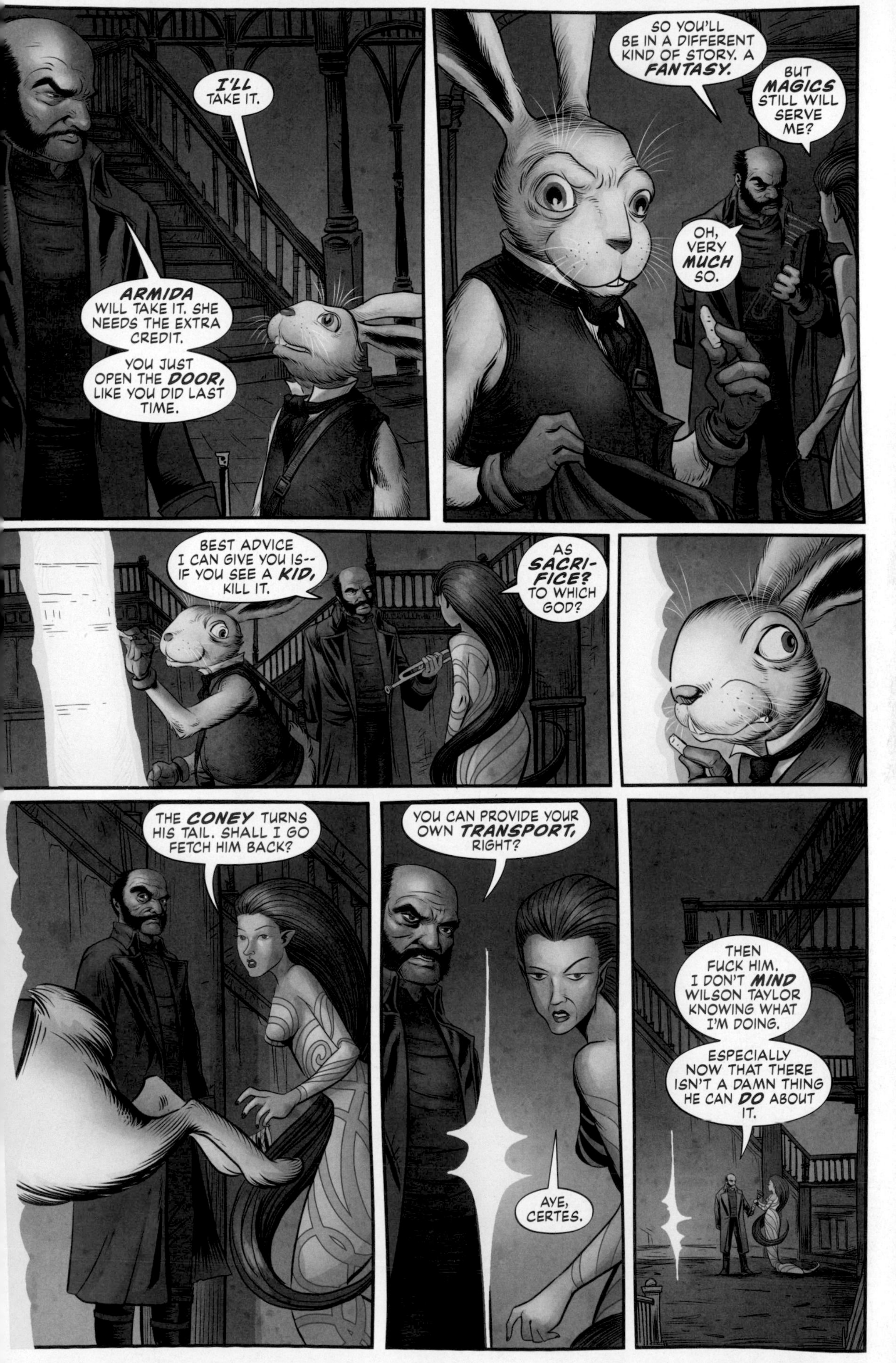
I'LL TAKE IT.
ARMIDA WILL TAKE IT. SHE NEEDS THE EXTRA CREDIT.
YOU JUST OPEN THE DOOR, LIKE YOU DID LAST TIME.
SO YOU'LL BE IN A DIFFERENT KIND OF STORY. A FANTASY.
BUT MAGICS STILL WILL SERVE ME?
OH, VERY MUCH SO.
BEST ADVICE I CAN GIVE YOU IS-- IF YOU SEE A KID, KILL IT.
AS SACRI-FICE? TO WHICH GOD?
THE CONEY TURNS HIS TAIL. SHALL I GO FETCH HIM BACK?
YOU CAN PROVIDE YOUR OWN TRANSPORT, RIGHT?
AYE, CERTES.
THEN FUCK HIM. I DON'T MIND WILSON TAYLOR KNOWING WHAT I'M DOING.
ESPECIALLY NOW THAT THERE ISN'T A DAMN THING HE CAN DO ABOUT IT.

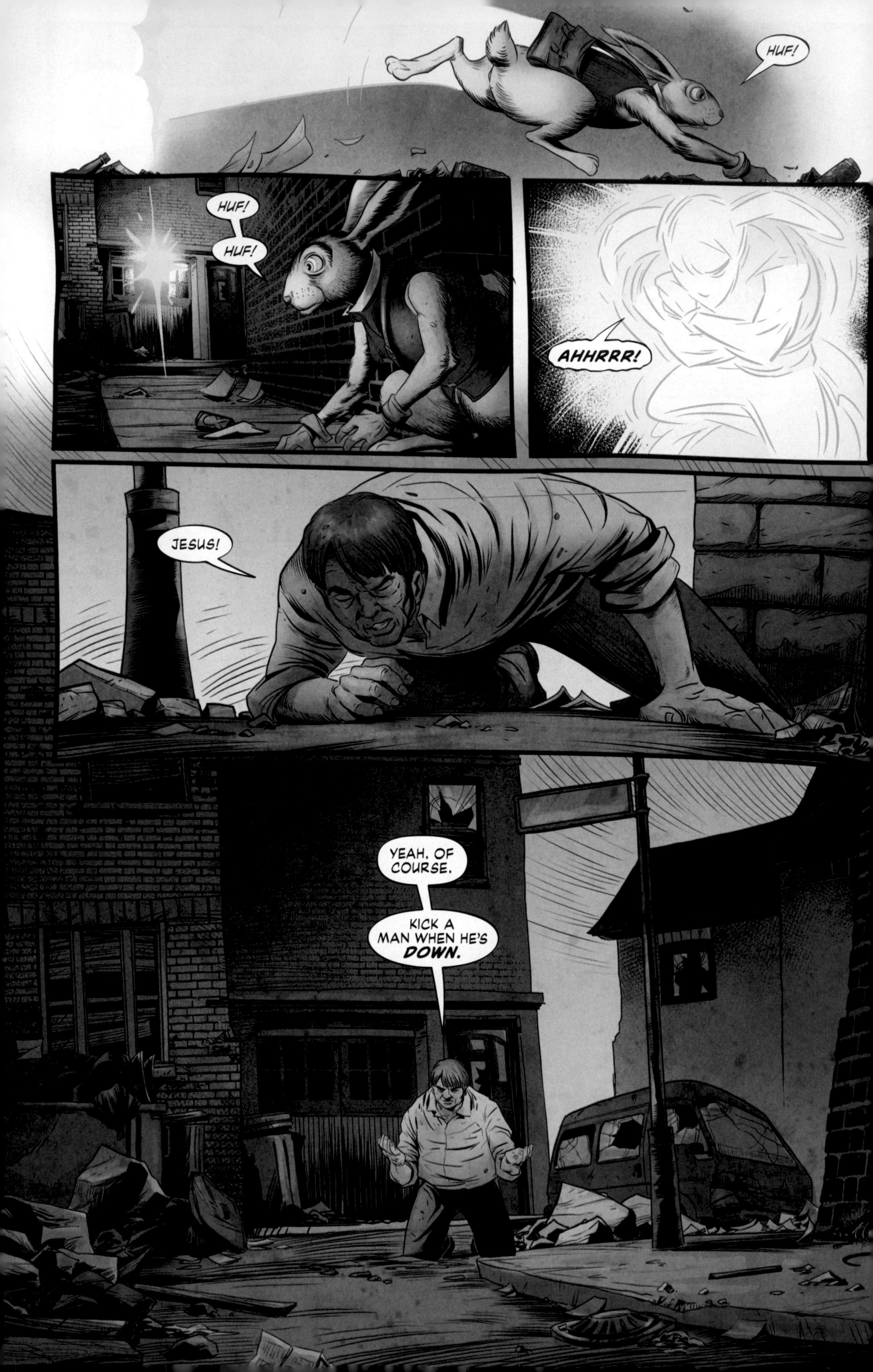
HUF!
HUF!
HUF!
AHHRRR!
JESUS!
YEAH. OF COURSE.
KICK A MAN WHEN HE'S *DOWN.*

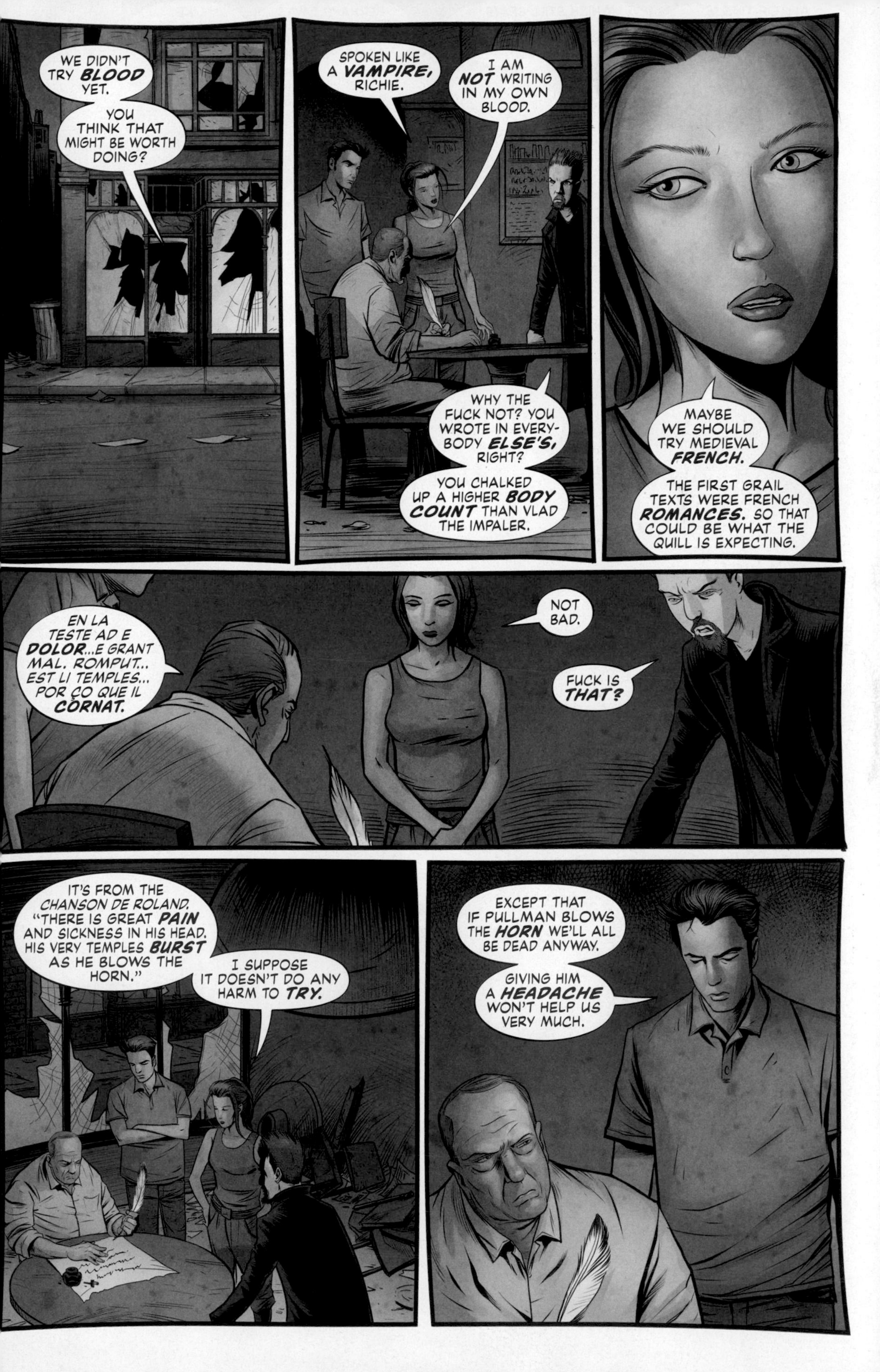
WE DIDN'T TRY BLOOD YET.
YOU THINK THAT MIGHT BE WORTH DOING?
SPOKEN LIKE A VAMPIRE, RICHIE.
I AM NOT WRITING IN MY OWN BLOOD.
WHY THE FUCK NOT? YOU WROTE IN EVERY-BODY ELSE'S, RIGHT?
YOU CHALKED UP A HIGHER BODY COUNT THAN VLAD THE IMPALER.
MAYBE WE SHOULD TRY MEDIEVAL FRENCH.
THE FIRST GRAIL TEXTS WERE FRENCH ROMANCES. SO THAT COULD BE WHAT THE QUILL IS EXPECTING.
EN LA TESTE AD E DOLOR...E GRANT MAL. ROMPUT... EST LI TEMPLES... POR ÇO QUE IL CÒRNAT.
NOT BAD.
FUCK IS THAT?
IT'S FROM THE CHANSON DE ROLAND. "THERE IS GREAT PAIN AND SICKNESS IN HIS HEAD. HIS VERY TEMPLES BURST AS HE BLOWS THE HORN."
I SUPPOSE IT DOESN'T DO ANY HARM TO TRY.
EXCEPT THAT IF PULLMAN BLOWS THE HORN WE'LL ALL BE DEAD ANYWAY.
GIVING HIM A HEADACHE WON'T HELP US VERY MUCH.

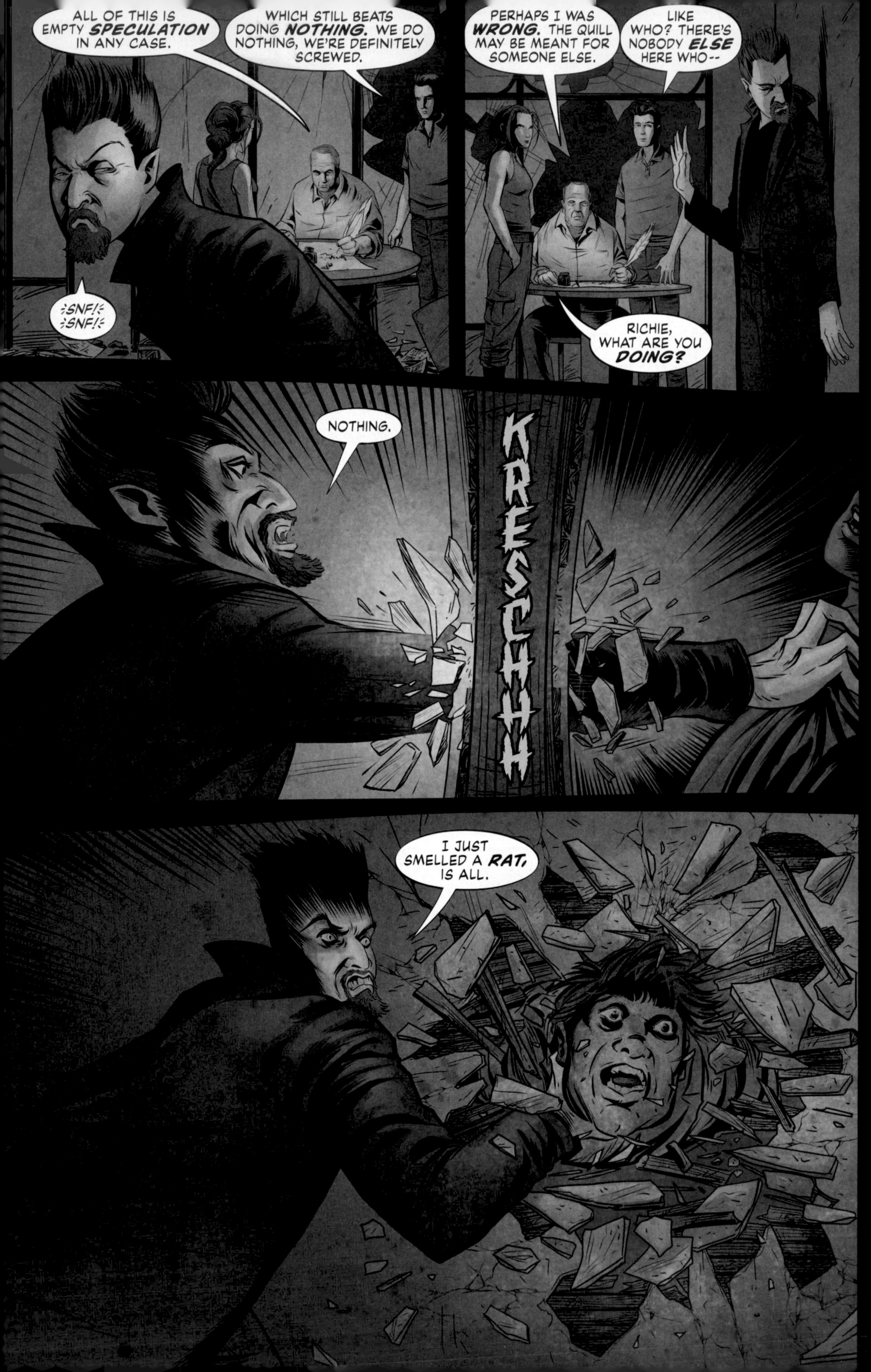
ALL OF THIS IS EMPTY SPECULATION IN ANY CASE.
WHICH STILL BEATS DOING NOTHING. WE DO NOTHING, WE'RE DEFINITELY SCREWED.
SNF! SNF!
PERHAPS I WAS WRONG. THE QUILL MAY BE MEANT FOR SOMEONE ELSE.
LIKE WHO? THERE'S NOBODY ELSE HERE WHO--
RICHIE, WHAT ARE YOU DOING?
NOTHING.
KRESCHHH
I JUST SMELLED A RAT, IS ALL.

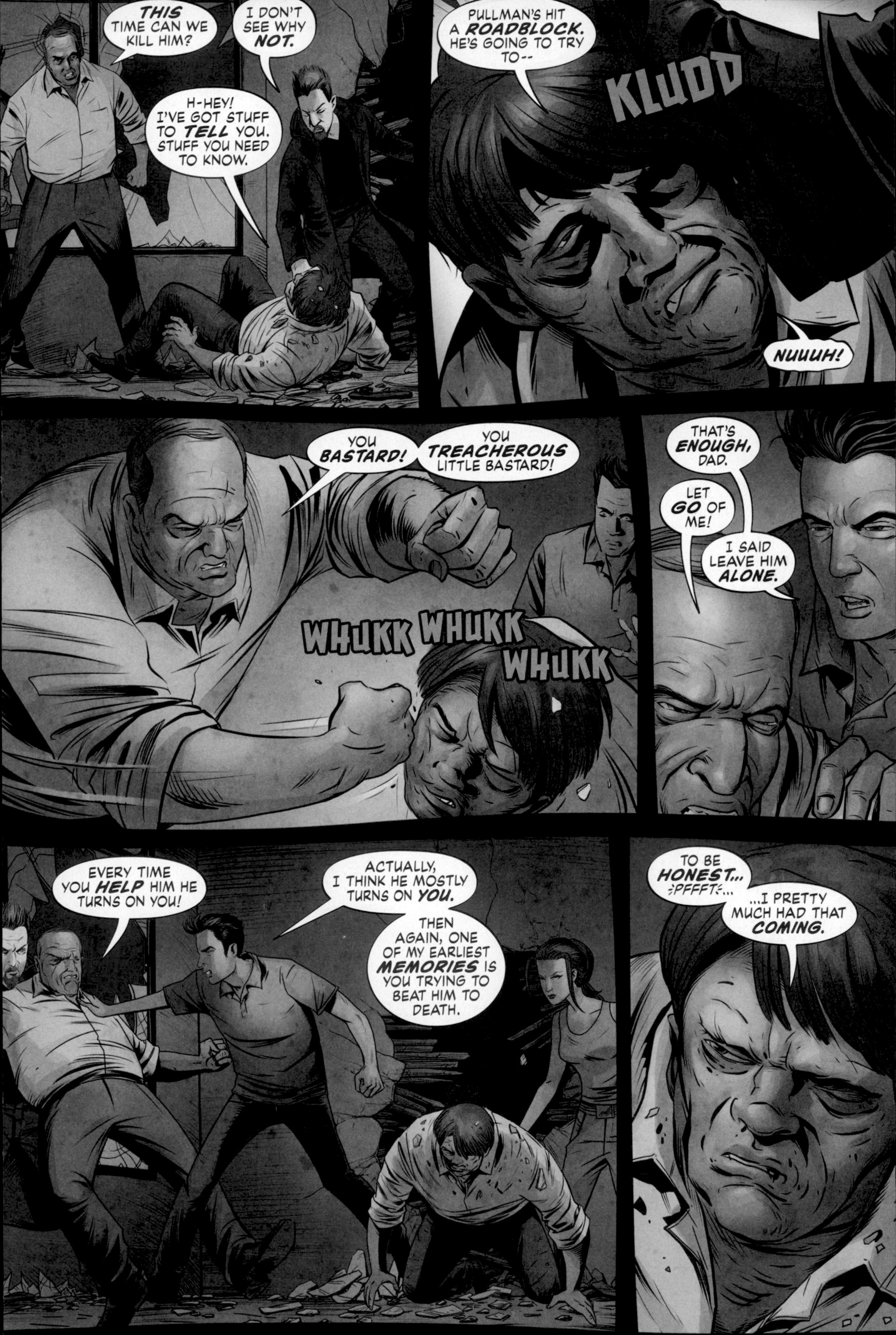
THIS TIME CAN WE KILL HIM?
I DON'T SEE WHY NOT.
H-HEY! I'VE GOT STUFF TO TELL YOU. STUFF YOU NEED TO KNOW.
PULLMAN'S HIT A ROADBLOCK. HE'S GOING TO TRY TO--
KLUDD
NUUUH!
YOU BASTARD!
YOU TREACHEROUS LITTLE BASTARD!
WHUKK WHUKK WHUKK
THAT'S ENOUGH, DAD.
LET GO OF ME!
I SAID LEAVE HIM ALONE.
EVERY TIME YOU HELP HIM HE TURNS ON YOU!
ACTUALLY, I THINK HE MOSTLY TURNS ON YOU.
THEN AGAIN, ONE OF MY EARLIEST MEMORIES IS YOU TRYING TO BEAT HIM TO DEATH.
TO BE HONEST...
PFFFT...
...I PRETTY MUCH HAD THAT COMING.

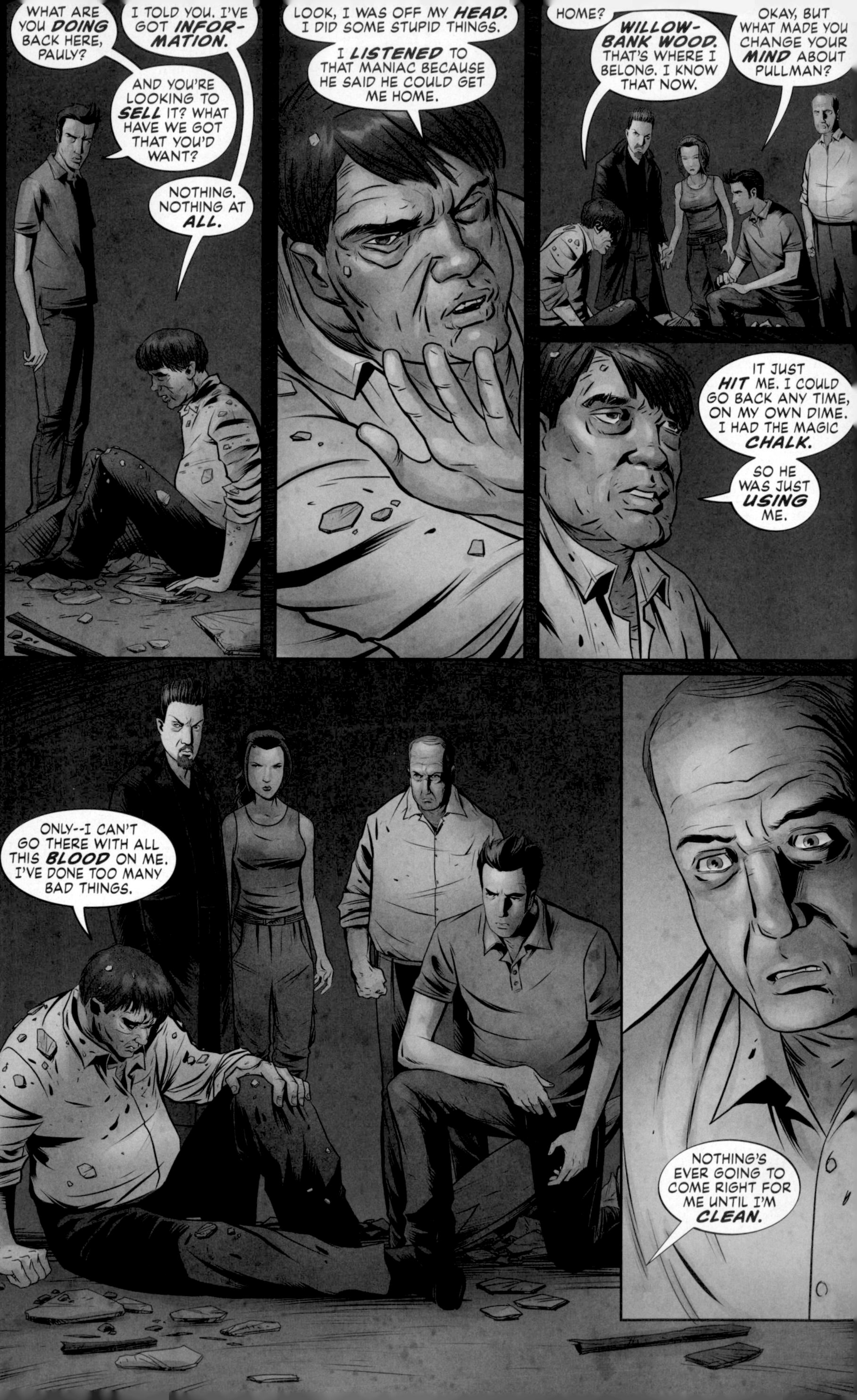

WHAT ARE YOU **DOING** BACK HERE, PAULY?
I TOLD YOU. I'VE GOT **INFORMATION.**
AND YOU'RE LOOKING TO **SELL** IT? WHAT HAVE WE GOT THAT YOU'D WANT?
NOTHING. NOTHING AT **ALL.**
LOOK, I WAS OFF MY **HEAD.** I DID SOME STUPID THINGS.
I **LISTENED** TO THAT MANIAC BECAUSE HE SAID HE COULD GET ME HOME.
HOME?
WILLOW-BANK WOOD. THAT'S WHERE I BELONG. I KNOW THAT NOW.
OKAY, BUT WHAT MADE YOU CHANGE YOUR **MIND** ABOUT PULLMAN?
IT JUST **HIT** ME. I COULD GO BACK ANY TIME, ON MY OWN DIME. I HAD THE MAGIC **CHALK.**
SO HE WAS JUST **USING** ME.
ONLY--I CAN'T GO THERE WITH ALL THIS **BLOOD** ON ME. I'VE DONE TOO MANY BAD THINGS.
NOTHING'S EVER GOING TO COME RIGHT FOR ME UNTIL I'M **CLEAN.**

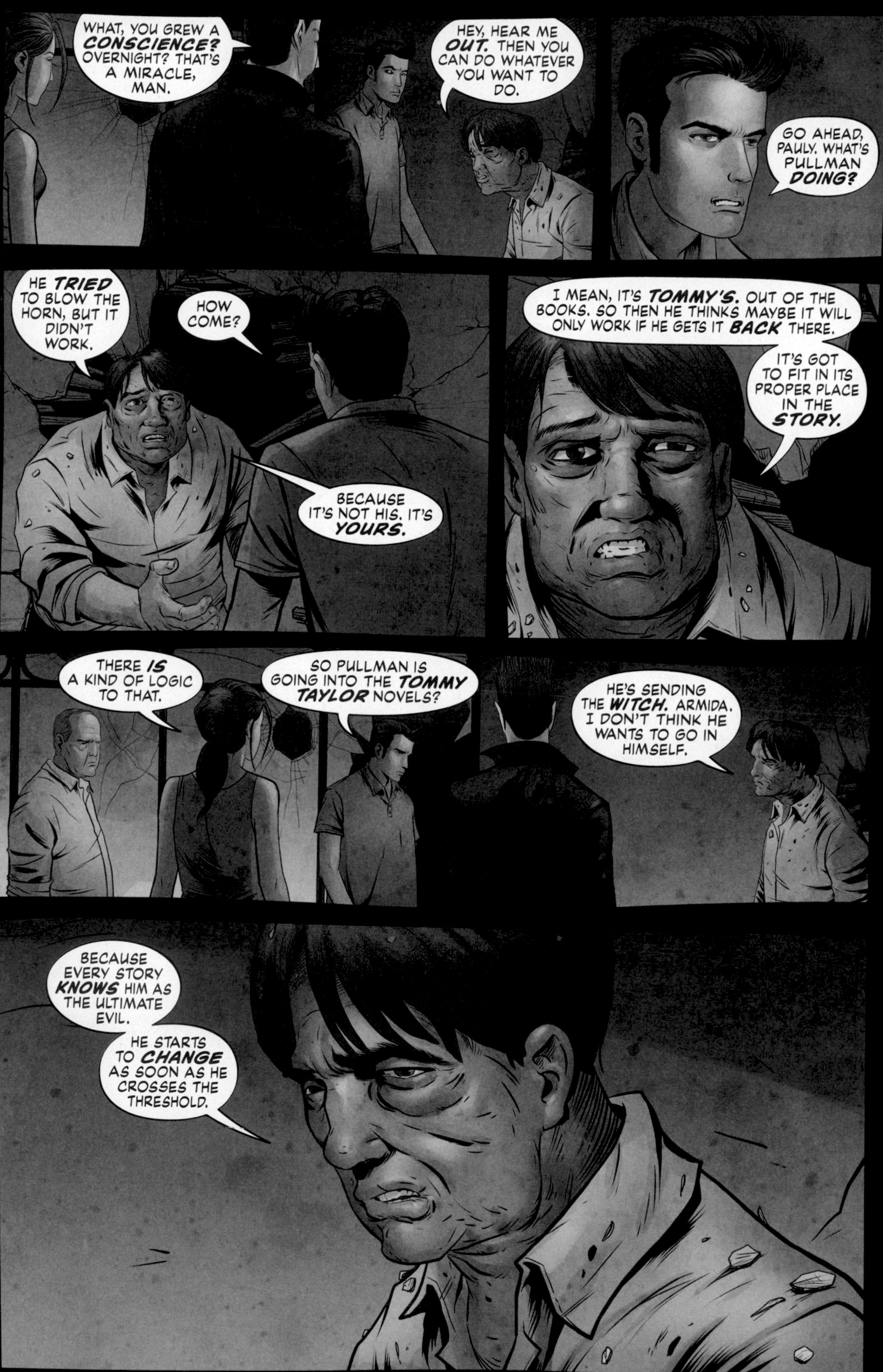
WHAT, YOU GREW A CONSCIENCE? OVERNIGHT? THAT'S A MIRACLE, MAN.
HEY, HEAR ME OUT. THEN YOU CAN DO WHATEVER YOU WANT TO DO.
GO AHEAD, PAULY. WHAT'S PULLMAN DOING?
HE TRIED TO BLOW THE HORN, BUT IT DIDN'T WORK.
HOW COME?
BECAUSE IT'S NOT HIS. IT'S YOURS.
I MEAN, IT'S TOMMY'S. OUT OF THE BOOKS. SO THEN HE THINKS MAYBE IT WILL ONLY WORK IF HE GETS IT BACK THERE.
IT'S GOT TO FIT IN ITS PROPER PLACE IN THE STORY.
THERE IS A KIND OF LOGIC TO THAT.
SO PULLMAN IS GOING INTO THE TOMMY TAYLOR NOVELS?
HE'S SENDING THE WITCH. ARMIDA. I DON'T THINK HE WANTS TO GO IN HIMSELF.
BECAUSE EVERY STORY KNOWS HIM AS THE ULTIMATE EVIL.
HE STARTS TO CHANGE AS SOON AS HE CROSSES THE THRESHOLD.

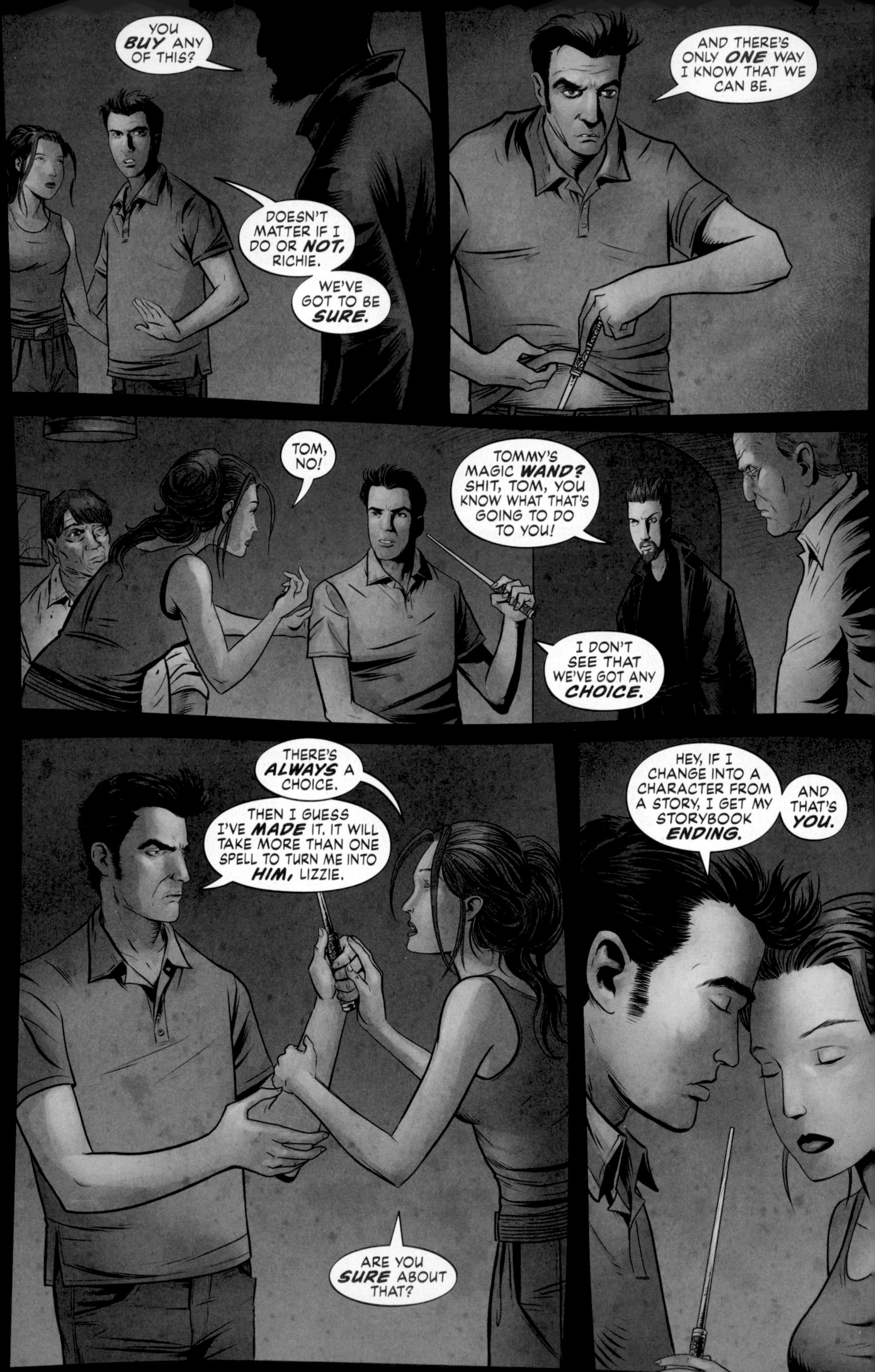
YOU BUY ANY OF THIS?
DOESN'T MATTER IF I DO OR NOT, RICHIE.
WE'VE GOT TO BE SURE.
AND THERE'S ONLY ONE WAY I KNOW THAT WE CAN BE.
TOM, NO!
TOMMY'S MAGIC WAND? SHIT, TOM, YOU KNOW WHAT THAT'S GOING TO DO TO YOU!
I DON'T SEE THAT WE'VE GOT ANY CHOICE.
THERE'S ALWAYS A CHOICE.
THEN I GUESS I'VE MADE IT. IT WILL TAKE MORE THAN ONE SPELL TO TURN ME INTO HIM, LIZZIE.
ARE YOU SURE ABOUT THAT?
HEY, IF I CHANGE INTO A CHARACTER FROM A STORY, I GET MY STORYBOOK ENDING.
AND THAT'S YOU.

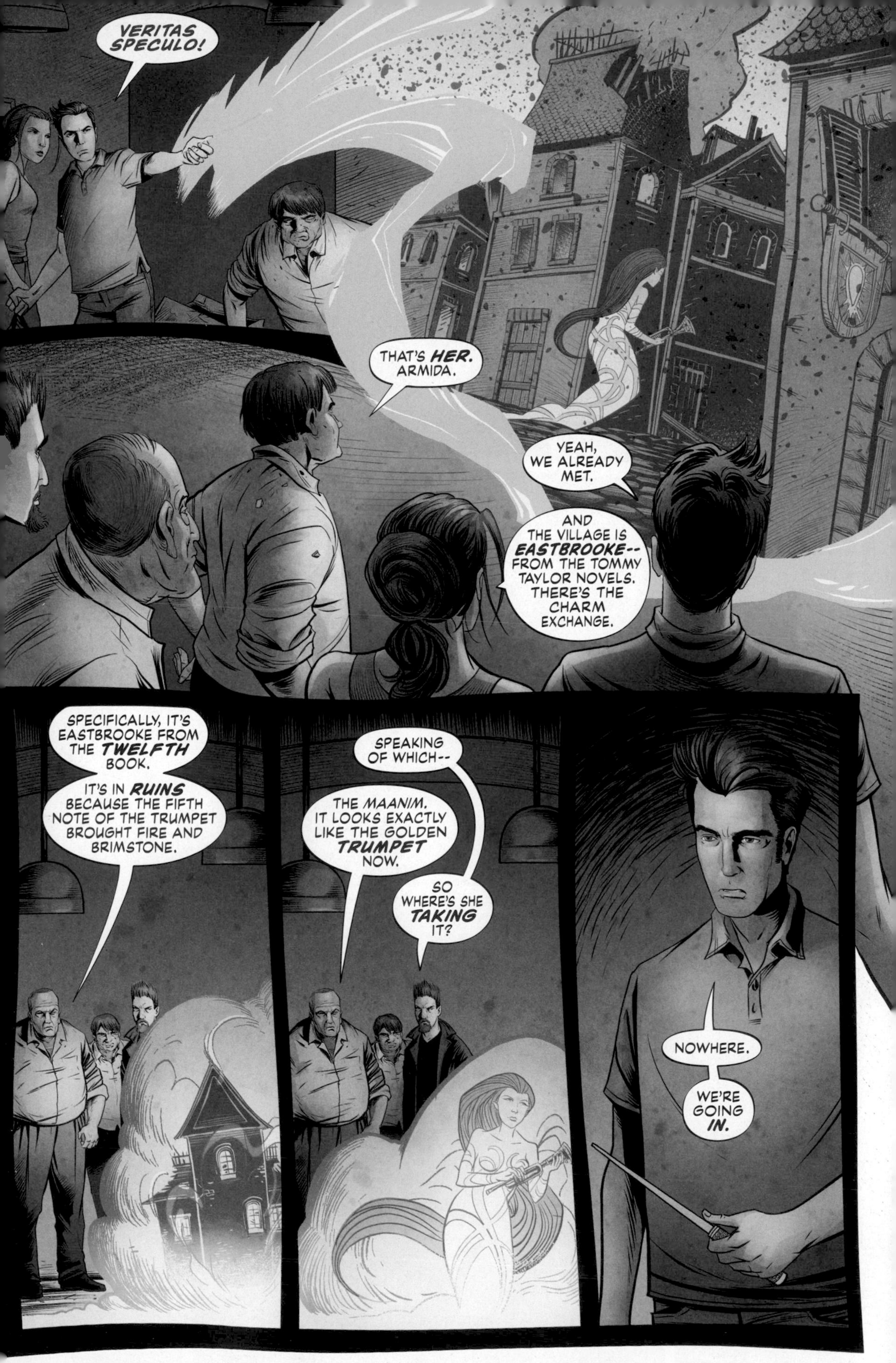
VERITAS SPECULO!
THAT'S HER. ARMIDA.
YEAH, WE ALREADY MET.
AND THE VILLAGE IS EASTBROOKE-- FROM THE TOMMY TAYLOR NOVELS. THERE'S THE CHARM EXCHANGE.
SPECIFICALLY, IT'S EASTBROOKE FROM THE TWELFTH BOOK.
IT'S IN RUINS BECAUSE THE FIFTH NOTE OF THE TRUMPET BROUGHT FIRE AND BRIMSTONE.
SPEAKING OF WHICH--
THE MAANIM. IT LOOKS EXACTLY LIKE THE GOLDEN TRUMPET NOW.
SO WHERE'S SHE TAKING IT?
NOWHERE.
WE'RE GOING IN.

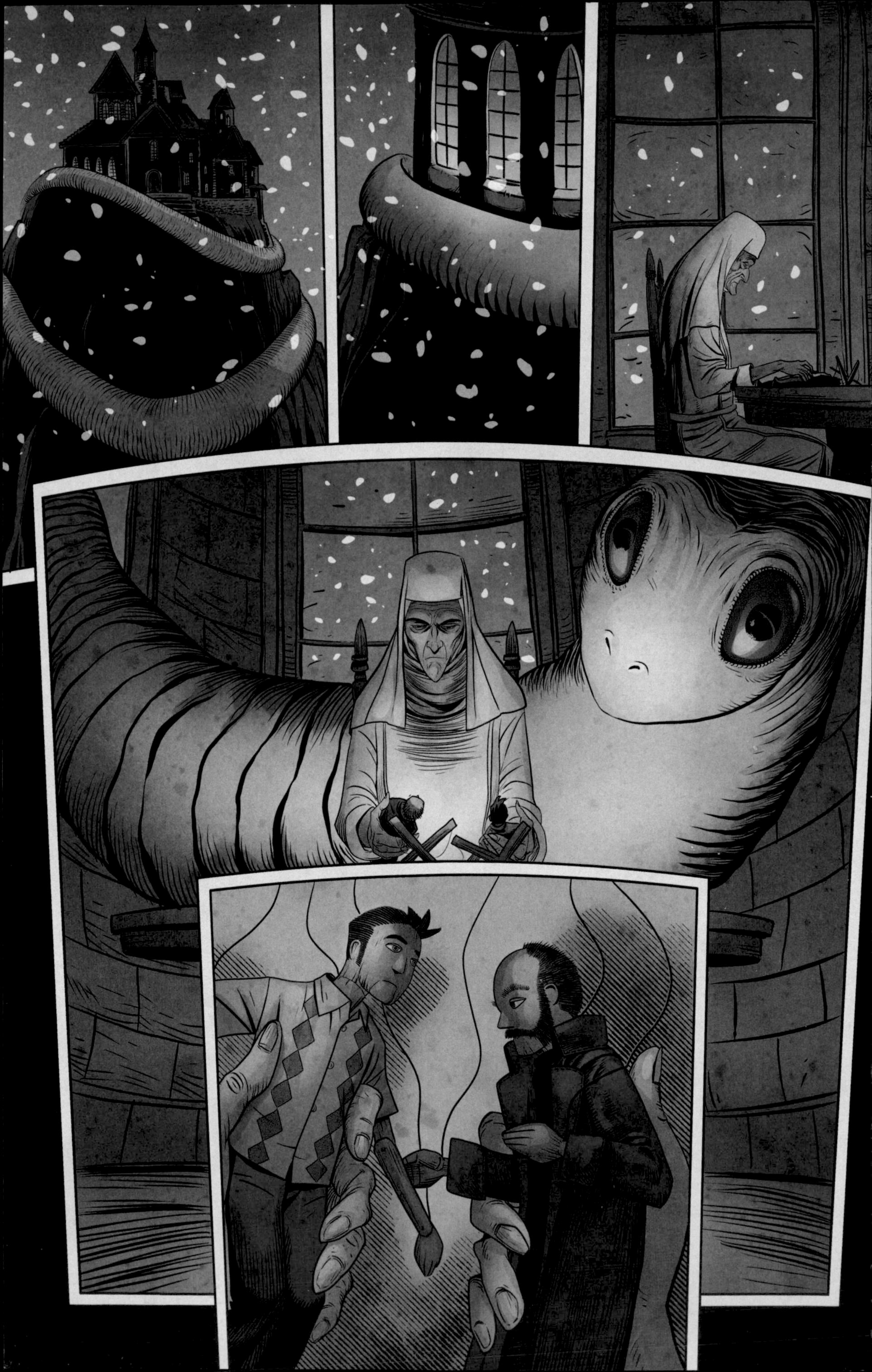

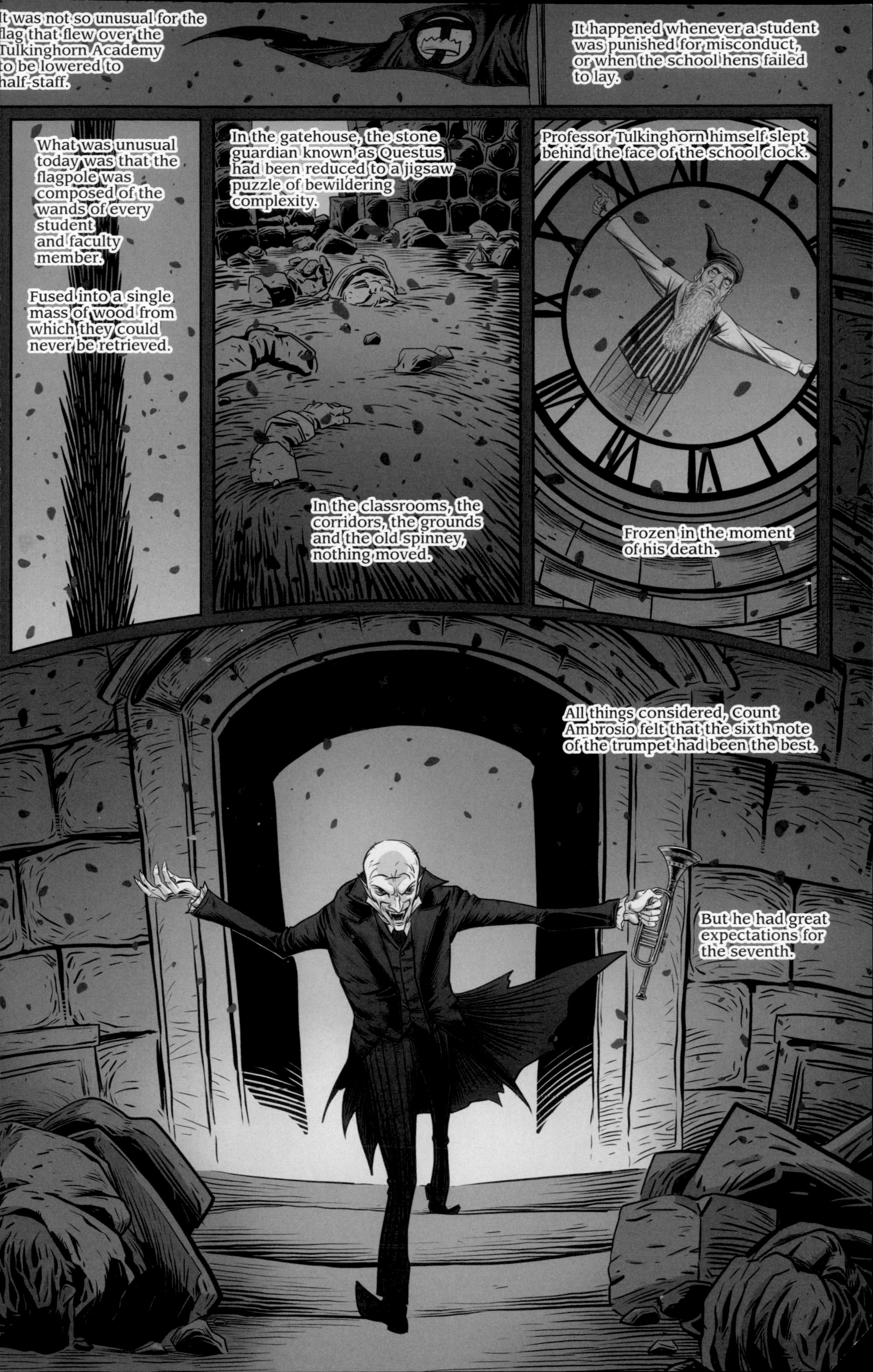
It was not so unusual for the flag that flew over the Tulkinghorn Academy to be lowered to half-staff.
It happened whenever a student was punished for misconduct, or when the school hens failed to lay.
What was unusual today was that the flagpole was composed of the wands of every student and faculty member.
Fused into a single mass of wood from which they could never be retrieved.
In the gatehouse, the stone guardian known as Questus had been reduced to a jigsaw puzzle of bewildering complexity.
In the classrooms, the corridors, the grounds and the old spinney, nothing moved.
Professor Tulkinghorn himself slept behind the face of the school clock.
Frozen in the moment of his death.
All things considered, Count Ambrosio felt that the sixth note of the trumpet had been the best.
But he had great expectations for the seventh.

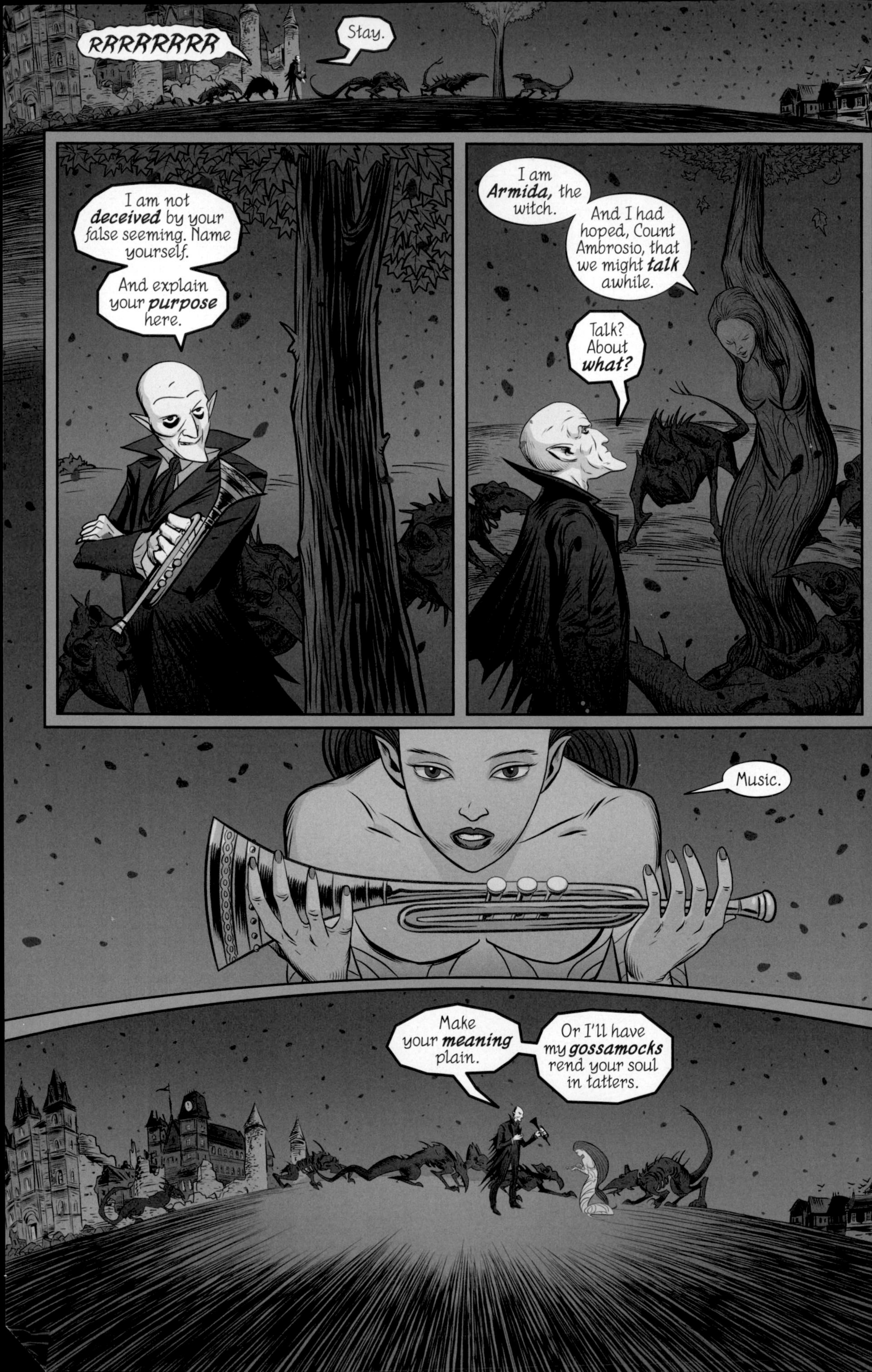
RRRRRRRR
Stay.
I am not deceived by your false seeming. Name yourself.
And explain your purpose here.
I am Armida, the witch.
And I had hoped, Count Ambrosio, that we might talk awhile.
Talk? About what?
Music.
Make your meaning plain.
Or I'll have my gossamocks rend your soul in tatters.

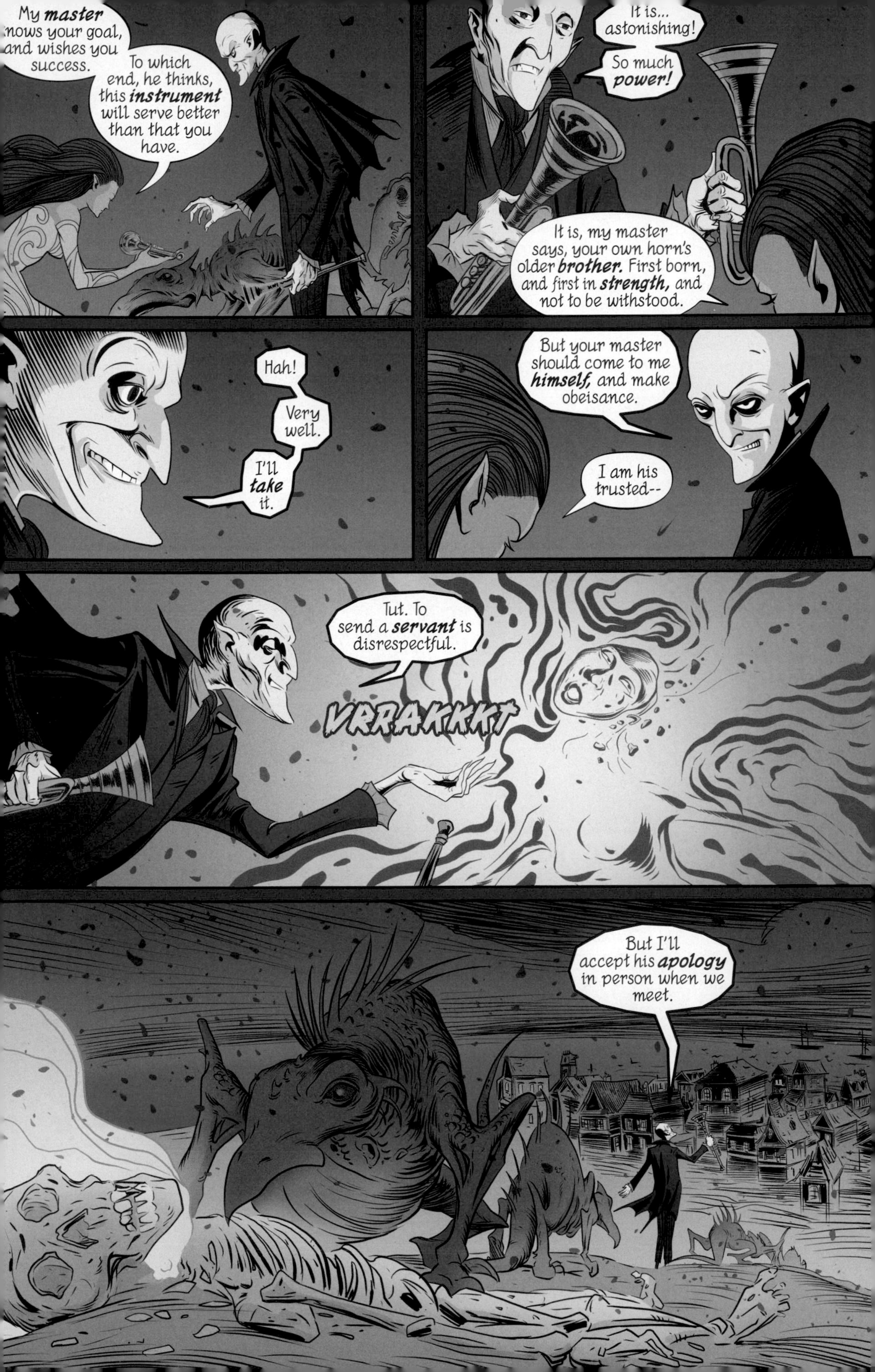
My master nows your goal, and wishes you success.
To which end, he thinks, this instrument will serve better than that you have.
It is... astonishing!
So much power!
It is, my master says, your own horn's older brother. First born, and first in strength, and not to be withstood.
Hah!
Very well.
I'll take it.
But your master should come to me himself, and make obeisance.
I am his trusted--
Tut. To send a servant is disrespectful.
VRRAKKKT
But I'll accept his apology in person when we meet.

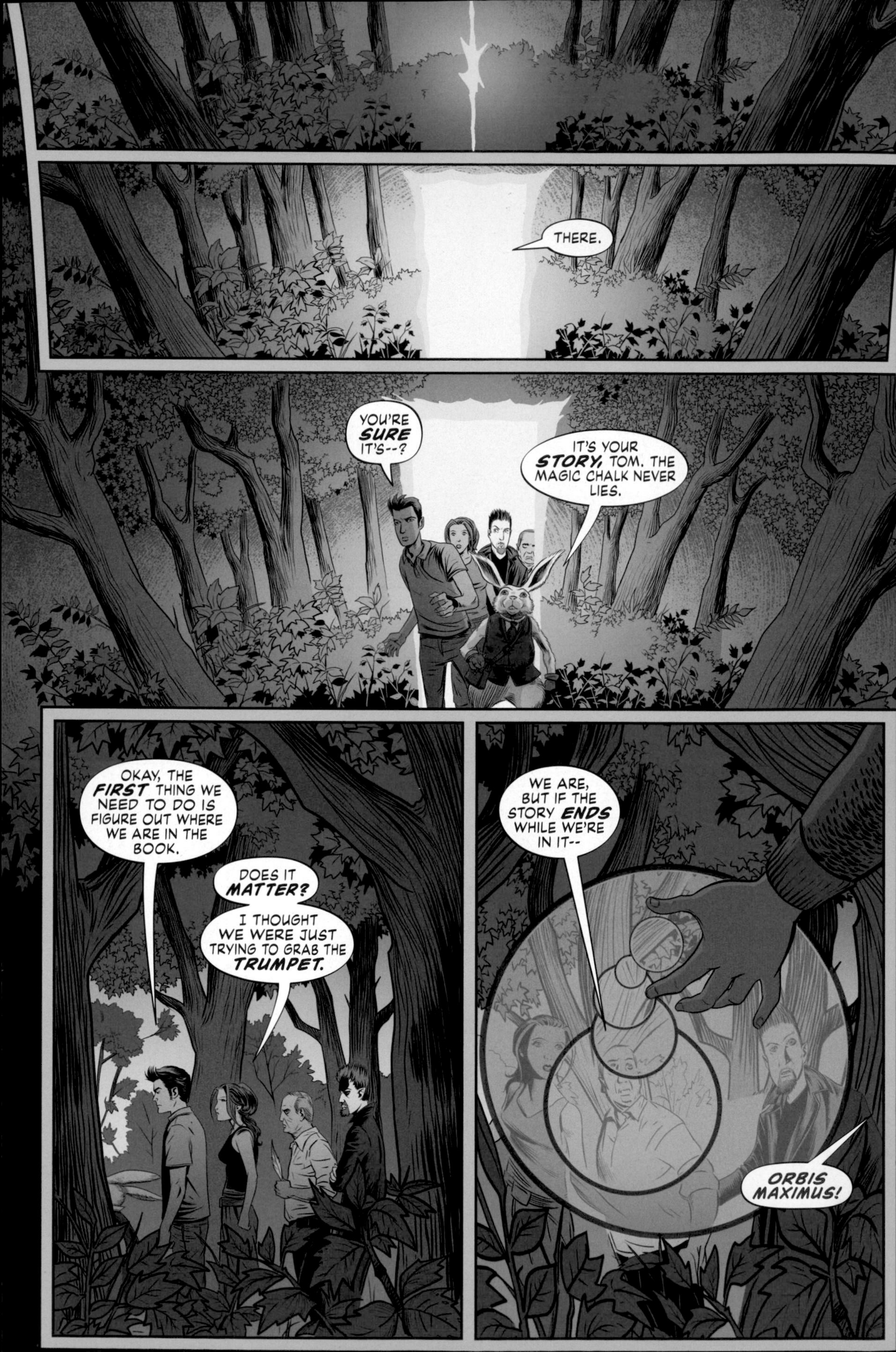
THERE.
YOU'RE SURE IT'S--?
IT'S YOUR STORY, TOM. THE MAGIC CHALK NEVER LIES.
OKAY, THE FIRST THING WE NEED TO DO IS FIGURE OUT WHERE WE ARE IN THE BOOK.
DOES IT MATTER?
I THOUGHT WE WERE JUST TRYING TO GRAB THE TRUMPET.
WE ARE, BUT IF THE STORY ENDS WHILE WE'RE IN IT--
ORBIS MAXIMUS!

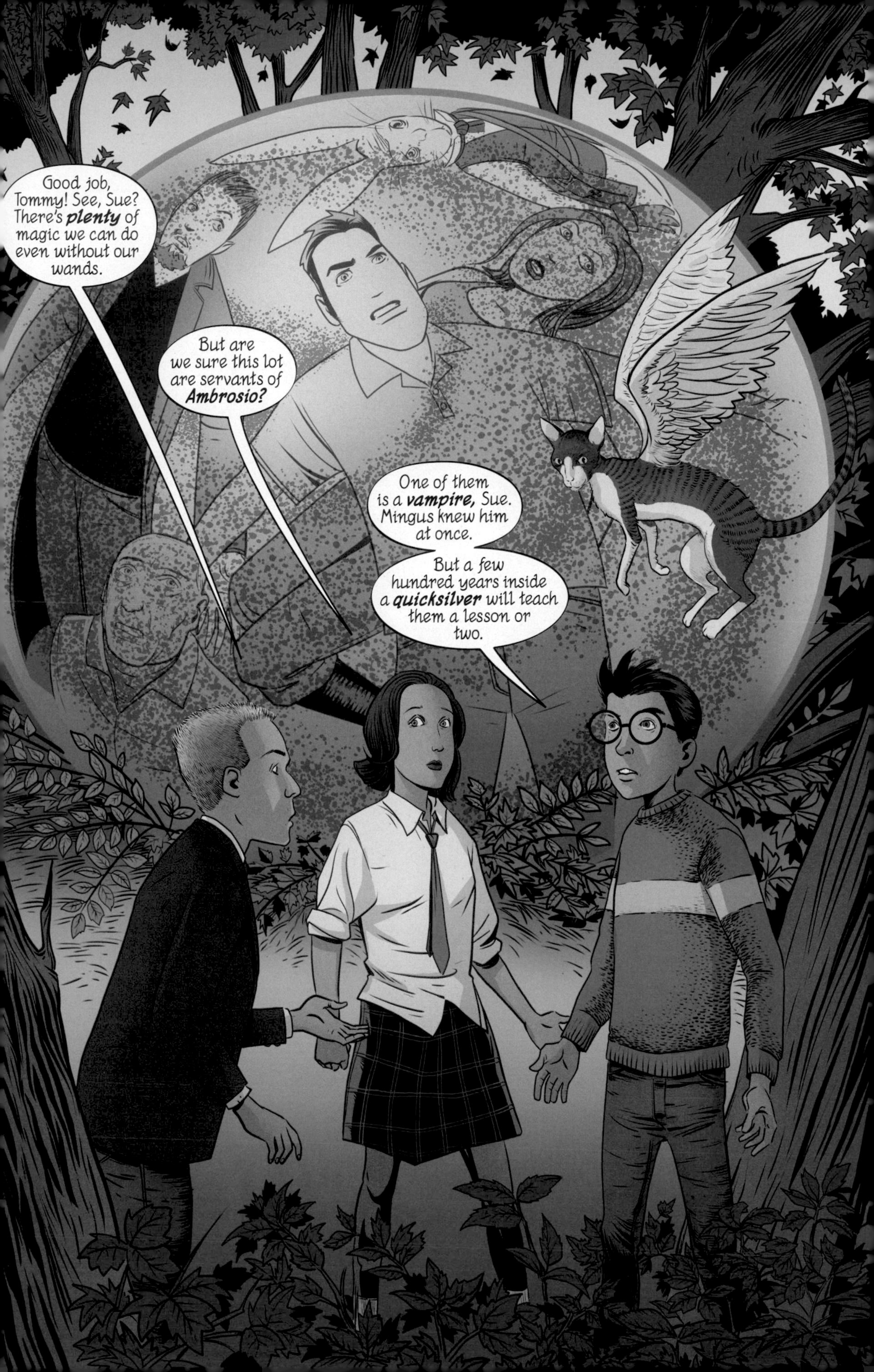
Good job, Tommy! See, Sue? There's **plenty** of magic we can do even without our wands.
But are we sure this lot are servants of **Ambrosio?**
One of them is a **vampire,** Sue. Mingus knew him at once.
But a few hundred years inside a **quicksilver** will teach them a lesson or two.

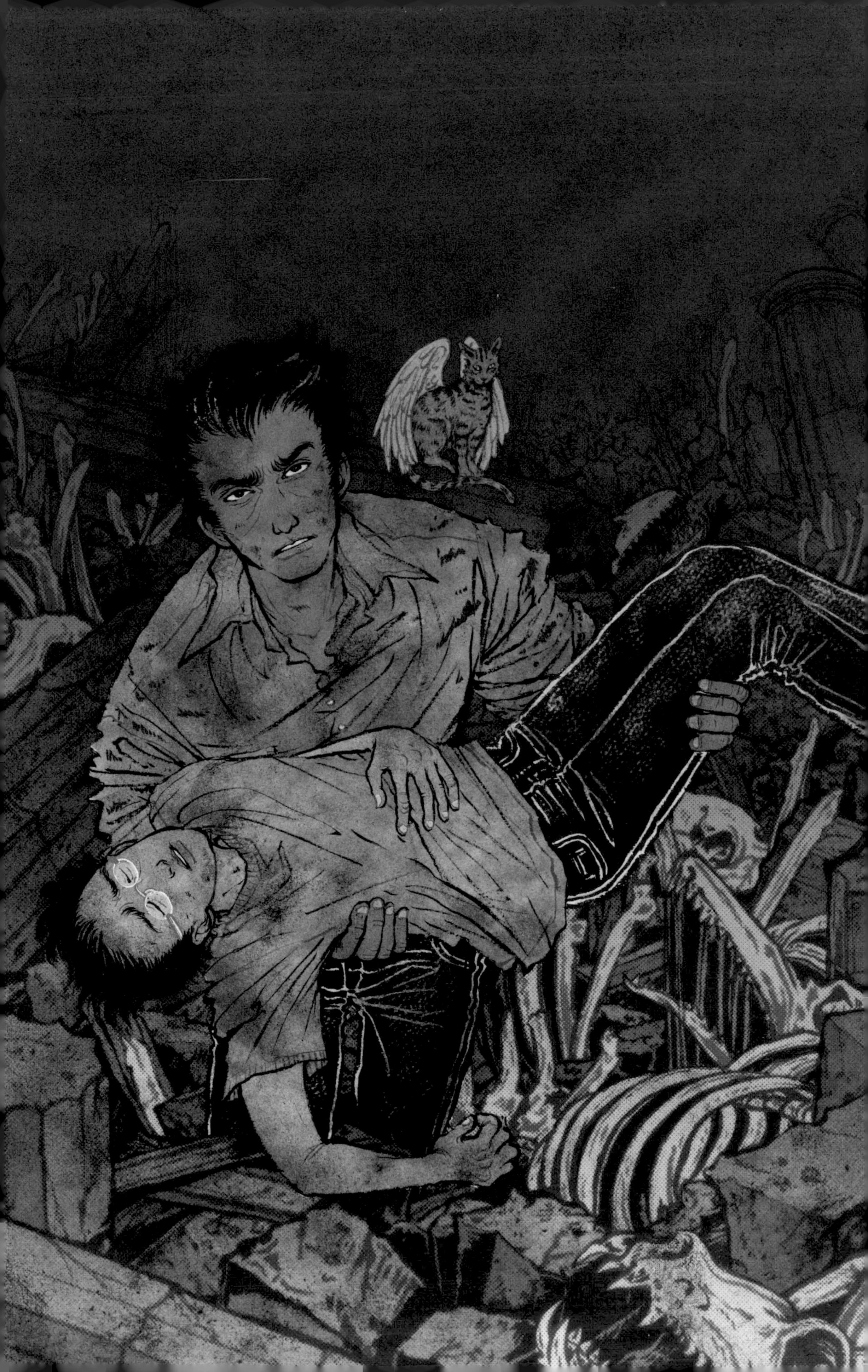

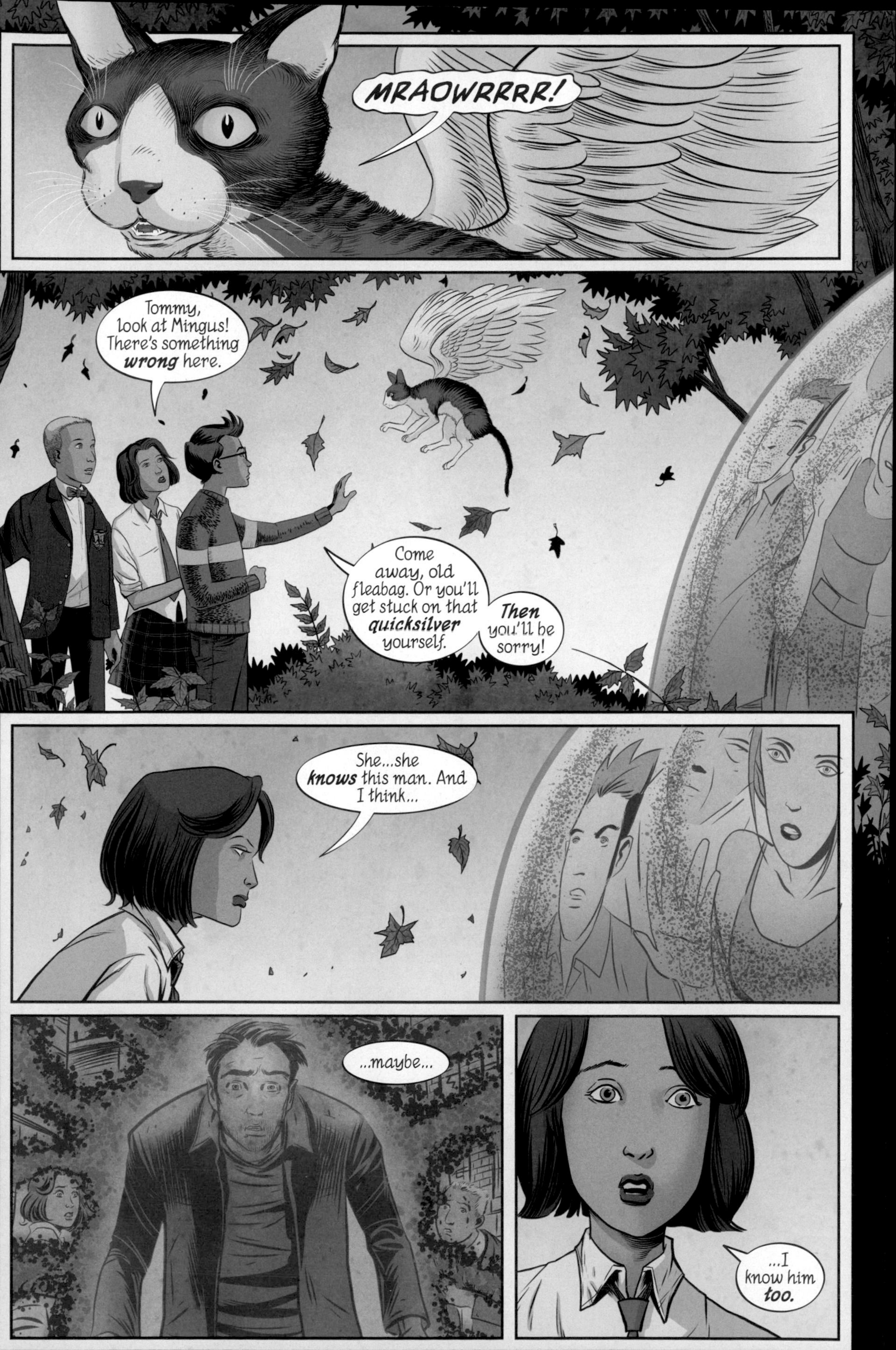
MRAOWRRRR!
Tommy, look at Mingus! There's something **wrong** here.
Come away, old fleabag. Or you'll get stuck on that **quicksilver** yourself.
Then you'll be sorry!
She...she **knows** this man. And I think...
...maybe...
...I know him **too.**

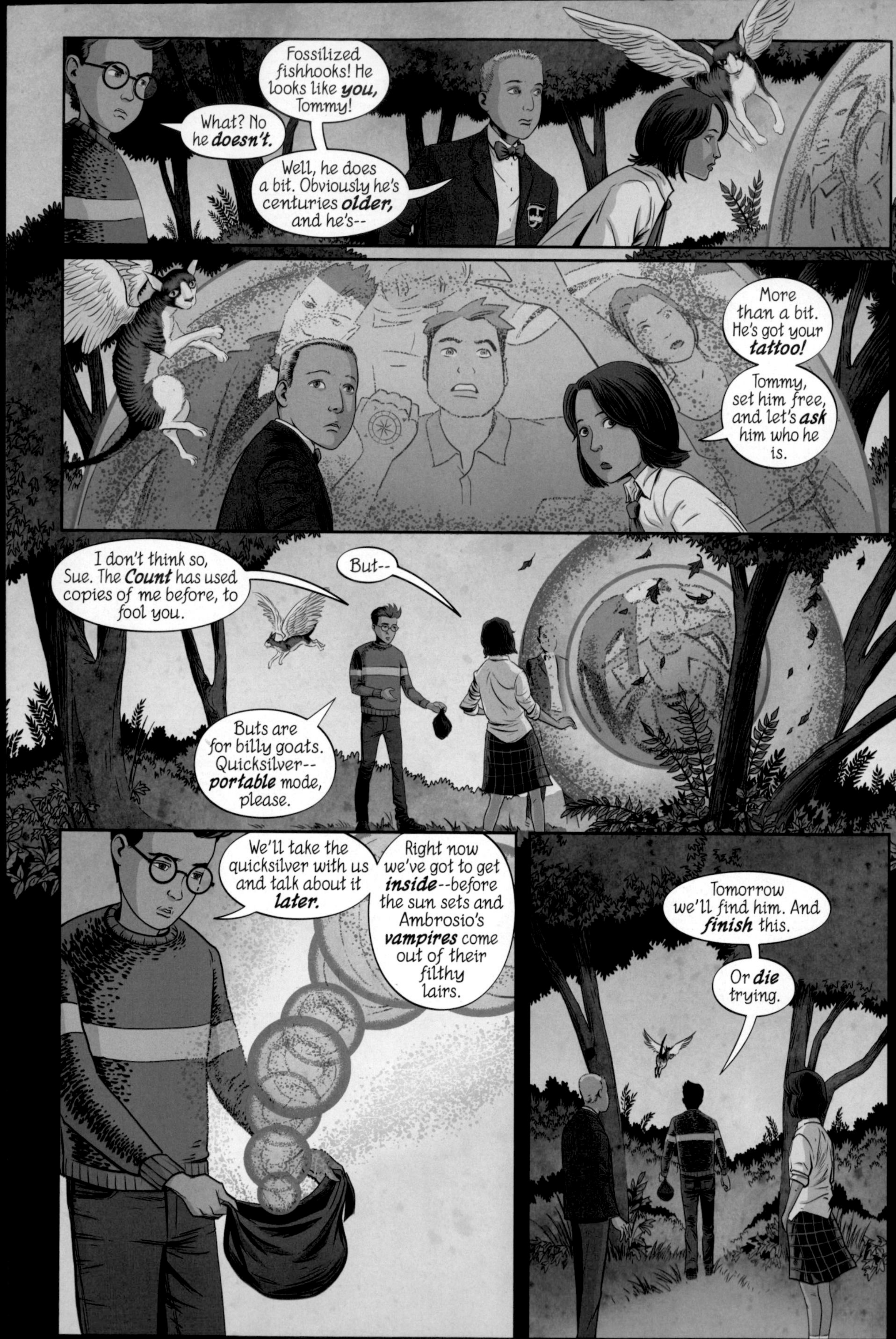
Fossilized fishhooks! He looks like **you,** Tommy!
What? No he **doesn't.**
Well, he does a bit. Obviously he's centuries **older,** and he's--
More than a bit. He's got your **tattoo!**
Tommy, set him free, and let's **ask** him who he is.
I don't think so, Sue. The **Count** has used copies of me before, to fool you.
But--
Buts are for billy goats. Quicksilver-- **portable** mode, please.
We'll take the quicksilver with us and talk about it **later.**
Right now we've got to get **inside**--before the sun sets and Ambrosio's **vampires** come out of their filthy lairs.
Tomorrow we'll find him. And **finish** this.
Or **die** trying.

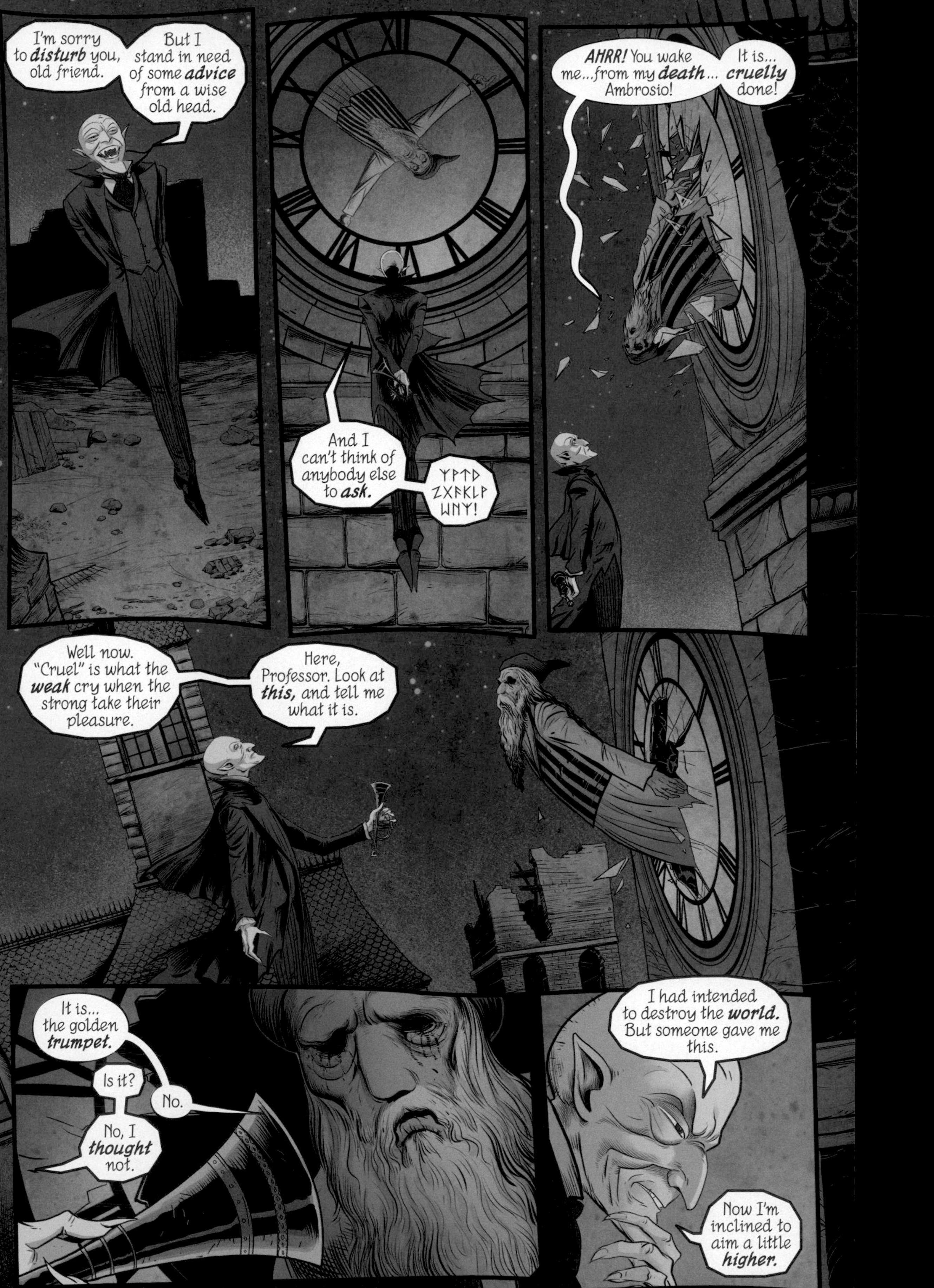
I'm sorry to **disturb** you, old friend.
But I stand in need of some **advice** from a wise old head.
And I can't think of anybody else to **ask.**
AHRR! You wake me...from my **death**... Ambrosio!
It is... **cruelly** done!
Well now. "Cruel" is what the **weak** cry when the strong take their pleasure.
Here, Professor. Look at **this,** and tell me what it is.
It is... the golden **trumpet.**
Is it?
No.
No, I **thought** not.
I had intended to destroy the **world.** But someone gave me this.
Now I'm inclined to aim a little **higher.**

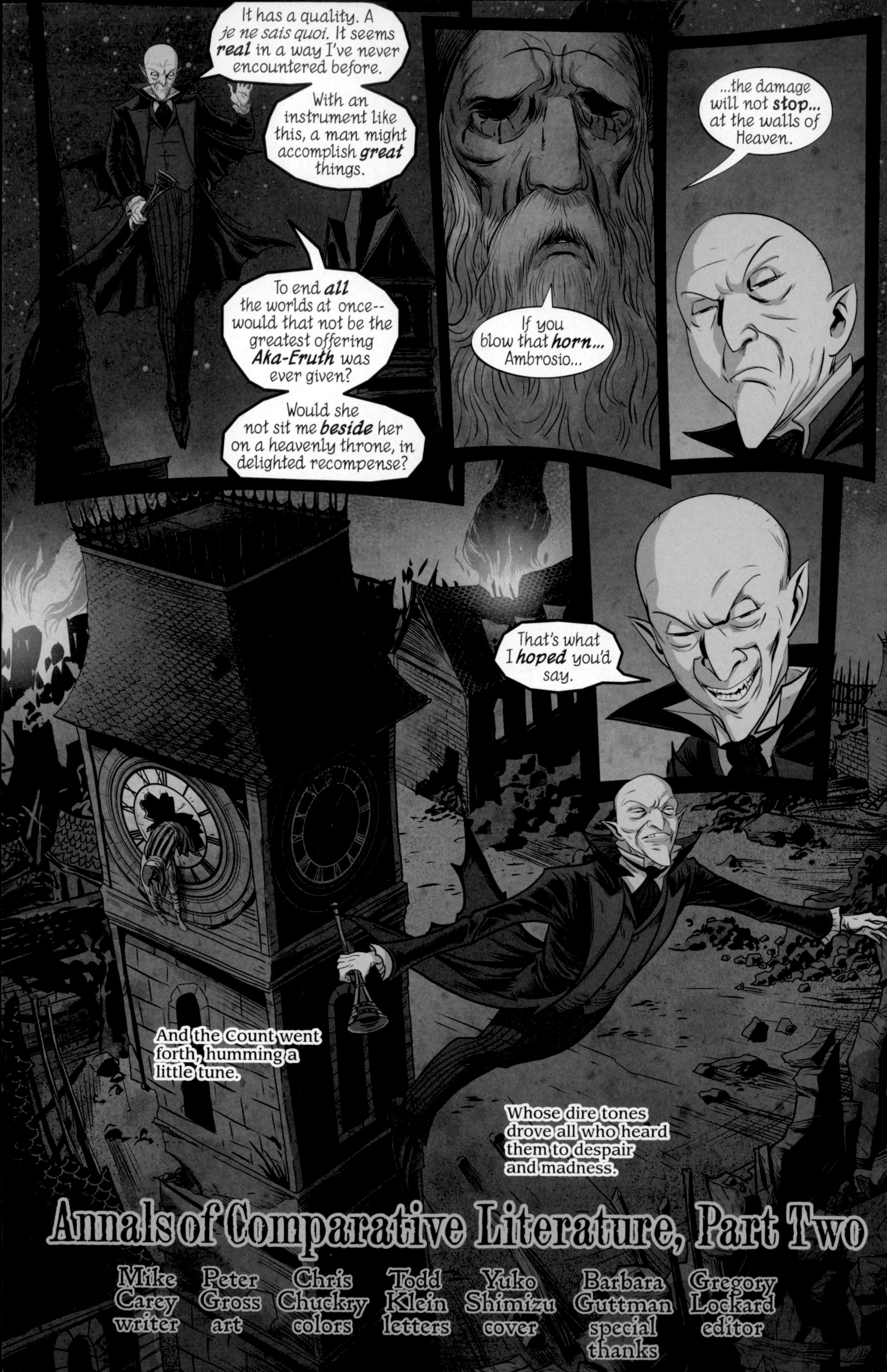

It has a quality. A *je ne sais quoi*. It seems **real** in a way I've never encountered before.
With an instrument like this, a man might accomplish **great** things.
To end **all** the worlds at once-- would that not be the greatest offering **Aka-Eruth** was ever given?
Would she not sit me **beside** her on a heavenly throne, in delighted recompense?
If you blow that **horn...** Ambrosio...
...the damage will not **stop...** at the walls of Heaven.
That's what I **hoped** you'd say.
And the Count went forth, humming a little tune.
Whose dire tones drove all who heard them to despair and madness.
Annals of Comparative Literature, Part Two
Mike Carey writer
Peter Gross art
Chris Chuckry colors
Todd Klein letters
Yuko Shimizu cover
Barbara Guttman special thanks
Gregory Lockard editor

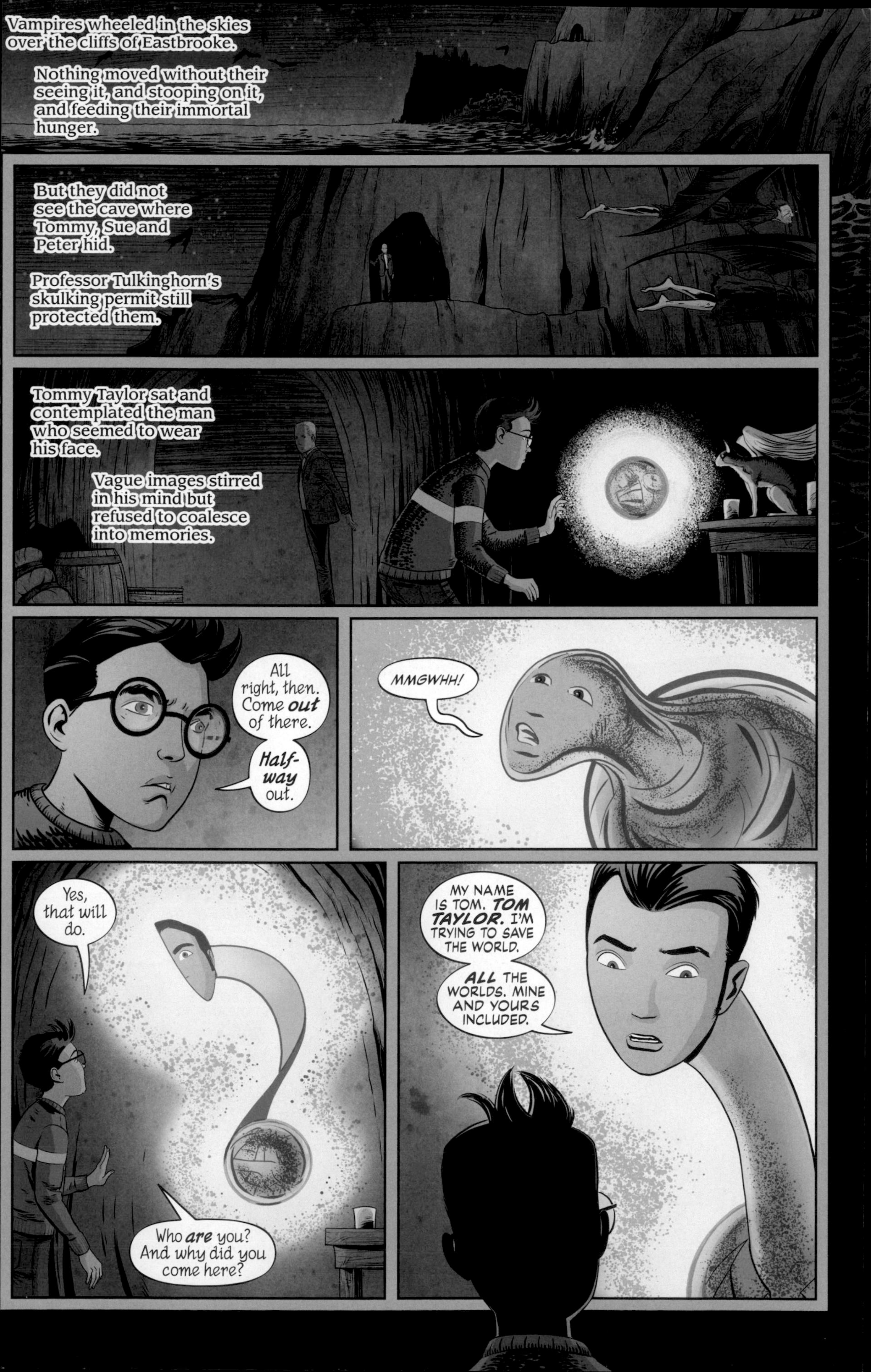

Vampires wheeled in the skies over the cliffs of Eastbrooke.
Nothing moved without their seeing it, and stooping on it, and feeding their immortal hunger.
But they did not see the cave where Tommy, Sue and Peter hid.
Professor Tulkinghorn's skulking permit still protected them.
Tommy Taylor sat and contemplated the man who seemed to wear his face.
Vague images stirred in his mind but refused to coalesce into memories.
All right, then. Come out of there.
Half-way out.
MMGWHH!
Yes, that will do.
Who are you? And why did you come here?
MY NAME IS TOM. TOM TAYLOR. I'M TRYING TO SAVE THE WORLD.
ALL THE WORLDS. MINE AND YOURS INCLUDED.

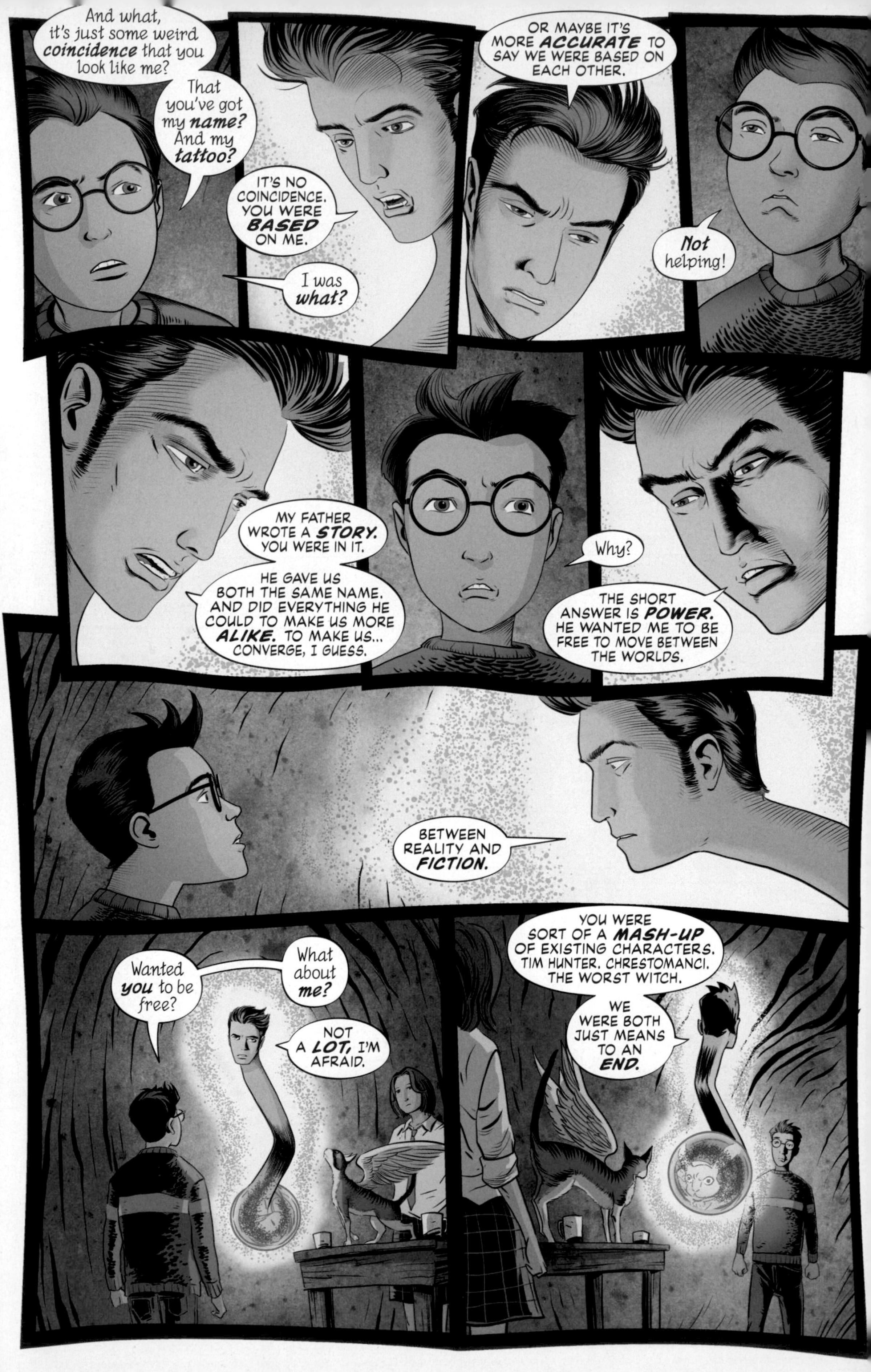

And what, it's just some weird coincidence that you look like me?
That you've got my name? And my tattoo?
IT'S NO COINCIDENCE. YOU WERE BASED ON ME.
I was what?
OR MAYBE IT'S MORE ACCURATE TO SAY WE WERE BASED ON EACH OTHER.
Not helping!
MY FATHER WROTE A STORY. YOU WERE IN IT.
HE GAVE US BOTH THE SAME NAME. AND DID EVERYTHING HE COULD TO MAKE US MORE ALIKE. TO MAKE US... CONVERGE, I GUESS.
Why?
THE SHORT ANSWER IS POWER. HE WANTED ME TO BE FREE TO MOVE BETWEEN THE WORLDS.
BETWEEN REALITY AND FICTION.
Wanted you to be free?
What about me?
NOT A LOT, I'M AFRAID.
YOU WERE SORT OF A MASH-UP OF EXISTING CHARACTERS. TIM HUNTER. CHRESTOMANCI. THE WORST WITCH.
WE WERE BOTH JUST MEANS TO AN END.

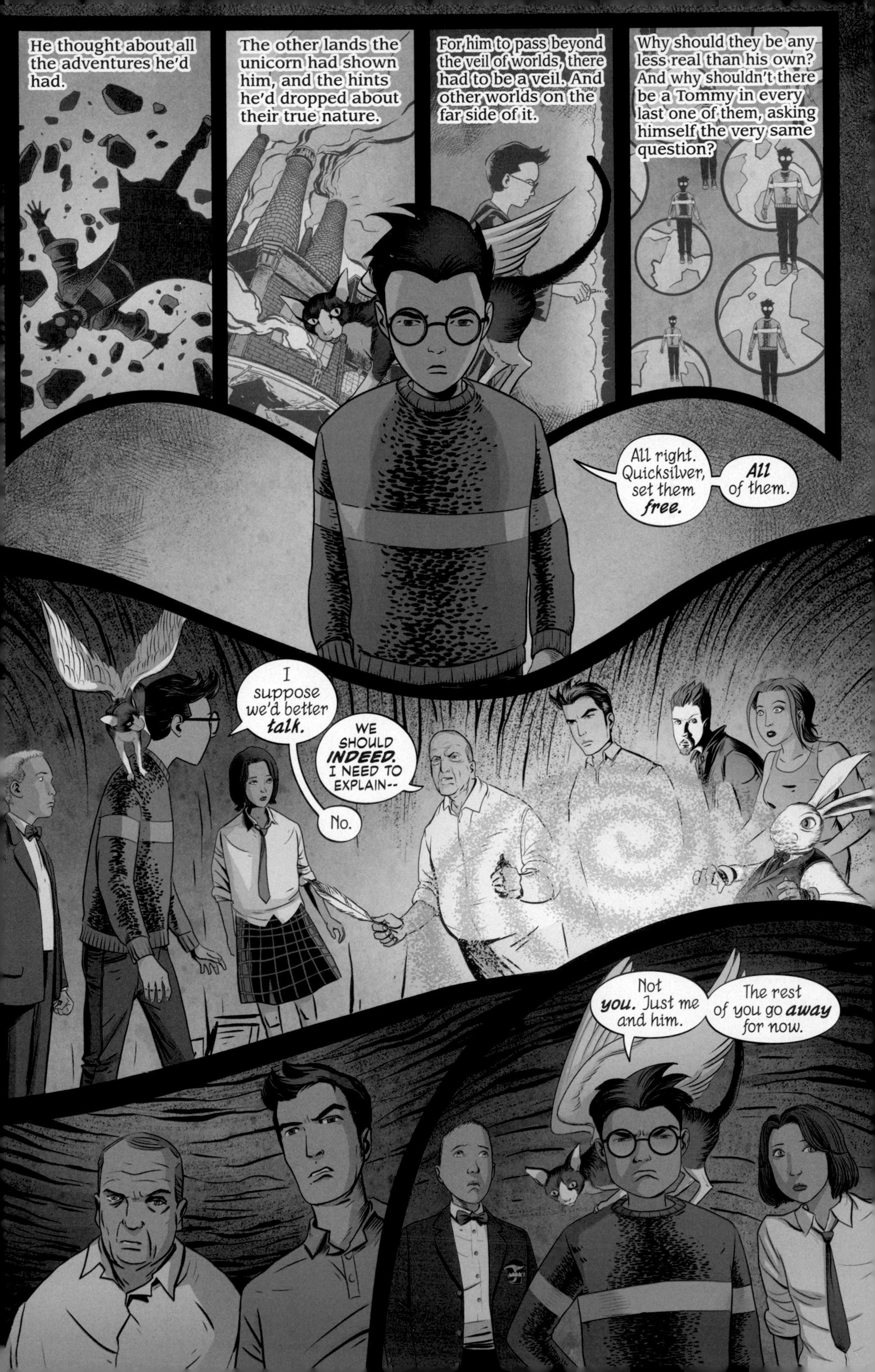
He thought about all the adventures he'd had.
The other lands the unicorn had shown him, and the hints he'd dropped about their true nature.
For him to pass beyond the veil of worlds, there had to be a veil. And other worlds on the far side of it.
Why should they be any less real than his own? And why shouldn't there be a Tommy in every last one of them, asking himself the very same question?
All right. Quicksilver, set them free.
All of them.
I suppose we'd better talk.
WE SHOULD INDEED. I NEED TO EXPLAIN--
No.
Not you. Just me and him.
The rest of you go away for now.

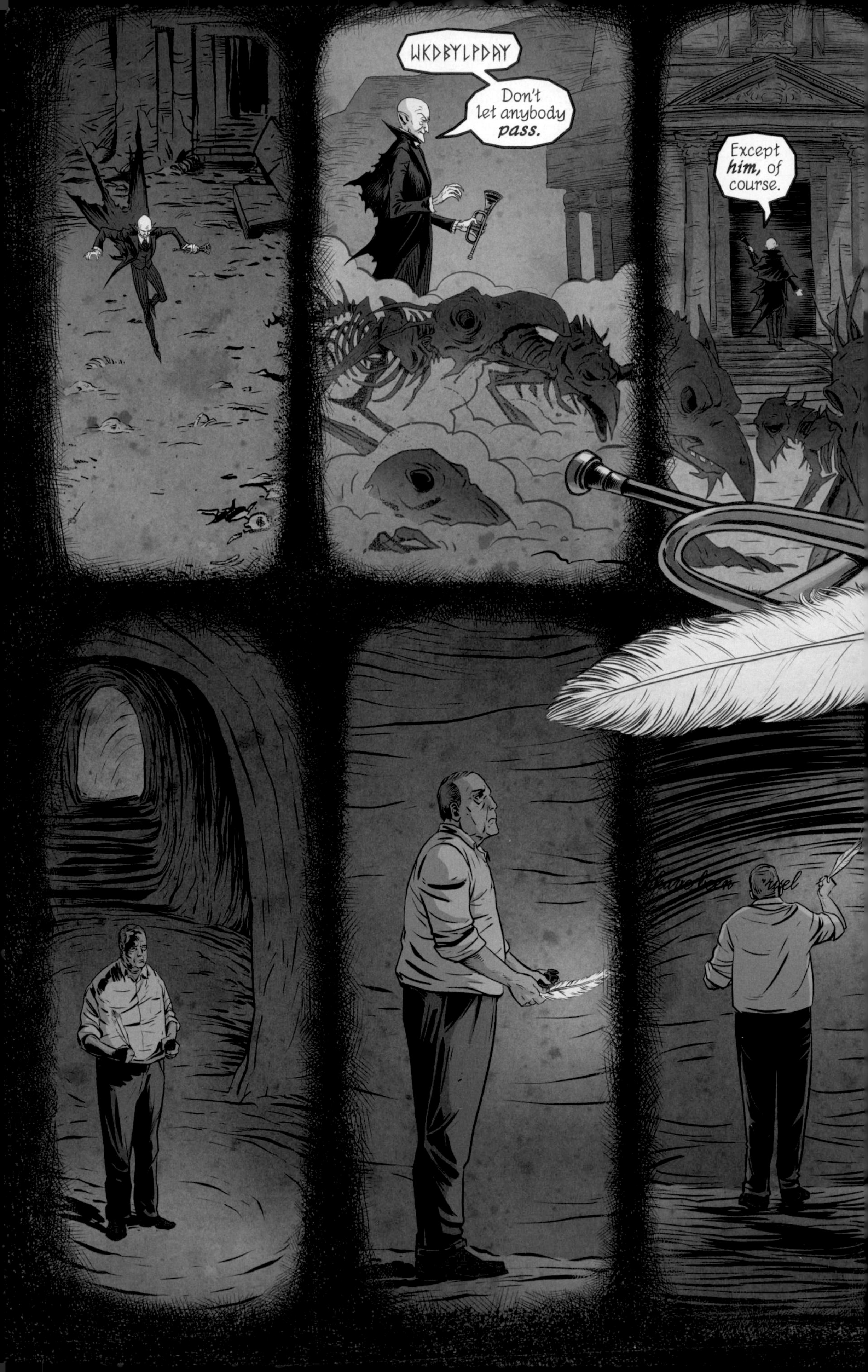
WKDBYLPDAY
Don't let anybody **pass.**
Except **him,** of course.

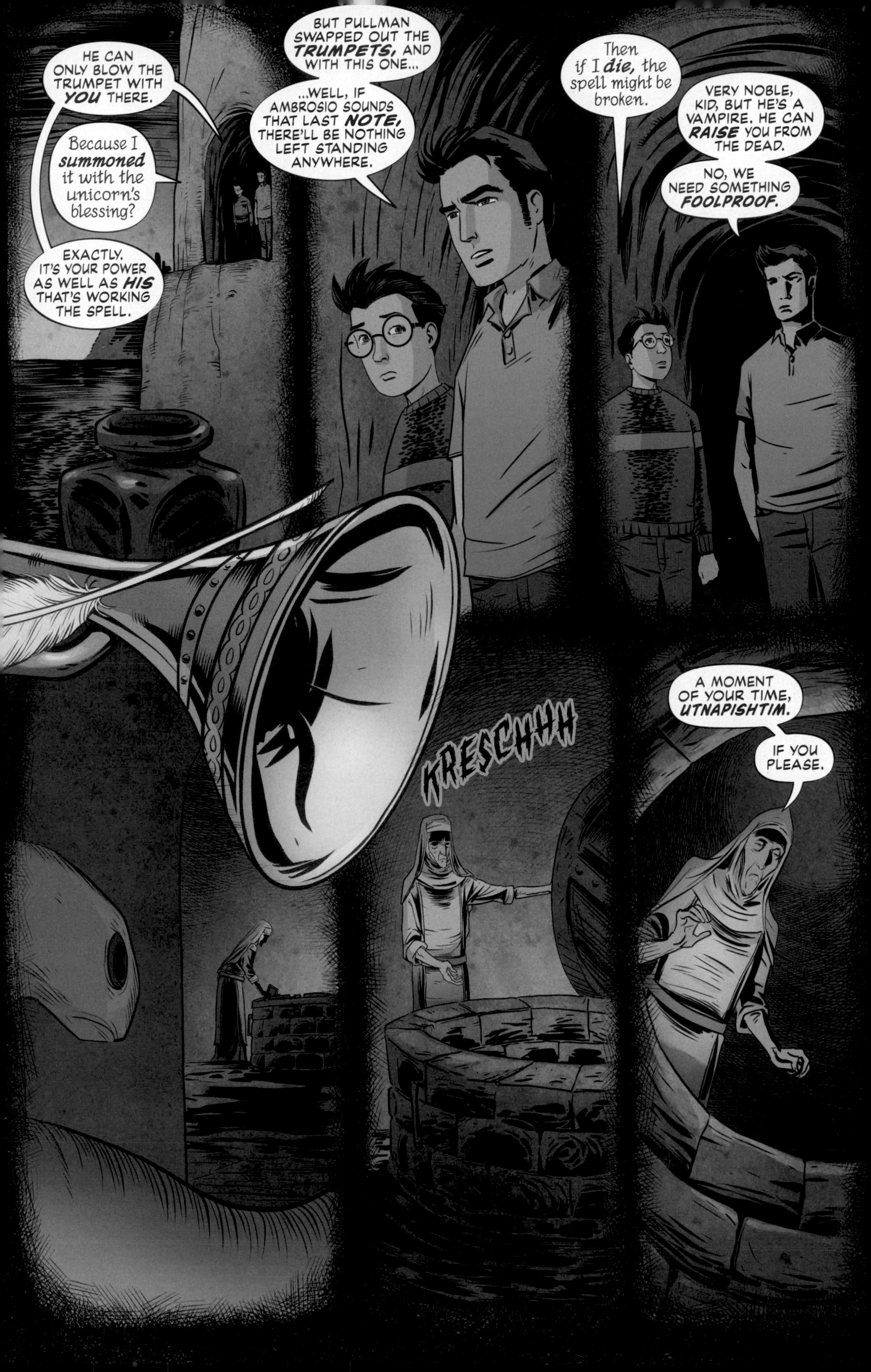
HE CAN ONLY BLOW THE TRUMPET WITH YOU THERE.
Because I summoned it with the unicorn's blessing?
EXACTLY. IT'S YOUR POWER AS WELL AS HIS THAT'S WORKING THE SPELL.
BUT PULLMAN SWAPPED OUT THE TRUMPETS, AND WITH THIS ONE...
...WELL, IF AMBROSIO SOUNDS THAT LAST NOTE, THERE'LL BE NOTHING LEFT STANDING ANYWHERE.
Then if I die, the spell might be broken.
VERY NOBLE, KID, BUT HE'S A VAMPIRE. HE CAN RAISE YOU FROM THE DEAD.
NO, WE NEED SOMETHING FOOLPROOF.
KRESCHHH
A MOMENT OF YOUR TIME, UTNAPISHTIM.
IF YOU PLEASE.

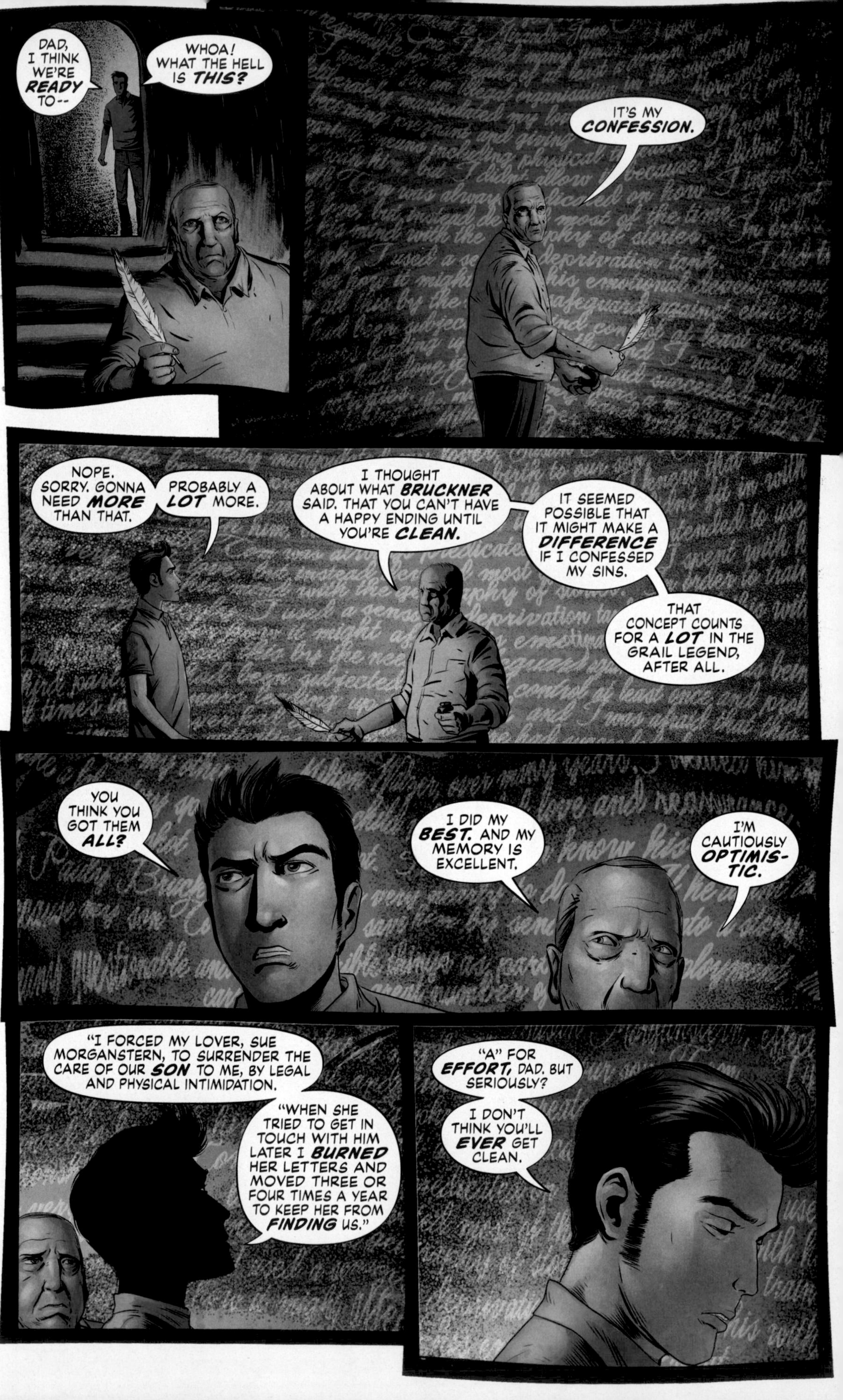
DAD, I THINK WE'RE READY TO--
WHOA! WHAT THE HELL IS THIS?
IT'S MY CONFESSION.
NOPE. SORRY. GONNA NEED MORE THAN THAT.
PROBABLY A LOT MORE.
I THOUGHT ABOUT WHAT BRUCKNER SAID. THAT YOU CAN'T HAVE A HAPPY ENDING UNTIL YOU'RE CLEAN.
IT SEEMED POSSIBLE THAT IT MIGHT MAKE A DIFFERENCE IF I CONFESSED MY SINS.
THAT CONCEPT COUNTS FOR A LOT IN THE GRAIL LEGEND, AFTER ALL.
YOU THINK YOU GOT THEM ALL?
I DID MY BEST. AND MY MEMORY IS EXCELLENT.
I'M CAUTIOUSLY OPTIMISTIC.
"I FORCED MY LOVER, SUE MORGANSTERN, TO SURRENDER THE CARE OF OUR SON TO ME, BY LEGAL AND PHYSICAL INTIMIDATION.
"WHEN SHE TRIED TO GET IN TOUCH WITH HIM LATER I BURNED HER LETTERS AND MOVED THREE OR FOUR TIMES A YEAR TO KEEP HER FROM FINDING US."
"A" FOR EFFORT, DAD. BUT SERIOUSLY?
I DON'T THINK YOU'LL EVER GET CLEAN.

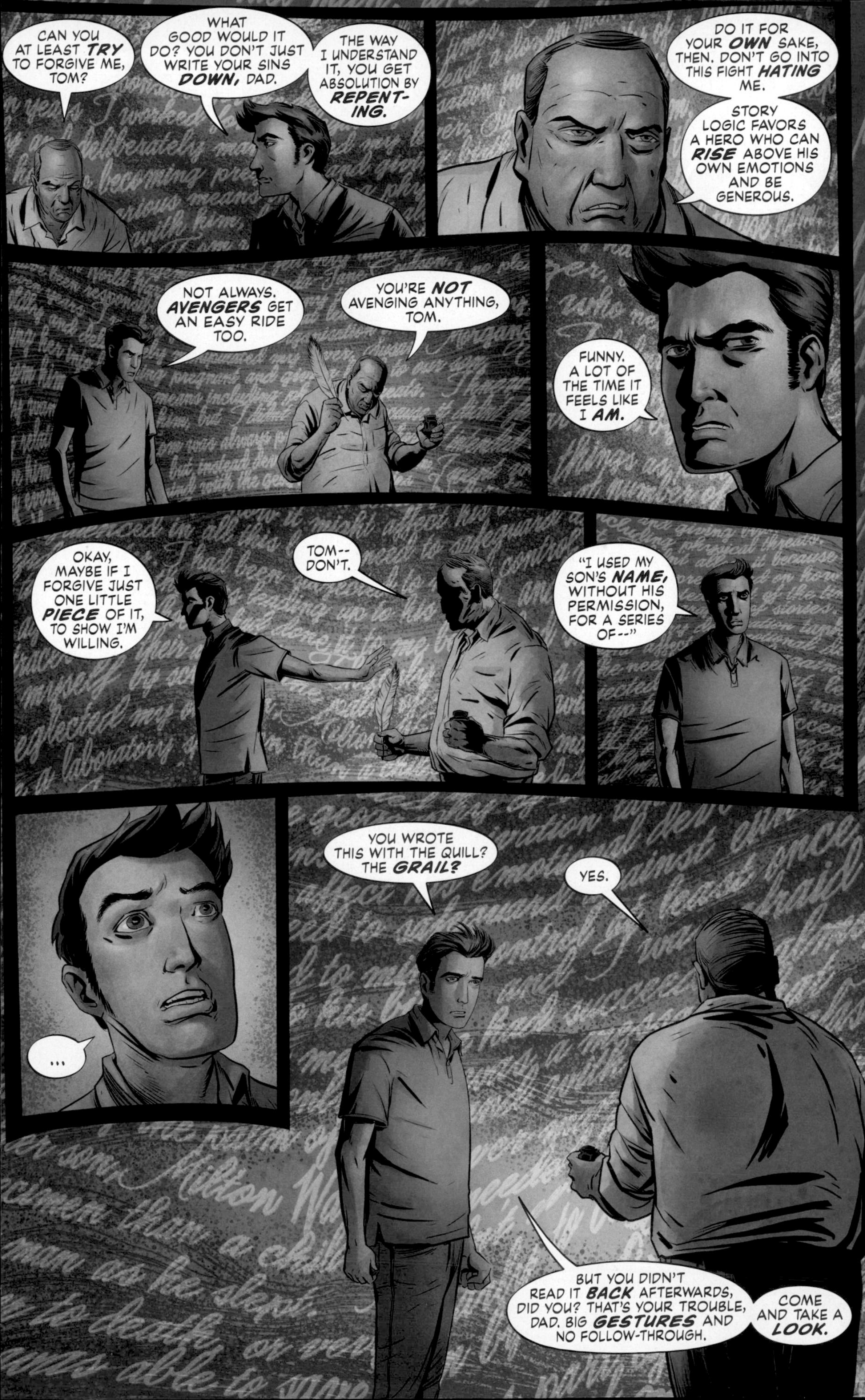
CAN YOU AT LEAST TRY TO FORGIVE ME, TOM?
WHAT GOOD WOULD IT DO? YOU DON'T JUST WRITE YOUR SINS DOWN, DAD.
THE WAY I UNDERSTAND IT, YOU GET ABSOLUTION BY REPENT-ING.
DO IT FOR YOUR OWN SAKE, THEN. DON'T GO INTO THIS FIGHT HATING ME.
STORY LOGIC FAVORS A HERO WHO CAN RISE ABOVE HIS OWN EMOTIONS AND BE GENEROUS.
NOT ALWAYS. AVENGERS GET AN EASY RIDE TOO.
YOU'RE NOT AVENGING ANYTHING, TOM.
FUNNY. A LOT OF THE TIME IT FEELS LIKE I AM.
OKAY, MAYBE IF I FORGIVE JUST ONE LITTLE PIECE OF IT, TO SHOW I'M WILLING.
TOM-- DON'T.
"I USED MY SON'S NAME, WITHOUT HIS PERMISSION, FOR A SERIES OF--"
...
YOU WROTE THIS WITH THE QUILL? THE GRAIL?
YES.
BUT YOU DIDN'T READ IT BACK AFTERWARDS, DID YOU? THAT'S YOUR TROUBLE, DAD. BIG GESTURES AND NO FOLLOW-THROUGH.
COME AND TAKE A LOOK.

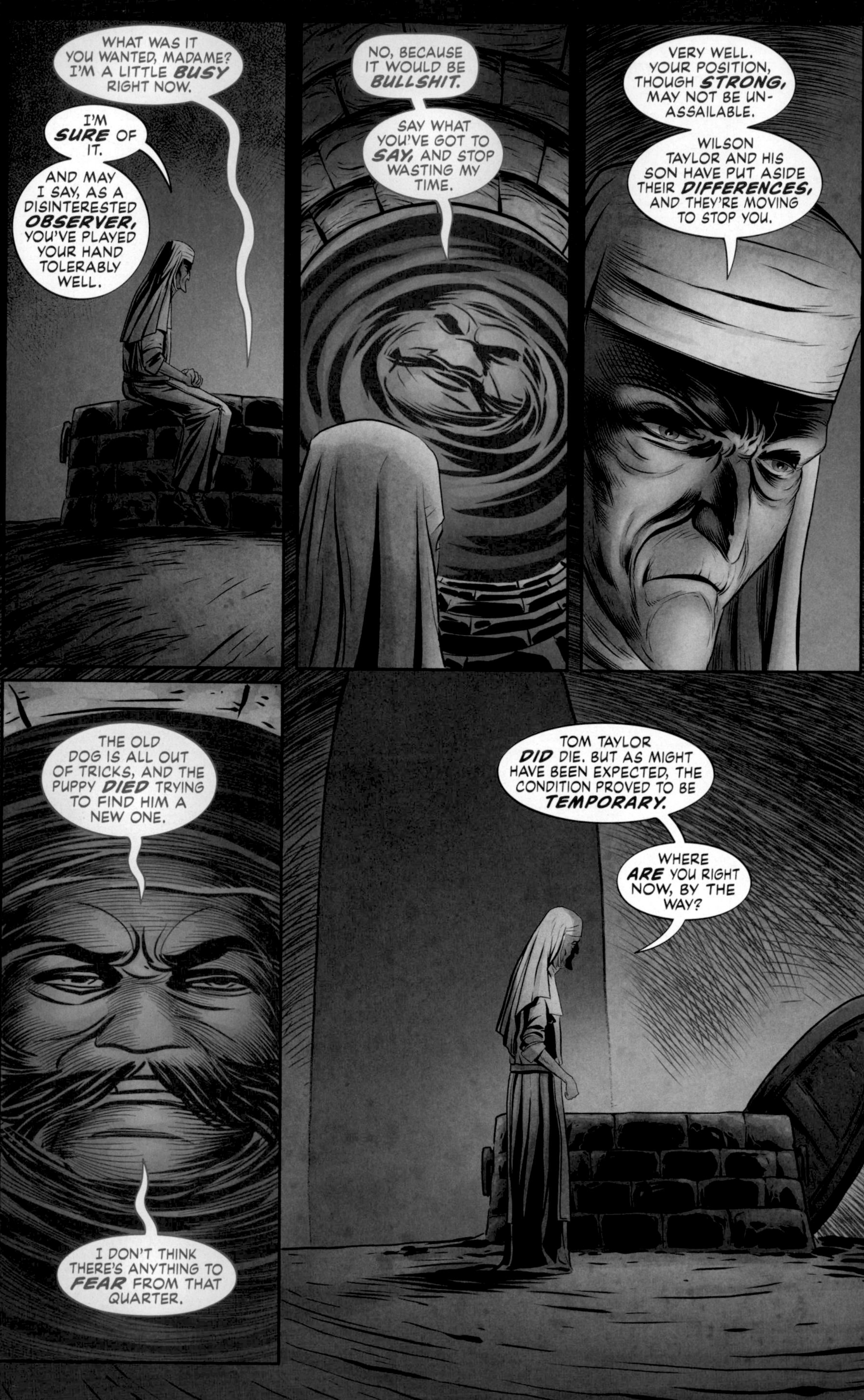
WHAT WAS IT YOU WANTED, MADAME? I'M A LITTLE BUSY RIGHT NOW.
I'M SURE OF IT.
AND MAY I SAY, AS A DISINTERESTED OBSERVER, YOU'VE PLAYED YOUR HAND TOLERABLY WELL.
NO, BECAUSE IT WOULD BE BULLSHIT.
SAY WHAT YOU'VE GOT TO SAY, AND STOP WASTING MY TIME.
VERY WELL. YOUR POSITION, THOUGH STRONG, MAY NOT BE UN-ASSAILABLE.
WILSON TAYLOR AND HIS SON HAVE PUT ASIDE THEIR DIFFERENCES, AND THEY'RE MOVING TO STOP YOU.
THE OLD DOG IS ALL OUT OF TRICKS, AND THE PUPPY DIED TRYING TO FIND HIM A NEW ONE.
I DON'T THINK THERE'S ANYTHING TO FEAR FROM THAT QUARTER.
TOM TAYLOR DID DIE. BUT AS MIGHT HAVE BEEN EXPECTED, THE CONDITION PROVED TO BE TEMPORARY.
WHERE ARE YOU RIGHT NOW, BY THE WAY?

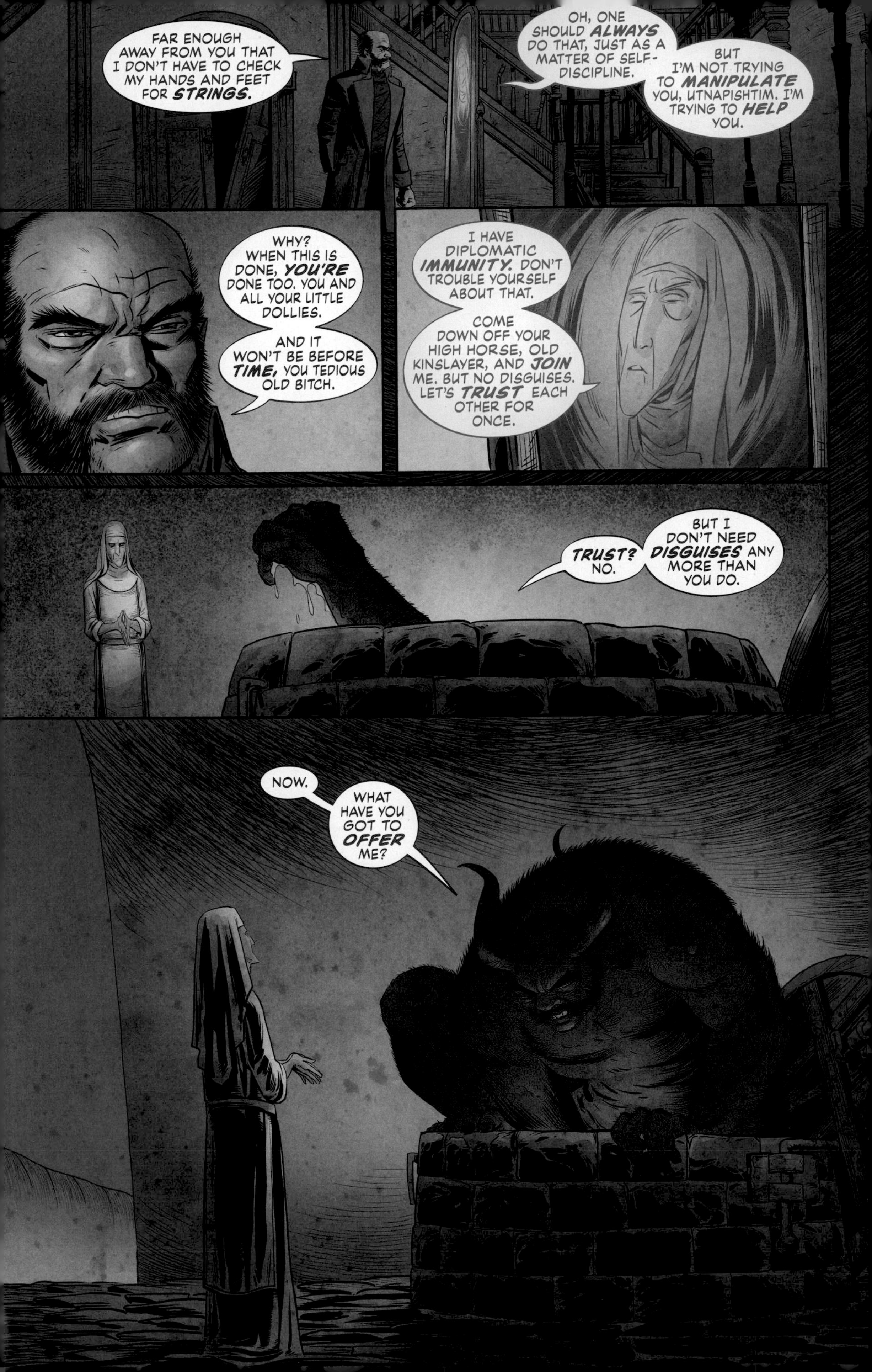
FAR ENOUGH AWAY FROM YOU THAT I DON'T HAVE TO CHECK MY HANDS AND FEET FOR STRINGS.
OH, ONE SHOULD ALWAYS DO THAT, JUST AS A MATTER OF SELF-DISCIPLINE.
BUT I'M NOT TRYING TO MANIPULATE YOU, UTNAPISHTIM. I'M TRYING TO HELP YOU.
WHY? WHEN THIS IS DONE, YOU'RE DONE TOO. YOU AND ALL YOUR LITTLE DOLLIES.
AND IT WON'T BE BEFORE TIME, YOU TEDIOUS OLD BITCH.
I HAVE DIPLOMATIC IMMUNITY. DON'T TROUBLE YOURSELF ABOUT THAT.
COME DOWN OFF YOUR HIGH HORSE, OLD KINSLAYER, AND JOIN ME. BUT NO DISGUISES. LET'S TRUST EACH OTHER FOR ONCE.
TRUST? NO.
BUT I DON'T NEED DISGUISES ANY MORE THAN YOU DO.
NOW.
WHAT HAVE YOU GOT TO OFFER ME?

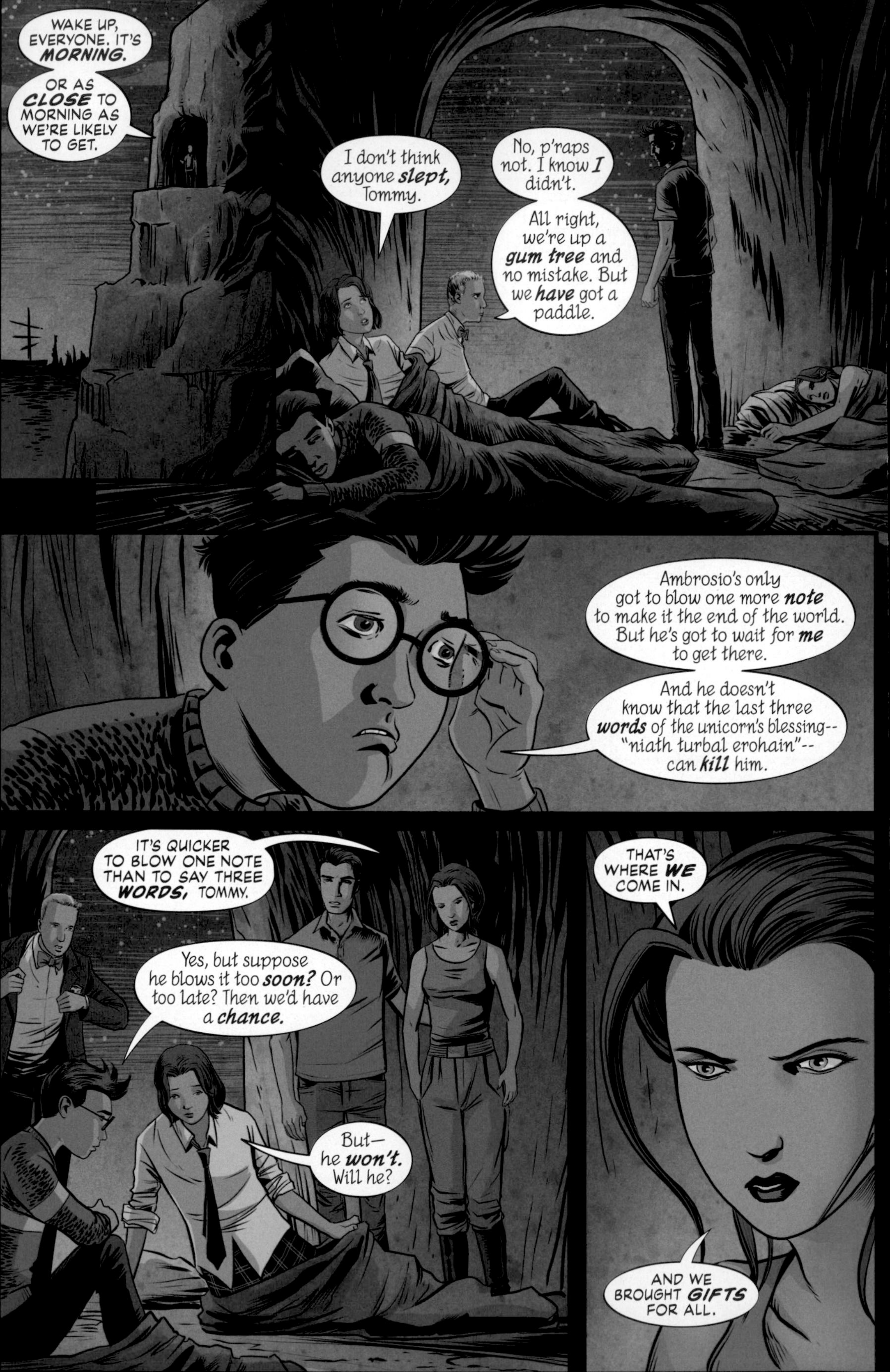
WAKE UP, EVERYONE. IT'S MORNING.
OR AS CLOSE TO MORNING AS WE'RE LIKELY TO GET.
I don't think anyone slept, Tommy.
No, p'raps not. I know I didn't.
All right, we're up a gum tree and no mistake. But we have got a paddle.
Ambrosio's only got to blow one more note to make it the end of the world. But he's got to wait for me to get there.
And he doesn't know that the last three words of the unicorn's blessing-- "niath turbal erohain"-- can kill him.
IT'S QUICKER TO BLOW ONE NOTE THAN TO SAY THREE WORDS, TOMMY.
Yes, but suppose he blows it too soon? Or too late? Then we'd have a chance.
But— he won't. Will he?
THAT'S WHERE WE COME IN.
AND WE BROUGHT GIFTS FOR ALL.

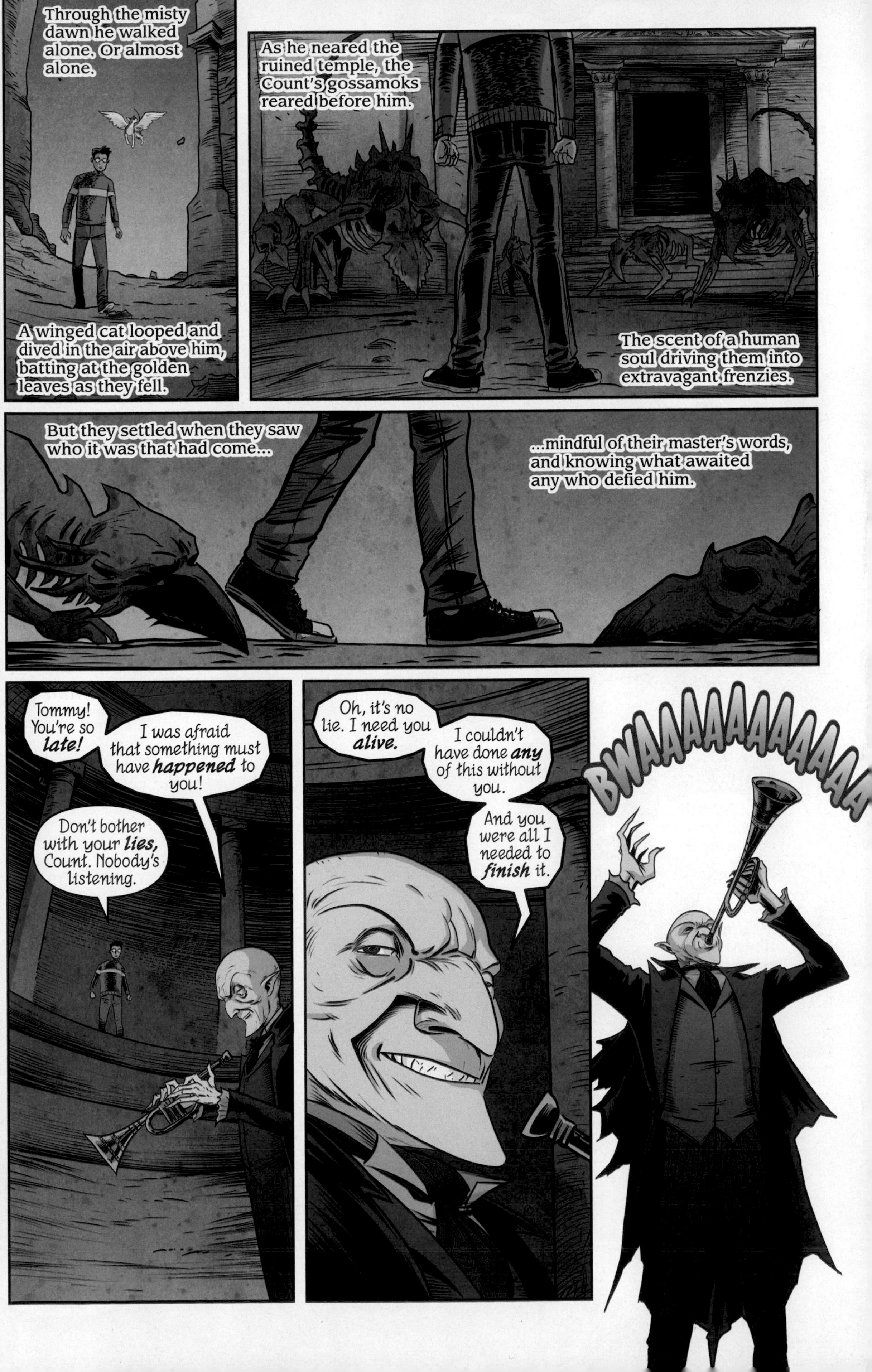

Through the misty dawn he walked alone. Or almost alone.
A winged cat looped and dived in the air above him, batting at the golden leaves as they fell.
As he neared the ruined temple, the Count's gossamoks reared before him.
The scent of a human soul driving them into extravagant frenzies.
But they settled when they saw who it was that had come...
...mindful of their master's words, and knowing what awaited any who defied him.
Tommy! You're so late!
I was afraid that something must have happened to you!
Don't bother with your lies, Count. Nobody's listening.
Oh, it's no lie. I need you alive.
I couldn't have done any of this without you.
And you were all I needed to finish it.
BWAAAAAAAAAAA

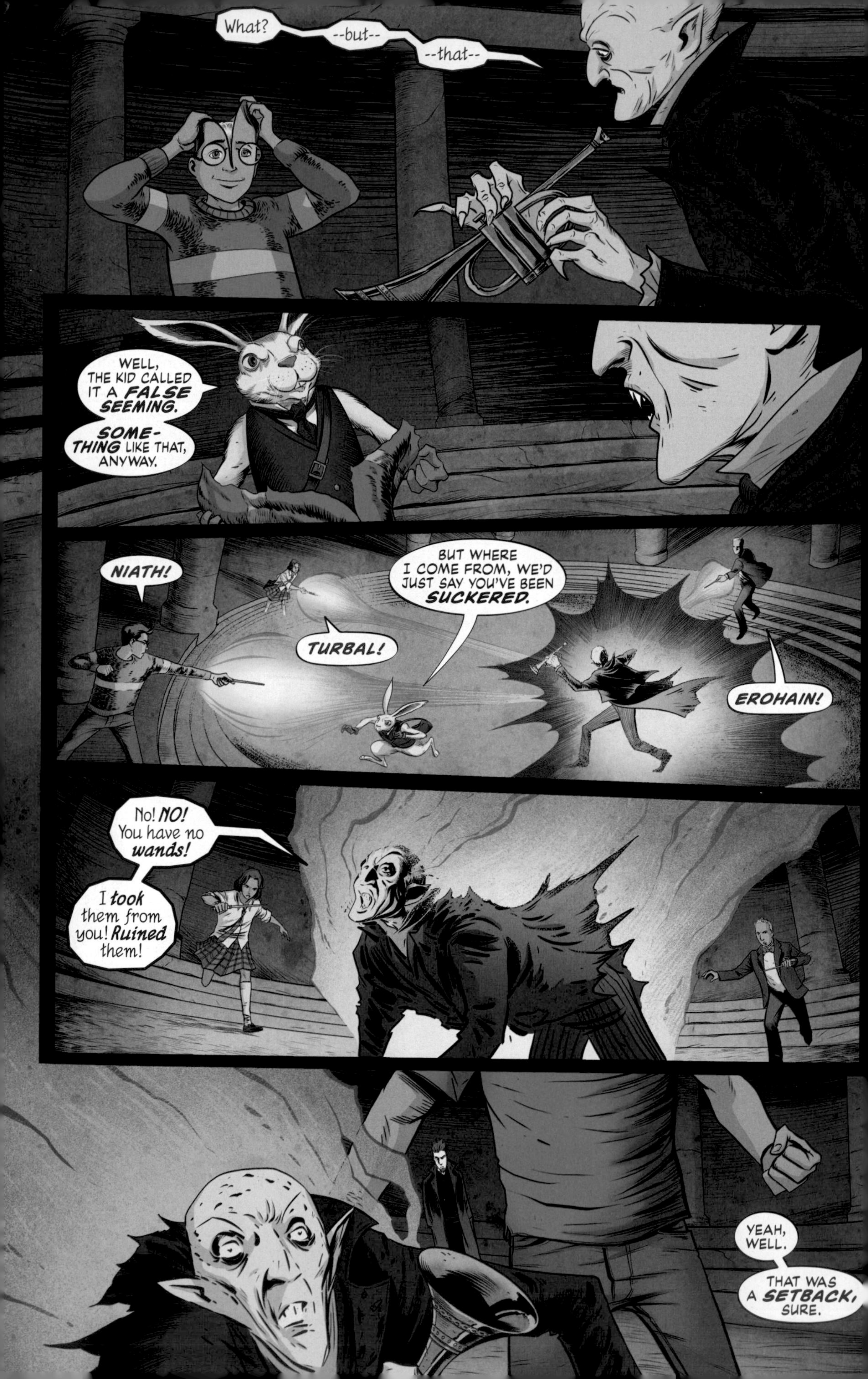
What?
--but--
--that--
WELL, THE KID CALLED IT A FALSE SEEMING.
SOMETHING LIKE THAT, ANYWAY.
NIATH!
TURBAL!
BUT WHERE I COME FROM, WE'D JUST SAY YOU'VE BEEN SUCKERED.
EROHAIN!
No! NO! You have no wands!
I took them from you! Ruined them!
YEAH, WELL.
THAT WAS A SETBACK, SURE.

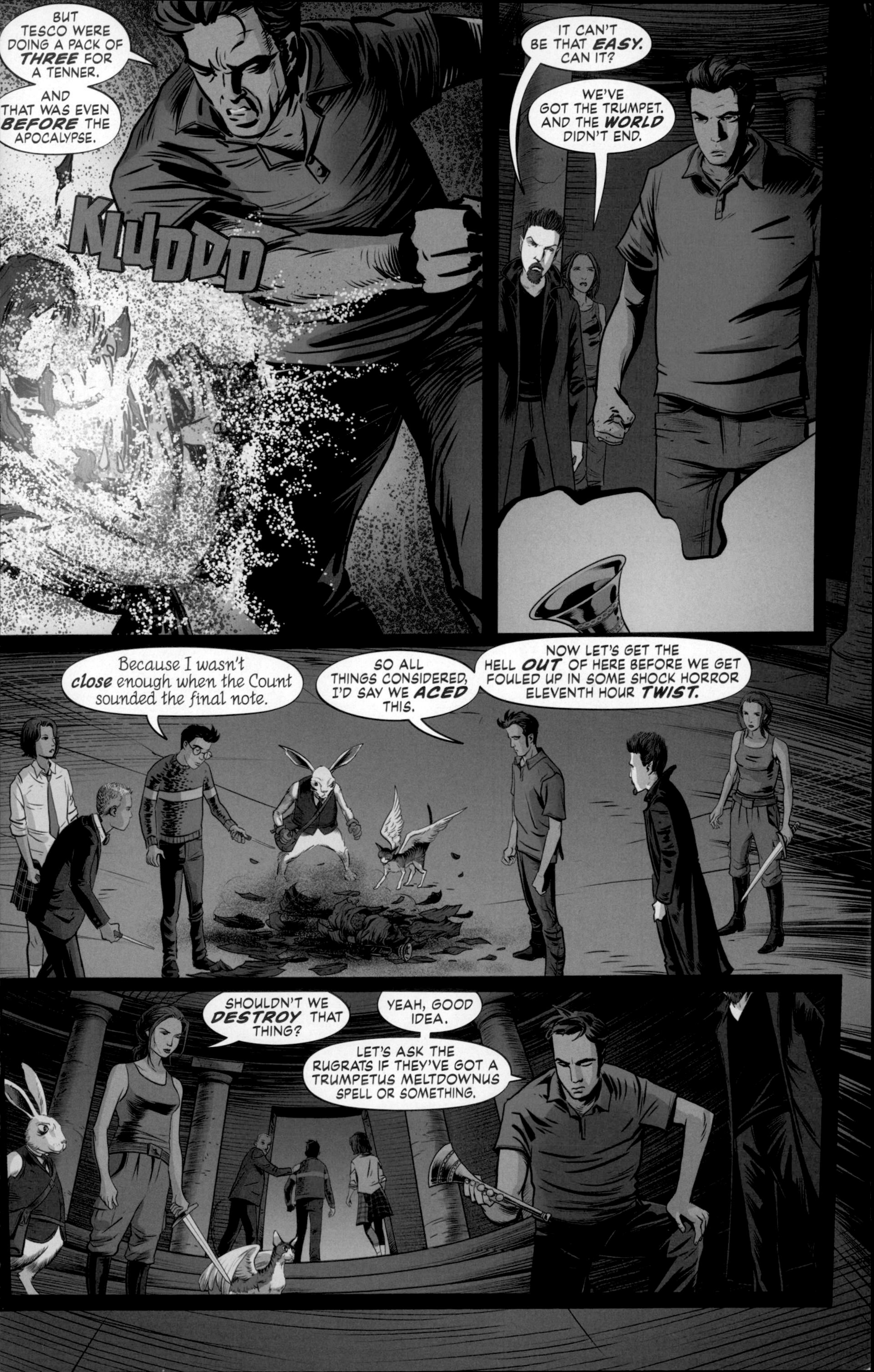

BUT TESCO WERE DOING A PACK OF THREE FOR A TENNER.
AND THAT WAS EVEN BEFORE THE APOCALYPSE.
KLUDDD
IT CAN'T BE THAT EASY. CAN IT?
WE'VE GOT THE TRUMPET. AND THE WORLD DIDN'T END.
Because I wasn't close enough when the Count sounded the final note.
SO ALL THINGS CONSIDERED, I'D SAY WE ACED THIS.
NOW LET'S GET THE HELL OUT OF HERE BEFORE WE GET FOULED UP IN SOME SHOCK HORROR ELEVENTH HOUR TWIST.
SHOULDN'T WE DESTROY THAT THING?
YEAH, GOOD IDEA.
LET'S ASK THE RUGRATS IF THEY'VE GOT A TRUMPETUS MELTDOWNUS SPELL OR SOMETHING.

YOU KNOW, I'VE HAD ENOUGH OF *MAGIC* TO LAST ME A LIFETIME.

I THINK I'D PREFER TO GET A BALLPEEN *HAMMER* AND--

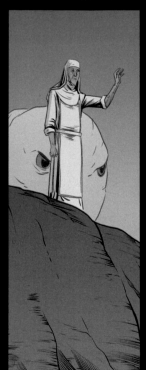

...

Oh no!

They're *frozen!* It must be a spell.

But if it was magic, we'd *feel* it. And Ambrosio is--

BLAM!

BLAM!

BLAM!

BLAM!

R-Reparo!

REPARO!

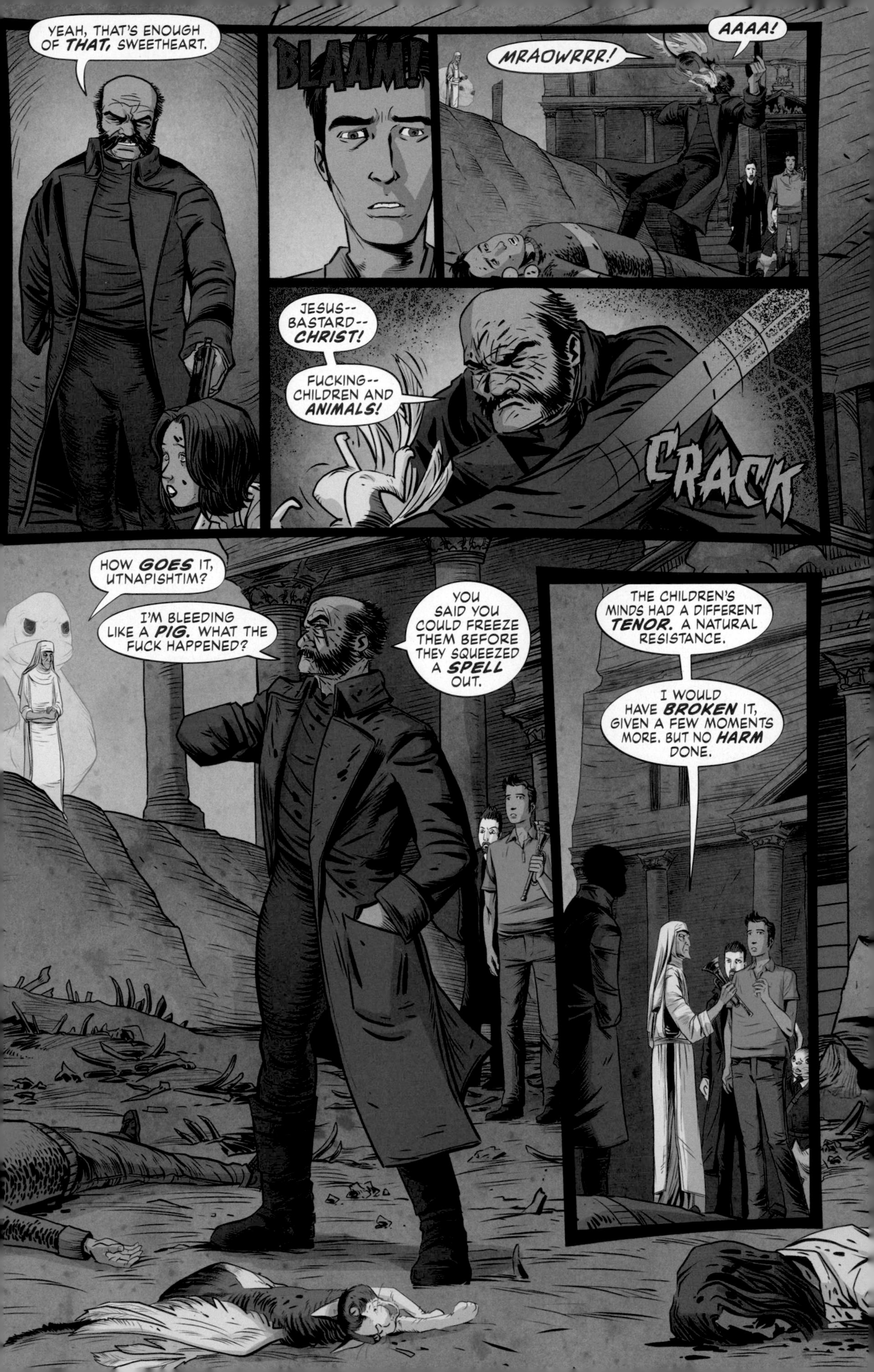

YEAH, THAT'S ENOUGH OF **THAT,** SWEETHEART.
BLAAM!
MRAOWRRR!
AAAA!
JESUS-- BASTARD-- **CHRIST!**
FUCKING-- CHILDREN AND **ANIMALS!**
CRACK
HOW **GOES** IT, UTNAPISHTIM?
I'M BLEEDING LIKE A **PIG.** WHAT THE FUCK HAPPENED?
YOU SAID YOU COULD FREEZE THEM BEFORE THEY SQUEEZED A **SPELL** OUT.
THE CHILDREN'S MINDS HAD A DIFFERENT **TENOR.** A NATURAL RESISTANCE.
I WOULD HAVE **BROKEN** IT, GIVEN A FEW MOMENTS MORE. BUT NO **HARM** DONE.

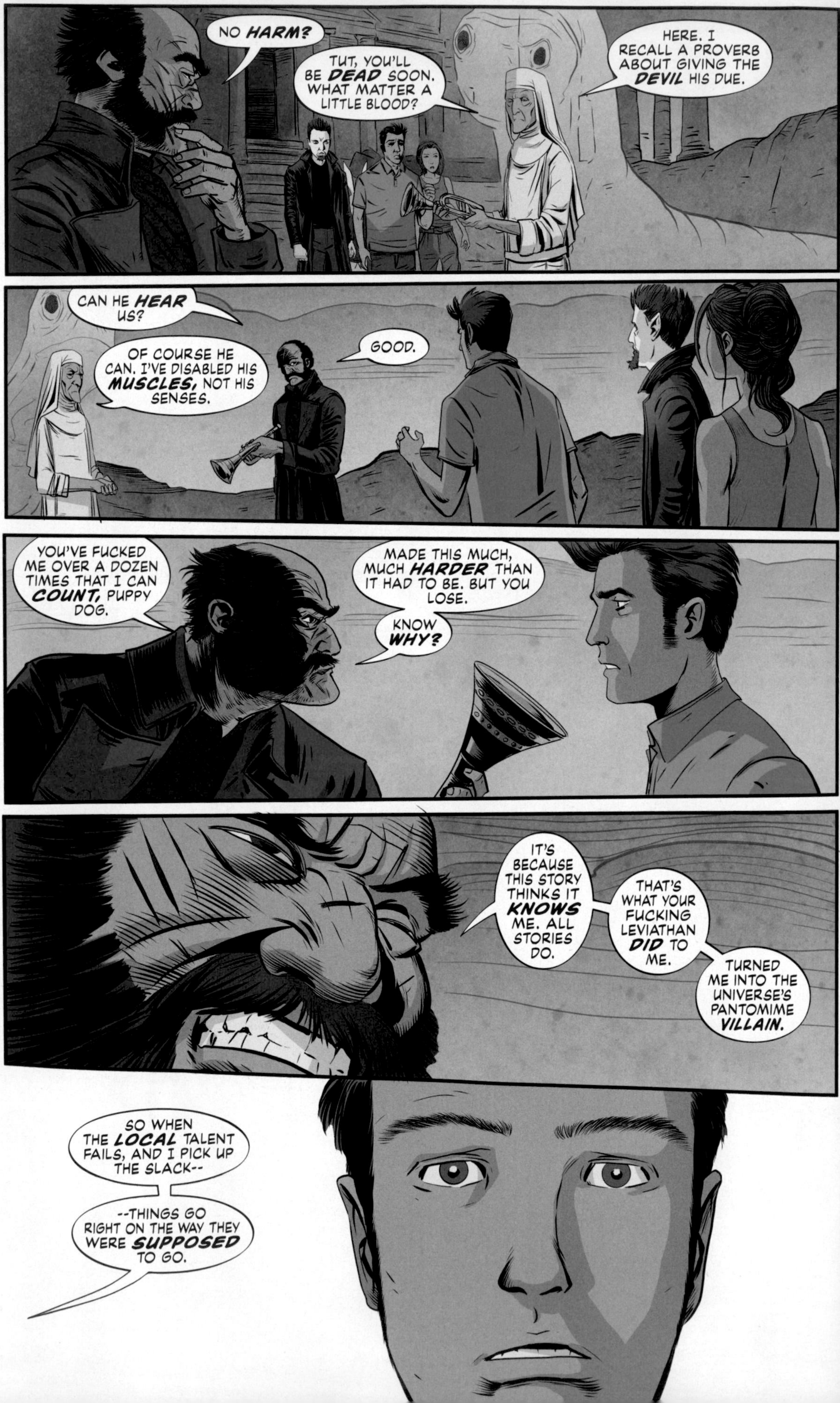
NO HARM?
TUT, YOU'LL BE DEAD SOON. WHAT MATTER A LITTLE BLOOD?
HERE. I RECALL A PROVERB ABOUT GIVING THE DEVIL HIS DUE.
CAN HE HEAR US?
OF COURSE HE CAN. I'VE DISABLED HIS MUSCLES, NOT HIS SENSES.
GOOD.
YOU'VE FUCKED ME OVER A DOZEN TIMES THAT I CAN COUNT, PUPPY DOG.
MADE THIS MUCH, MUCH HARDER THAN IT HAD TO BE. BUT YOU LOSE.
KNOW WHY?
IT'S BECAUSE THIS STORY THINKS IT KNOWS ME. ALL STORIES DO.
THAT'S WHAT YOUR FUCKING LEVIATHAN DID TO ME.
TURNED ME INTO THE UNIVERSE'S PANTOMIME VILLAIN.
SO WHEN THE LOCAL TALENT FAILS, AND I PICK UP THE SLACK--
--THINGS GO RIGHT ON THE WAY THEY WERE SUPPOSED TO GO.

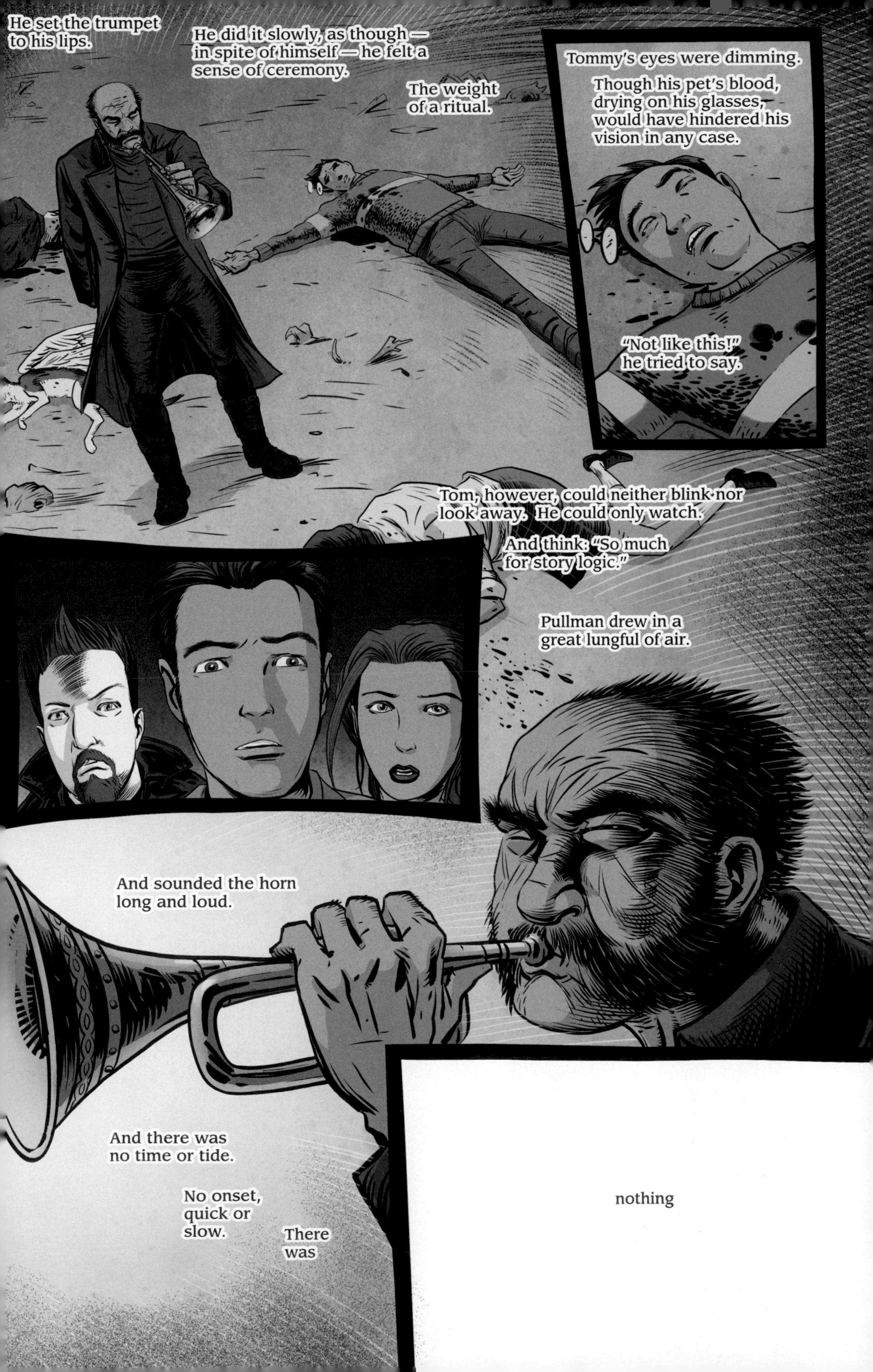
He set the trumpet to his lips.
He did it slowly, as though — in spite of himself — he felt a sense of ceremony.
The weight of a ritual.
Tommy's eyes were dimming.
Though his pet's blood, drying on his glasses, would have hindered his vision in any case.
"Not like this!" he tried to say.
Tom, however, could neither blink nor look away. He could only watch.
And think: "So much for story logic."
Pullman drew in a great lungful of air.
And sounded the horn long and loud.
And there was no time or tide.
No onset, quick or slow.
There was
nothing

The same nothing,
all at once, and
everywhere.

Not spilling from one place into
another. Just suddenly and
inexorably there.

And once it was there, it
made itself at home.

Eliminating, with a single
shrug of its vast non-being,
the possibility that
anything else —

— or the potential for
anything else —

— had ever
existed.

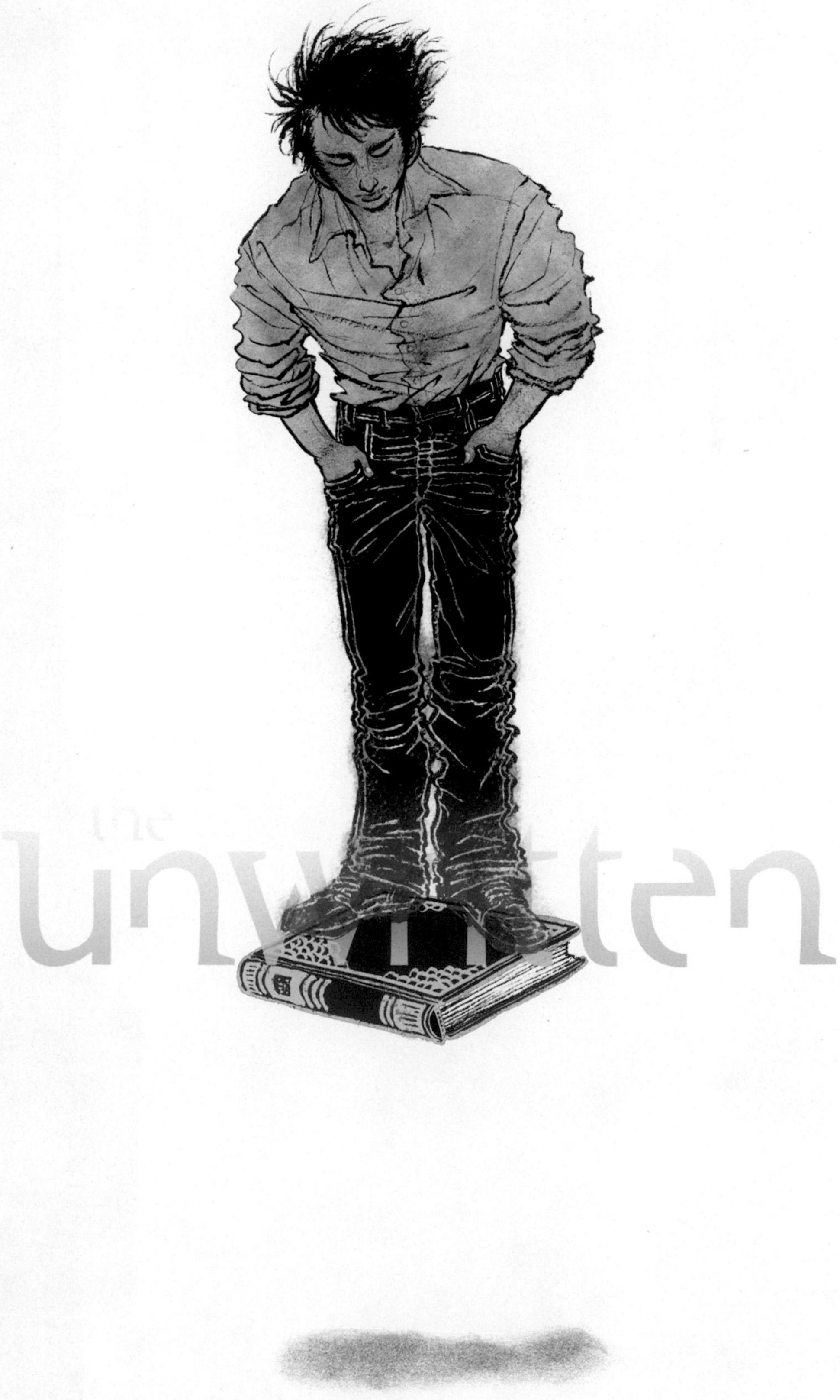
the

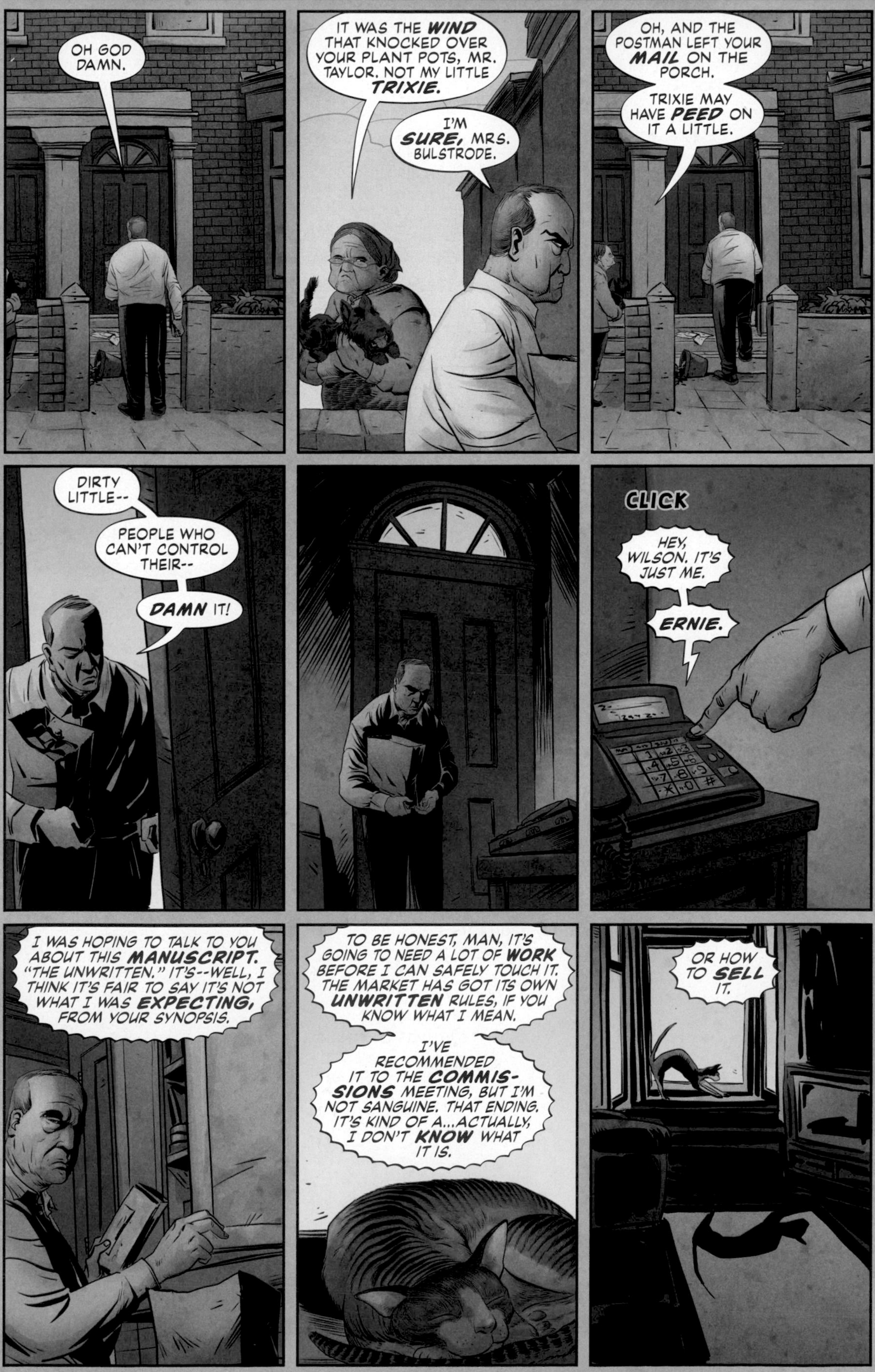
OH GOD DAMN.
IT WAS THE WIND THAT KNOCKED OVER YOUR PLANT POTS, MR. TAYLOR. NOT MY LITTLE TRIXIE.
I'M SURE, MRS. BULSTRODE.
OH, AND THE POSTMAN LEFT YOUR MAIL ON THE PORCH.
TRIXIE MAY HAVE PEED ON IT A LITTLE.
DIRTY LITTLE--
PEOPLE WHO CAN'T CONTROL THEIR--
DAMN IT!
CLICK
HEY, WILSON. IT'S JUST ME.
ERNIE.
I WAS HOPING TO TALK TO YOU ABOUT THIS MANUSCRIPT. "THE UNWRITTEN." IT'S--WELL, I THINK IT'S FAIR TO SAY IT'S NOT WHAT I WAS EXPECTING, FROM YOUR SYNOPSIS.
TO BE HONEST, MAN, IT'S GOING TO NEED A LOT OF WORK BEFORE I CAN SAFELY TOUCH IT. THE MARKET HAS GOT ITS OWN UNWRITTEN RULES, IF YOU KNOW WHAT I MEAN.
I'VE RECOMMENDED IT TO THE COMMISSIONS MEETING, BUT I'M NOT SANGUINE. THAT ENDING. IT'S KIND OF A...ACTUALLY, I DON'T KNOW WHAT IT IS.
OR HOW TO SELL IT.

And there was no time or tide. No onset,
quick or slow. There was nothing.

The same nothing, all at
once, and everywhere.

Not spilling from one place into another.
Just suddenly and inexorably there.

And once it was there,
it made itself at home.

Eliminating, with a single shrug of its vast
non-being, the possibility that anything else —

— or the potential for anything else —

— had ever existed.

But it **had,** hadn't it?

That was the point.

That was the **tragedy.**

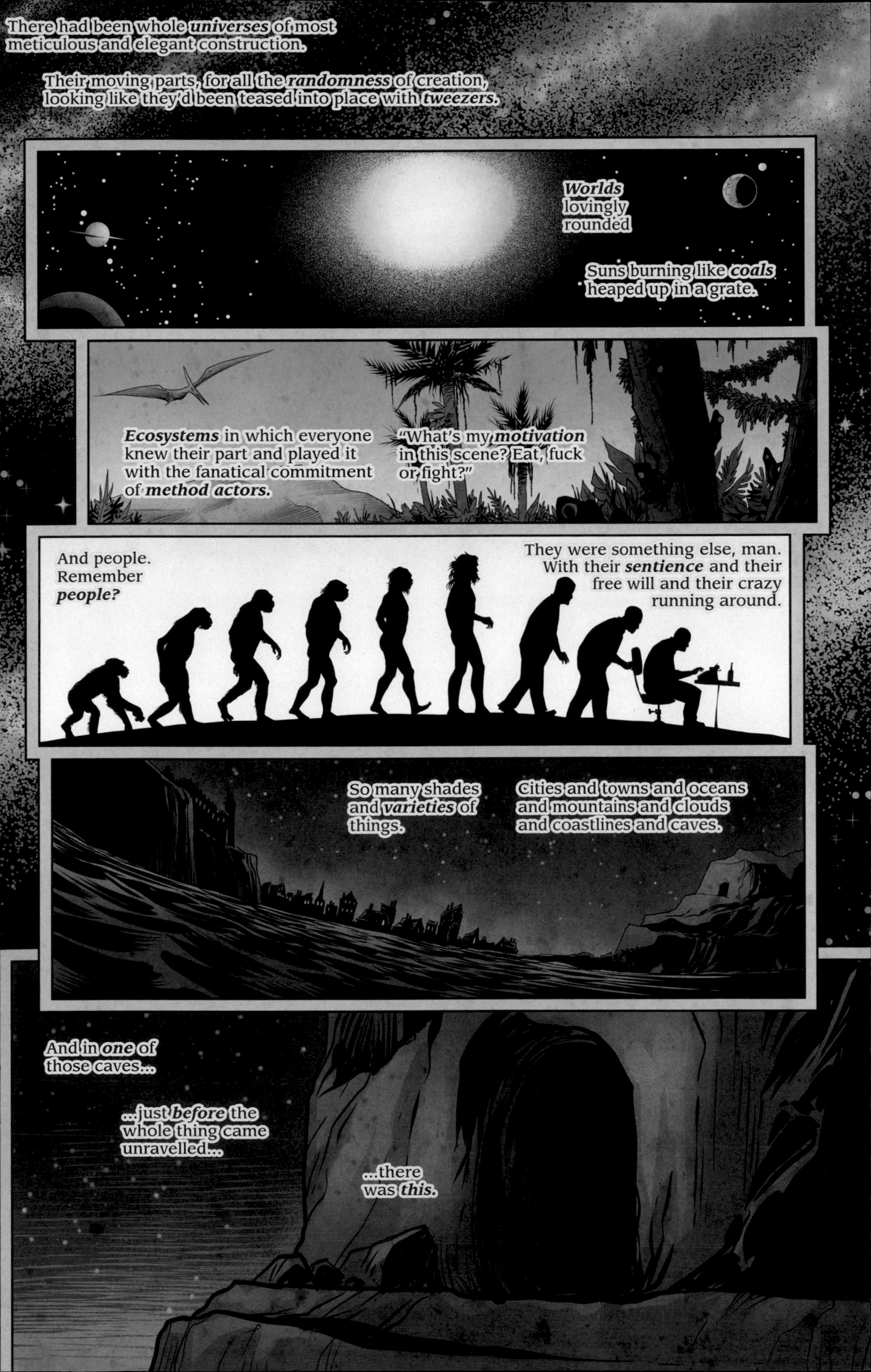

There had been whole universes of most meticulous and elegant construction.
Their moving parts, for all the randomness of creation, looking like they'd been teased into place with tweezers.
Worlds lovingly rounded
Suns burning like coals heaped up in a grate.
Ecosystems in which everyone knew their part and played it with the fanatical commitment of method actors.
"What's my motivation in this scene? Eat, fuck or fight?"
And people. Remember people?
They were something else, man. With their sentience and their free will and their crazy running around.
So many shades and varieties of things.
Cities and towns and oceans and mountains and clouds and coastlines and caves.
And in one of those caves...
...just before the whole thing came unravelled...
...there was this.

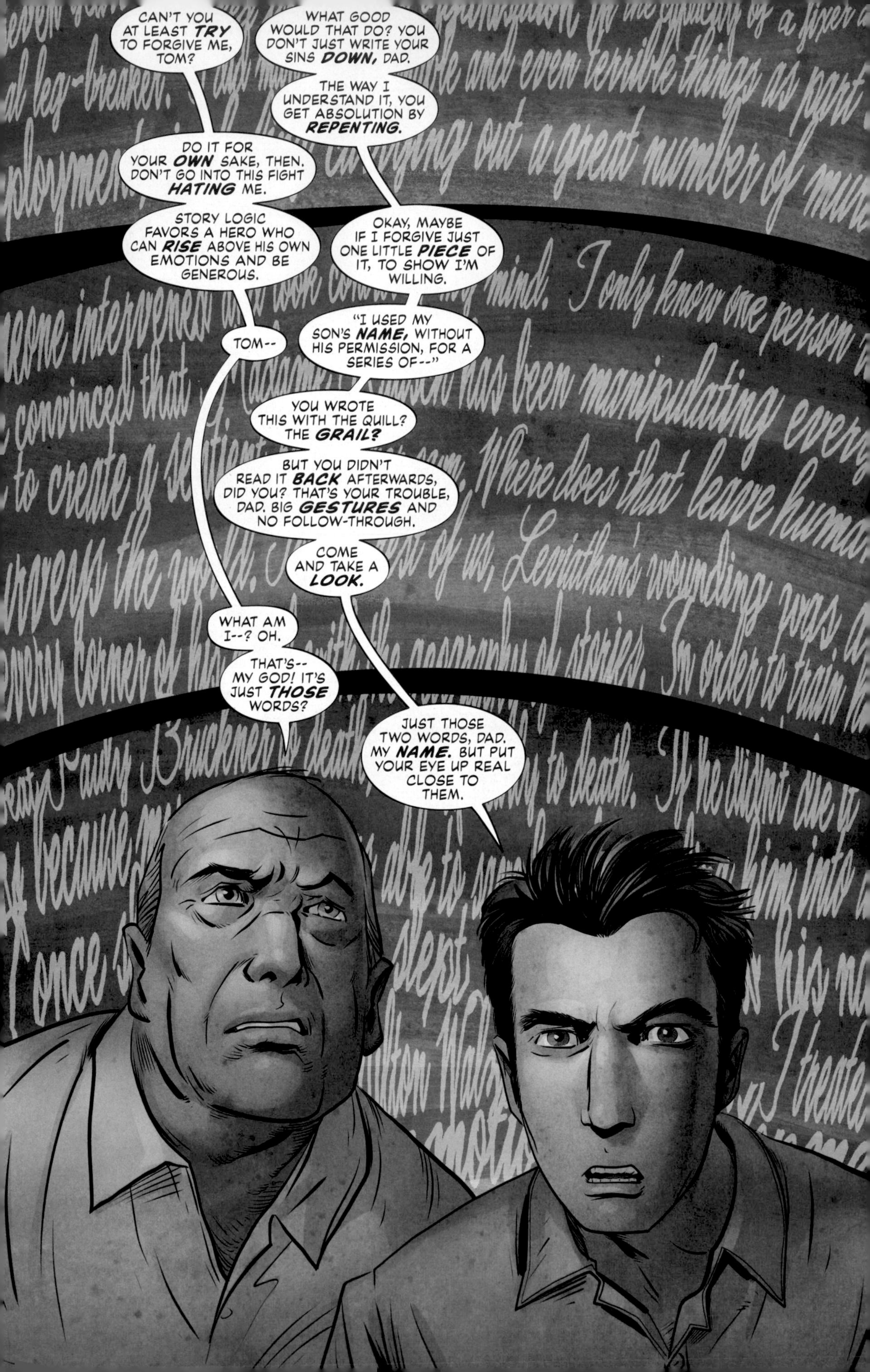
CAN'T YOU AT LEAST TRY TO FORGIVE ME, TOM?
WHAT GOOD WOULD THAT DO? YOU DON'T JUST WRITE YOUR SINS DOWN, DAD.
THE WAY I UNDERSTAND IT, YOU GET ABSOLUTION BY REPENTING.
DO IT FOR YOUR OWN SAKE, THEN. DON'T GO INTO THIS FIGHT HATING ME.
STORY LOGIC FAVORS A HERO WHO CAN RISE ABOVE HIS OWN EMOTIONS AND BE GENEROUS.
OKAY, MAYBE IF I FORGIVE JUST ONE LITTLE PIECE OF IT, TO SHOW I'M WILLING.
TOM--
"I USED MY SON'S NAME, WITHOUT HIS PERMISSION, FOR A SERIES OF--"
YOU WROTE THIS WITH THE QUILL? THE GRAIL?
BUT YOU DIDN'T READ IT BACK AFTERWARDS, DID YOU? THAT'S YOUR TROUBLE, DAD. BIG GESTURES AND NO FOLLOW-THROUGH.
COME AND TAKE A LOOK.
WHAT AM I--? OH.
THAT'S-- MY GOD! IT'S JUST THOSE WORDS?
JUST THOSE TWO WORDS, DAD. MY NAME. BUT PUT YOUR EYE UP REAL CLOSE TO THEM.

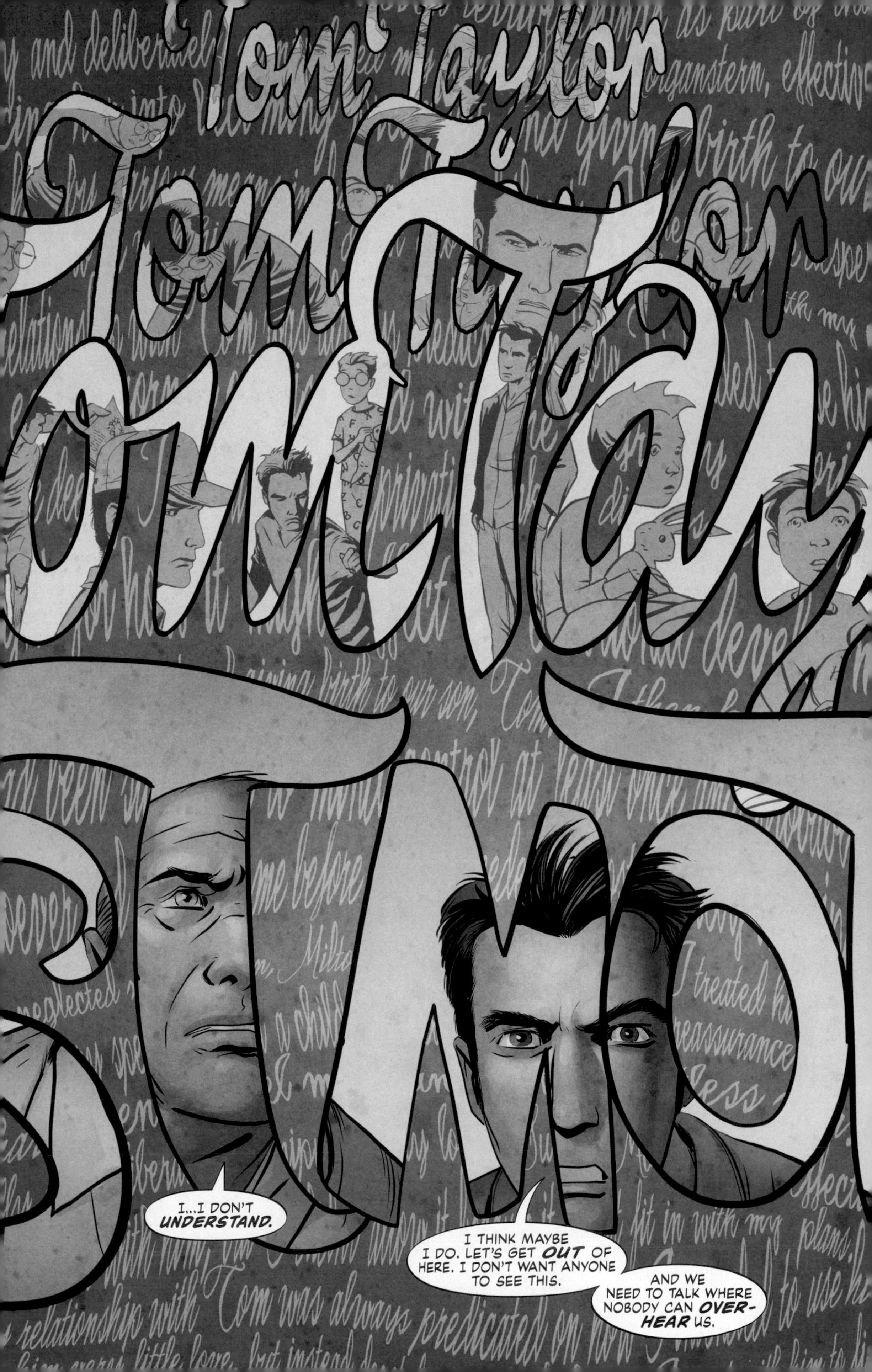
Tom Taylor
I...I DON'T UNDERSTAND.
I THINK MAYBE I DO. LET'S GET OUT OF HERE. I DON'T WANT ANYONE TO SEE THIS.
AND WE NEED TO TALK WHERE NOBODY CAN OVER-HEAR US.

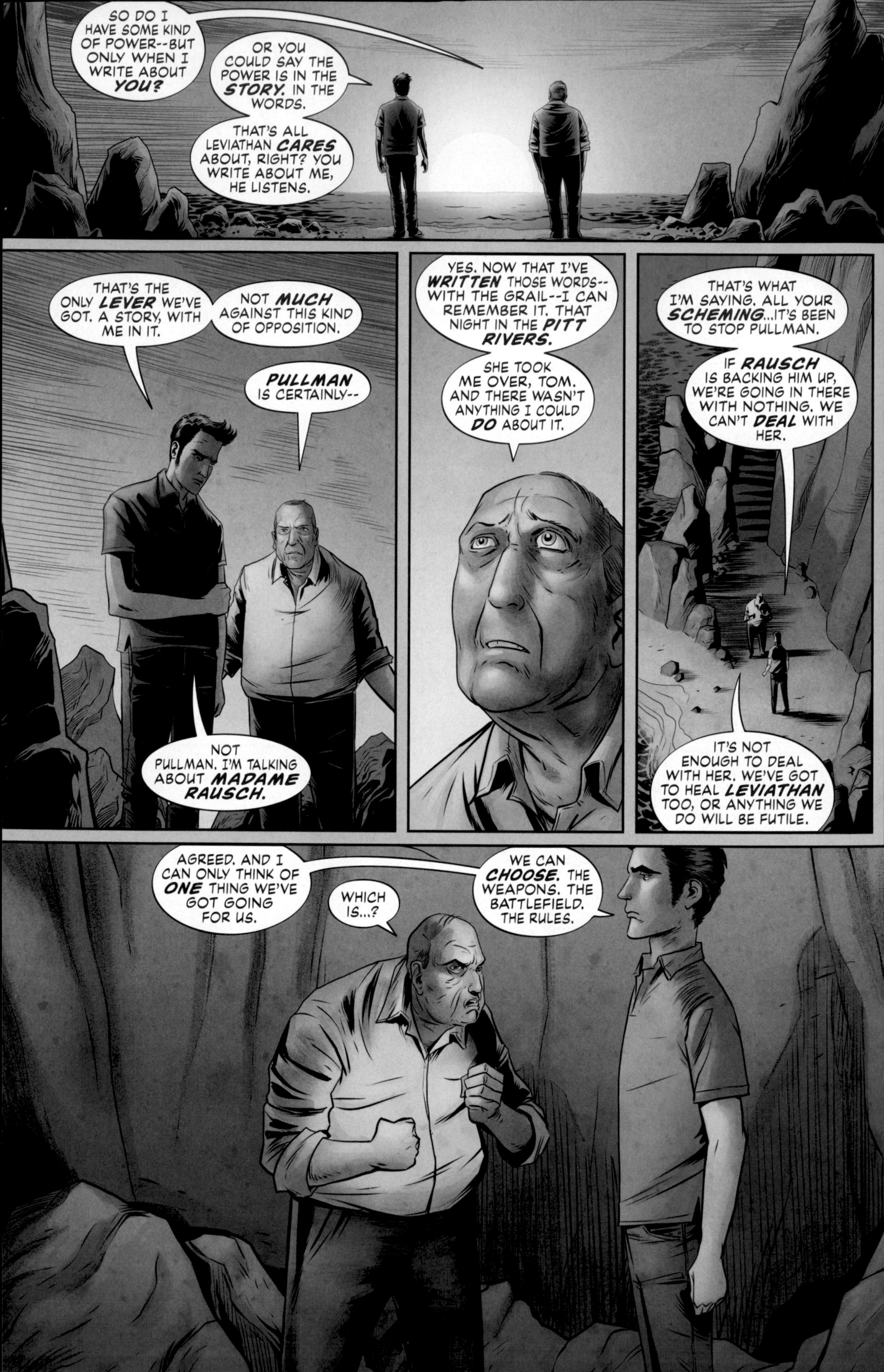

SO DO I HAVE SOME KIND OF POWER--BUT ONLY WHEN I WRITE ABOUT YOU?
OR YOU COULD SAY THE POWER IS IN THE STORY. IN THE WORDS.
THAT'S ALL LEVIATHAN CARES ABOUT, RIGHT? YOU WRITE ABOUT ME, HE LISTENS.
THAT'S THE ONLY LEVER WE'VE GOT. A STORY, WITH ME IN IT.
NOT MUCH AGAINST THIS KIND OF OPPOSITION.
PULLMAN IS CERTAINLY--
NOT PULLMAN. I'M TALKING ABOUT MADAME RAUSCH.
YES. NOW THAT I'VE WRITTEN THOSE WORDS--WITH THE GRAIL--I CAN REMEMBER IT. THAT NIGHT IN THE PITT RIVERS.
SHE TOOK ME OVER, TOM. AND THERE WASN'T ANYTHING I COULD DO ABOUT IT.
THAT'S WHAT I'M SAYING. ALL YOUR SCHEMING...IT'S BEEN TO STOP PULLMAN.
IF RAUSCH IS BACKING HIM UP, WE'RE GOING IN THERE WITH NOTHING. WE CAN'T DEAL WITH HER.
IT'S NOT ENOUGH TO DEAL WITH HER. WE'VE GOT TO HEAL LEVIATHAN TOO, OR ANYTHING WE DO WILL BE FUTILE.
AGREED. AND I CAN ONLY THINK OF ONE THING WE'VE GOT GOING FOR US.
WHICH IS...?
WE CAN CHOOSE. THE WEAPONS. THE BATTLEFIELD. THE RULES.

WELL, WE KNOW WHAT MADAME *WANTS.* WHAT SHE'S BEEN AIMING FOR ALL THIS TIME.

THE END OF THE *WORLD.*

SO SUPPOSE WE LET HER *HAVE* IT. BAIT AND SWITCH.

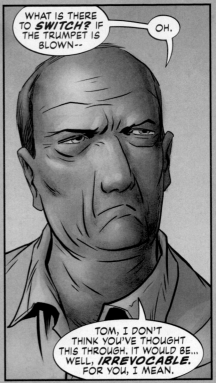

WHAT IS THERE TO *SWITCH?* IF THE TRUMPET IS BLOWN--

OH.

TOM, I DON'T THINK YOU'VE THOUGHT THIS THROUGH. IT WOULD BE... WELL, *IRREVOCABLE.* FOR YOU, I MEAN.

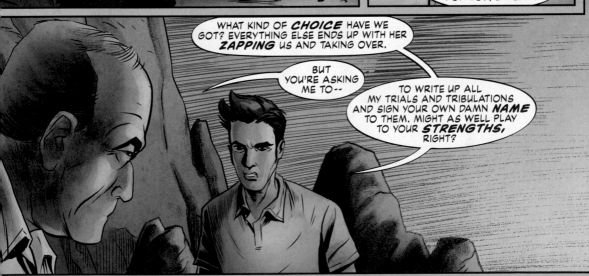

WHAT KIND OF *CHOICE* HAVE WE GOT? EVERYTHING ELSE ENDS UP WITH HER *ZAPPING* US AND TAKING OVER.

BUT YOU'RE ASKING ME TO--

TO WRITE UP ALL MY TRIALS AND TRIBULATIONS AND SIGN YOUR OWN DAMN *NAME* TO THEM. MIGHT AS WELL PLAY TO YOUR *STRENGTHS,* RIGHT?

ANYWAY, IT'S MY CALL. I'M THE MAGIC *INGREDIENT,* AFTER ALL.

BUT WE DON'T SAY A *WORD* TO ANYONE ELSE.

BECAUSE THEY WOULDN'T *AGREE.* YOU WANT TO SPRING IT ON THEM WHEN IT'S TOO LATE TO SAY *NO.*

WHICH IS HOW WE *ROLL,* ISN'T IT?

I LEARNED FROM THE *BEST,* DAD.

"Wake up, everyone," Tommy said. "It's morning. Or as close to morning as we're likely to get."

"I don't think anyone slept, Tommy," Peter Price exclaimed ruefully, rubbing his shoulder.

"No, p'raps not," Tommy murmured, staring down at the desolate beach below. "I know I didn't." He stilled his somber thoughts with an effort and smiled at his friends. "All right, we're up a gum tree and no mistake. But we have got a paddle. Ambrosio's only got to blow one more note to make it be the end of the world. But he's got to wait for me to get there. And he doesn't know that the last three words of the unicorn's blessing can kill him!"

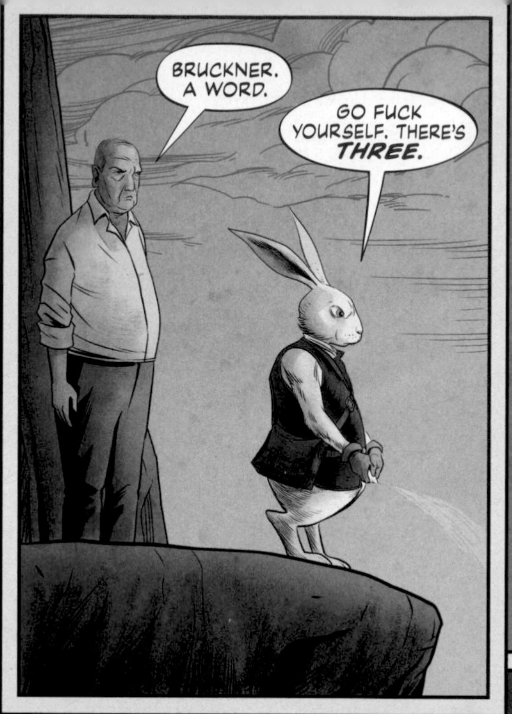
BRUCKNER. A WORD.
GO FUCK YOURSELF. THERE'S THREE.

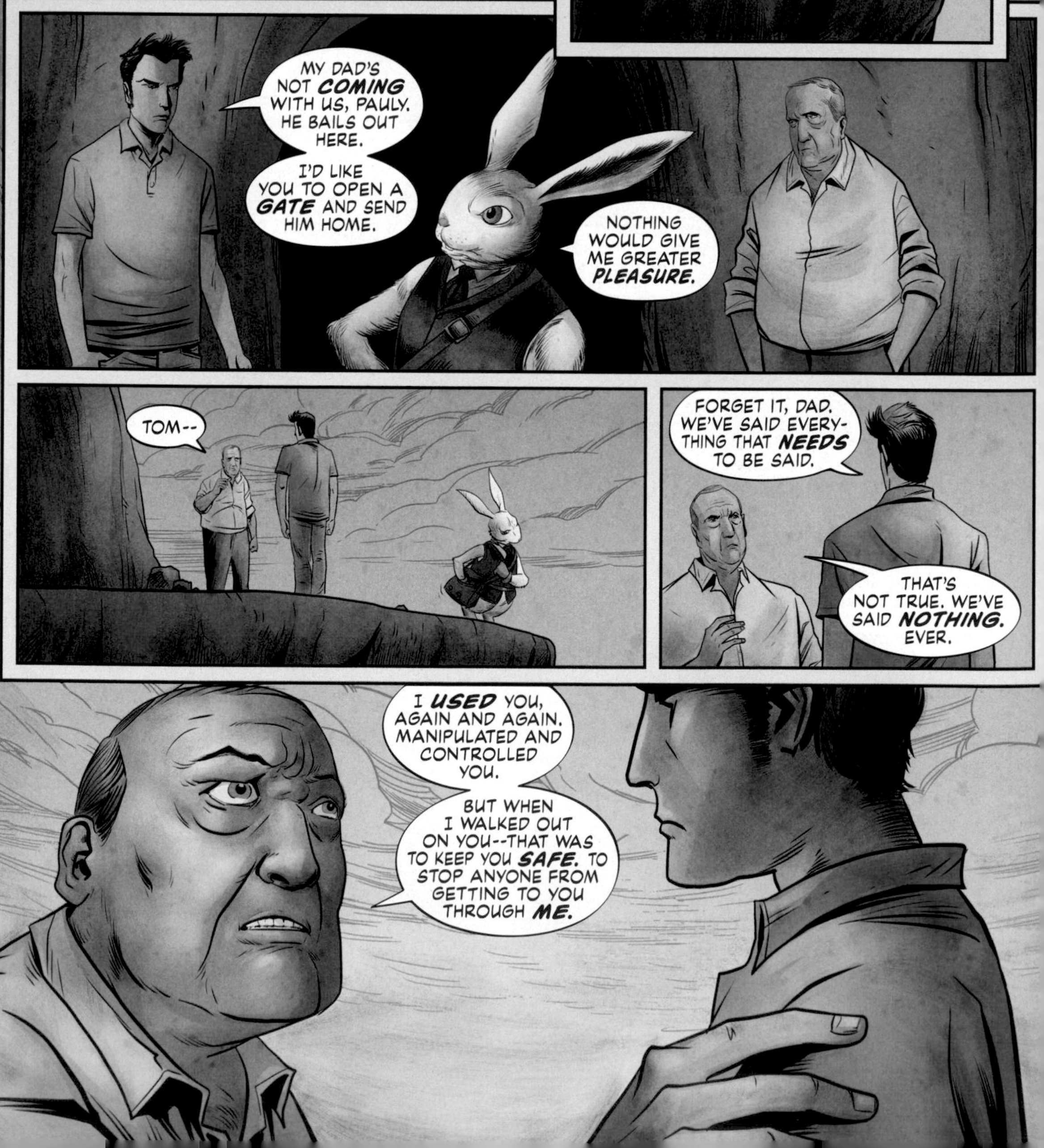
MY DAD'S NOT COMING WITH US, PAULY. HE BAILS OUT HERE.
I'D LIKE YOU TO OPEN A GATE AND SEND HIM HOME.
NOTHING WOULD GIVE ME GREATER PLEASURE.
TOM--
FORGET IT, DAD. WE'VE SAID EVERYTHING THAT NEEDS TO BE SAID.
THAT'S NOT TRUE. WE'VE SAID NOTHING. EVER.
I USED YOU, AGAIN AND AGAIN. MANIPULATED AND CONTROLLED YOU.
BUT WHEN I WALKED OUT ON YOU--THAT WAS TO KEEP YOU SAFE. TO STOP ANYONE FROM GETTING TO YOU THROUGH ME.

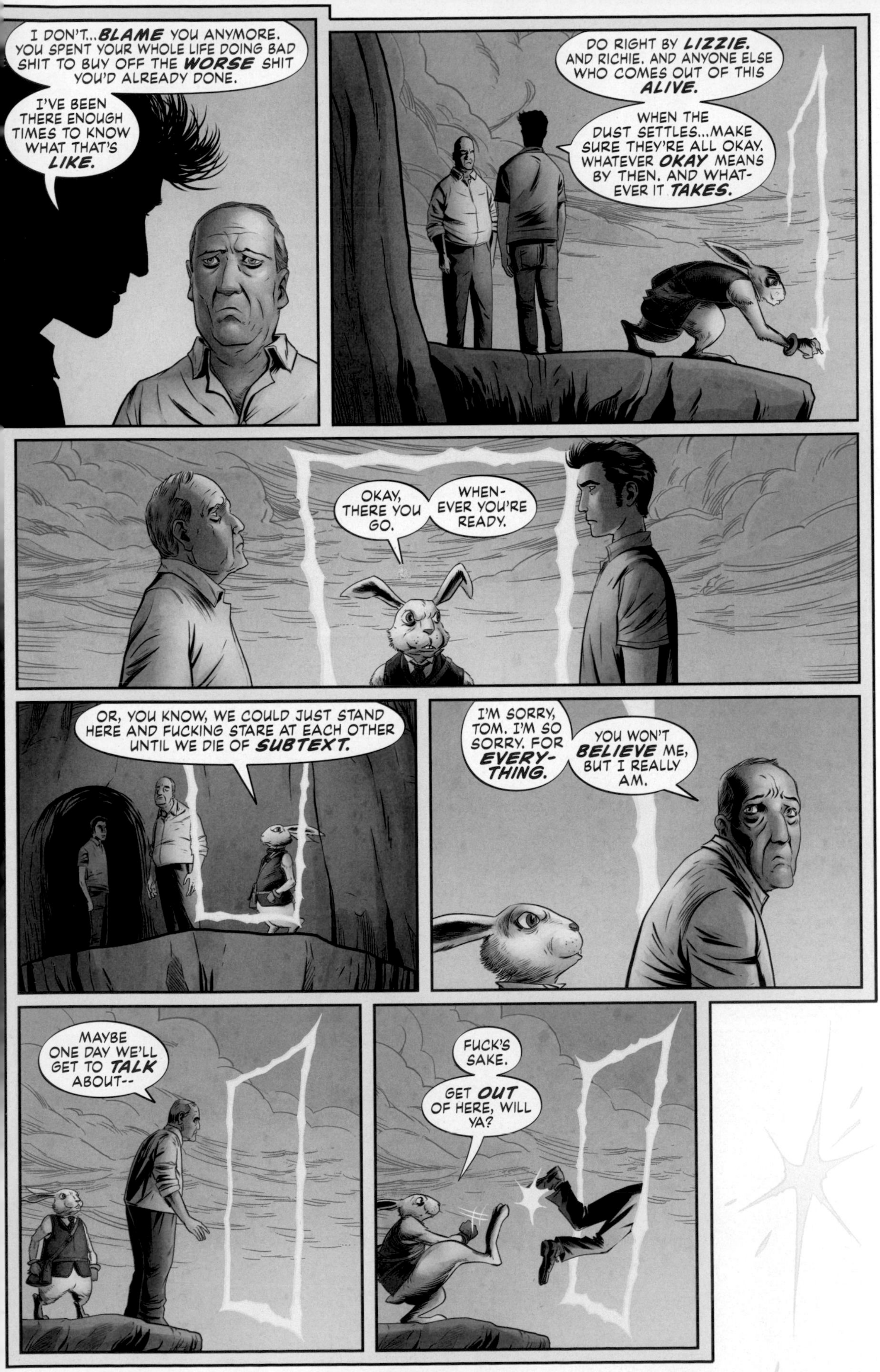
I DON'T...BLAME YOU ANYMORE. YOU SPENT YOUR WHOLE LIFE DOING BAD SHIT TO BUY OFF THE WORSE SHIT YOU'D ALREADY DONE.
I'VE BEEN THERE ENOUGH TIMES TO KNOW WHAT THAT'S LIKE.
DO RIGHT BY LIZZIE. AND RICHIE. AND ANYONE ELSE WHO COMES OUT OF THIS ALIVE.
WHEN THE DUST SETTLES...MAKE SURE THEY'RE ALL OKAY. WHATEVER OKAY MEANS BY THEN. AND WHAT-EVER IT TAKES.
OKAY, THERE YOU GO.
WHEN-EVER YOU'RE READY.
OR, YOU KNOW, WE COULD JUST STAND HERE AND FUCKING STARE AT EACH OTHER UNTIL WE DIE OF SUBTEXT.
I'M SORRY, TOM. I'M SO SORRY. FOR EVERY-THING.
YOU WON'T BELIEVE ME, BUT I REALLY AM.
MAYBE ONE DAY WE'LL GET TO TALK ABOUT--
FUCK'S SAKE.
GET OUT OF HERE, WILL YA?

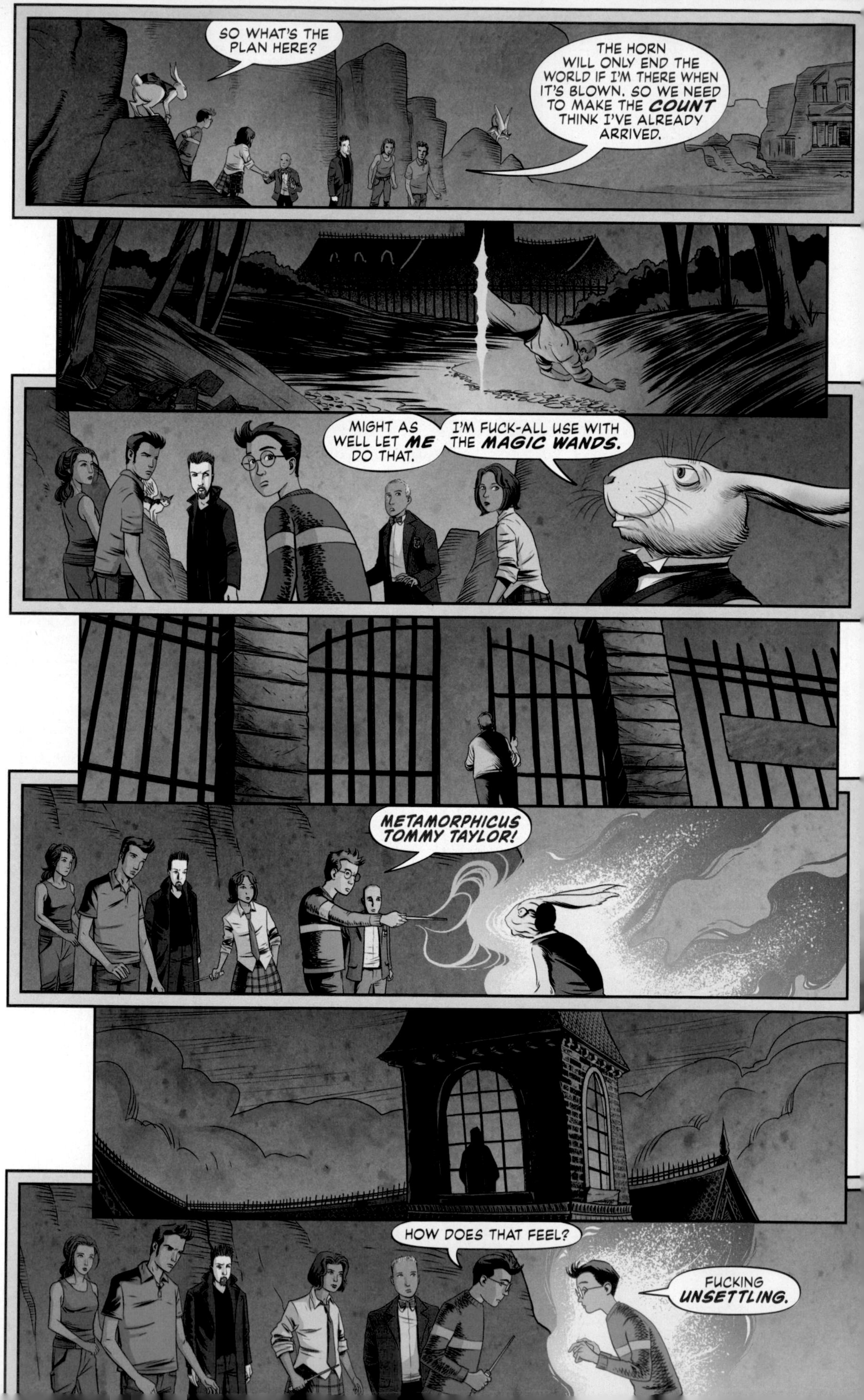
SO WHAT'S THE PLAN HERE?
THE HORN WILL ONLY END THE WORLD IF I'M THERE WHEN IT'S BLOWN. SO WE NEED TO MAKE THE COUNT THINK I'VE ALREADY ARRIVED.
MIGHT AS WELL LET ME DO THAT.
I'M FUCK-ALL USE WITH THE MAGIC WANDS.
METAMORPHICUS TOMMY TAYLOR!
HOW DOES THAT FEEL?
FUCKING UNSETTLING.

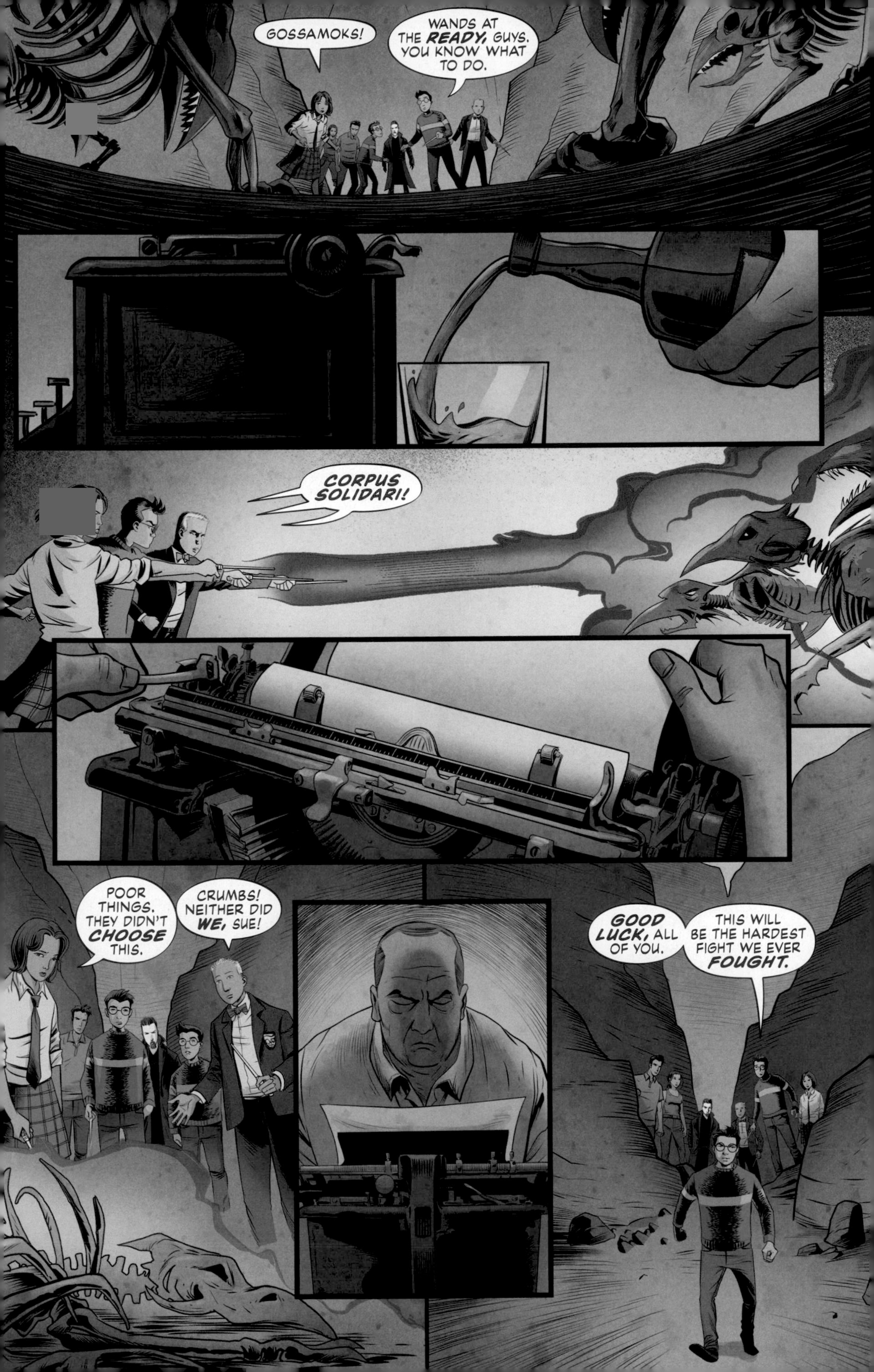
GOSSAMOKS!
WANDS AT THE READY, GUYS. YOU KNOW WHAT TO DO.
CORPUS SOLIDARI!
POOR THINGS. THEY DIDN'T CHOOSE THIS.
CRUMBS! NEITHER DID WE, SUE!
GOOD LUCK, ALL OF YOU.
THIS WILL BE THE HARDEST FIGHT WE EVER FOUGHT.

They went into that last battle without much hope.

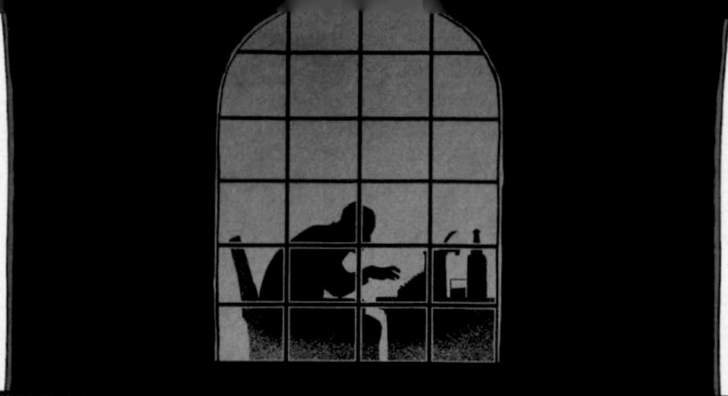

Behind this enemy, they knew, stood another enemy. And a third, even more formidable, behind him.

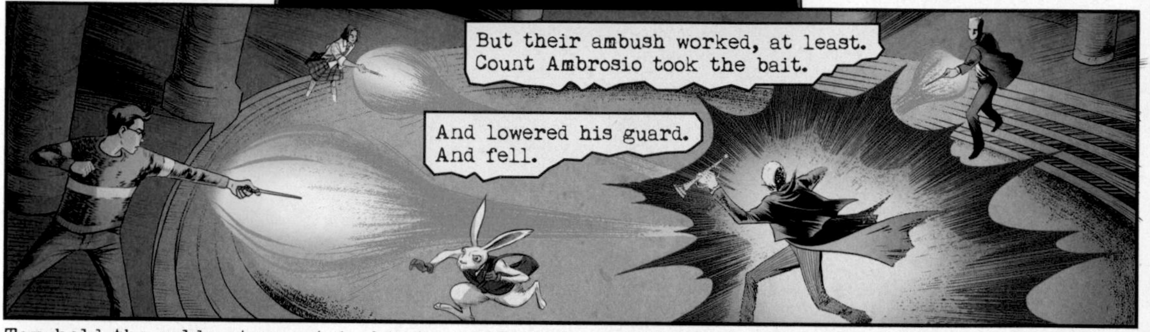
But their ambush worked, at least. Count Ambrosio took the bait.
And lowered his guard. And fell.

Tom held the golden trumpet in his hands. Felt the weight and the heft of it. Its solid mass and cold, unyielding metal.

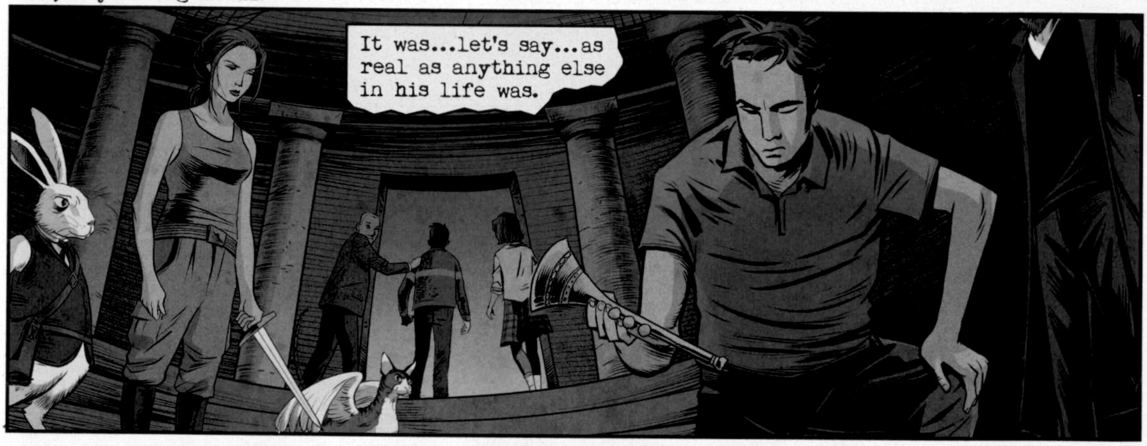
It was...let's say...as real as anything else in his life was.

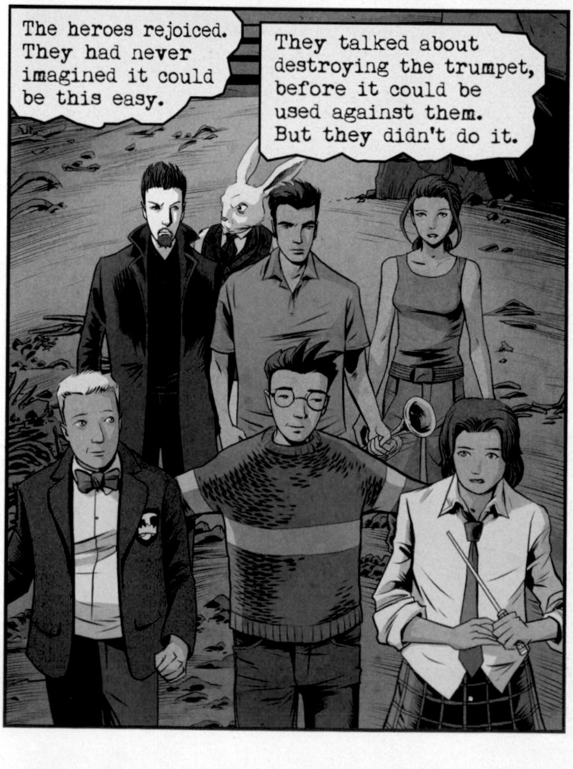
The heroes rejoiced. They had never imagined it could be this easy.
They talked about destroying the trumpet, before it could be used against them. But they didn't do it.

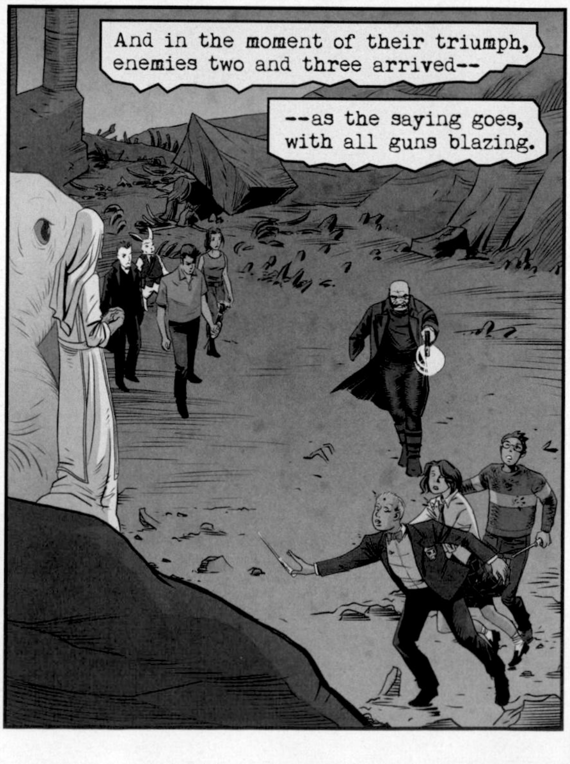
And in the moment of their triumph, enemies two and three arrived--
--as the saying goes, with all guns blazing.

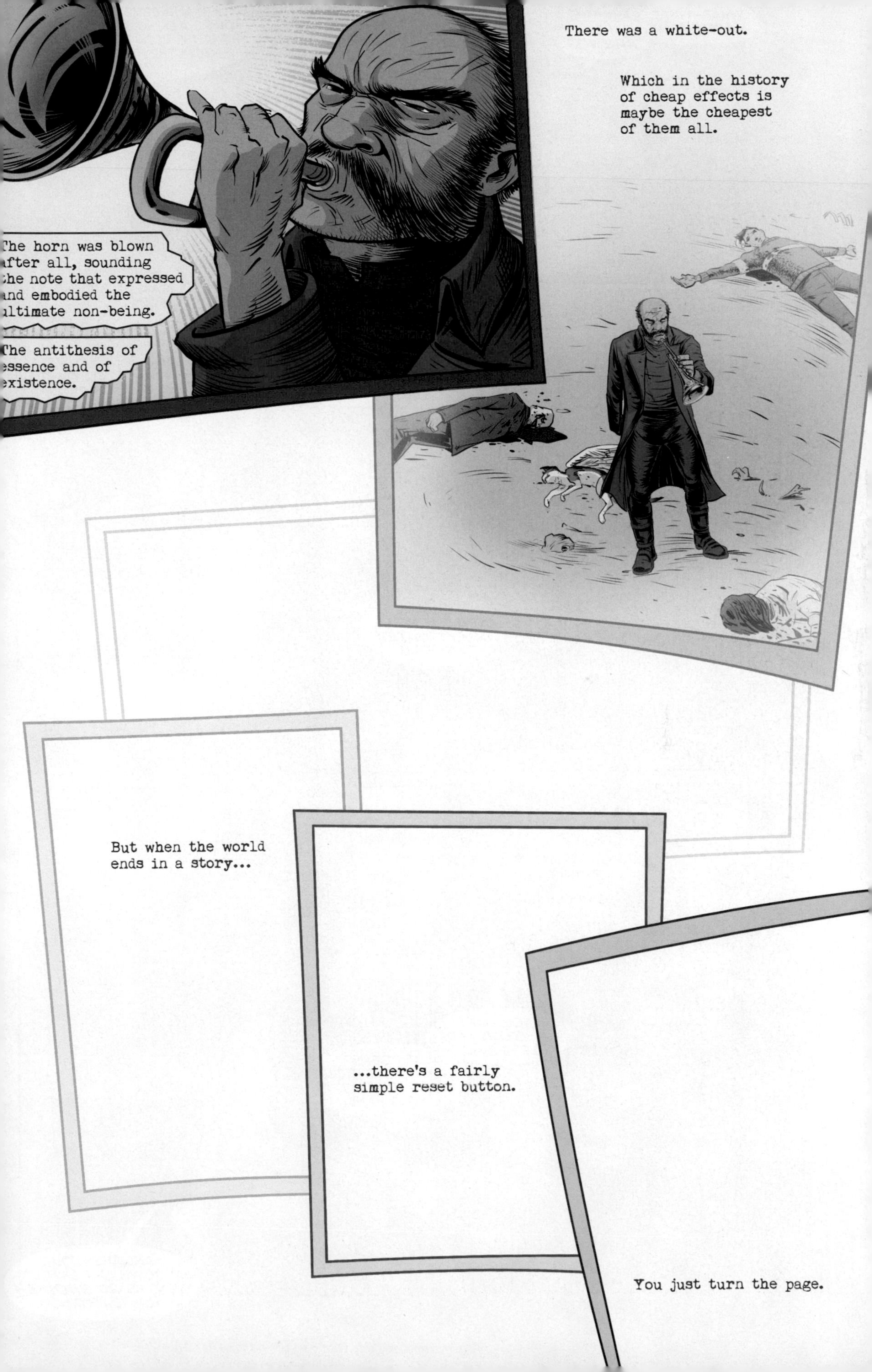

The horn was blown after all, sounding the note that expressed and embodied the ultimate non-being.
The antithesis of essence and of existence.
There was a white-out.
Which in the history of cheap effects is maybe the cheapest of them all.
But when the world ends in a story...
...there's a fairly simple reset button.
You just turn the page.

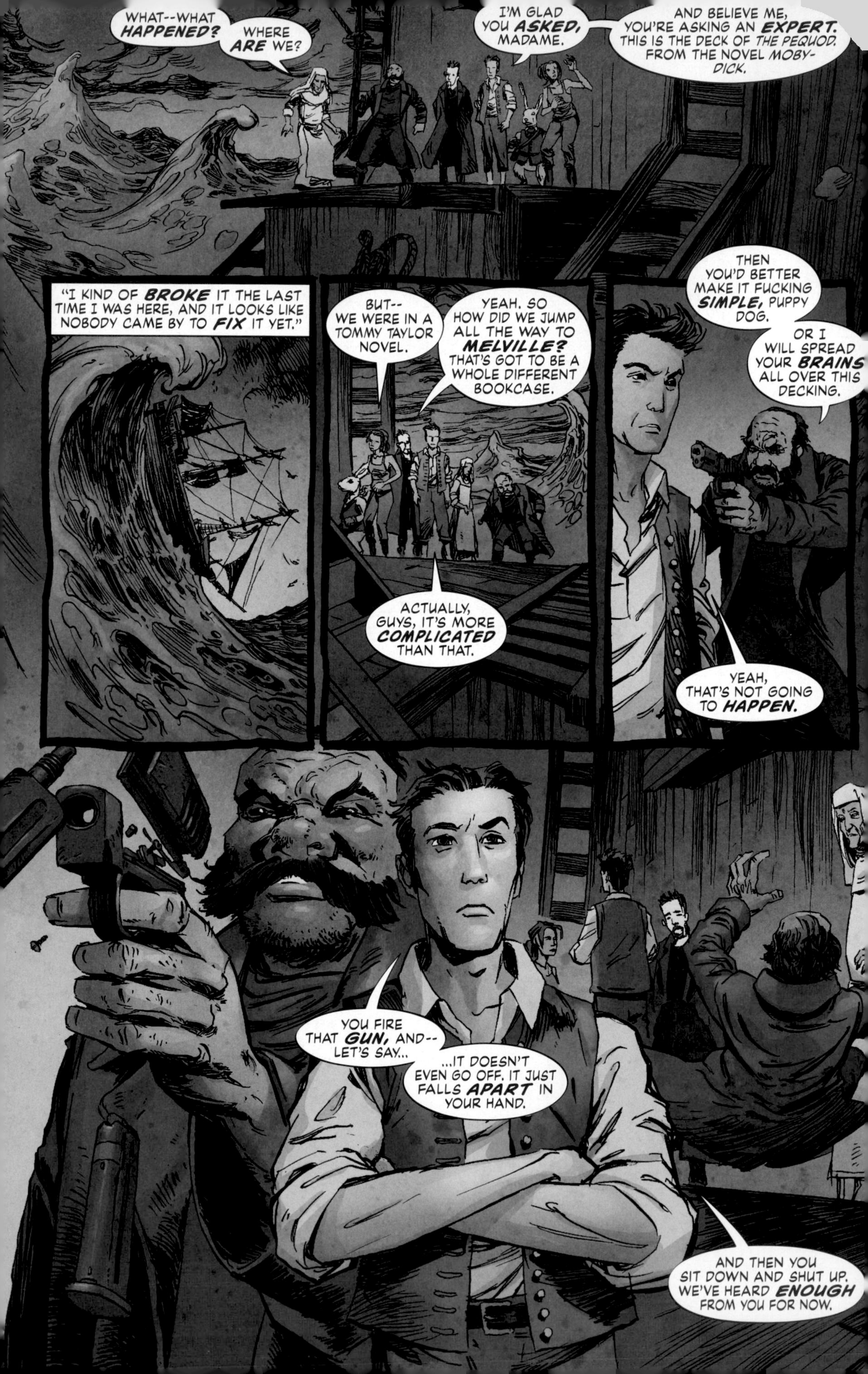
WHAT--WHAT HAPPENED?
WHERE ARE WE?
I'M GLAD YOU ASKED, MADAME.
AND BELIEVE ME, YOU'RE ASKING AN EXPERT. THIS IS THE DECK OF THE PEQUOD. FROM THE NOVEL MOBY-DICK.
"I KIND OF BROKE IT THE LAST TIME I WAS HERE, AND IT LOOKS LIKE NOBODY CAME BY TO FIX IT YET."
BUT-- WE WERE IN A TOMMY TAYLOR NOVEL.
YEAH. SO HOW DID WE JUMP ALL THE WAY TO MELVILLE? THAT'S GOT TO BE A WHOLE DIFFERENT BOOKCASE.
ACTUALLY, GUYS, IT'S MORE COMPLICATED THAN THAT.
THEN YOU'D BETTER MAKE IT FUCKING SIMPLE, PUPPY DOG.
OR I WILL SPREAD YOUR BRAINS ALL OVER THIS DECKING.
YEAH, THAT'S NOT GOING TO HAPPEN.
YOU FIRE THAT GUN, AND-- LET'S SAY...
...IT DOESN'T EVEN GO OFF. IT JUST FALLS APART IN YOUR HAND.
AND THEN YOU SIT DOWN AND SHUT UP. WE'VE HEARD ENOUGH FROM YOU FOR NOW.

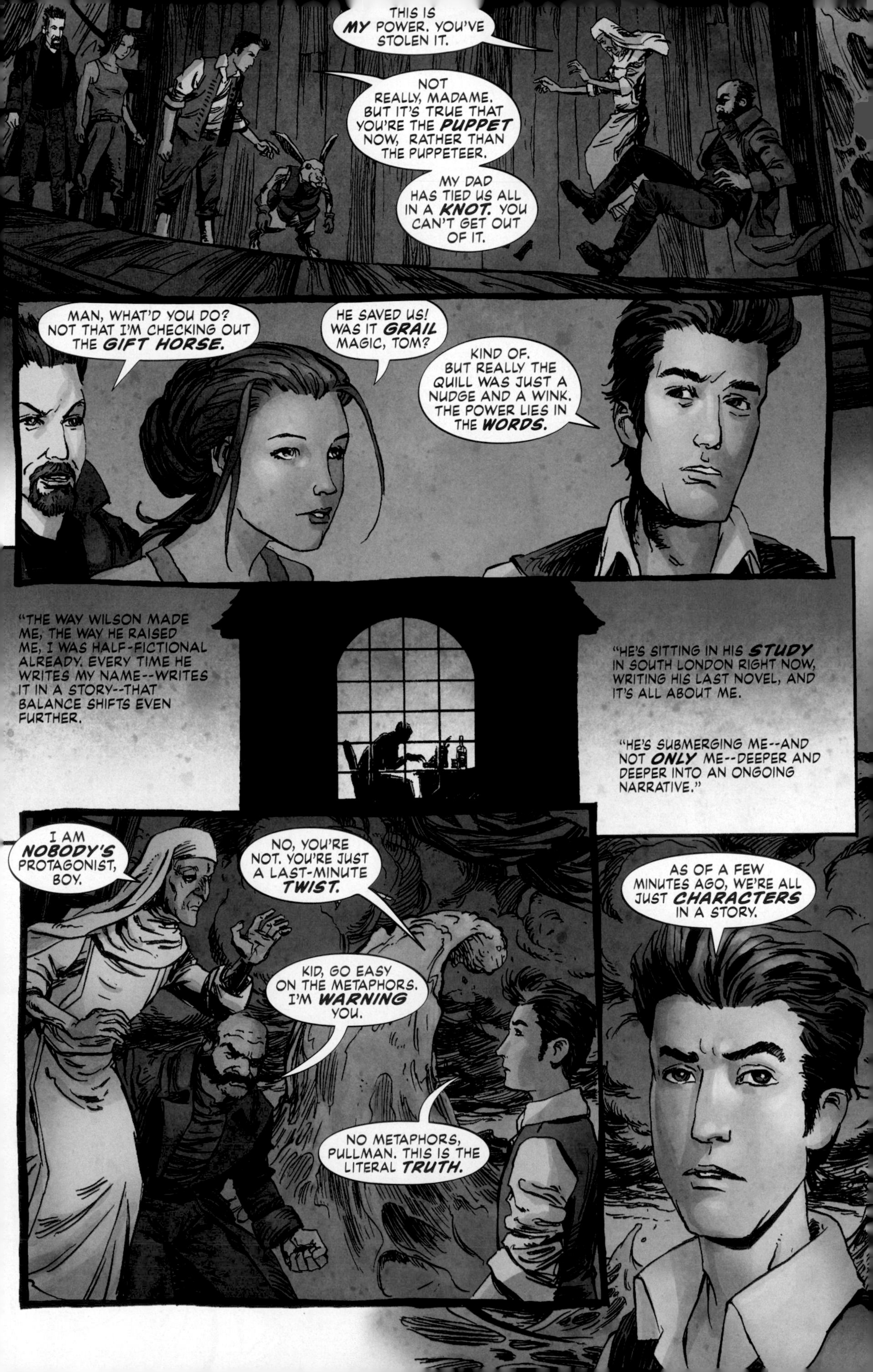
THIS IS MY POWER. YOU'VE STOLEN IT.
NOT REALLY, MADAME. BUT IT'S TRUE THAT YOU'RE THE PUPPET NOW, RATHER THAN THE PUPPETEER.
MY DAD HAS TIED US ALL IN A KNOT. YOU CAN'T GET OUT OF IT.
MAN, WHAT'D YOU DO? NOT THAT I'M CHECKING OUT THE GIFT HORSE.
HE SAVED US! WAS IT GRAIL MAGIC, TOM?
KIND OF. BUT REALLY THE QUILL WAS JUST A NUDGE AND A WINK. THE POWER LIES IN THE WORDS.
"THE WAY WILSON MADE ME, THE WAY HE RAISED ME, I WAS HALF-FICTIONAL ALREADY. EVERY TIME HE WRITES MY NAME--WRITES IT IN A STORY--THAT BALANCE SHIFTS EVEN FURTHER.
"HE'S SITTING IN HIS STUDY IN SOUTH LONDON RIGHT NOW, WRITING HIS LAST NOVEL, AND IT'S ALL ABOUT ME.
"HE'S SUBMERGING ME--AND NOT ONLY ME--DEEPER AND DEEPER INTO AN ONGOING NARRATIVE."
I AM NOBODY'S PROTAGONIST, BOY.
NO, YOU'RE NOT. YOU'RE JUST A LAST-MINUTE TWIST.
KID, GO EASY ON THE METAPHORS. I'M WARNING YOU.
NO METAPHORS, PULLMAN. THIS IS THE LITERAL TRUTH.
AS OF A FEW MINUTES AGO, WE'RE ALL JUST CHARACTERS IN A STORY.

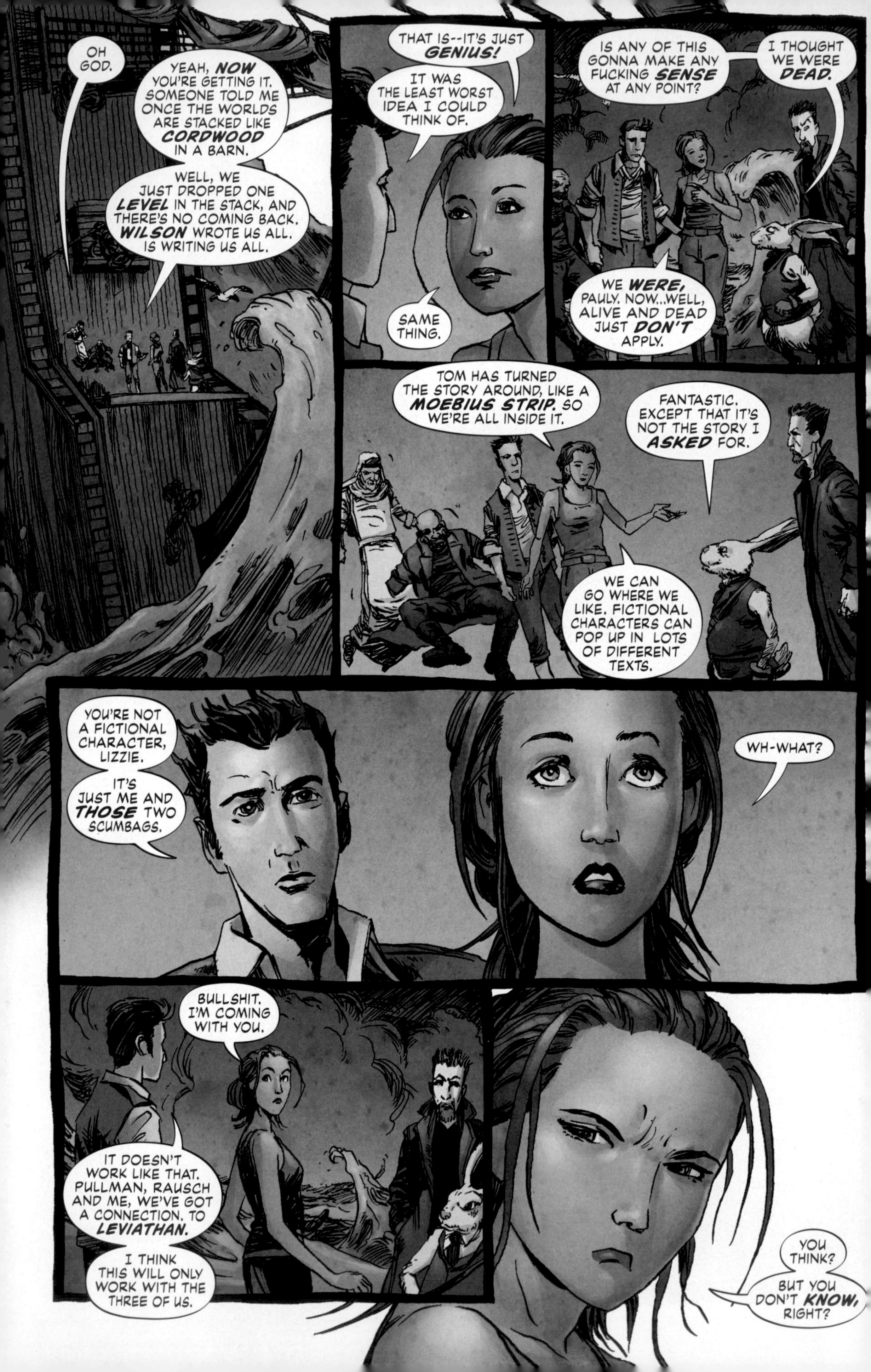
OH GOD.
YEAH, NOW YOU'RE GETTING IT. SOMEONE TOLD ME ONCE THE WORLDS ARE STACKED LIKE CORDWOOD IN A BARN.
WELL, WE JUST DROPPED ONE LEVEL IN THE STACK, AND THERE'S NO COMING BACK. WILSON WROTE US ALL. IS WRITING US ALL.
THAT IS--IT'S JUST GENIUS!
IT WAS THE LEAST WORST IDEA I COULD THINK OF.
SAME THING.
IS ANY OF THIS GONNA MAKE ANY FUCKING SENSE AT ANY POINT?
I THOUGHT WE WERE DEAD.
WE WERE, PAULY. NOW...WELL, ALIVE AND DEAD JUST DON'T APPLY.
TOM HAS TURNED THE STORY AROUND, LIKE A MOEBIUS STRIP. SO WE'RE ALL INSIDE IT.
FANTASTIC. EXCEPT THAT IT'S NOT THE STORY I ASKED FOR.
WE CAN GO WHERE WE LIKE. FICTIONAL CHARACTERS CAN POP UP IN LOTS OF DIFFERENT TEXTS.
YOU'RE NOT A FICTIONAL CHARACTER, LIZZIE.
IT'S JUST ME AND THOSE TWO SCUMBAGS.
WH-WHAT?
BULLSHIT. I'M COMING WITH YOU.
IT DOESN'T WORK LIKE THAT. PULLMAN, RAUSCH AND ME, WE'VE GOT A CONNECTION. TO LEVIATHAN.
I THINK THIS WILL ONLY WORK WITH THE THREE OF US.
YOU THINK?
BUT YOU DON'T KNOW, RIGHT?

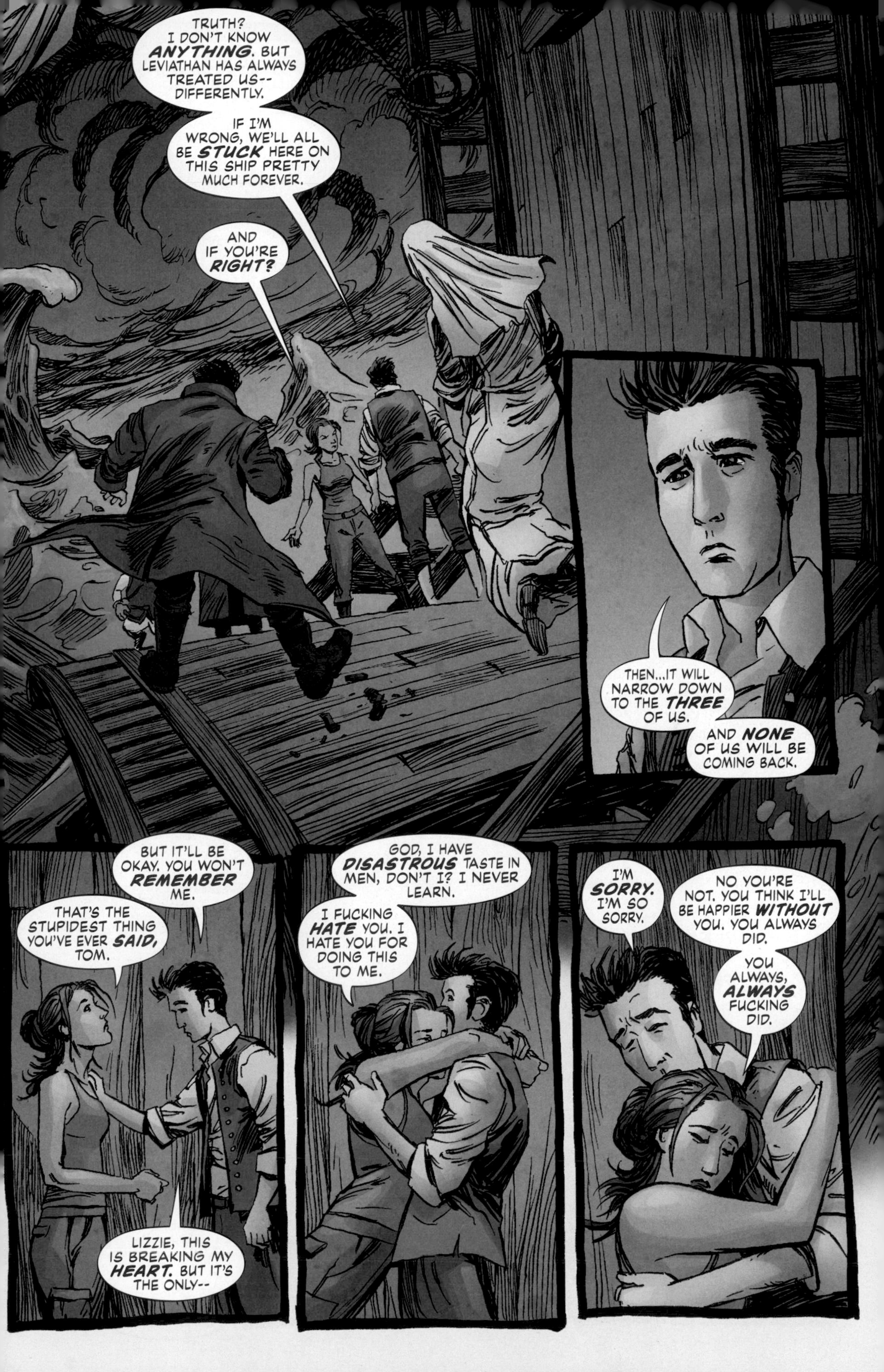
TRUTH? I DON'T KNOW ANYTHING. BUT LEVIATHAN HAS ALWAYS TREATED US-- DIFFERENTLY.
IF I'M WRONG, WE'LL ALL BE STUCK HERE ON THIS SHIP PRETTY MUCH FOREVER.
AND IF YOU'RE RIGHT?
THEN...IT WILL NARROW DOWN TO THE THREE OF US.
AND NONE OF US WILL BE COMING BACK.
BUT IT'LL BE OKAY. YOU WON'T REMEMBER ME.
THAT'S THE STUPIDEST THING YOU'VE EVER SAID, TOM.
LIZZIE, THIS IS BREAKING MY HEART. BUT IT'S THE ONLY--
GOD, I HAVE DISASTROUS TASTE IN MEN, DON'T I? I NEVER LEARN.
I FUCKING HATE YOU. I HATE YOU FOR DOING THIS TO ME.
I'M SORRY. I'M SO SORRY.
NO YOU'RE NOT. YOU THINK I'LL BE HAPPIER WITHOUT YOU. YOU ALWAYS DID.
YOU ALWAYS, ALWAYS FUCKING DID.

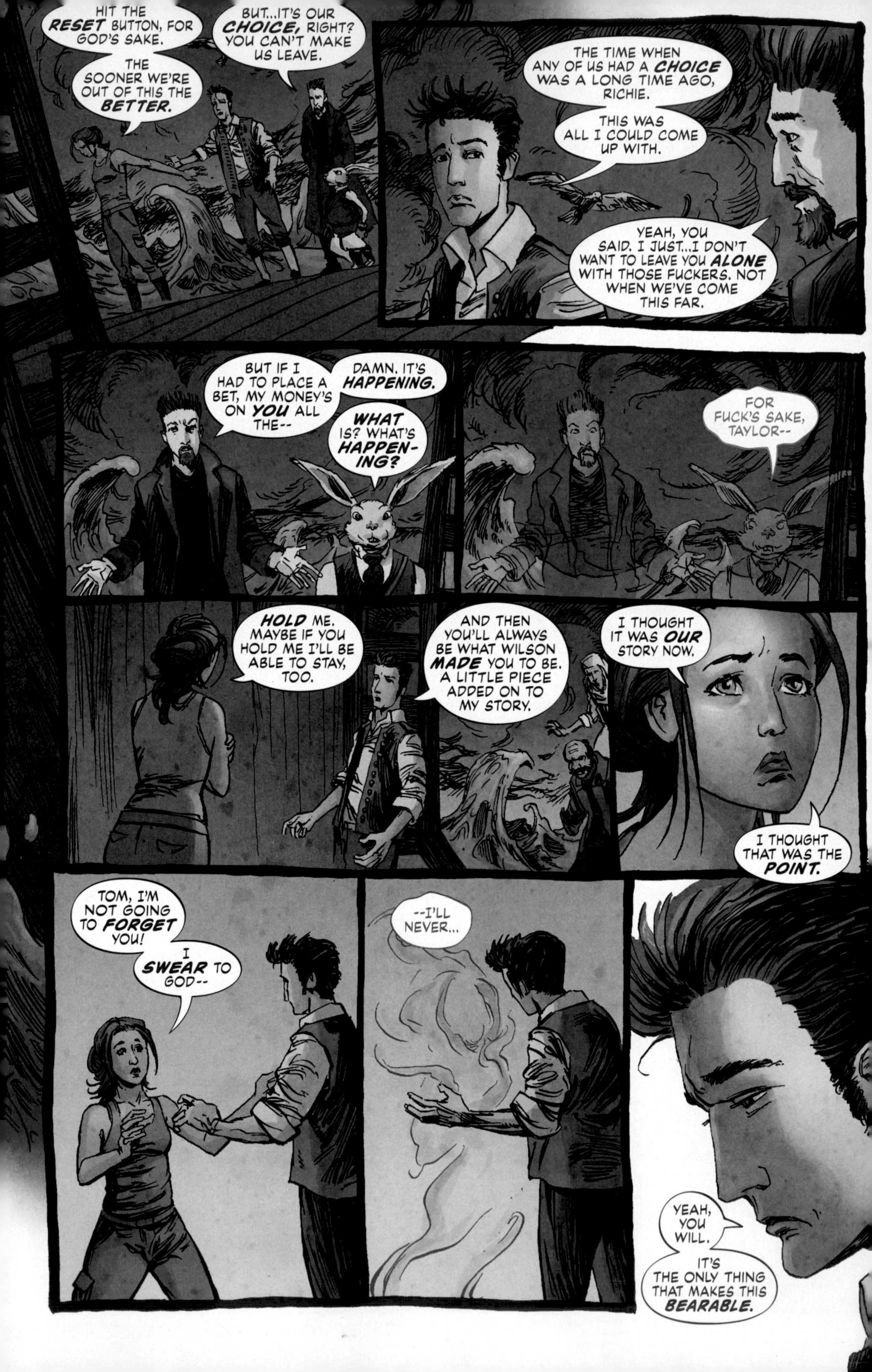
HIT THE RESET BUTTON, FOR GOD'S SAKE.
THE SOONER WE'RE OUT OF THIS THE BETTER.
BUT...IT'S OUR CHOICE, RIGHT? YOU CAN'T MAKE US LEAVE.
THE TIME WHEN ANY OF US HAD A CHOICE WAS A LONG TIME AGO, RICHIE.
THIS WAS ALL I COULD COME UP WITH.
YEAH, YOU SAID. I JUST...I DON'T WANT TO LEAVE YOU ALONE WITH THOSE FUCKERS. NOT WHEN WE'VE COME THIS FAR.
BUT IF I HAD TO PLACE A BET, MY MONEY'S ON YOU ALL THE--
DAMN. IT'S HAPPENING.
WHAT IS? WHAT'S HAPPEN-ING?
FOR FUCK'S SAKE, TAYLOR--
HOLD ME. MAYBE IF YOU HOLD ME I'LL BE ABLE TO STAY, TOO.
AND THEN YOU'LL ALWAYS BE WHAT WILSON MADE YOU TO BE. A LITTLE PIECE ADDED ON TO MY STORY.
I THOUGHT IT WAS OUR STORY NOW.
I THOUGHT THAT WAS THE POINT.
TOM, I'M NOT GOING TO FORGET YOU!
I SWEAR TO GOD--
--I'LL NEVER...
YEAH, YOU WILL.
IT'S THE ONLY THING THAT MAKES THIS BEARABLE.

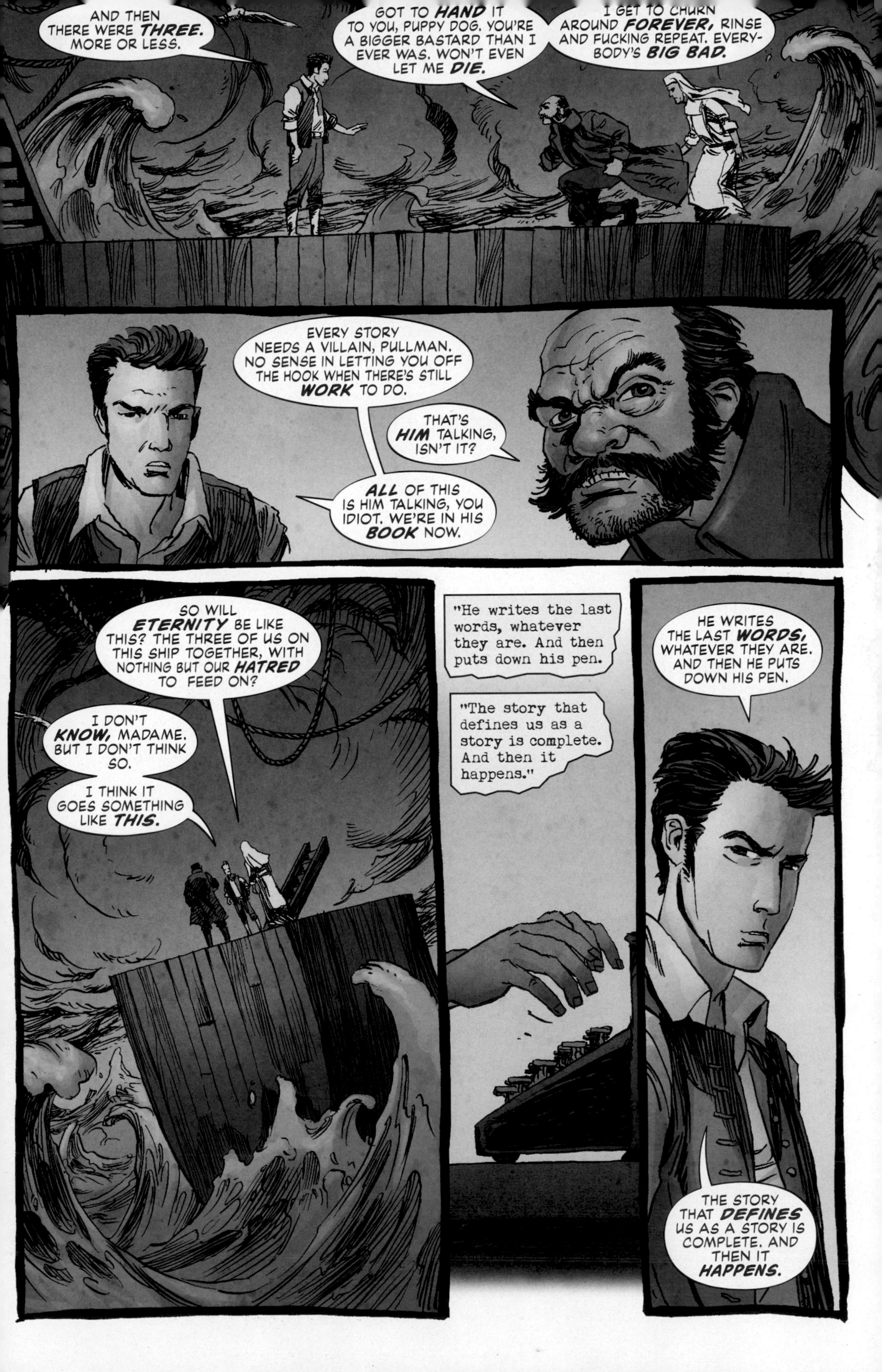
AND THEN THERE WERE THREE. MORE OR LESS.
GOT TO HAND IT TO YOU, PUPPY DOG. YOU'RE A BIGGER BASTARD THAN I EVER WAS. WON'T EVEN LET ME DIE.
I GET TO CHURN AROUND FOREVER, RINSE AND FUCKING REPEAT. EVERYBODY'S BIG BAD.
EVERY STORY NEEDS A VILLAIN, PULLMAN. NO SENSE IN LETTING YOU OFF THE HOOK WHEN THERE'S STILL WORK TO DO.
THAT'S HIM TALKING, ISN'T IT?
ALL OF THIS IS HIM TALKING, YOU IDIOT. WE'RE IN HIS BOOK NOW.
SO WILL ETERNITY BE LIKE THIS? THE THREE OF US ON THIS SHIP TOGETHER, WITH NOTHING BUT OUR HATRED TO FEED ON?
I DON'T KNOW, MADAME. BUT I DON'T THINK SO.
I THINK IT GOES SOMETHING LIKE THIS.
"He writes the last words, whatever they are. And then puts down his pen.
"The story that defines us as a story is complete. And then it happens."
HE WRITES THE LAST WORDS, WHATEVER THEY ARE. AND THEN HE PUTS DOWN HIS PEN.
THE STORY THAT DEFINES US AS A STORY IS COMPLETE. AND THEN IT HAPPENS.

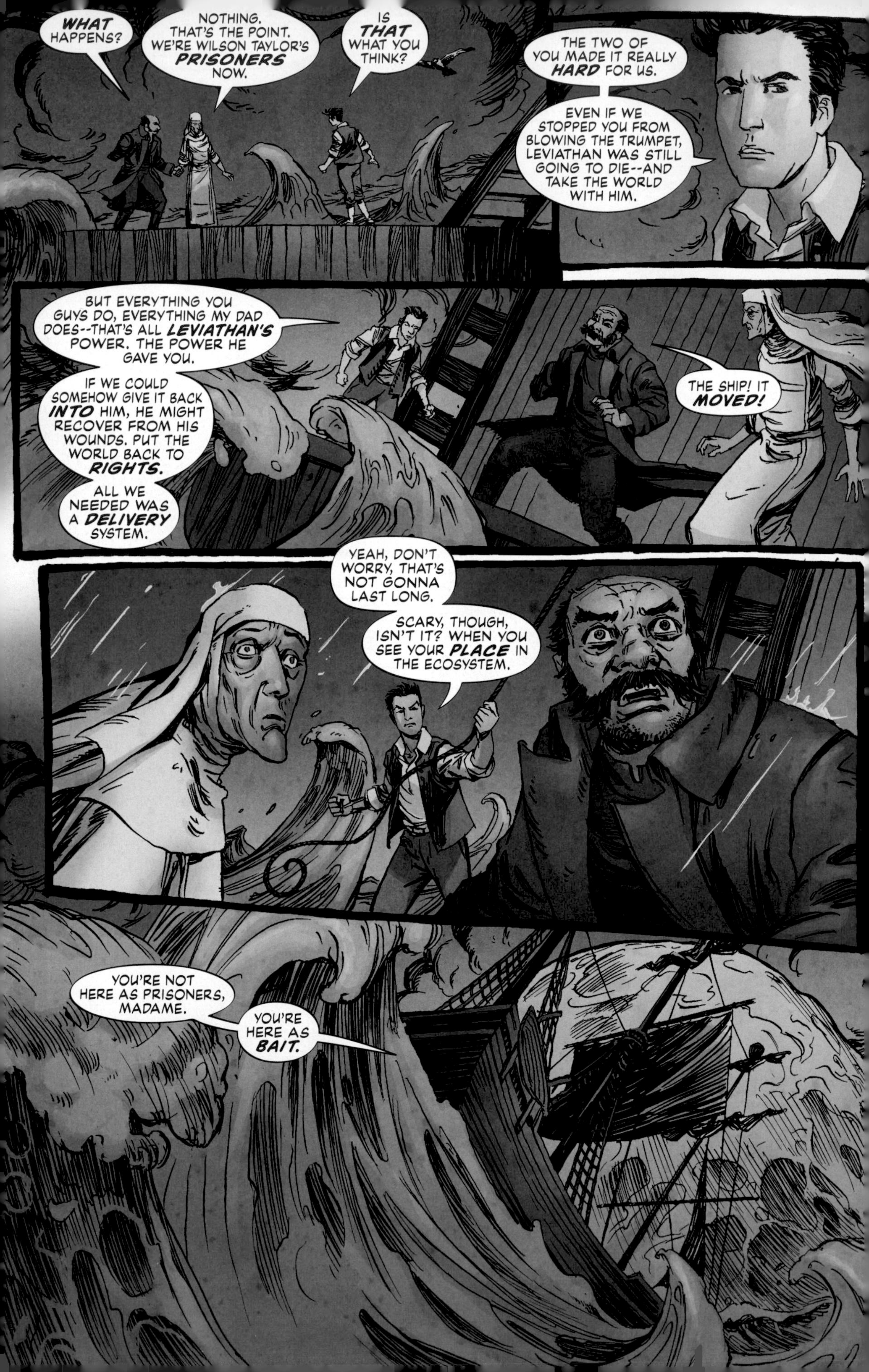

WHAT HAPPENS?
NOTHING. THAT'S THE POINT. WE'RE WILSON TAYLOR'S PRISONERS NOW.
IS THAT WHAT YOU THINK?
THE TWO OF YOU MADE IT REALLY HARD FOR US.
EVEN IF WE STOPPED YOU FROM BLOWING THE TRUMPET, LEVIATHAN WAS STILL GOING TO DIE--AND TAKE THE WORLD WITH HIM.
BUT EVERYTHING YOU GUYS DO, EVERYTHING MY DAD DOES--THAT'S ALL LEVIATHAN'S POWER. THE POWER HE GAVE YOU.
IF WE COULD SOMEHOW GIVE IT BACK INTO HIM, HE MIGHT RECOVER FROM HIS WOUNDS. PUT THE WORLD BACK TO RIGHTS.
ALL WE NEEDED WAS A DELIVERY SYSTEM.
THE SHIP! IT MOVED!
YEAH, DON'T WORRY, THAT'S NOT GONNA LAST LONG.
SCARY, THOUGH, ISN'T IT? WHEN YOU SEE YOUR PLACE IN THE ECOSYSTEM.
YOU'RE NOT HERE AS PRISONERS, MADAME.
YOU'RE HERE AS BAIT.

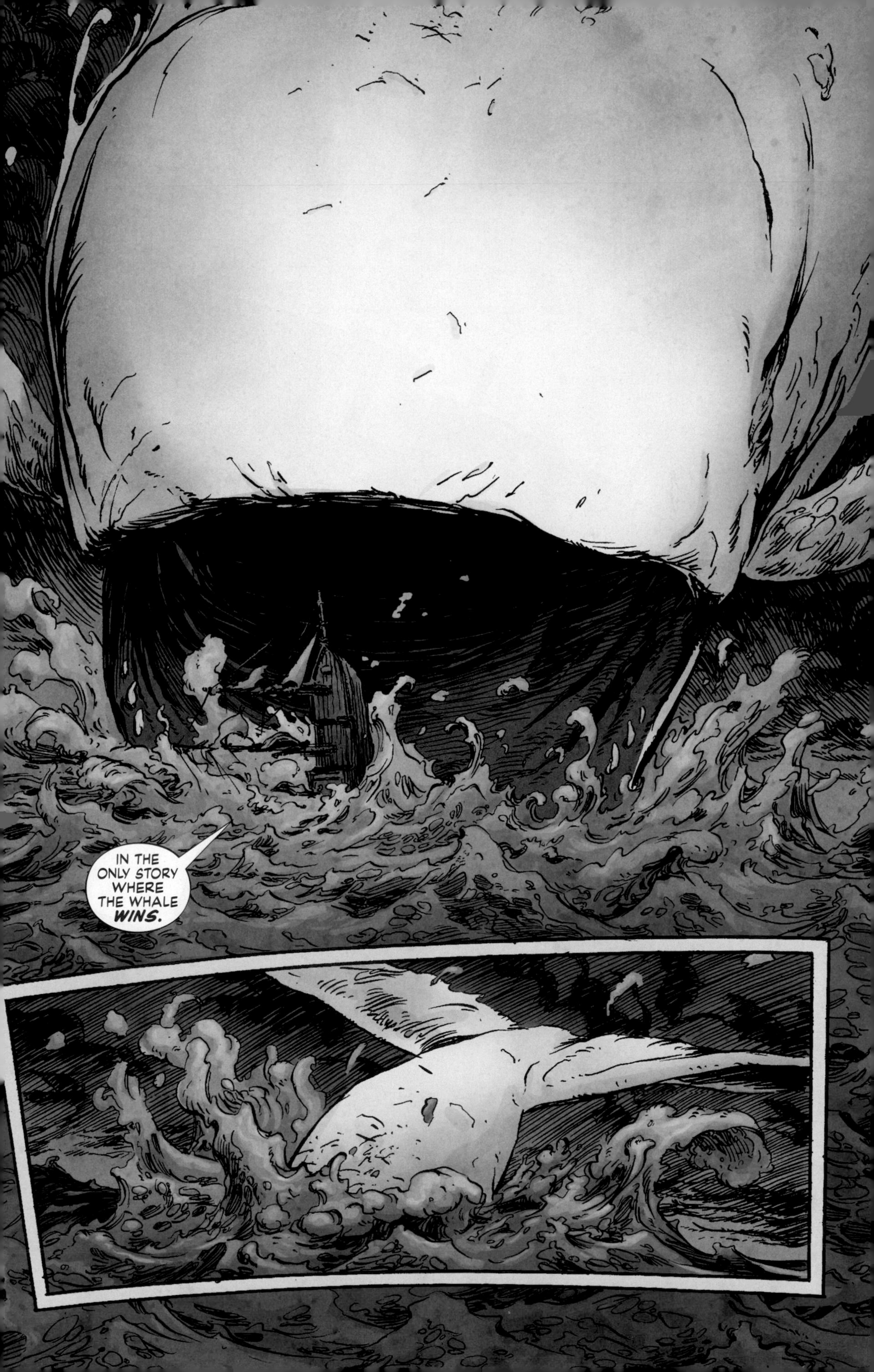
IN THE ONLY STORY WHERE THE WHALE *WINS.*

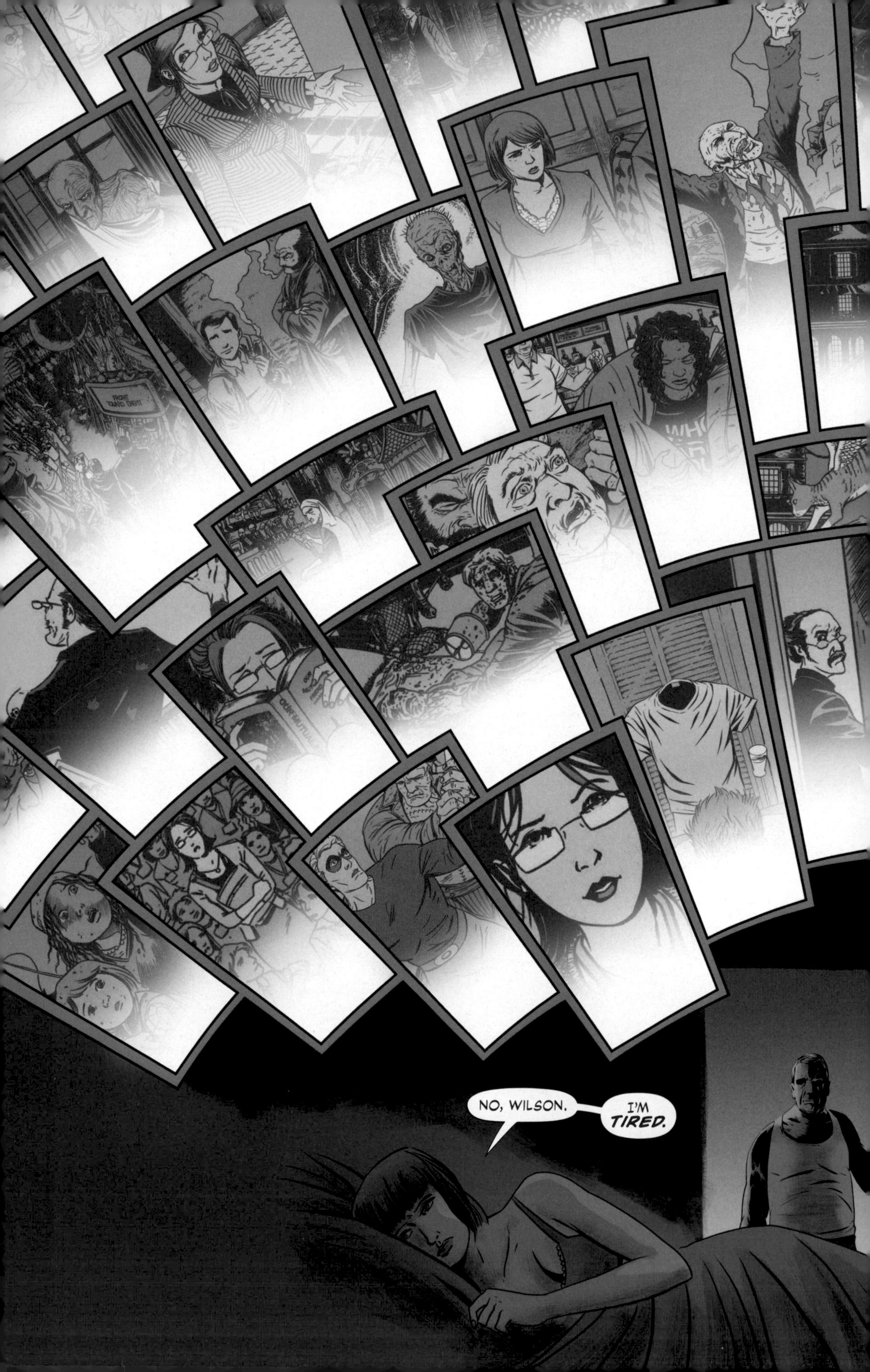
NO, WILSON.
I'M TIRED.

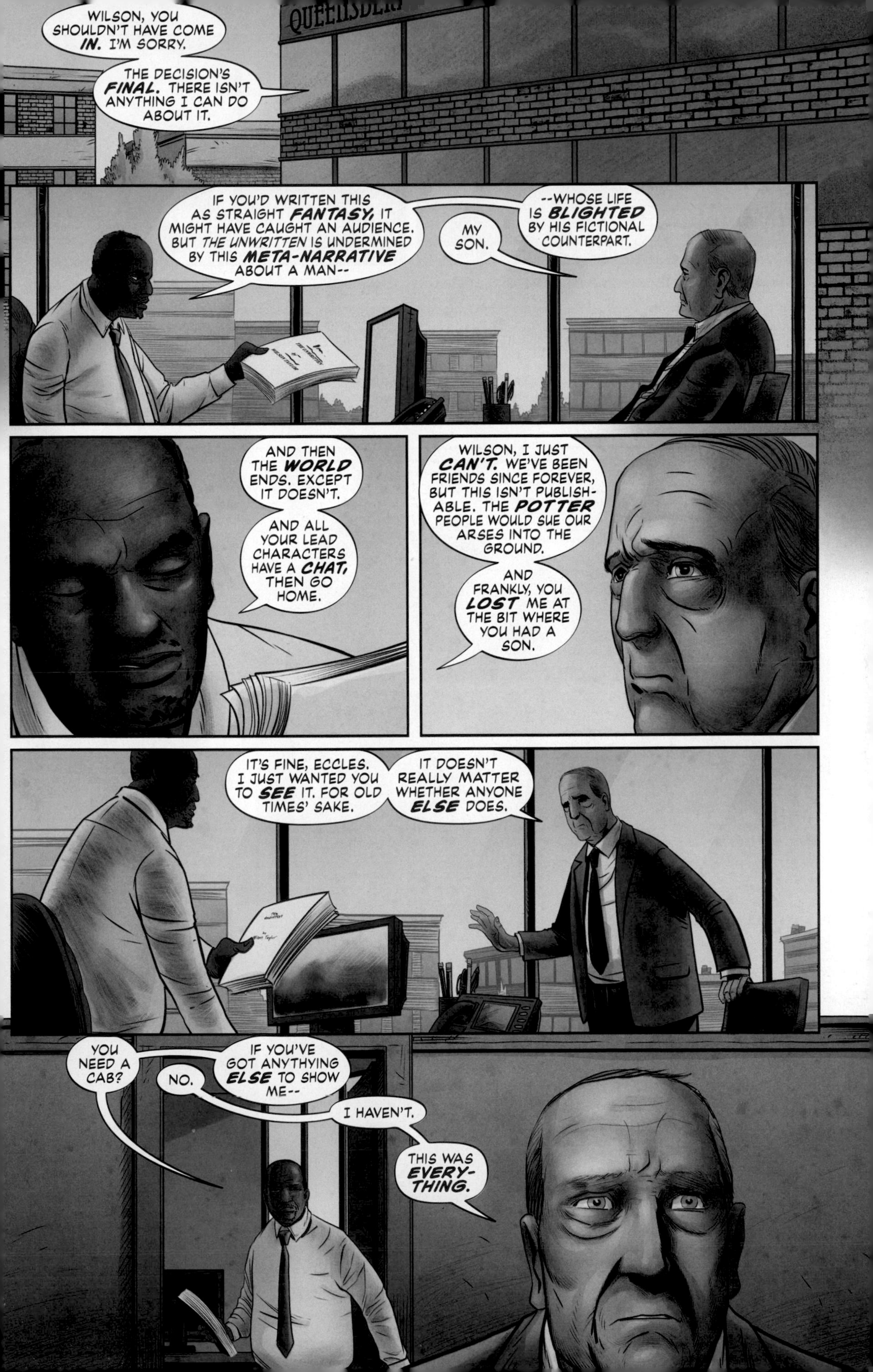
QUEENSBERY
WILSON, YOU SHOULDN'T HAVE COME IN. I'M SORRY.
THE DECISION'S FINAL. THERE ISN'T ANYTHING I CAN DO ABOUT IT.
IF YOU'D WRITTEN THIS AS STRAIGHT FANTASY, IT MIGHT HAVE CAUGHT AN AUDIENCE. BUT THE UNWRITTEN IS UNDERMINED BY THIS META-NARRATIVE ABOUT A MAN--
MY SON.
--WHOSE LIFE IS BLIGHTED BY HIS FICTIONAL COUNTERPART.
AND THEN THE WORLD ENDS. EXCEPT IT DOESN'T.
AND ALL YOUR LEAD CHARACTERS HAVE A CHAT, THEN GO HOME.
WILSON, I JUST CAN'T. WE'VE BEEN FRIENDS SINCE FOREVER, BUT THIS ISN'T PUBLISH-ABLE. THE POTTER PEOPLE WOULD SUE OUR ARSES INTO THE GROUND.
AND FRANKLY, YOU LOST ME AT THE BIT WHERE YOU HAD A SON.
IT'S FINE, ECCLES. I JUST WANTED YOU TO SEE IT. FOR OLD TIMES' SAKE.
IT DOESN'T REALLY MATTER WHETHER ANYONE ELSE DOES.
YOU NEED A CAB?
IF YOU'VE GOT ANYTHYING ELSE TO SHOW ME--
NO.
I HAVEN'T.
THIS WAS EVERY-THING.

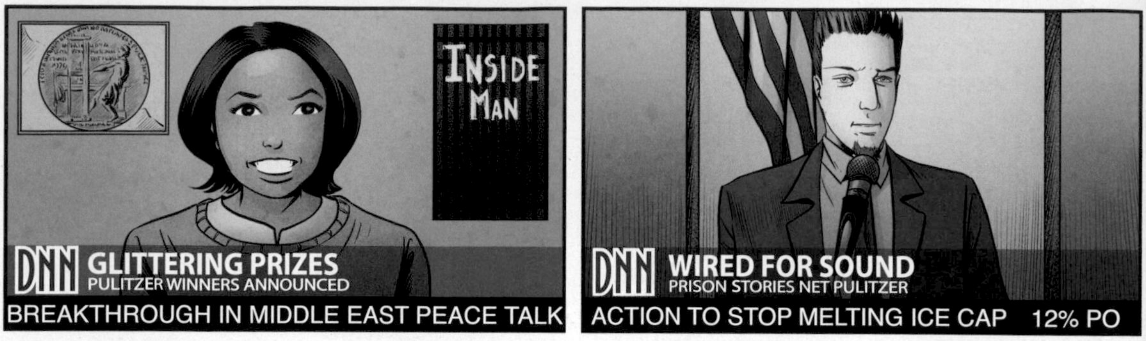
INSIDE MAN
DNN GLITTERING PRIZES
PULITZER WINNERS ANNOUNCED
BREAKTHROUGH IN MIDDLE EAST PEACE TALK
DNN WIRED FOR SOUND
PRISON STORIES NET PULITZER
ACTION TO STOP MELTING ICE CAP 12% PO

JOURNALIST RICHARD SAVOY, WHO WRITES REGULAR CONTENT FOR SITES SUCH AS DIGITAL WINDOW AND THE HUFFINGTON POST, YESTERDAY BECAME THE FIRST JOURNALIST EVER TO WIN A PULITZER WITHOUT WRITING A SINGLE WORD FOR TRADITIONAL PRINT AND BROADCAST MEDIA.

IN HIS ACCEPTANCE SPEECH, THE 29-YEAR-OLD SAID THAT HIS WORK WAS A TINY PART OF A GENERATIONAL SHIFT IN HOW NEWS STORIES ARE PRODUCED AND CONSUMED.

"WE DON'T BUY NEWS IN A STORE ANY MORE, OR EVEN GO TO A BOX ON THE WALL FOR IT. IT HAS TO FOLLOW US WHEREVER WE GO. IT HAS TO HOVER AT OUR SHOULDERS AND AT OUR FINGERTIPS. WE FIND THE NEWS--AND MAKE IT--WHEREVER WE GO."

SAVOY'S PULITZER WAS AWARDED FOR THE SERIES OF ARTICLES HE WROTE ABOUT CONDITIONS IN FRANCE'S DONOSTIA PRISON, PUBLISHED UNDER THE COLLECTIVE TITLE ***INSIDE MAN.***

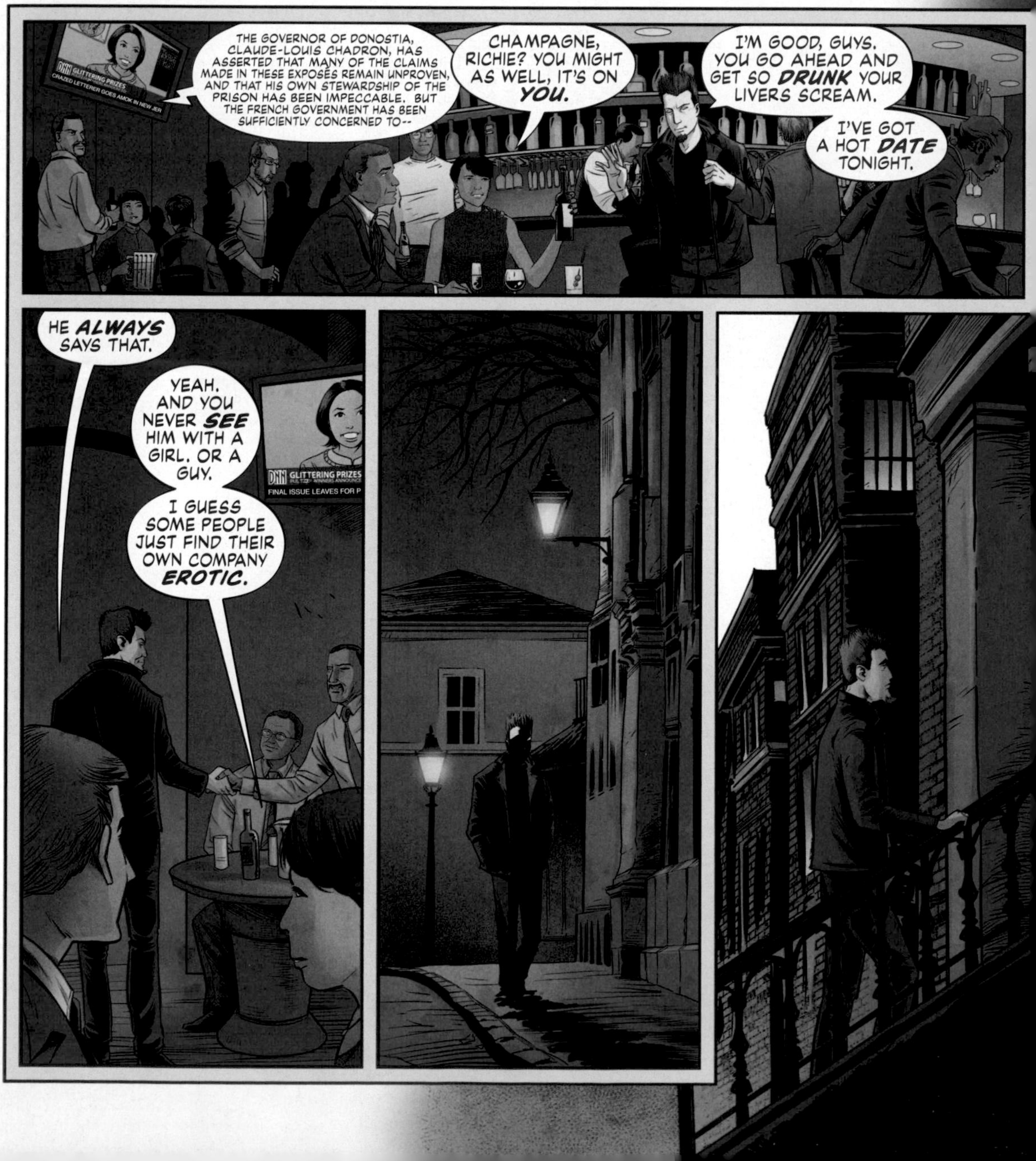
DNN GLITTERING PRIZES
CRAZED LETTERER GOES AMOK IN NEW JER
THE GOVERNOR OF DONOSTIA, CLAUDE-LOUIS CHADRON, HAS ASSERTED THAT MANY OF THE CLAIMS MADE IN THESE EXPOSÉS REMAIN UNPROVEN, AND THAT HIS OWN STEWARDSHIP OF THE PRISON HAS BEEN IMPECCABLE. BUT THE FRENCH GOVERNMENT HAS BEEN SUFFICIENTLY CONCERNED TO--
CHAMPAGNE, RICHIE? YOU MIGHT AS WELL, IT'S ON ***YOU.***
I'M GOOD, GUYS. YOU GO AHEAD AND GET SO ***DRUNK*** YOUR LIVERS SCREAM.
I'VE GOT A HOT ***DATE*** TONIGHT.
HE ***ALWAYS*** SAYS THAT.
YEAH. AND YOU NEVER ***SEE*** HIM WITH A GIRL. OR A GUY.
DNN GLITTERING PRIZES
PULITZER WINNERS ANNOUNCED
FINAL ISSUE LEAVES FOR P
I GUESS SOME PEOPLE JUST FIND THEIR OWN COMPANY ***EROTIC.***

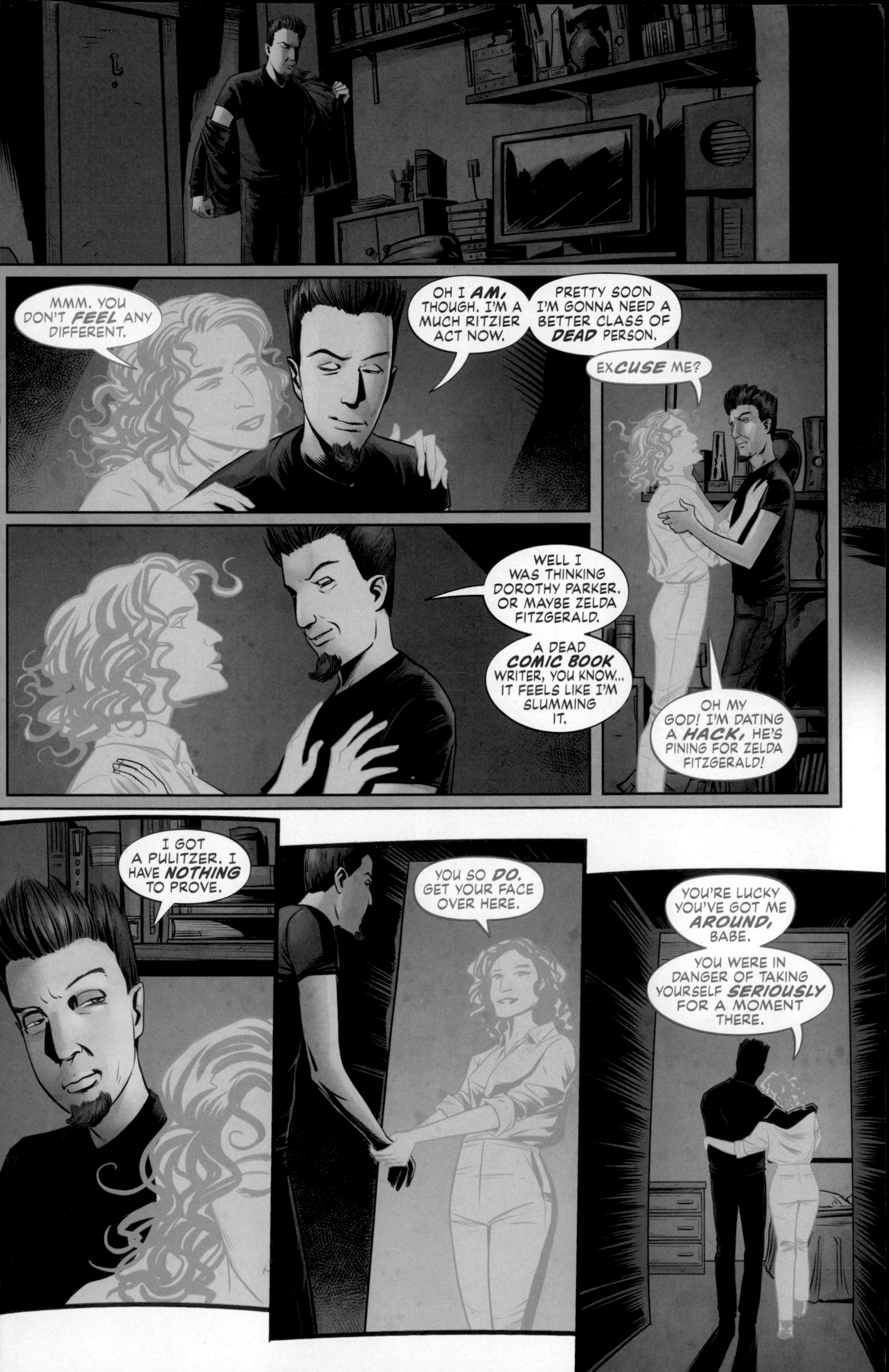
MMM. YOU DON'T *FEEL* ANY DIFFERENT.
OH I *AM,* THOUGH. I'M A MUCH RITZIER ACT NOW.
PRETTY SOON I'M GONNA NEED A BETTER CLASS OF *DEAD* PERSON.
EX*CUSE* ME?
WELL I WAS THINKING DOROTHY PARKER. OR MAYBE ZELDA FITZGERALD.
A DEAD *COMIC BOOK* WRITER, YOU KNOW... IT FEELS LIKE I'M SLUMMING IT.
OH MY GOD! I'M DATING A *HACK,* HE'S PINING FOR ZELDA FITZGERALD!
I GOT A PULITZER. I HAVE *NOTHING* TO PROVE.
YOU SO *DO.* GET YOUR FACE OVER HERE.
YOU'RE LUCKY YOU'VE GOT ME *AROUND,* BABE.
YOU WERE IN DANGER OF TAKING YOURSELF *SERIOUSLY* FOR A MOMENT THERE.

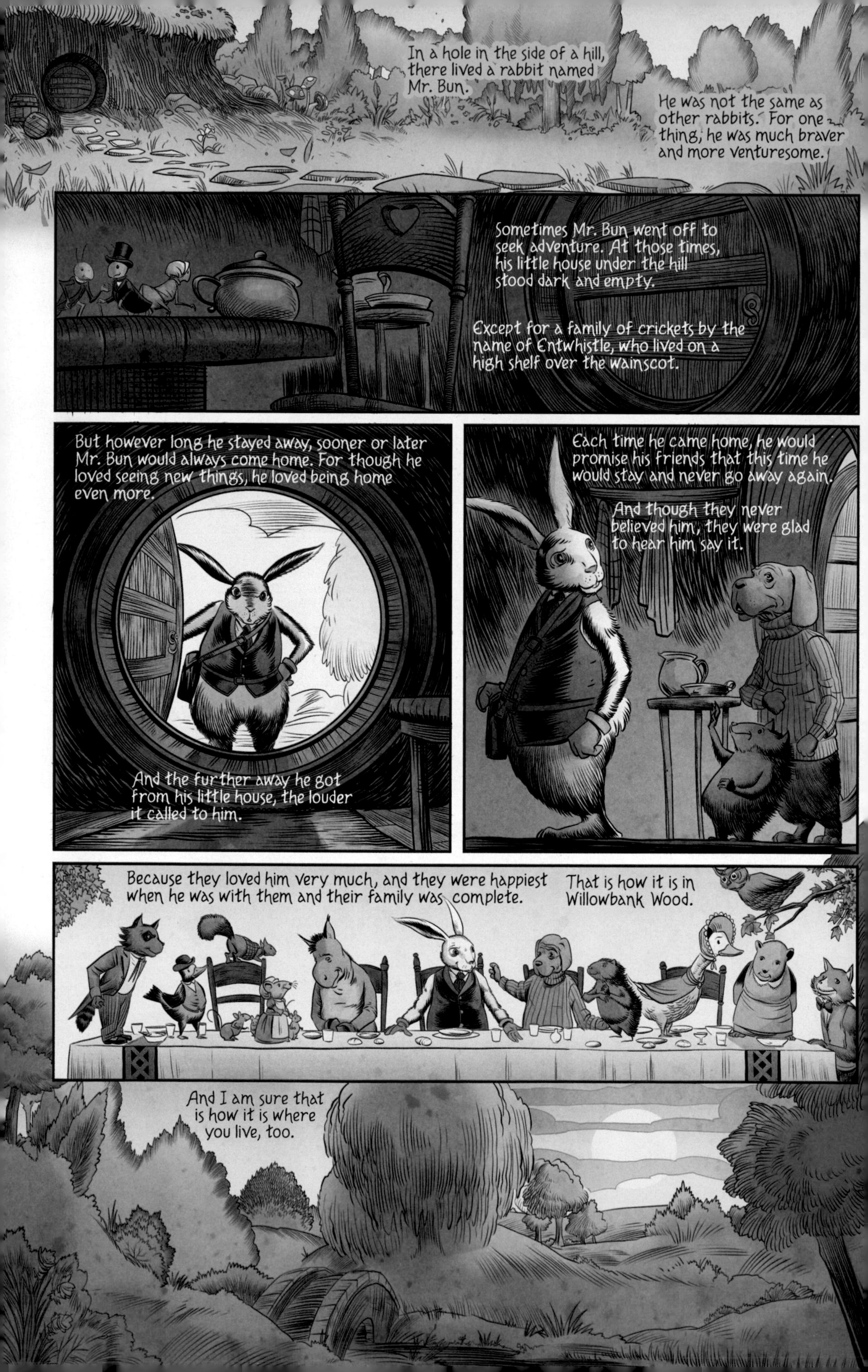
In a hole in the side of a hill, there lived a rabbit named Mr. Bun.
He was not the same as other rabbits. For one thing, he was much braver and more venturesome.
Sometimes Mr. Bun went off to seek adventure. At those times, his little house under the hill stood dark and empty.
Except for a family of crickets by the name of Entwhistle, who lived on a high shelf over the wainscot.
But however long he stayed away, sooner or later Mr. Bun would always come home. For though he loved seeing new things, he loved being home even more.
And the further away he got from his little house, the louder it called to him.
Each time he came home, he would promise his friends that this time he would stay and never go away again.
And though they never believed him, they were glad to hear him say it.
Because they loved him very much, and they were happiest when he was with them and their family was complete.
That is how it is in Willowbank Wood.
And I am sure that is how it is where you live, too.

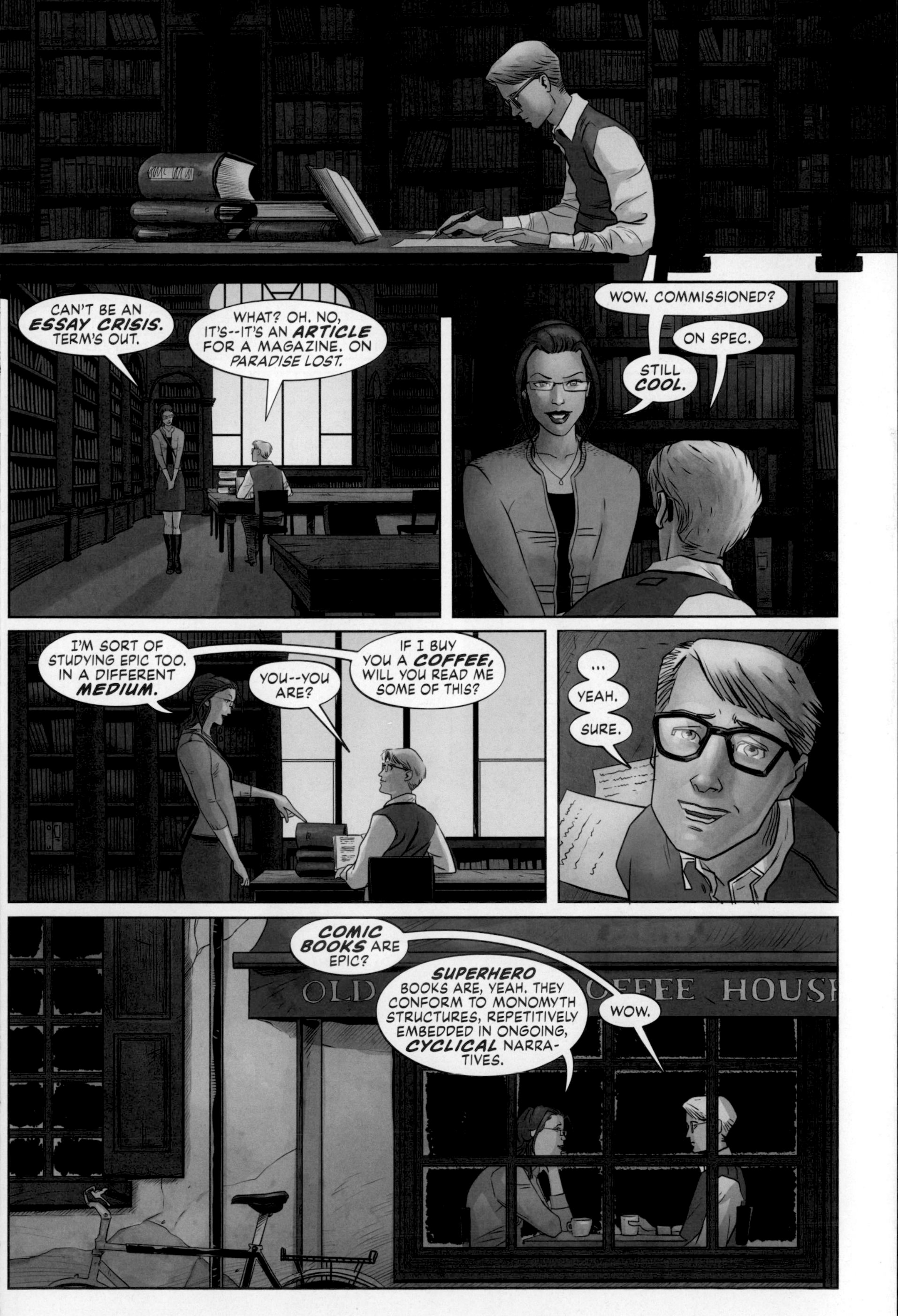

CAN'T BE AN ESSAY CRISIS. TERM'S OUT.
WHAT? OH. NO, IT'S--IT'S AN ARTICLE FOR A MAGAZINE. ON PARADISE LOST.
WOW. COMMISSIONED?
ON SPEC.
STILL COOL.
I'M SORT OF STUDYING EPIC TOO. IN A DIFFERENT MEDIUM.
YOU--YOU ARE?
IF I BUY YOU A COFFEE, WILL YOU READ ME SOME OF THIS?
...
YEAH.
SURE.
OLD COFFEE HOUS
COMIC BOOKS ARE EPIC?
SUPERHERO BOOKS ARE, YEAH. THEY CONFORM TO MONOMYTH STRUCTURES, REPETITIVELY EMBEDDED IN ONGOING, CYCLICAL NARRATIVES.
WOW.

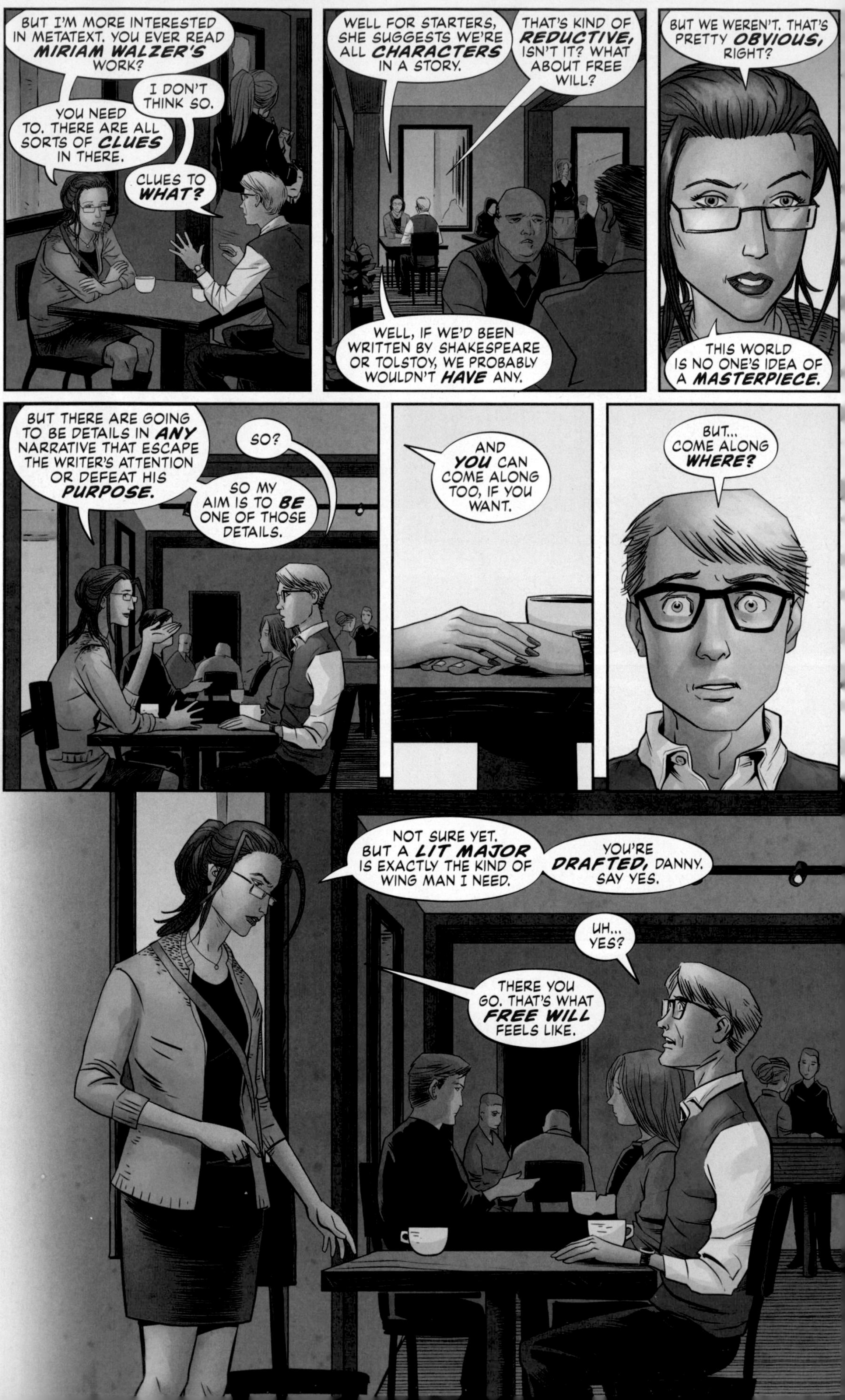
BUT I'M MORE INTERESTED IN METATEXT. YOU EVER READ MIRIAM WALZER'S WORK?
I DON'T THINK SO.
YOU NEED TO. THERE ARE ALL SORTS OF CLUES IN THERE.
CLUES TO WHAT?
WELL FOR STARTERS, SHE SUGGESTS WE'RE ALL CHARACTERS IN A STORY.
THAT'S KIND OF REDUCTIVE, ISN'T IT? WHAT ABOUT FREE WILL?
WELL, IF WE'D BEEN WRITTEN BY SHAKESPEARE OR TOLSTOY, WE PROBABLY WOULDN'T HAVE ANY.
BUT WE WEREN'T. THAT'S PRETTY OBVIOUS, RIGHT?
THIS WORLD IS NO ONE'S IDEA OF A MASTERPIECE.
BUT THERE ARE GOING TO BE DETAILS IN ANY NARRATIVE THAT ESCAPE THE WRITER'S ATTENTION OR DEFEAT HIS PURPOSE.
SO?
SO MY AIM IS TO BE ONE OF THOSE DETAILS.
AND YOU CAN COME ALONG TOO, IF YOU WANT.
BUT... COME ALONG WHERE?
NOT SURE YET. BUT A LIT MAJOR IS EXACTLY THE KIND OF WING MAN I NEED.
YOU'RE DRAFTED, DANNY. SAY YES.
UH... YES?
THERE YOU GO. THAT'S WHAT FREE WILL FEELS LIKE.

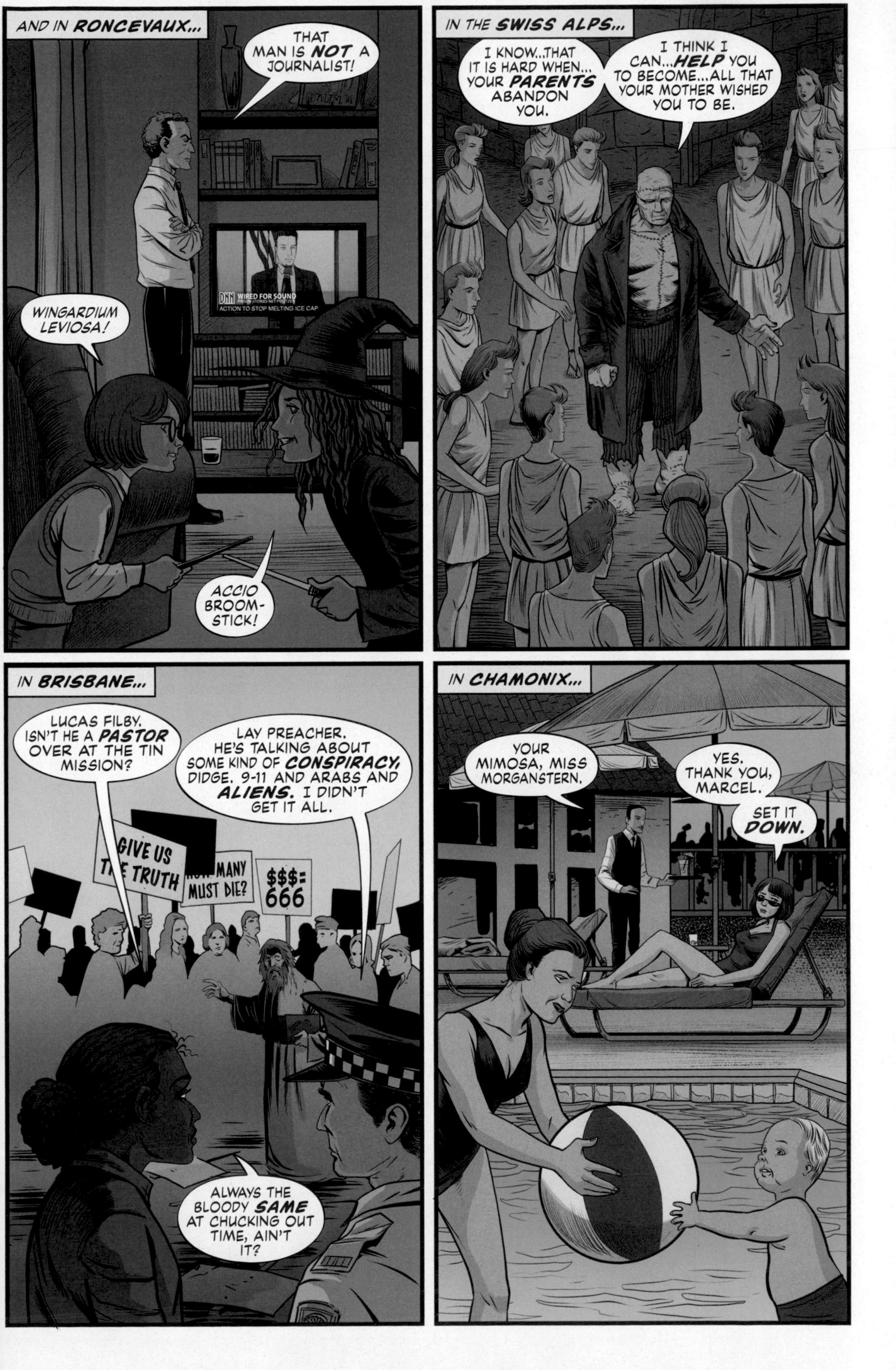
AND IN RONCEVAUX...
THAT MAN IS NOT A JOURNALIST!
DNN WIRED FOR SOUND
ACTION TO STOP MELTING ICE CAP
WINGARDIUM LEVIOSA!
ACCIO BROOM-STICK!
IN THE SWISS ALPS...
I KNOW...THAT IT IS HARD WHEN... YOUR PARENTS ABANDON YOU.
I THINK I CAN...HELP YOU TO BECOME...ALL THAT YOUR MOTHER WISHED YOU TO BE.
IN BRISBANE...
LUCAS FILBY. ISN'T HE A PASTOR OVER AT THE TIN MISSION?
LAY PREACHER. HE'S TALKING ABOUT SOME KIND OF CONSPIRACY, DIDGE. 9-11 AND ARABS AND ALIENS. I DIDN'T GET IT ALL.
GIVE US
TRUTH
MANY MUST DIE?
$$$= 666
ALWAYS THE BLOODY SAME AT CHUCKING OUT TIME, AIN'T IT?
IN CHAMONIX...
YOUR MIMOSA, MISS MORGANSTERN.
YES. THANK YOU, MARCEL.
SET IT DOWN.

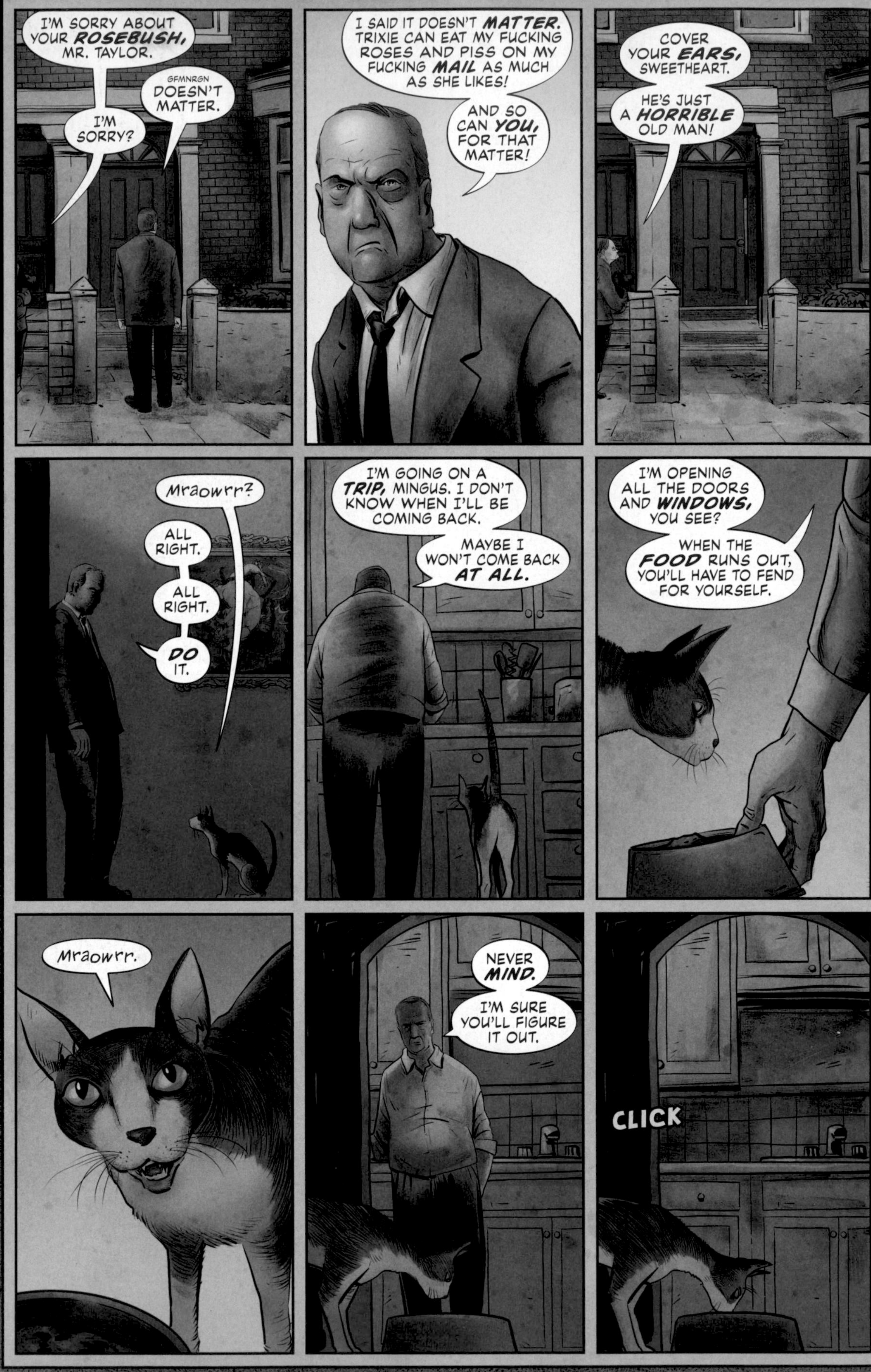
I'M SORRY ABOUT YOUR ROSEBUSH, MR. TAYLOR.
I'M SORRY?
GFMNRGN
DOESN'T MATTER.
I SAID IT DOESN'T MATTER. TRIXIE CAN EAT MY FUCKING ROSES AND PISS ON MY FUCKING MAIL AS MUCH AS SHE LIKES!
AND SO CAN YOU, FOR THAT MATTER!
COVER YOUR EARS, SWEETHEART.
HE'S JUST A HORRIBLE OLD MAN!
Mraowrr?
ALL RIGHT.
ALL RIGHT.
DO IT.
I'M GOING ON A TRIP, MINGUS. I DON'T KNOW WHEN I'LL BE COMING BACK.
MAYBE I WON'T COME BACK AT ALL.
I'M OPENING ALL THE DOORS AND WINDOWS, YOU SEE?
WHEN THE FOOD RUNS OUT, YOU'LL HAVE TO FEND FOR YOURSELF.
Mraowrr.
NEVER MIND.
I'M SURE YOU'LL FIGURE IT OUT.
CLICK

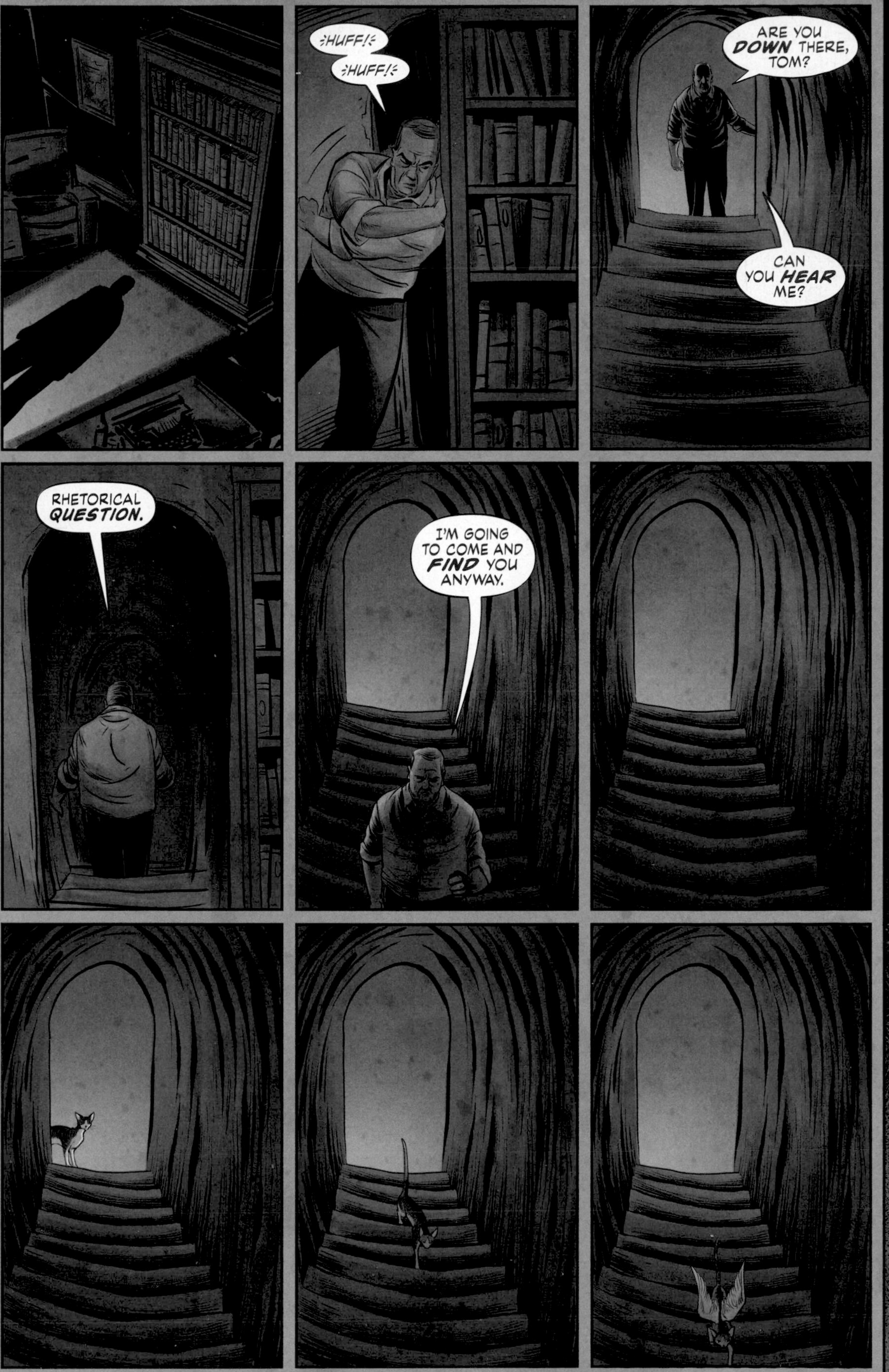

HUFF!
HUFF!
ARE YOU DOWN THERE, TOM?
CAN YOU HEAR ME?
RHETORICAL QUESTION.
I'M GOING TO COME AND FIND YOU ANYWAY.

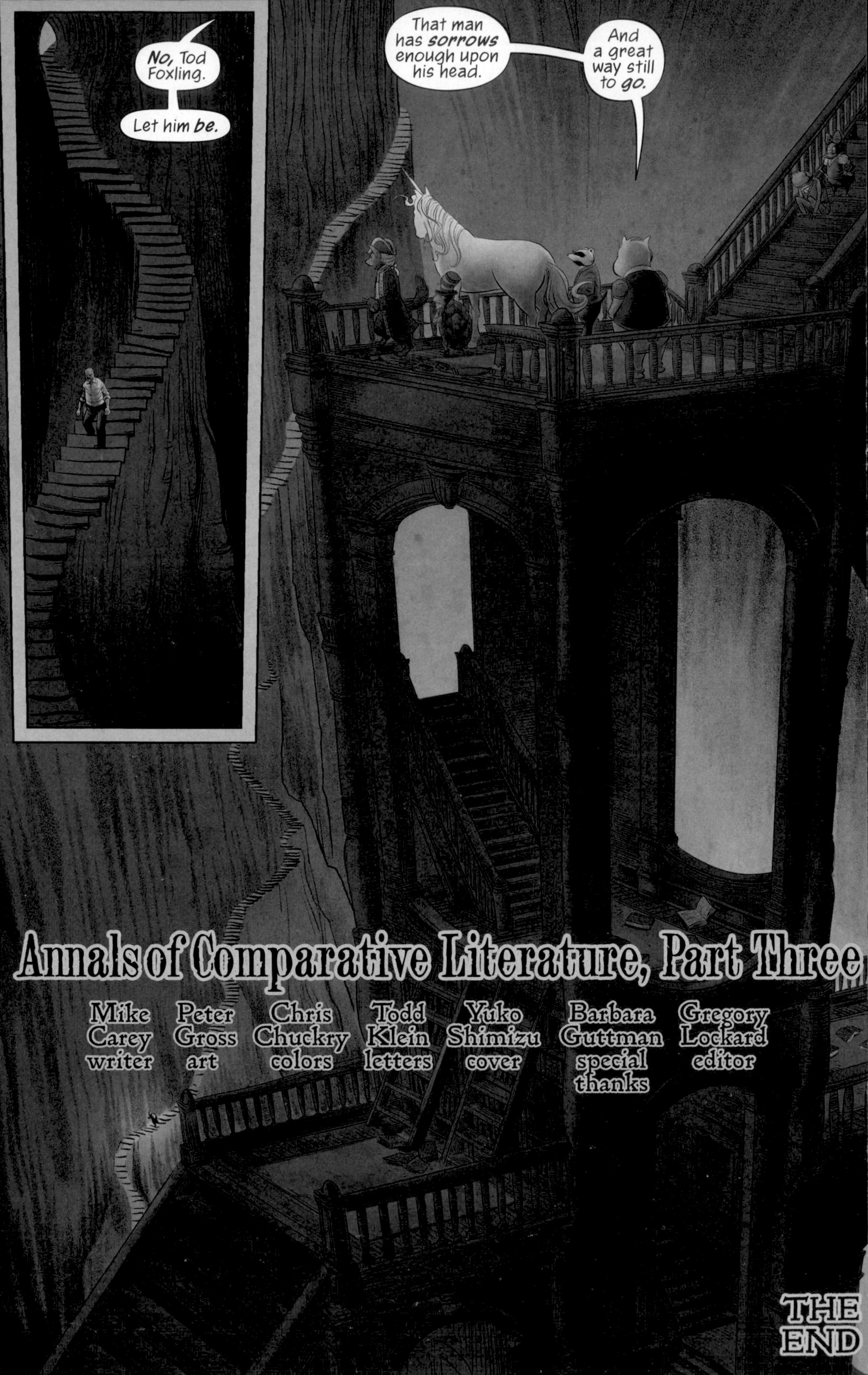

No, Tod Foxling.
Let him be.
That man has sorrows enough upon his head.
And a great way still to go.
Annals of Comparative Literature, Part Three
Mike Carey writer
Peter Gross art
Chris Chuckry colors
Todd Klein letters
Yuko Shimizu cover
Barbara Guttman special thanks
Gregory Lockard editor
THE END